Maureen Attwooll and Jack W[illegible] experts on Weymouth's history, [illegible] to the understanding and appreciation of [illegible] has been immense. They are well-known for their lectures on the town, and they have worked together on a number of projects. They have already written the definitive history of the town, *Weymouth, An Illustrated History,* (Dovecote Press, 1983).

Maureen Attwooll was educated at Weymouth Grammar School. She is on the staff of Dorset County Library and has worked at Weymouth Library for a number of years.

Jack West was also at the Grammar School. He was Weymouth's chief Librarian from 1949 to 1974, after which he served as Curator of the Weymouth and Portland Museum Service until his retirement in 1981.

Frontispiece
Weymouth Esplanade in about 1800, drawn by Eric Ricketts

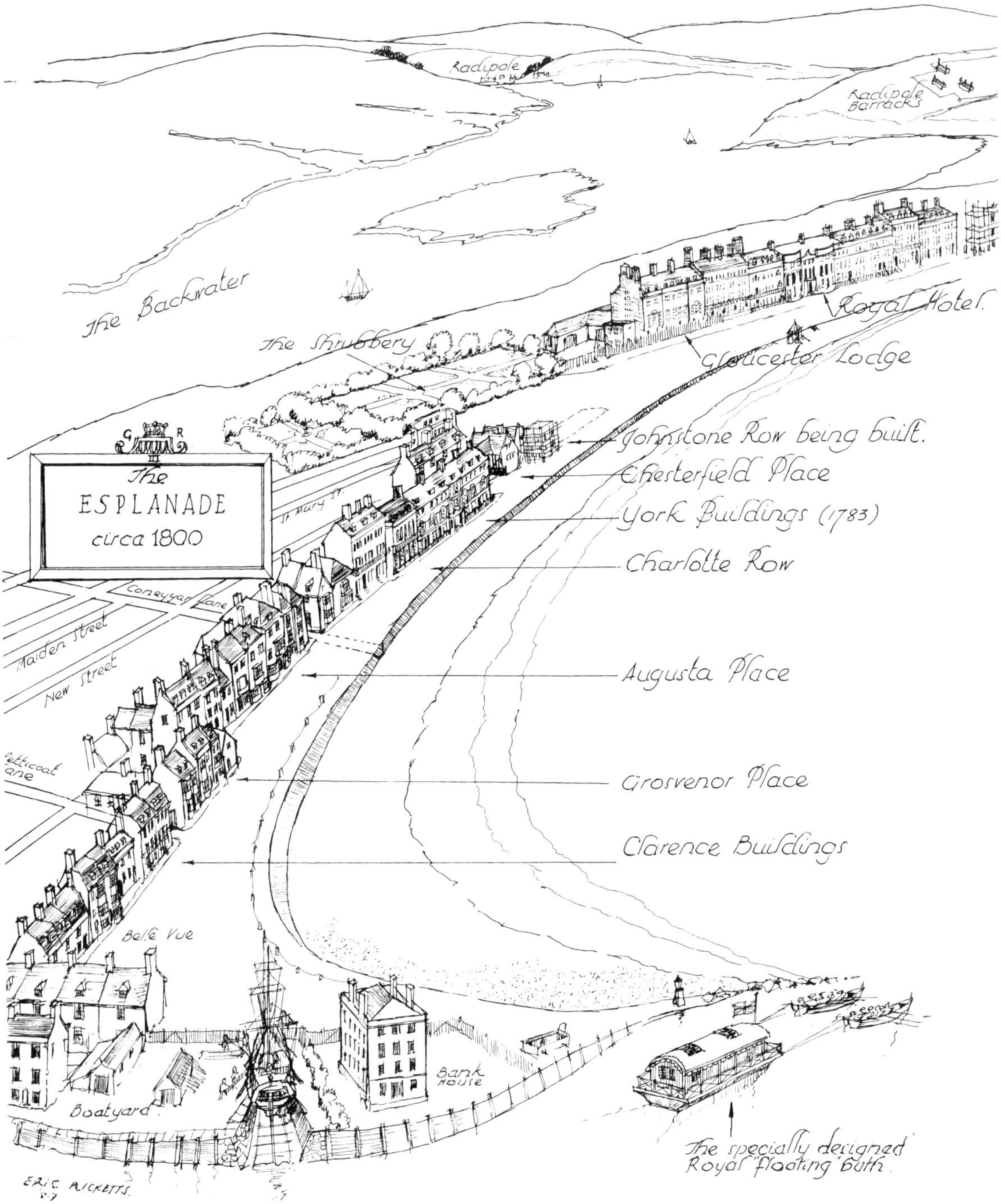

The ESPLANADE circa 1800
G R
Radipole
Radipole Barracks
The Backwater
The Shrubbery
Royal Hotel
Gloucester Lodge
Johnstone Row being built.
Chesterfield Place
York Buildings (1783)
Charlotte Row
Augusta Place
Grosvenor Place
Clarence Buildings
St Mary St.
Coneygar Lane
Maiden Street
New Street
Petticoat Lane
Belle Vue
Boatyard
Bank House
The specially designed Royal "floating" bath
ERIC RICKETTS

SEASIDE WEYMOUTH

A Celebration in Pictures

Maureen Attwooll and Jack West

DOVECOTE PRESS

First published in 1989 by The Dovecote Press Ltd
Stanbridge, Wimborne, Dorset BH21 4JD

ISBN 0 946159 68 8

Typeset by Character Graphics, Taunton, Somerset
Printed and bound by Biddles Ltd, Guildford and King's Lynn

Introduction

The story of *Seaside Weymouth* begins in the 18th century at a time when Sea Bathing was being advocated by physicians as a cure for all the ills of the age. This new medical treatment was to bring prosperity to many small coastal towns as fashionable society, already accustomed to 'taking the cure' at the established inland spas, turned its attention to the developing seaside health and pleasure resorts. These offered the experience of bathing in the sea along with the more dubious benefits to be gained from drinking prescribed courses of sea water. Weymouth's special claim to fame is that during the years 1789-1805 the town was King George III's favourite health resort, where he spent fourteen long summer holidays by the sea.

The King was by no means one of the first visitors to bathe in the sea at Weymouth – as early as the 1740's there were already two 'bathing houses' in use. By the end of the century the growth of the sea bathing industry and the popularity of 'Royal Weymouth' had brought about great changes in the town, where for hundreds of years the main source of income had come from trade through the twin ports of Weymouth and Melcombe Regis. Around the harbour were clustered the houses, commercial premises, inns and markets of the inhabitants, but there was to be a complete 'about face' as those same inhabitants began to realise the full potential of the area then considered merely as the back of the town – the smooth golden sands and calm waters of Weymouth Bay. The land where the new developments were to take place lay behind, or seaward of Melcombe, on what is now 'The Esplanade'. North of where the King's Statue stands today was then empty waste ground, and the entire beach was used as the town rubbish dump.

The first visitors lodged in the town area, and one of the resort's earliest patrons was Ralph Allen, of Prior Park, Bath, who in 1750 purchased a harbour-side house for his regular summer visits. This was on the south, or Weymouth, side of the harbour, which became less popular in later years when 'The Esplanade' was developed on the more fashionable north, or Melcombe side. Allen was a wealthy and influential man with a wide circle of friends; he attracted other visitors and Weymouth's reputation grew. The local newspapers began publishing weekly lists of 'fashionable arrivals' and noted that 'families of distinction' were spending summer weeks at Weymouth during the 'season' from June to October each year.

In 1765 another important and very significant visitor expressed "great satisfaction at the reception and entertainment he met with" at Weymouth. This was William Henry, 1st Duke of Gloucester, and a younger brother of King George III. Gloucester's liking for the town was consolidated in 1780 when he began building his own summer home – 'Gloucester Lodge' – facing the sea. It was here that King George III and the Royal Family stayed each time they holidayed at Weymouth.

Where the King went society followed, and the years 1789-1805 brought 'Royal Weymouth' real fame as England's premier health and pleasure resort. There was a great upsurge in building as new terraces of houses appeared on that most desirable site – 'The Esplanade', facing the sands and bay.

Georgian seaside holidays were somewhat sedate. Sea bathing was a medical treatment and doctors strongly recommended that it should only take place early in the morning, warning that a bathe late in the day would "occasion great depression of the spirits". It was something of a ritual, the intending bather being trundled out into deep water in one of the thirty or so horse-drawn bathing machines lined up on the sands. The 'dip' might be followed by a stroll along 'The Esplanade', or perhaps a carriage ride to a local beauty spot. Gentlemen could meet at one of the libraries for a card game or to peruse the newspapers displayed there. Evening entertainments included Balls, the well-ordered social scene being organised by a 'Master of Ceremonies', as well as Royal Receptions at the Assembly Rooms when the King and his family were in residence. The Theatre Royal on 'The Esplanade' provided plays and variety bills. King George III's holidays were enlivened by numerous (and often boisterous) trips to sea, and by regular troop reviews. Thousands of soldiers saw duty at Weymouth as England was at war with France during almost the entire period of the royal visits, and the threat of invasion was ever present. The Royal Family paid regular visits to the local gentry and the King and Princesses enjoyed horseback rides in the hills around the town.

King George III's final visit to Weymouth in 1805 and the sale of the royal property on his death in 1820 brought about a slowing-down in the building boom, but Weymouth continued to bask in its new prosperity and the nobility and gentry were still attracted to a resort once favoured by royalty.

The change from genteel health and pleasure resort to family holiday town came towards the end of the 19th century. The railway reached Weymouth in 1857, and soon cheap rail fares and statutory holidays combined to bring a trip to the seaside within the reach of the masses for the very first time. The Victorians did not want to spend long leisurely weeks of 'the season' by the sea – their holidays were shorter and they wanted cheaper accommodation. Day trips to the seaside by train became popular. The character of the resort altered and soon thousands of holidaymakers were thronging the sands and Esplanade, enjoying outdoor band concerts, sandcastle building, Punch and Judy, donkey rides, paddling and sea bathing. Modesty was preserved and enforced, and bathing machines and the larger bathing saloons remained in use until well into the 20th century.

Weymouth is a well-illustrated town, and both Georgian artists and Victorian photographers recorded their impressions of life at the seaside. The early 1900s saw the great era of picture postcard collecting (halfpenny postage, half the cost of a letter), and from that time hundreds of photographs exist to portray all the different aspects which have contributed to the story of *Seaside Weymouth*.

This selection of pictures attempts to show both the constant features and the passing whims of the past 200 years. Many are of the sands and bay, because Weymouth's popularity today still depends very much on what it was advertising back in 1785 as "The general Tranquillity of the Bay, the Clearness of the Water, the Softness and almost imperceptible Descent of its Shore . . ." (plus, hopefully, a good measure of sunshine added!).

Acknowledgements

For permission to reproduced illustrations in this celebration of more than two hundred years of life at 'Seaside Weymouth' we are grateful to the following.

David Chambers. Nos. 7, 19, 32, 38, 42, 48, 50, 103.

Dorset County Library. Nos. 4, 6, 11, 12, 13, 14, 15, 16, 17, 18, 22, 24, 25, 31, 34, 39, 40, 41, 44, 45, 51, 58, 59, 60, 62, 75, 79, 80, 81, 82, 83, 85, 88, 105.

Dorset County Library – "The Graham Herbert Collection" Nos. 1, 2, 3, 21, 23, 28, 37, 52, 57, 61, 63, 64, 65, 69, 70, 71, 72, 73, 87, 90, 91, 92, 93, 94, 95, 96, 97, 98, 99, 100, 101, 102.

Hunting Aerofilms Ltd. No. 89.

Bill Macey. No. 104.

The Mitchell Library, Sydney, N.S.W. Nos. 5, 20.

H.M.S. Osprey Photographic Section. No. 35.

Mrs Kynaston Thompson. Nos. 27, 36.

Weymouth Museum. Nos. 8, 9, 10, 26, 53.

Mr and Mrs Harry Wrate. Nos. 47, 74.

(Items from the authors' own collection. Nos. 29, 30, 33, 43, 46, 49, 54, 55, 56, 66, 67, 68, 76, 77, 78, 84, 86.)

We are especially grateful to Mrs Mollie Herbert for having made the items from the 'Graham Herbert Collection' available to us.

We also wish to thank two people who have helped in very special ways – Eric Ricketts, who drew the splendid 'Bird's eye' map of Weymouth Esplanade in 1800, and David Chambers, who not only provided illustrations for this book but also gave a great deal of practical help.

As always, we owe a great debt to our publisher for his help and guidance, and last but not least, thanks to our families, who have once more been surrounded by 'local history' for many weeks.

1. In the 1750s, Ralph Allen of Bath, one of Weymouth's first regular visitors, bought the bow-fronted building in the centre of this photograph of Trinity Road as his summer home. This side of the town became less fashionable with the development of The Esplanade in Melcombe Regis.

2. The southern side of the harbour was described in 1774 as being: " . . . situated at the foot of an high hill that rises on the south of it, fronting the harbour, and the ground between it and the hill being narrow, it contains but one narrow and irregular street, near a mile in length . . . "

Although the health and pleasure resort developed on the opposite side of the harbour, a local physician still felt able to recommend the older part of the town to visitors in the 1790s: "There are yet some good Houses, and convenient Lodgings, to be had on this side of the Harbour, suited to those who are desirous of retirement, and whose Indispositions are not such as to prevent their crossing the Water to the Bathing Machines etc. on the other side, at Melcombe Regis, or rather New Weymouth . . . "

'Old' Weymouth is illustrated here – the line of the 'narrow and irregular street' which existed until after the Second World War. Most of these buildings, some of which had been damaged in air raids, were cleared in the 1960s and North Quay was re-developed.

3. The opening of Assembly Rooms on the Esplanade in the 1770s was to cause the demise of Mr DeLa Motte's Assembly Rooms in Trinity Street on the Weymouth side of the harbour. In a converted and extended 17th century building, they had provided entertainment for the resort's early visitors, but as society flocked to newly-fashionable Melcombe, they lost popularity. By the 1780s these were already known as 'The Old Rooms'. The building now houses the offices of the Devenish company.

4. Across the harbour, the first purpose built hotel on the land fronting what was to become Weymouth Esplanade was the Royal Hotel. Opened in 1773, it had been built on the empty waste ground north of the town by Andrew Sproule, a speculative developer from Bath. An attractive bow-fronted building with first floor Assembly Rooms, its early name was 'Stacie's Hotel' after the first manager, but when George III began attending events there regularly, 'Royal Hotel' became a popular alternative name. The building was demolished in 1891.

5. *Above:* Gloucester Lodge, built in 1780. Then, it had a side entrance and long gardens stretching down to what is now Frederick Place. Here, to stay in his brother's house, came King George III in June 1789.

Two fine Venetian windows are an important feature facing the Esplanade, and perhaps 200 years ago, King George III gazed out of them rather apprehensively at the cold waters of Weymouth Bay prior to taking his first-ever sea dip!

By the time of King's second visit four more houses in Gloucester Row had been leased to provide much-needed extra accommodation for the royal party. The King purchased Gloucester Lodge from his brother in 1801 and it remained a royal property until 1820 when it was sold following his death.

The drawing is by actor James Winston, who performed before the Royal Family in Weymouth in 1802.

6, 7. *Opposite:* In Victorian times the building was converted to an hotel. The original side entrance and courtyard were lost when the large extension was built at the southern end in the mid-nineteenth century. A new entrance was constructed between the two Venetian windows, facing the Esplanade.

The lower photograph shows the building as it is now, closed and awaiting conversion into flats. A dramatic fire in 1927 destroyed much of the interior, but the facade was little damaged. During rebuilding work an extra storey and roof with double row of attics were added, bringing the heights of the Lodge and its Victorian extension almost level. Over the years a succession of verandahs constructed along the front of the hotel have obscured one of the Venetian windows.

8. More 18th century developments along Weymouth Esplanade. Stacie's Hotel of the early 1770s is in the background of this print, part of Gloucester Row. The terrace in the centre is York Buildings of 1785.

A row of posts marks The Esplanade, walling of which did not begin until 1800. It follows a much straighter shoreline than today – reclamation in the early 1800s provided land for building and curved the Esplanade seawards at its southern end.

This is one of a series of twelve engravings published locally in 1790 by John Love, Weymouth librarian and bookseller.

9. A companion print, from the opposite direction. The thin strip of land which then led into Melcombe was 'The Narrows', aptly named with the Bay on one side and the Backwater on the other. Here in later years were to be built the Esplanade terraces, but Gloucester Row stands alone in 1790. The area behind the 'Narrows' was not reclaimed from the Backwater until well into the 19th century.

Bathing machines are shown in both prints, and a local medical man noted approvingly that they were placed "immediately under the Windows of the Lodging Houses, pretty nearly in the centre of them; a Convenience better adapted to the Wish of the Sick and debilitated than is to be met with elsewhere".

10. King George III (1738-1820) brought fame to Weymouth when he, Queen Charlotte and three of their daughters stayed at Gloucester Lodge for the first time in the summer of 1789. All thirteen royal children were to visit Weymouth at one time or another, and the King and Queen spent fourteen long holidays by the sea between 1789 and 1805.

The King's first visit here was to convalesce after a debilitating and much misunderstood illness, which led to symptoms of mental derangement so severe that he had been diagnosed as mad by baffled doctors who attended him. But the King recovered, enjoyed his spell of rural and seaside life, and returned to Weymouth again and again, bringing great prosperity and fame to the growing resort.

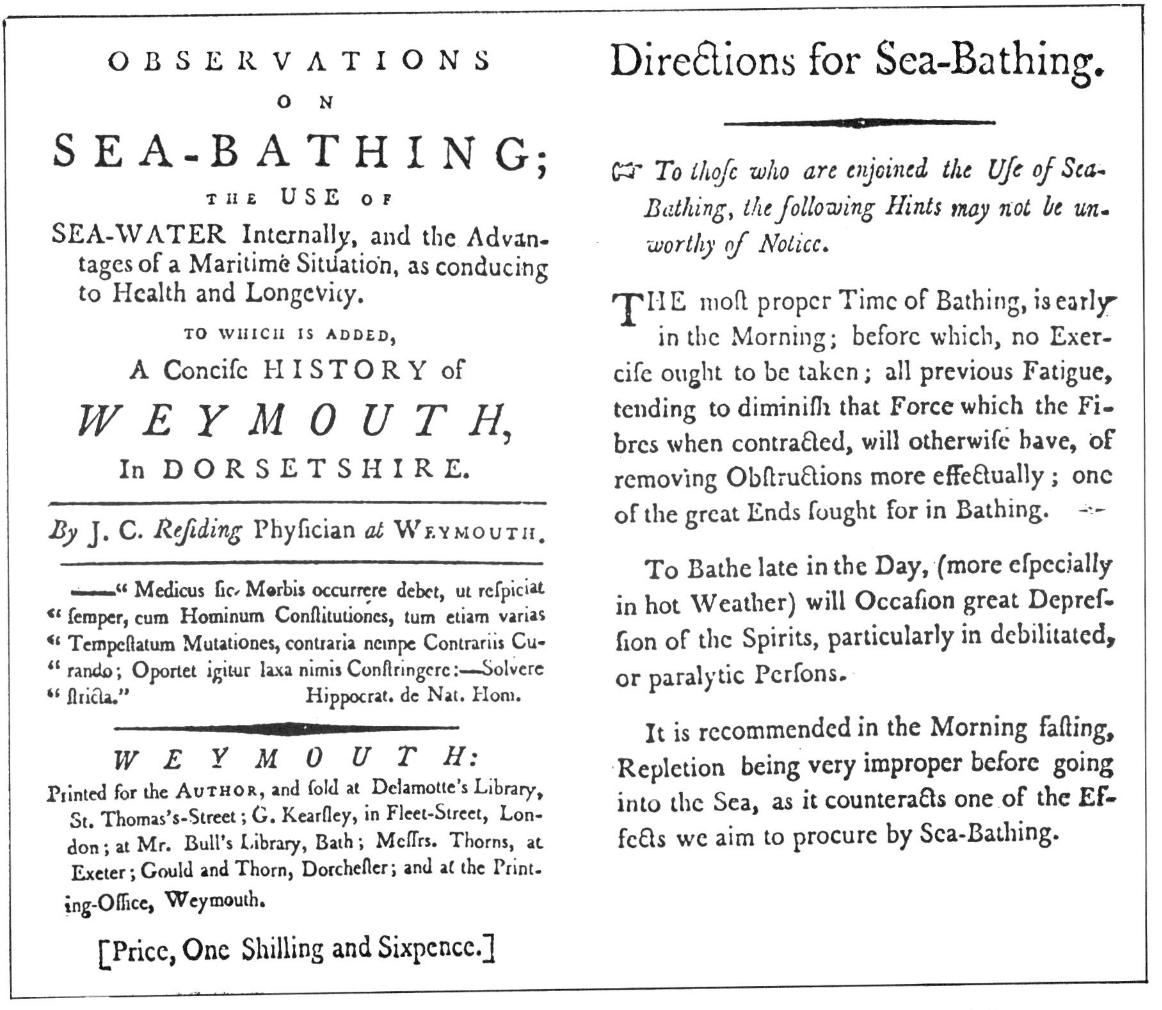

OBSERVATIONS
ON
SEA-BATHING;
THE USE OF
SEA-WATER Internally, and the Advantages of a Maritime Situation, as conducing to Health and Longevity.

TO WHICH IS ADDED,
A Concise HISTORY of
WEYMOUTH,
In DORSETSHIRE.

By J. C. *Residing* Physician *at* WEYMOUTH.

——"Medicus sic Morbis occurrere debet, ut respiciat "semper, cum Hominum Constitutiones, tum etiam varias "Tempestatum Mutationes, contraria nempe Contrariis Curando; Oportet igitur laxa nimis Constringere:—Solvere "stricta." Hippocrat. de Nat. Hom.

WEYMOUTH:
Printed for the AUTHOR, and sold at Delamotte's Library, St. Thomas's-Street; G. Kearsley, in Fleet-Street, London; at Mr. Bull's Library, Bath; Messrs. Thorns, at Exeter; Gould and Thorn, Dorchester; and at the Printing-Office, Weymouth.

[Price, One Shilling and Sixpence.]

Directions for Sea-Bathing.

☞ *To those who are enjoined the Use of Sea-Bathing, the following Hints may not be unworthy of Notice.*

THE most proper Time of Bathing, is early in the Morning; before which, no Exercise ought to be taken; all previous Fatigue, tending to diminish that Force which the Fibres when contracted, will otherwise have, of removing Obstructions more effectually; one of the great Ends sought for in Bathing.

To Bathe late in the Day, (more especially in hot Weather) will Occasion great Depression of the Spirits, particularly in debilitated, or paralytic Persons.

It is recommended in the Morning fasting, Repletion being very improper before going into the Sea, as it counteracts one of the Effects we aim to procure by Sea-Bathing.

11. It was to bathe in the sea that King George III came to Weymouth, and these guidelines concerning the use of sea water were published in the 1790s.

12. A cartoon to commemorate a historic occasion – King George III's first bathe in the sea at Weymouth, July 7th, 1789. Stripped of wig and clothes (it was customary for gentlemen to bathe naked in the 18th century), the King waits to be immersed by the 'dippers'. It is only 7 a.m. but crowds line the Esplanade, a band (looking rather seasick) stands by to play the National Anthem as soon as the royal head goes under the water, to shouts of "Long live the King" from the assembled population.

Assembly Room
Long live the King

13. *Above:* Octagonal bathing machines at Weymouth in the early years of this century, with the King's Bathing Machine (the only one known to have survived to the present day) in the foreground.

The intending bather ascended the steps facing the shore and disrobed inside the machine. A horse was hitched to the front of it (facing the sea) and trundled it out until a sufficient depth of water was reached. Once the horse had been unhitched and taken back to the shore, the bather was able to descend the seaward facing steps for a health giving dip in the briny.

Those nervous of sampling the benefits of sea bathing alone could hire, for an extra fee, the services of one of the attendants or 'dippers' employed by the bathing machine companies. When the bathe was complete, the whole process was repeated in reverse and the bather was jolted uncomfortably back to the beach again.

14. *Below:* Crowds turned out to see the King wherever he went in Weymouth and he must have welcomed the privacy offered by the Floating Bathing Machine which was introduced in 1792. This vessel was usually moored at the pier and offered a sea-water bathe below sea level, with dressing rooms above.

The watercolour shows the Floating Bathing Machine moored at the Nothe some years after the Royal visits and before the Nothe Fort of the 1860s was built. Only a 'Camera Obscura' stands on the Nothe Headland.

HOT AND COLD BATHS,

Exceedingly commodious, supplied from sea water, are constructed upon the quay, southward of the Esplanade, ; which may be used at any time, by day or night, at the following rates :

A hot bath before six in the evening, or an hour's notice - -	3s. 6d.
At a later hour - - -	4s. 0d.
For each guide attending -	0s. 6d.

The Cold Bath is chiefly used by persons incapable of using the bathing machines, either from lameness or very uncommon timidity.

THE BATHING MACHINES,

As we have already observed, are upwards of forty in number. Some of these have umbrellas, and are chiefly used by the ladies ; the rates as follow :

An umbrella machine with a guide	1s. 6d
A gentleman's bathing machine	0s. 6d.
For each guide - - -	0s. 6d.

N. B. At the baths a sedan is always in waiting ; and the baths are freshly filled for every lady or gentleman that uses them.

15. A guidebook of 1800 provided bathing information for the visitor.

16. 'Maids in their proper element' (probably three of the Royal Princesses) enjoy the privacy of a sea-water bathe inside the Floating Bathing Machine.

17. One of three 'Umbrella Machines' specially designed for the Royal Family in 1791. The large oblong machines were painted red, white and blue, and had 'modesty hoods' fitted over the seaward-facing doors. These could be lowered to provide a clammy and claustrophobic enclosed 'bathing-pool' when the bather descended the steps into the water!

18. *Above:* Entertainment in the growing resort was limited. The colonnaded building on the left of this drawing once housed John Harvey's Library and Card Assembly in Charlotte Row. Harvey's 'Rooms' were not quite as prestigious as those in the Royal Hotel, but were still a fashionable meeting place for visiting society. Adjacent to Harvey's is York Buildings, once a very fine example of a Georgian terrace.

19. *Below:* York Buildings today, much altered and minus one house at its northern end. Only the central bow-windowed feature and the house at the southern end remain as they were first built.

20. Since 1770 the tiny theatre on Weymouth Esplanade had provided the main venue for an evening out. It seated more than 400 people, Georgian playgoers being entertained in some discomfort, packed together on hard backless benches. King George III and the Royal Family were very frequent patrons of what became known as the 'Theatre Royal'. To the left of the theatre can be seen Ryall's Toyshop in Augusta Place, where Queen Charlotte and her daughters shopped for trinkets.

The sketch dates from 1802. The 'Theatre Royal' was demolished long ago and the building now housing the 'Theatre Royal Bars' stands on the site.

THEATRE ROYAL

New Concert Hall, St. Nicholas Street, Weymouth.

LESSEE AND MANAGER, - - MR. BELTON.

Doors open at quarter past 7, the curtain will rise at quarter to 8 o'Clock.

21. A second 'Theatre Royal' opened in a converted chapel building in St. Nicholas Street in the 1860s, but this one had no 'Royal' connections and closed before the end of the century. Ending its days as a store, the building was demolished in 1968 and only this little landmark remained to remind passers-by of the site's theatrical history. The entrance arch did not survive further demolitions in the 1980s.

22. As the resort's popularity grew the Esplanade developed apace: its southern end was considerably changed by the plans of Sir William Pulteney in the early 1800s, when a large area of land was reclaimed from the sea. On this new ground 'The Rings' were laid out (shown here in the foreground of a picture by John Upham in 1821), and Pulteney and Devonshire Buildings were erected between 1812 and 1819.

23, 24. King George III's visits to Weymouth are commemorated by two monuments. *Above:* The King's Statue unveiled in 1810, was the design of James Hamilton, local architect, builder and stone mason, whose work can be seen in many of the buildings of Georgian Weymouth. The photograph, of the 1950s, shows W.H. Smith's bookshop-style windows, before the arrival of the plate-glass era.

Below: The second 'monument' to the visits of King George III is the Osmington White Horse of 1808, the chalk cutting which is the subject of many a local legend. It is a very appropriate tribute to the King who so much enjoyed riding horseback on the hills around Weymouth.

25. The seaside saying that 'the price of food goes up when the visitors arrive' is a very old one – it is known that the Royal Family had produce sent down from the gardens at Windsor and Kew rather than pay the prices asked by Weymouth shopkeepers. Cartoonists were soon portraying the Royal 'meanness', showing the King and Queen preparing their own suppers – "Frying Sprats" and "Toasting Muffins".

26. *Overleaf:* Long after the Royal visits had ended, Weymouth remained a genteel health resort. In the early Victorian period Henry Burn painted this view of The Esplanade, looking north. The building with a roofline higher than its neighbours is now known as the Fairhaven Bars, but for over a century was the Victoria Hotel.

ALBION

27. *Above:* Shown here are the Ionic columns of the Hot and Cold Sea Water Baths at the top end of St. Thomas Street, opened in the early 1840s. Earlier visitors too nervous or too ill to plunge into the sea had enjoyed a similar facility on the Quay.

This building had another impressive entrance in St. Mary Street. In winter, a Hot Sea Water Bath cost 6d., but the charge went up to 1/- in the season!

28. The Baths were demolished in 1927 and this building rose on the site. It too offered facilities for the visitor in the way of shops and a restaurant, but will be remembered by many a holidaymaker who rushed for the shelter of the Clinton Arcade on a rainy day! This passage through to St. Mary Street was almost considered as a public right of way, but it was closed once a year (on Good Friday) to maintain the owners' rights.

On the left the mansard roof of the old buildings in Coburg Place can be seen in both photographs.

29-30. Small engravings, the originals no more than 4″ x 3″, were popular souvenirs in the days before the introduction of the picture postcard. These two Victorian Esplanade scenes show Royal Terrace and Frederick Place (both built on the former gardens of Gloucester Lodge) and Victoria Terrace.

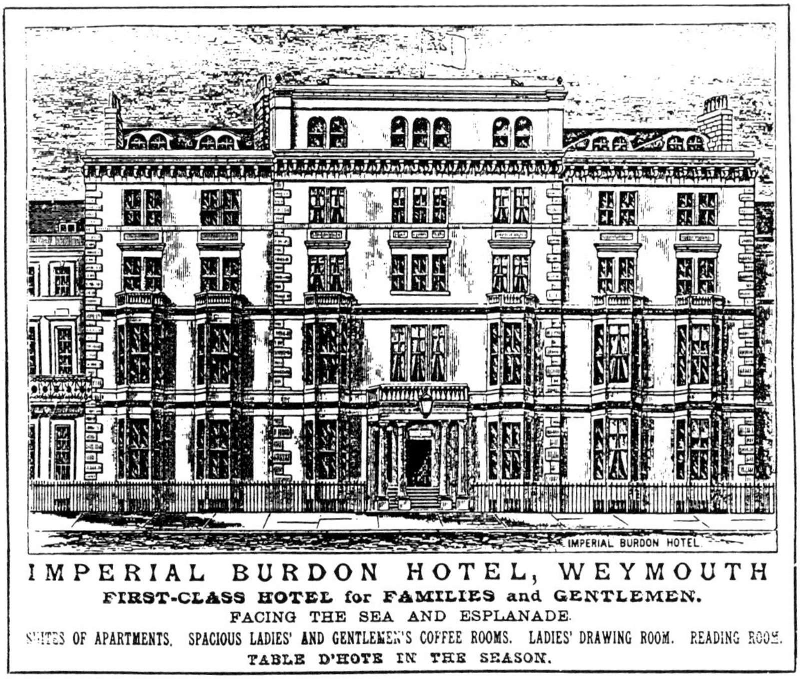

31. Architecturally, the Georgian atmosphere of The Esplanade was maintained well into the Victorian era, and Victoria Terrace, of 1855, blends well with the earlier terraces to the south. With the building of Victoria Terrace the long row of houses facing the sea, begun before King George III visited Weymouth, was now virtually complete.

This is the central feature of Victoria Terrace – the Burdon Hotel (now The Prince Regent) advertising its facilities in the 1880s.

32. At the time this engraving was made, both the Pier and the Nothe Fort were new features of the harbourside. The Pier had been extended seawards in stages during the early nineteenth century, but the final extensions culminating in the rounded 'Pier Head' shown here were carried out in 1859-60.

The Nothe Fort, part of the fortifications of Portland Harbour, was built during the years 1860-1869, and was used by the military until after the Second World War. It is now maintained as an historical showpiece, and is open to visitors.

33. *Above*: Apart from improved berthing facilities, the Pier of 1860 remained little changed until more land was reclaimed in the early 1900s, to provide a site for the new Pavilion Theatre, opened in 1908.

34. *Below:* Increased trade required improved harbour facilities, and in 1931 work commenced on replacing the old pile pier with a modern stone and concrete structure. Here the new works are shown extending seawards. Although proposals were put forward in the late 19th century for a 'promenade pier' in the vicinity of the Jubilee Clock, they were later dropped, and Weymouth has never had the traditional cast-iron seaside pleasure pier popular in other resorts.

35. The latest major extensions to the Pier, carried out to provide facilities for handling 'Roll-on-Roll-off' traffic were commenced in 1967, and eventually resulted in the largest reclamation of land from the sea since the first modest schemes of the early 1800s. The total area of land reclaimed is clearly seen in this aerial photograph. Remember that when King George III was visiting Weymouth the 'Esplanade' ran almost straight from 'Gloucester Lodge' to the harbourside. The modern 'Alexandra Gardens' and everything seaward has been reclaimed since 1800. Compare this aerial photograph of the 1980s with the frontispiece map.

36. The railway reached Dorchester in 1847, but it was another ten years before the final eight miles of track to Weymouth resulted in this photograph of the Station on 'Opening Day', 29th January, 1857. The large roof spanning the tracks was removed in the 1950s.

37. This remarkable 'aerial' photograph of the layout of Weymouth Station was taken from the top of Christchurch spire, shortly before the church was demolished in 1956. On the right are the lines running into the station: to the left are the 'goods' facilities, including a transit shed and sidings, and in the distance are the storage sidings laid down following the construction of Radipole Park Drive in 1926.

38. The old 'Brunel' station, dating from 1857, was demolished and this modern station, designed to handle the passenger traffic of the 1980s opened in 1986.

39. *Above:* Victorian holidaymakers enjoying Esplanade and sands. The photograph was taken shortly before the demolition of the first Royal Hotel (in the centre of the picture) in 1891. Everyone is rather overdressed by today's standards, but it is a very recognizable seaside scene.

40. *Below:* In 1890 a new version of the Bathing Machine appeared on the beach – the Bathing Saloon where a cubicle could be hired at a cheaper rate than an individual machine. Strict regulations were enforced in Victorian times regarding the distance between the Ladies' Saloon and the Gentlemen's Saloon. In the foreground of the picture is a regular feature of seaside entertainment – the outdoor concert platform. Here, in about 1900, Mr. Ballard Brown's Entertainers were putting on a show for the visitors.

41. Val Vaux's Vaudeville Pavilion troupe pose for a publicity photograph in about 1920. The removable beach theatre features on many pre-war views of Weymouth sands.

42. The simple lines of the first Royal Hotel proved to be too plain for the Victorians, who pulled it down in 1891. A few years later this larger and more elaborate Royal Hotel rose on the site. A small extension later closed the gap shown here, and a ground floor balcony has been added.

44. *Overleaf*: 'Weymouth from the Nothe' has always been a favourite subject for photographers. This striking picture of 1895 shows the veteran paddle steamer *Premier* alongside the pier, whilst the train at the Landing Stage awaits the arrival of the Jersey Boat. A typical luxury yacht of the period is moored alongside the Nothe Walk.

43. The Jubilee Clock appeared on Weymouth seafront in 1888, (a little behind time for Queen Victoria's Golden Jubilee celebrations of 1887!) It has never been moved – when first erected this stone platform was actually on the beach, with steps leading down to the sands. Later extension of the Esplanade seawards has surrounded and covered the original base of the clock. A rather wintry scene of the early 1900s.

45., 46. *Above*: Esplanade extensions of the 1920s provided a wider roadway for traffic and more room for pedestrians on the 'prom'. Another important reason for this wide sweep around the Jubilee Clock was to prevent the encroachment of shingle onto Weymouth's great asset – its golden sands.

Below: A first glimpse of Weymouth seafront for many thousands of holidaymakers who have streamed out of Weymouth railway station for more than a century – the view up King Street towards the Jubilee Clock.

47., 48. The early 1900s had heralded the start of a new craze – picture postcard collecting – and one made more popular because postcards could be sent for a halfpenny, half the cost of a letter. These two comic cards are typical of the Edwardian period (although in later years vulgar comic cards were to cause vigilant local Watch Committees some problems).

Mixed bathing, unheard of in Victorian times, was now becoming acceptable, and obviously a cause for celebration!

49. 'The Swans' have been a popular subject for postcard publishers since the early 1900s when this photograph was taken, but its background is equally interesting, showing the Weymouth and Portland Railway Viaduct and the shoreline of Commercial Road before the 1920s reclamation of land for Melcombe Regis Gardens and Radipole Park Drive.

50. *Below*: The sands at Weymouth about 1910. Some of the bathing machines date back to the Georgian era; the 'oblong' and 'octagonal' machines can be seen in many of the earliest drawings of 'Seaside Weymouth'. Both types had large wheels which enabled them to be drawn out into deep water. The survivors were all sold off in 1916 and many had a further lease of life as garden sheds or summer-houses.

New machines provided after the First World War were fitted with small iron wheels, provided solely to enable them to be moved on and off the beach. They were stationary throughout the summer and never entered the water.

51., 52. The Weymouth Donkeys are still a feature of the sands today, but the Goat-Carts are now only a memory. The top photograph of about 1905 shows one of the goats and two of the small carriages, one of which survived in use until the 1950s. The lower photograph of the donkey pulling a miniature landau was taken in 1958.

53. No holiday is complete without 'A Present from Weymouth' – commemorative china has been popular since the nineteenth century.

54. *Below* From early in the 19th century Bath Chairs, used to transport the invalid and aged around Weymouth, were a common sight, but not one is known to have survived to the present day. This photograph dates from the early 1900s.

55. By 1907 there were bandstands at both ends of the Esplanade, one in the Alexandra Gardens and this newer bandstand which stood on the beach opposite Victoria Terrace. It was replaced in 1939 by the Pier Bandstand.

56., 57. The Victorian cast iron and glass shelters which are such attractive 'period pieces' today first appeared on the Esplanade late in the 1880s. The left hand photograph shows a detail of the delicate filigree cast ironwork. When erected, all the shelters had small 'balconies' overlooking the beach, but Esplanade widening has left most of them centrally placed on the promenade.

58., 59. Weymouth's first 'Bandstand', shown in the engraving as a kind of circular open tent, was in place in the centre of 'The Rings' by 1871. These gardens, laid out on land reclaimed from the sea around 1810, remained in private ownership until 1867 when the site was purchased by a wealthy visitor and presented to the Weymouth Corporation as a public open space. Named The Alexandra Gardens in 1880, this is still one of the best known features of 'Seaside Weymouth'.

The photograph shows the permanent 'Bandstand' erected in 1891 and the thatched shelters of 1904 around the sides of the gardens.

60. Rain always threatened audiences enjoying band concerts in the Gardens, so the glass 'Kursaal' was built around the Bandstand in 1913. It was a strange structure, draughty on a breezy day, hot in bright sunshine and hardly the 'Miniature Crystal Palace' it was described as by an over-enthusiastic local reporter!

The helter-skelter in the background was a brief visitor to the sands in the 1920s.

61. The 'Kursaal' survived until 1924, when it was replaced by the 'Alexandra Concert Hall', which occupied the major part of the Gardens.

62. *Above*: Much of the glass was removed in the late 1930s. More generally known as 'The Alexandra Gardens Theatre', it was one of the major entertainment centres during the summer season for almost forty years, and many well-known show personalities have appeared on its stage.

63. *Left*: A temporary visitor to the Alexandra Gardens in 1953 was the 'Guinness Clock' originally featured at the 'Festival of Britain' two years before. It was a great crowd-puller and one of the more spectacular free entertainments laid on for the holidaymakers.

64. Inside the Alexandra Gardens Theatre, where mural-painted walls helped distract the eye from the complex pattern of metal struts above.

65. Competition from the newly opened 'Weymouth Pavilion' in the early 1960s marked the end of the road for the 'Alexandra Gardens Theatre' and it was converted to an Amusement Arcade. Shown here in 1967, the building is little changed today.

66. The Nothe public gardens were laid out in the 1880s and later extended. The area has always been subject to land slippage, and a section of the sea wall in this 1920s picture had been engulfed. The Alexandra Gardens bandstand was moved here in 1924.

This postcard's main interest lies in its view of a Georgian bathing machine – on the left – in use as a summer house, which was the fate of many others removed from the beach during the First World War.

67. The gardens at Greenhill were also begun over one hundred years ago. This Edwardian layout of high hedges and walks was described as "a pleasant retreat from the bustling scenes on the Front and Esplanade".

68., 69. In 1908 the Pavilion Theatre opened, built on reclaimed land on the seaward side of Weymouth Pier. It was a real seaside confection and a striking landmark viewed from either the harbour or the Esplanade. After closure during the Second World War, the theatre opened again in the early 1950s under a new name – "The Ritz".

70. As 'The Ritz', the theatre had a very short life. The mainly wooden building caught fire during refurbishment on 13th April, 1954 and burned down. Practically the whole of Weymouth turned out to watch the fire-fighting operation, as this congested scene shows.

71. Two days after the fire, showing the tangled girders of the auditorium. The building behind the theatre, untouched by the blaze, was the Ritz Palm Court ballroom. It had been built on the site of an Edwardian roller skating rink.

72. *Below*: It was six years before a new 'Pavilion' rose on the same spot, shown here almost ready for opening day in 1960. The ornamental pier toll house to the right of the theatre was removed later the same year. Major reclamation work has now completely altered the area in front of the building.

73. *Below right*: Decorative seashell panels were an attractive feature of the Pavilion, but twenty years' exposure to the vagaries of seaside weather damaged them beyond repair and they have now been covered over.

74. Paddle steamers became a feature of the traditional Weymouth holiday from 1845 onwards, when Captain Cosens introduced the first of his fleet of pleasure boats. Excursions were made to Portland Harbour, Lulworth Cove, Swanage, Bournemouth and even the Isle of Wight, and on a rather more limited scale, westwards as far as Torquay.

The Cosens Boats saw service in two Wars, but rising costs following the Second World War meant that they could not be replaced when too old for service, and the last 'paddler' was withdrawn in 1967. They are still remembered with great affection by thousands of visitors, and the annual visit by the *Waverley*, not a Weymouth boat, but the last Paddle Steamer still in service in Great Britain, is always a 'sell-out'.

75. One of the Cosens Fleet, the paddle steamer *Victoria*, laden with holiday makers, reverses out of harbour on an afternoon excursion to Lulworth Cove about 1910.

76., 77. Paddle-steamers could take holidaymakers on day-trips to other seaside-resorts, but on land such excursions were restricted to those places which could be reached by horse-drawn carriages. The 'wagonettes' which took visitors into the surrounding countryside are shown here in front of the King's Statue, and a trip to Osmington Mills or Upwey Wishing Well often included a 'Cream Tea'. A few of these vehicles endured after the coming of the motor coach, but by the 1920s, when the lower photograph was taken, only one wagonette survives amidst an assembly of charabancs and motor-buses.

Very much a part of the seaside scene since the 1870s is the 'Cabmen's Shelter' adjoining the Esplanade, more familiarly known today as the 'Tea Cabin'.

78. *Above*: One of the last surviving wagonettes, the 'Royal Pearl' was still operating in the 1930s and is shown here in front of the Gloucester Hotel, ready to set off for Upwey Wishing Well.

79. *Left*: Specially designed buses were available for the summer season and the 'toast-racks' which ran from the Pavilion Theatre to Bowleaze Cove were a popular feature of the years prior to the Second World War.

80. *Below*: Off to the Puddle Valley by 'Rambler' coach return fare of 4/- (20p). By the 1930s, motor-coaches were bringing in an ever increasing proportion of the summer visitors to Weymouth, and motor-coach tours were part of the seaside holiday.

81. Weymouth sands in the 1920s, the scene dominated by the helter-skelter – beyond it are swings, a roundabout and the Vaudeville Theatre.

82. On a site to the south in the twenties and thirties was the Skee Ball Pavilion. The game was played in a bowling alley – a bump in the alley caused the ball to leap in the air and enter a target. The building was removed shortly after the Second World War.

FREE

83. The magnificent sweep of Weymouth Bay led to the town advertising itself as 'The Naples of England' from Victorian times until well into the 1920s.

This photograph of 1923 was taken before work began on the second stage of widening the Esplanade. The completed extension from the Jubilee Clock southwards stops just opposite the Tea Cabin.

ICES

84. Until after the Second World War, modesty prevailed on Weymouth Beach. Family Bathing Machines, cubicled Bathing Saloons and hired Bathing Tents provided changing facilities for bathers. Another development of the 1920s was the bungalows or chalets at Greenhill which were also available for hire.

85. Sea bathing advice, 1920s-style.

Weymouth Bathing Saloon Company, Ltd.

SPLENDID SEA BATHING from 4 Large Saloons and 30 Family Machines situated on the SANDS at WEYMOUTH.

The Saloons will accommodate 58 persons, with a separate cubicle for each.
Each Family Machine will accommodate 4 persons in comfort.
All Saloons and Machines are in perfect order, and great care is taken to ensure cleanliness.
No Towel or Costume will be issued before being thoroughly cleansed.

TARIFF MOST REASONABLE.

Civility and attention may be depended upon from the Employees.

TICKETS MUST BE OBTAINED AT THE TICKET OFFICE.

Saloons and Machines will be available for Bathers during May and June from 7.30 a.m. to 5.30 p.m., and during July, August and September from 7.15 a.m. to 5.30 p.m., except on Sundays, when the time will be 7.15 a.m. till noon, or later when tide and weather are suitable.

Evening Bathing from Small Machines when tide is suitable.

WEYMOUTH IS RENOWNED FOR ITS COMFORTABLE AND PERFECTLY SAFE BATHING.

86. Almost certainly photographed in 1939, the last summer season at Weymouth before the outbreak of World War II. A beach scene so crowded that some holidaymakers cannot even see the sea, such is the proliferation of refreshment and souvenir stalls, bathing tents and bathing pavilions plus a row of modern bathing machines near the water's edge!

87. Cinema entertainment was once very much a part of seaside Weymouth. Moving pictures were first shown in this building as early as 1909 when it was the Jubilee Hall. The interior was rebuilt and reopened in 1926 as the Regent Theatre, renamed the Gaumont in the 1950s and the Odeon in the 1960s (when this photograph of the restored interior was taken). By 1976 it was the New Invicta, incorporating bingo. Now solely a bingo hall, it awaits demolition as part of the 1980s town centre redevelopment of St. Thomas Street.

Two other cinemas closed long ago – The Belle Vue (now the Elim Church) and The Palladium (now the Steam House Cafe). Only the Cannon in Gloucester Street (built on the site of the Georgian Royal Mews) still operates today.

88. This view of American Troops marching along Weymouth Esplanade in the early summer of 1944 has become almost a classic record of wartime Weymouth. The sands had been stripped of every bathing machine or structure which might give cover to an invading army, and extensive barbed-wire defences were everywhere. The whole of the Esplanade was one long fortification, but the end was in sight, and the Allied armies were preparing to cross the Channel to land in Normandy

89. *Opposite page*: This photograph of September 1954 shows how life at the seaside returned to normal in the post-war years. The Pier Bandstand of 1939 breaks the gentle curve of the bay, one of many criticisms levelled against this structure. The bus shelter in front of the King's Statue has only a short span of life left before this open area gives way to the Statue Gardens as we know them today. The 1920s extension round the Jubilee Clock is shown in dramatic detail – remember the sands once reached the base of the clock. There is no underpass or roundabout at the Clock Tower – such wonders are yet to be devised!

The Esplanade bears little physical resemblance to the one used by King George III back in 1789, but it is still the main feature of 'Seaside Weymouth'.

90., 91. The Pier Bandstand, opened in 1939, was apparently designed under a false idea that it never rained at Weymouth. On a sunny day it was ideal for such functions as the choosing of 'Miss Weymouth', an annual August ritual. On summer evenings it was perfect for dancing. But when it rained, the inadequate shelters along each side of the auditorium became more than a little overcrowded!

The Pier Bandstand was finally demolished in 1987, leaving only the entrance standing on the actual Esplanade as a reminder of this passing attraction.

92. Traditional entertainment – "That's the way to do it!" squeals Mr Punch to a packed audience on Weymouth Sands in the 1950s.

93. Jack Hayward's sand models delighted residents and visitors for more than thirty years. Cathedral models were his speciality, using only sand and sea water.

94. The loco of the miniature railway chugs its way along the western shore of Radipole Lake towards the 'Station' near Westham Road Bridge in 1958. Vehicles alongside belong to the fairground, and the overhanging girder to the Weymouth and Portland Railway Viaduct which was removed in the 1970s.

The fairground has transferred to the other side of the Lake and the miniature railway runs no more. This whole area has changed with the construction of the Weymouth relief road along this shore, the traffic roundabout, subway and new road bridge across Radipole Lake.

95. A Carnival Day in the 1950s, with floats making their way along a rain-soaked Esplanade! Weymouth Carnival grew out of the Weymouth Hospitals Carnival in the 1930s.

96. Regattas and yachting have always been a feature of seaside Weymouth and from time to time the sands have been occupied by various classes of sailing craft. The National Dinghy Championships were just one of the many such events held here in the years since World War II.

97. On the night of 18th/19th July, 1955, at the height of the summer season, 11 inches of rain fell in the area of Hardy's Monument on the hills above Portesham. The following day the floods hit the valley of the River Wey and there was extensive flooding throughout the entire Borough.

This photograph of Park Street shows how Radipole Lake had risen and flooded across the public gardens near Westham Bridge into the neighbouring streets.

98. *Above*: Weymouth at the height of its popularity on a warm sunny day in the 1960s. One cannot but wonder what the pioneers of 'Seaside Weymouth' such as Ralph Allen would have made of this.

99. *Opposite page*: The cross-Channel steamers *Caesarea* and *Sarnia* were familiar sights at Weymouth during the 1960s, and here the *Caesarea* leaves harbour in April, 1961. Both ships were rendered out-of-date by the introduction of 'Roll-on-Roll-off' car ferries in 1973 and the *Caesarea* left Weymouth in 1975. In the foreground is one of the last of the Cosens paddle-steamers, undergoing a pre-season overhaul on the Nothe slipway.

100. *Above*: The *Caesarea*, *Sarnia* and cross-Channel cargo vessel *Sambur* in 1961. Weymouth Harbour provides endless diversion for the visitor, with an ever changing range of ships and yachts.

101. The tradition of the professional sandmodellers at Weymouth continues. After Jack Hayward came Fred Darrington, seen here at work on his version of 'The Last Supper'. Weymouth sand is ideal for this type of modelling, but it is the special skill of the individual modeller which produces such spectacular results.

102. One of Weymouth's features for more than a century has been the 'Harbour Tramway' which takes the trains from the yards near Weymouth Station, through the streets to the harbour. Extensively used during the years Weymouth was a busy cargo port, it continued in use for passenger trains until the introduction of electric trains to Weymouth in 1988.

103. The harbour ferry which plies to and fro between the Nothe Steps and the Pavilion all day during the season.

105. *Overleaf*: 'Seaside Weymouth' in about 1900.

104. The electric trains from Waterloo were not the only new transport feature introduced to Weymouth in 1988. The 'Seafront Express' arrived on the Esplanade, conveying passengers of all ages from the vicinity of the Jubilee Clock to the far end of the Esplanade near the car parks at Lodmoor.

RICAN
DIO

YMOUTH
ATHING
ACHINES.
SALOONS
OFFICE.

maniac

Titre original : *Egomaniac*

Collection créée par Hugues de Saint Vincent et dirigée
par Arthur de Saint Vincent
Ouvrage dirigé par Sylvie Gand

Photo de couverture : Fred Goudon
Mannequin de couverture : Clément Becq
Couverture : Sommer Stein, Perfect Pear Creative

Pour la présente édition,

Collection dirigée par Franck Spengler
34-36 rue La Pérouse
75116 PARIS
www.hugoetcie.fr

ISBN : 9782755644418
Dépôt légal : février 2020
Imprimé en Espagne

EGO maniac

Traduit de l'anglais (américain)
par Karine Forestier

VI KEELAND

Hugo Poche

NEW ROMANCE®

Parfois ce que l'on cherche arrive
quand on ne le cherche plus.

Inconnu

CHAPITRE 1

DREW

Je déteste le réveillon du 31 décembre.

Deux heures dans les embouteillages et on n'a même pas parcouru les quinze kilomètres entre l'aéroport de La Guardia et chez moi. Il est plus de vingt-deux heures. Pourquoi tous ces gens ne sont-ils pas déjà en train de faire la fête ? La tension que mes deux semaines à Hawaï avaient réussi à apaiser est de retour, en embuscade, qui me vrille de plus en plus fort le ventre tandis que le taxi avance à la vitesse d'un escargot vers le nord de la ville.

Je m'efforce de ne pas songer à tout le travail qui m'attend pour mon retour, l'interminable litanie des problèmes d'autrui qui accentuent les miens.

Elle m'a trompé.

Il m'a trompée.

Obtenez-moi la garde exclusive des enfants.

Elle n'aura pas la maison de Vail.

Tout ce qu'elle veut, c'est mon argent.

Elle ne m'a pas taillé une seule pipe en trois ans.

Écoute, trouduc, tu as cinquante ans, tu es chauve, arrogant et taillé comme un œuf. Elle a vingt-trois ans, elle est sexy et ses seins sont si fermes qu'ils lui pointent presque sous le menton. Tu veux le sauver, ce mariage ? Rentre à la maison avec dix mille balles en cash, et ordonne-lui de se mettre à genoux. Tu l'auras, ta pipe. Et elle, son argent de poche. Arrêtons de faire semblant que cette association était autre chose que ce qu'elle est en réalité. Ça ne te convient pas ? Contrairement à ta future ex-femme, je prends les règlements par chèque. Mets-le à l'ordre de Drew M. Jagger, avocat du barreau.

Je me frotte la nuque, pris d'un léger accès de claustrophobie à l'arrière de mon Uber, et tourne les yeux vers la vitre. Une vieille dame nous dépasse, appuyée sur sa canne.

– Je vais descendre ici, j'aboie au chauffeur.

– Mais… et vos bagages ?

Je suis déjà en train de pousser ma portière.

– Ouvrez-moi le coffre, ce n'est pas comme si on avançait, de toute façon.

La circulation est complètement arrêtée et je ne suis plus qu'à deux pâtés d'immeubles du mien. Je jette un pourboire de cent dollars au chauffeur et attrape ma valise dans le coffre, avant de prendre une longue goulée de Manhattan.

J'aime cette ville autant que je la déteste.

Le 575 Park Avenue est un immeuble d'avant-guerre restauré, situé à l'angle sud-ouest de la 63e rue ;

une adresse qui donne aux gens des a priori vous concernant. Quelqu'un portant le même patronyme que moi occupait ce bâtiment avant qu'il ne soit converti en copro hors de prix. Raison pour laquelle j'ai été autorisé à garder mon cabinet au rez-de-chaussée quand les autres baux commerciaux ont été annulés il y a des années. De plus, je vis au dernier étage.

– Bon retour, monsieur Jagger, m'accueille le portier en uniforme qui m'ouvre tout grand la porte du hall.

– Merci, Ed. J'ai raté quelque chose pendant mon absence ?

– Non. Rien de neuf. Cela dit, j'ai jeté un coup d'œil à vos travaux l'autre jour. Ça m'a l'air de bien avancer.

– Ils utilisent l'entrée de service sur la 63e, comme prévu ?

Ed hoche la tête.

– Absolument. Je les ai à peine entendus, ces derniers jours.

Je lâche mon bagage une fois dans l'appartement, puis redescends en ascenseur pour aller vérifier l'état de mon cabinet. Les deux semaines qui viennent de s'écouler, pendant que moi je séjournais à Honolulu, mon espace professionnel a subi une rénovation complète. Les fissures dans les hauts plafonds de plâtre devaient être rebouchées et le tout repeint, un nouveau sol posé pour remplacer le vieux parquet trop usé.

Une épaisse bâche de plastique est encore fixée par de l'adhésif autour de l'encadrement des portes quand j'entre. Le peu de meubles que je n'ai pas stockés au garde-meuble est lui aussi couvert de bâches. *Merde. Ils n'ont pas encore fini.* L'entrepreneur m'avait promis qu'il ne resterait plus que les finitions d'ici à ce que je revienne de vacances. J'avais raison d'être sceptique.

Allumant la lumière, je suis soulagé de constater que l'aire d'accueil est complètement terminée, elle. Enfin une soirée de 31 décembre sans horribles surprises. Ça change.

Je balaie les lieux d'un rapide regard, satisfait de ce que je découvre, et je m'apprête à repartir quand je remarque un rai de lumière qui filtre sous la porte de la petite salle des archives, au bout du couloir.

Sans réfléchir plus avant, je m'y dirige pour l'éteindre.

Alors voilà, je mesure un mètre quatre-vingt-dix pour un bon quintal et peut-être est-ce juste à cause de mon état d'esprit du moment, ou du fait que je ne m'attends pas à voir quiconque ici, en tout cas quand j'ouvre la porte de la pièce et que je la trouve là, eh bien, j'ai la trouille de ma vie.

Elle hurle.

Je recule dans le couloir.

Elle se perche sur la chaise et se met à me brailler dessus en agitant son téléphone portable en l'air.

– J'appelle la police !

Les doigts tremblants, elle appuie sur le 9, puis le 1, et reste suspendue au-dessus du même chiffre, qui compléterait le numéro des secours.

– Sortez maintenant ou je les appelle !

Je pourrais lui sauter dessus et envoyer valser son téléphone avant qu'elle ait le temps de se rendre compte qu'elle n'a pas composé le dernier 1. Mais comme elle a l'air terrifiée, je recule d'un pas supplémentaire et lève les mains dans un geste de reddition.

– Je ne vous veux pas de mal, lui promets-je de ma voix la plus apaisante, la plus calme. Inutile d'appeler la police. C'est mon bureau, ici.

– Vous me prenez pour une imbécile ? Vous venez de faire irruption dans *mon* bureau.

– Votre bureau ? Vous avez dû prendre le mauvais chemin à l'angle de Dingo et de Tarée.

Elle vacille sur sa chaise et tend les deux bras pour recouvrer son équilibre. Et puis… sa jupe tombe à ses pieds.

– Dehors !

Elle s'accroupit et ramasse la jupe, qu'elle remonte jusqu'à sa taille tout en me tournant le dos.

– Vous prenez des médicaments, madame ?

– Des médicaments ? Madame ? Non, mais vous plaisantez, là ?

– Vous savez quoi ? (Je désigne le téléphone qu'elle a toujours à la main.) Pourquoi vous ne composeriez pas le numéro, histoire que les flics viennent. Qu'ils vous reconduisent dans l'asile de fous dont vous vous êtes échappée.

Elle écarquille les yeux.

Pour une folle, maintenant que j'y regarde de plus près, elle est carrément mignonne. La tignasse rousse flamboyante ramassée au sommet de son crâne semble en accord avec sa personnalité explosive. Enfin, vu l'expression de ses yeux bleus étincelants, je ne suis pas fâché de m'être abstenu de le lui faire remarquer.

Elle appuie sur le 1 et entreprend de rapporter le délit dont elle m'accuse, à savoir l'entrée par effraction dans mon propre bureau.

– Je souhaite signaler un cambriolage.

– Un cambriolage ?

Je hausse un sourcil et regarde autour de moi. Une chaise pliante isolée et une table en métal merdique, elle aussi pliante, constituent le seul ameublement de la pièce.

– Je vais voler quoi, exactement ? Votre tempérament de vainqueur ?

Elle corrige sa déclaration à la police.

– Une effraction. Je souhaite signaler une entrée par effraction au 575 Park Avenue. (Elle se tait et écoute.) Non, je ne pense pas qu'il soit armé. Mais il est grand. Très grand. Au moins un mètre quatre-vingt-cinq. Peut-être plus.

Je ricane.

– Et costaud. N'oubliez pas de leur préciser que je suis costaud aussi. Vous voulez que je vous montre mes biscotos ? Et vous devriez peut-être aussi leur dire que j'ai les yeux verts. Je ne voudrais pas que la police me confonde avec les autres « très grands » voleurs qui traînent dans MON BUREAU.

Même après avoir raccroché, elle reste debout sur sa chaise, à me toiser d'un air mauvais.

– Il y a une souris ? je lui demande.

– Une souris ?

– Vu que vous avez sauté sur cette chaise…

Je m'esclaffe.

– Vous trouvez ça drôle ?

– Bizarrement, oui. Et je ne m'explique pas du tout pourquoi, figurez-vous. Je devrais plutôt être furax : je rentre de deux semaines de vacances pour trouver une squatteuse dans mon bureau, merde.

– Une « squatteuse » ? Je ne suis pas une squatteuse. C'est mon bureau. J'ai emménagé ici il y a une semaine.

De nouveau, elle tangue sur son perchoir.

– Pourquoi vous ne descendez pas de là ? Vous allez tomber et vous faire mal.

– Qu'est-ce qui me dit que vous n'allez pas m'attaquer si je descends ?

Je secoue la tête et réprime le rire qui monte.

– Ma belle, regardez un peu comment je suis bâti. Et regardez-vous. Rester perchée là-dessus, ça vous protège de que dalle. Si j'avais voulu vous frapper, vous seriez déjà par terre et dans les vapes.

– Je suis des cours de krav-maga deux fois par semaine.

– Deux fois par semaine ? Ah bon ? Merci de m'avertir.

– Pas besoin de vous moquer de moi. Je pourrais vous faire mal, qu'est-ce que vous en savez ? Pour un intrus, je vous trouve bien malpoli.

– Descendez.

Au bout d'une bonne minute de bataille de regards, yeux dans les yeux, elle descend de sa chaise.

– Vous voyez ? Vous êtes aussi en sécurité au sol que vous l'étiez là-haut.

– Qu'est-ce que vous êtes venu chercher ici ?

– Vous n'avez pas appelé la police, en fait, pas vrai ? J'ai failli vous croire pendant une seconde.

– Non. Mais je peux les appeler.

– Pourquoi vous iriez faire ça ? Pour qu'ils vous arrêtent pour être entrée ici par effraction ?

Elle désigne du doigt son bureau de fortune. Pour la première fois, je remarque les papiers qui jonchent la pièce.

– Je vous l'ai dit. C'est mon bureau. Je travaille tard ce soir, parce que les ouvriers ont fait tellement de bruit aujourd'hui que je n'ai pas pu terminer tout ce que j'avais à faire. Pourquoi quelqu'un s'amuserait à entrer quelque part par effraction pour travailler à 22 h 30 un 31 décembre ?

Les ouvriers ? *Mes ouvriers ?* Il y a quelque chose qui cloche.

– Vous étiez ici aujourd'hui avec les ouvriers ?

– Oui.

Je me gratte le menton ; j'hésite à la croire.

– Comment s'appelle le contremaître ?

– Tommy.

Merde. Elle dit la vérité. Enfin, au moins une partie de ce qu'elle raconte doit être vrai.

– Vous dites que vous avez emménagé il y a une semaine ?

– Exact.

– Et vous avez loué cet endroit à qui, précisément ?

– John Cougar.

Je hausse les deux sourcils à la fois.

– John Cougar ? Et il n'avait pas amené Mellencamp[1], par hasard ?

– Qu'est-ce que j'en sais, moi ?

Aïe, ça ne sent vraiment pas bon.

– Et vous avez payé John Cougar ?

– Bien sûr. C'est le principe de la location d'un espace de bureau. Deux mois de caution, premier et dernier mois de loyer.

Je ferme les yeux et secoue la tête.

– Merde.

– Quoi ?

– Vous vous êtes fait avoir. Ça vous a coûté combien, en tout ? Deux mois de caution, premier et dernier mois de loyer ? Soit quatre mois au total ?

– Dix mille dollars.

– Je vous en prie, dites-moi que vous n'avez pas payé en liquide

La connexion semble enfin s'établir et son joli minois se vide de ses couleurs.

1. Il s'agit d'un artiste américain qui commence sa carrière sous le pseudonyme de John Cougar. Après ses premiers succès, il adopte le nom de John Cougar Mellencamp qu'il simplifie, à la fin des années quatre-vingt, en John Mellencamp.

– Il a dit que sa banque était fermée le soir et qu'il ne pouvait pas me donner les clés tant que mon chèque n'était pas encaissé. Que si je le payais en liquide, je pouvais emménager sur-le-champ.

– Vous avez versé quarante mille dollars en liquide à un John Cougar ?

– Non !

– Ouf.

– Je lui ai versé dix mille dollars en espèces.

– Je croyais que vous aviez dit avoir payé quatre mois.

– Effectivement. Le loyer se montait à deux mille cinq cents pour le mois.

C'est le pompon. De toutes les conneries que j'ai entendues jusqu'à maintenant, qu'elle croie pouvoir louer un espace sur Park Avenue pour deux mille cinq cents dollars par mois, c'est la cerise sur le gâteau. J'éclate de rire.

– Qu'est-ce qu'il y a de si drôle ?

– Vous, vous n'êtes pas de New York, c'est ça ?

– Non, je viens d'arriver de l'Oklahoma. Quel rapport ?

Je m'approche d'un pas.

– Ça me fait de la peine de devoir vous l'apprendre, miss Oklahoma, mais vous vous êtes fait rouler dans la farine. Cet endroit est mon bureau. Je l'occupe depuis trois ans. Et avant ça, mon père y a travaillé pendant trente ans. J'étais en congés ces deux dernières semaines et j'ai fait effectuer des travaux de rénovation durant mon absence. Quelqu'un qui a pris le nom d'un chanteur vous a arnaquée et convaincue de lui payer en liquide la location d'un bureau qu'il n'avait aucun droit de louer. Le portier s'appelle Ed. Traversez le hall principal du bâtiment, il confirmera tout ce que je viens de vous dire.

– Ce n'est pas possible.

– Qu'est-ce que vous faites, pour avoir besoin d'un bureau ?

– Je suis psychologue.

Je lui tends la main.

– Je suis avocat. Faites-moi voir votre contrat.

Son visage blêmit.

– Il ne l'a pas encore apporté. Il m'a dit que le propriétaire était en vacances au Brésil et que je pouvais m'installer, qu'il repasserait le premier du mois pour collecter le loyer et me donner le contrat à signer.

– Vous avez été victime d'une arnaque.

– Mais je lui ai versé dix mille dollars !

– Autre indice qui aurait dû vous faire tiquer : pour deux mille cinq cents dollars par mois, vous ne pourriez même pas louer un placard, sur Park Avenue. Vous n'avez pas trouvé étrange de mettre la main sur un endroit pareil pour des clopinettes ?

– J'ai cru faire une bonne affaire.

Je secoue la tête.

– Une affaire, oui. Mais une mauvaise.

Elle se couvre la bouche.

– Je crois que je vais vomir.

CHAPITRE 2

EMERIE

Mais quelle crétine !

Un léger coup retentit à la porte de la salle de bains.

– Tout va bien ?

– Oui, je vais bien.

Je suis humiliée. Stupide. Naïve. *Complètement fauchée*. Mais je vais bien.

Je me lave le visage et me regarde dans le miroir. Bon sang, qu'est-ce que je vais faire, maintenant ? Ma ligne de téléphone fixe allait enfin être installée cette semaine et j'étais sur le point de recevoir mes cartes de visite et autres courriers à en-tête. *Mes belles cartes de visite*. Avec le joli logo et l'adresse chic sur Park Avenue. *Aaargh*. Encore deux cent cinquante dollars jetés par la fenêtre. Je penche la tête vers le fond du lavabo, incapable de supporter plus longtemps ma tête de cruche.

Au bout d'un moment, j'entrouvre la porte des toilettes et sors. Le locataire légitime est adossé contre le mur ; il m'attend. Évidemment, il fallait qu'il soit super craquant. Parce que je ne pouvais pas me contenter de me ridiculiser devant un moche. *Ben non, ça, pas possible.*

– Vous êtes sûre que ça va bien ?

J'évite de croiser son regard.

– Non. Mais ça va aller. (J'hésite, puis j'ajoute :) Ça ne vous dérange pas si je retourne à mon bureau... enfin, votre bureau... pour ramasser mes affaires ?

– Bien sûr. Prenez votre temps.

Il n'y a pas grand-chose à remballer. Tous mes meubles allaient eux aussi m'être livrés cette semaine. À l'instar des dossiers de mon armoire de rangement. Ça aussi, il faudra que je l'annule. Punaise, où est-ce que je vais mettre toutes mes affaires ? Mon appartement n'est pas beaucoup plus grand que la salle des archives où j'étais assise quand le type est arrivé.

Alors que j'entasse mes dernières bricoles dans le carton que j'avais utilisé pour les apporter ici, il vient se planter dans l'encadrement de la porte. Je m'adresse à lui avant qu'il n'ait le temps d'ouvrir la bouche.

– Je suis vraiment navrée... d'être tombée dans le piège, de vous avoir menacé d'appeler les flics...

– Et d'avoir menacé mon intégrité physique grâce à vos talents de krav-maga, ne l'oubliez pas.

Je lève les yeux sur son sourire moqueur. Qui lui va bien. *Trop bien.* Son beau visage me rend nerveuse, mais pas nerveuse au sens où je me sens obligée de sauter sur une chaise et d'appeler la police. Non, le sourire de cet homme est arrogant et il me fait trembler les genoux – entre autres parties du corps.

– Je fais vraiment du krav-maga, vous savez.

– C'est bien. Vous m'avez fait un peu peur, quand je suis arrivé. Je parie que vous leur bottez les fesses, aux petites filles de votre cours.

Je me pétrifie au milieu de mon rangement.

– Des petites filles ? Mon instructeur est un homme.

Il croise les bras sur son torse. *Son torse large et musclé.*

– Et vous prenez des leçons depuis combien de temps ?

– Presque trois mois.

– Vous ne risquez pas de faire grand mal à un gars de ma taille avec trois mois de cours de krav-maga.

Peut-être est-ce l'heure tardive, ou le constat que je me suis fait arnaquer de mes économies de toute une vie et que je n'ai plus de bureau où recevoir mes patients, bref, sa remarque me fait perdre les pédales. Je fonds sur le pauvre homme qui s'attendait à tout sauf à ça. Je bondis littéralement sur ma chaise, puis sur la table pliante, et je lui saute dessus. *Je lui saute dessus.*

J'ai beau l'avoir pris au dépourvu, il m'a complètement maîtrisée en moins d'une fraction de seconde. Je ne sais même pas dire quel mouvement il a utilisé pour ça. J'ignore comment, il a réussi à me faire pivoter, si bien que je suis de dos contre son torse, avec mes bras liés derrière moi, entre nous.

Ça me rend folle de rage qu'il n'ait même pas l'air remonté quand il reprend la parole. Son souffle me chatouille le cou tandis qu'il me maintient immobile. Sa voix est basse et mesurée.

– C'était quoi, ça ?

– J'essayais de vous faire une petite démonstration.

Je sens son corps s'agiter derrière moi, sans qu'aucun son n'en sorte.

– Vous vous moquez de moi ? Encore ?

– Non, répond-il… en riant !

– Je connais des mouvements. Je vous jure. C'est juste que ce soir, je suis tourneboulée à cause de tout ce qui s'est passé.

Il ne m'a toujours pas relâchée. Au lieu de quoi, il se penche vers l'avant et passe la tête par-dessus mon épaule.

– Si on en est à se faire des démonstrations de mouvements, je serais ravi de vous montrer certains des miens, à l'occasion.

Tous les poils de mon corps se dressent, la chair de poule hérisse ma peau.

– Euh… je… je…

Il relâche enfin sa prise et il me faut une minute pour retrouver mes petites affaires. Plutôt que de lui faire face, le rouge aux joues, je continue à lui tourner le dos tandis que je rassemble mes derniers papiers et débranche mon chargeur de la prise sur le mur.

– J'ai des livraisons prévues et une ligne téléphonique qui doit être installée mardi. (Mes épaules s'affaissent à nouveau.) Et j'ai payé le double le garde-meuble pour être livrée cette semaine. Je vais tout annuler dès demain matin, mais au cas où ils se pointeraient quand même… si vous êtes ici, ça ne vous dérangerait pas de les renvoyer ?

– Pas de problème.

– Merci.

Je soulève mon carton, et là, je n'ai d'autre choix que de me tourner vers lui.

Contournant la table, il vient me le prendre des mains avant de me précéder dans l'aire d'accueil. Tout est plongé dans la pénombre à l'exception de la lumière de ce que j'avais cru être ma salle des archives, qui éclaire suffisamment le couloir pour que nous nous voyions. Nous nous arrêtons devant la porte de service que j'utilise depuis le début de la semaine. L'idée me vient que le faux agent immobilier m'a convaincue d'utiliser cette entrée pour éviter que je ne sois repérée trop vite. Il a prétendu qu'il ne fallait pas passer par l'entrée principale sur Park Avenue pour ne pas apporter de la poussière partout avec nos chaussures pendant les travaux. Et moi, j'ai avalé tout ce que m'a raconté cet arnaqueur.

– Vous avez un nom, Oklahoma ? Ou est-ce que je dois continuer à vous appeler « la squatteuse » ?

– Emerie. Emerie Rose.

– Joli. Rose, c'est votre nom de famille ou votre deuxième prénom ?

– Mon nom de famille.

Il passe le carton de ses deux bras sur un seul et me tend sa main libre.

– Drew. Drew Michael.

Je plisse les paupières.

– Deuxième prénom ou nom de famille ?

Son sourire illumine l'obscurité quand je place ma main dans la sienne. Ce ne sont pas des fossettes qu'il a, mais un sourire jusqu'aux oreilles.

– Deuxième prénom. Mon nom de famille, c'est Jagger.

– Enchantée, Drew Jagger.

Il ne lâche pas ma main.

– Vraiment ? Enchantée ? Vous êtes bien plus polie que je ne le serais dans les mêmes circonstances.

– Vous avez raison. À l'heure qu'il est, je regrette presque que vous ne soyez pas un cambrioleur, tout compte fait.

– Vous avez une voiture ? Il est tard et ce carton est plutôt lourd.

– Ça ira. Je vais prendre un taxi.

Il hoche la tête.

– Faites tout de même attention en montant et en sortant de voiture. Cette jupe, là, il semblerait qu'elle ait son petit caractère.

Cette fois, la pénombre ne suffira pas à masquer mon embarras.

– Avec toutes les hontes que j'ai subies ce soir, vous n'auriez pas pu m'épargner celle-là ? Faire comme si ça n'était pas arrivé ?

Sourire narquois.

– Impossible de faire comme si je n'avais pas vu vos fesses.

Je suis mince, mais mes fesses sont plutôt du genre imposant. Cela a toujours été un complexe pour moi.

– C'est censé vouloir dire quoi, ça ?

– C'était un compliment.

– Ah.

– Pourquoi votre jupe est tombée ? Vous avez perdu du poids récemment ou quoi ?

À ce stade, rien ne peut me gêner plus que je ne le suis déjà, alors je préfère éclater de rire et lui raconter la vérité.

– J'ai mangé un gros hamburger pour le dîner et ma jupe était trop serrée, alors je l'ai dégrafée. La porte était fermée à clé, je ne pensais pas que quelqu'un entrerait.

– Une femme qui mange des hamburgers et qui a une silhouette comme la vôtre ? N'en parlez pas aux New-Yorkaises, elles vont vous remettre dans un bus pour l'Oklahoma direct.

Il ponctue sa remarque d'un clin d'œil. Et moi, pathétique bécasse, je sens les battements de mon cœur s'accélérer.

Nous sortons dans la rue et Drew attend avec moi, mon carton sous le bras, jusqu'à ce qu'un taxi se gare le long du trottoir. Il se penche par la portière une fois que je suis installée à l'intérieur.

– Le réveillon du Nouvel An, c'est toujours naze. Demain, ça ira mieux. Faites la grasse matinée, commandez-vous un autre gros hamburger et tâchez de vous reposer. Retrouvons-nous au commissariat après-demain. 19e circonscription, sur la 67e rue. Disons huit heures du matin ? Parce que le 1er janvier, ça va être la folie chez les flics, avec tous les imbéciles saouls de la veille qu'ils auront à gérer.

La police. Je n'y avais même pas pensé. En effet, il va bien falloir que je dépose une plainte.

– Vous n'êtes pas obligé de m'accompagner. Je vous ai déjà assez dérangé.

Il hausse les épaules.

– Ils vont réclamer ma déposition, de toute façon. En plus, je suis assez pote avec l'un des gars. Ça vous aidera à passer plus vite.

– OK.

Il donne deux petits coups de phalange sur le toit du taxi et se penche pour parler au chauffeur.

– Prenez bien soin de la demoiselle, elle a passé une sale soirée.

Dès que nous sommes avalés par la circulation, les événements de l'heure écoulée me reviennent comme un boomerang. L'adrénaline qui était montée en flèche entame une chute libre.

Je me suis fait arnaquer de toutes mes économies.

Je n'ai plus de bureau.

J'ai donné ma nouvelle adresse à tous mes patients.

La tête se met à me tourner.

Où vais-je aller ?

Comment vais-je pouvoir verser un dépôt de garantie, si jamais je trouve un nouveau local ?

La nausée me reprend et je renverse la tête contre le siège de cuir. Les yeux fermés, je prends quelques profondes inspirations. Bizarrement, la première vision qui s'affiche est celle du beau brun aux lèvres sensuelles, adossé à l'encadrement de ma porte. De *sa* porte. Et avec cette image en tête, au milieu du tourbillon qui me propulse vers le bas et l'amorce d'une énorme crise d'angoisse, je ne peux empêcher mes lèvres de s'étirer sur un petit sourire.

CHAPITRE 3

DREW

Je tourne vers moi le cadran de ma montre. *Vingt minutes de retard.* Elle est sexy et une partie de mon cœur de pierre s'est ramollie en pensant à la manière dont elle s'est fait duper. Mais vingt minutes, merde ! Sachant que je facture mes services six cent soixante-quinze dollars de l'heure, je viens d'en perdre deux cent vingt-cinq, planté là, devant ce fichu commissariat de police. Un dernier regard au bout de la rue et je m'apprête à retourner à mon bureau quand un éclair de couleur tourne à l'angle.

Vert. J'ai toujours bien aimé le vert. Tout ce qui est vert est sympa : l'argent, l'herbe, ces grenouilles aux yeux qui leur sortent de la tête et que j'adorais chasser, gamin. Aujourd'hui, cela dit, je dirais que le vert passe de « teinte appréciée » à « couleur préférée » alors que j'admire les seins d'Emerie qui se balancent sous son pull. Pour un petit modèle, elle a du monde au balcon. Et ça s'accorde très joliment avec ses fesses rebondies.

– Pardon, je suis en retard ?

Son manteau est ouvert et ses joues pâles ont rosi sous l'effet de sa course depuis l'angle de la rue. Elle halète. Elle a l'air différente de l'autre soir. Ses longs cheveux ondulés sont lâchés et le soleil parsème de petits éclats dorés leur masse cuivrée. Elle tente de les apprivoiser tout en parlant.

– Je me suis trompée de train.

– J'étais sur le point de partir.

En baissant les yeux vers ma montre, je remarque de minuscules gouttes de sueur dans son décolleté. Je me racle la gorge en calculant depuis combien de temps j'attends.

– Trente-cinq minutes, ça vous fera trois cent cinquante dollars.

– Pardon ?

Toujours imperturbable, je hausse les épaules.

– Je facture six cent soixante-quinze dollars de l'heure. Vous m'avez fait perdre plus d'une demi-heure de mon temps. Ça vous fera donc trois cent cinquante dollars.

– Je vous signale que je suis fauchée. (Elle lève les mains d'un air exaspéré.) Votre bureau chicos que j'ai cru pouvoir louer, ça vous rappelle quelque chose ? Je ne vais quand même pas vous payer une somme pareille juste parce que je ne me suis pas réveillée assez tôt.

– Relax, je vous taquine. (Je marque une pause.) Attendez, je croyais que vous vous étiez trompée de train ?

Elle se mord la lèvre, l'air coupable, et désigne la porte du commissariat.

– On ferait mieux d'entrer, je vous ai déjà suffisamment fait attendre.

Je secoue la tête.

– Vous m'avez menti.

Elle lâche un soupir.

– Je vous présente mes excuses, je ne me suis pas réveillée. Je n'arrivais pas à m'endormir hier soir. Vous comprenez, tout ça, c'est encore comme un mauvais rêve, pour moi.

Je hoche la tête et, contrairement à mes habitudes, je n'insiste pas.

– Venez, allons voir s'il y a une chance pour qu'ils chopent cet escroc.

À l'intérieur du poste de police, l'officier d'accueil est au téléphone. Souriant, il lève deux doigts. Dès qu'il a expliqué à son interlocuteur que des prospectus de supermarchés volés dans sa boîte aux lettres, ça concerne la Poste et non le NYPD, il tend une main par-dessus son comptoir.

– Drew Jagger, qu'est-ce qui t'amène dans les bas-quartiers ? Tu t'encanailles ?

Je lui rends son sourire et lui serre la main.

– Quelque chose comme ça. Comment ça va, Frank ?

– Jamais été plus heureux. Je rentre chez moi, pas besoin de quitter mes chaussures à la porte, je laisse la lunette relevée aux toilettes après avoir pissé et je mange dans des assiettes en carton pour ne pas avoir à faire la vaisselle. La vie de célibataire, ça a du bon, mon pote.

Je me tourne vers Emerie.

– Je vous présente le sergent Frank Caruso. Il me fournit du travail aussi régulièrement qu'il change de femme. Frank, voici Emerie Rose. Elle a besoin de déposer une plainte. Mahoney ne serait pas de service aujourd'hui, par hasard ? Il pourrait peut-être l'aider.

– Il est en congé pour quelques semaines. Il s'est tordu la cheville en pourchassant un cambrioleur après effraction. Mais je vais jeter un œil, voir qui est au tableau d'affichage, histoire de lui appeler quelqu'un de sympa. Qu'est-ce qui se passe ? Problème domestique ? Un mari qui lui fait des misères ?

– Rien de tout ça. Emerie n'est pas une de mes clientes. Elle a loué un bureau dans mon immeuble il y a quelques semaines.

Frank lâche un sifflement admiratif.

– Un espace sur Park Avenue. Jolie et riche, en plus. Vous êtes célibataire, ma belle ?

– Tu n'apprends jamais de tes erreurs, mon vieux ?

– Quoi ? J'ai seulement essayé les moches et les fauchées, c'est peut-être ça, mon souci.

– Je suis quasi certain que c'est pas ça, non.

Frank balaie ma remarque d'un revers de la main.

– Bon, et c'est quoi, le problème de la petite dame ? Un proprio qui l'embête ?

– Elle a loué mon bureau pour deux mille cinq cents dollars par mois. Et elle a versé dix mille d'avance. Le problème, c'est qu'elle n'a pas eu affaire au propriétaire, mais à un arnaqueur qui s'est fait passer pour un agent immobilier pendant que j'étais absent le temps que le bureau soit rénové.

– Deux mille cinq cents dollars par mois ? Dans ton immeuble ?

– Elle débarque de l'Oklahoma.

Il reporte son attention sur Emerie.

– Ils ont pas le Monopoly, dans l'Oklahoma ? Vous ne pouviez pas vous douter que Park Avenue, c'était cinq fois plus cher qu'à Baltic ?

J'interromps le sergent Gros-Malin avant que la pauvre Emerie ne se sente encore plus mal qu'elle ne l'est déjà. Après tout, je me suis déjà moqué d'elle, l'autre soir, quand elle m'a fourni un accueil auquel je ne m'attendais pas. C'est bon, elle a eu sa dose. Frank lui donne de la paperasse à remplir pour commencer et nous indique une pièce à l'écart, où patienter. Sur le chemin, je m'arrête pour discuter avec un vieil ami et Emerie a presque fini de compléter ses formulaires quand je la rejoins.

Je referme la porte derrière moi.

– Vous faites dans les affaires criminelles ? demande-t-elle en levant les yeux.

– Non. Juste matrimoniales.

– Tous les flics semblent vous connaître.

– Mon associé travaillait dans cette juridiction. Certains de mes premiers clients étaient flics. Et quand vous êtes l'ami d'un gars en uniforme et que vous faites du bon boulot pour lui, toute la circonscription et même plus vous fait travailler. Ce sont des types loyaux. Du moins les uns envers les autres. En revanche, la profession connaît le taux de divorce le plus élevé de la ville.

Une minute plus tard, un inspecteur que je n'ai jamais vu entre et prend la déposition d'Emerie. Puis la mienne. Une fois qu'il en a terminé, il m'informe que je peux partir si je veux.

Ne me demandez pas pourquoi je traîne encore dans les parages une demi-heure plus tard, alors qu'Emerie tourne les pages de son deuxième album de photos de tronches patibulaires.

Elle passe à la suivante avec un soupir.

– Je n'en reviens pas du nombre de criminels qui ressemblent à des gens normaux.

– Ça aurait été plus difficile pour vous de filer dix mille dollars en liquide à un type s'il avait effectivement eu l'air d'un malfrat, c'est ça ?

– Sans doute, oui.

Je me gratte le menton.

– Dans quoi vous transportiez une somme pareille ? Un sac en papier kraft rempli de billets de cent ?

– Non.

Le ton trahit sa vexation, mais elle ne se fend d'aucune explication. Alors je la dévisage et j'attends. Elle lève les yeux au ciel.

– OK. Mais ça n'était pas un sac en papier kraft, il était blanc. De chez Wendy.

Je hausse les sourcils.

– Wendy ? Le *fast-food* ? Décidément, vous avez un truc avec les burgers, vous.

– J'avais mis le burger que je venais de m'acheter pour le déjeuner dans mon sac à main et je transportais le cash dedans parce que je ne voulais pas me le faire dérober dans le métro. Or je me suis dit qu'on essaierait plus logiquement de me voler mon portefeuille que mon déjeuner.

Bien vu.

– Pas mal pensé, pour une fille de l'Oklahoma.

Elle plisse les paupières.

– Je viens d'Oklahoma City, pas d'un trou paumé. Vous me croyez naïve sous prétexte que je ne suis pas de New York et que je prends de mauvaises décisions.

– Vous avez quand même donné dix mille balles à un faux agent immobilier dans un sac de chez Wendy.

Je n'ai pas pu m'en empêcher. On dirait que de la fumée va lui sortir des oreilles. Heureusement, un coup frappé à la porte m'épargne une volée de bois vert en provenance de l'Oklahoma. Frank passe la tête.

– T'as une seconde, l'avocat ?

– Bien sûr.

Frank ouvre la porte en grand, attend que je la franchisse et la referme derrière nous avant de parler.

– On a un petit problème, Drew.

Il a affiché son air de flic quand il désigne la porte fermée derrière laquelle se trouve Emerie.

– On engage toujours une procédure de vérification standard, quand un plaignant se présente.

– Ouais, et alors ?

– Figure-toi qu'elle a un mandat d'arrêt en souffrance, Oklahoma.

– Tu déconnes ?

– J'aimerais bien. Le nouveau système informatique nous oblige à renseigner la raison pour laquelle on enregistre un nouveau nom. L'inspecteur qui a pris sa déposition avait déjà entré son nom. Elle est déjà passée ici, au commissariat, quoi. C'est plus comme avant, maintenant, tout est traçable. Il va falloir qu'elle règle cette affaire. Moi, je quitte mon service dans une heure. Si tu veux, je peux la conduire au tribunal pour répondre des charges retenues contre elle, comme ça on n'a pas besoin de lui passer les menottes. C'est une amende pour non-comparution. Je suis sûr qu'elle peut déposer une demande de clémence et s'en tirer à bon compte.

– Elle est accusée de quoi ?

Frank m'adresse un sourire en coin.

– Attentat à la pudeur.

***

– Bon, racontez-moi toute l'histoire depuis le début.

On est assis sur un banc devant la salle du tribunal, à attendre que commence la séance de l'après-midi.

Emerie baisse la tête.

– Je suis vraiment obligée ?

– Vous allez devoir la raconter devant le juge, alors en ma qualité d'avocat, j'ai besoin de l'entendre en premier.

Menteur.

Elle sera sans doute furax en se rendant compte qu'une amende pour non-comparution ne requiert pas que l'on ressasse l'événement en question. On va entrer, plaider coupable, payer l'amende et on sera ressortis d'ici une heure. Mais ma journée est fichue, alors j'ai bien le droit de m'amuser un peu. En plus, j'aime assez le côté explosif de sa personnalité. Elle est encore plus sexy quand elle est en colère.

– OK. Eh bien, j'étais à New York pour l'été, en visite chez ma grand-mère. J'ai rencontré un type. On est sortis ensemble deux ou trois fois, on se rapprochait et il y a eu cette soirée d'août, il faisait particulièrement chaud et étouffant. Je venais de décrocher mon diplôme et je n'avais jamais rien fait de foufou, chez moi. Alors quand il a suggéré qu'on aille plonger tout nus dans la piscine municipale, je me suis dit : « Pourquoi pas ? Personne n'en saura jamais rien. »

– Continuez.

– On est allés au Y, sur la 82e rue, ils ont une piscine extérieure, et on a sauté par-dessus la barrière. Il faisait si sombre quand on s'est déshabillés que je ne pensais même pas que le gars me verrait.

– Donc vous vous êtes mise nue ? De quelle couleur étaient votre soutien-gorge et votre culotte ?

T'es sérieux, mec ? Faut être sacrément malade pour poser une question pareille. Mais dans mon imaginaire tordu, je la vois dans un petit string blanc et soutien-gorge en dentelle assorti.

L'espace d'un instant, elle a l'air paniquée.

– Vous avez vraiment besoin de savoir tout ça ? C'était il y a dix ans.

– C'est préférable. Plus je connaîtrai de détails, mieux c'est. Cela montrera au juge que vous vous rappelez bien cette nuit-là, et du coup, il pensera que vous avez des remords.

Emerie se ronge l'ongle du pouce, plongée dans ses pensées.

– Blancs ! Ils étaient blancs.

Sympa.

– String ou culotte ?

Ses joues rosissent et elle se cache le visage entre ses mains.

– String. Oh là là, ce que c'est embarrassant !

– Ce sera plus facile si vous me balancez tout maintenant.

– OK.

– Est-ce que vous vous êtes déshabillée vous-même, ou est-ce le gars qui s'en est chargé ?

– Je me suis déshabillée moi-même.

– D'accord. Et qu'est-ce qui s'est passé après ? Racontez-moi tout en détail. Sans rien omettre. Vous pensez peut-être que ça n'a pas d'importance, mais ça pourrait aider votre cas.

Elle hoche la tête.

– Une fois que je me suis déshabillée, j'ai posé mes vêtements en tas près de la clôture qu'on avait franchie. Jared, le garçon avec qui j'étais, a enlevé ses habits, les a posés près des miens et s'est dirigé vers le plongeoir le plus haut. Et il a fait une bombe.

– Et puis ?

– La police est arrivée.

– Vous n'étiez même pas encore dans le bassin ? Vous ne faisiez pas des cochonneries dans l'eau, rien du tout ?

– Non. Je n'ai même pas eu le temps de me tremper. Juste après que Jared est remonté à la surface, les sirènes se sont mises à hurler.

J'ai l'impression qu'on m'a privé de mon cadeau. Tout ça pour ça ? Même pas de pelotage ? Avant que j'aie le temps de lui poser d'autres questions, un employé du tribunal égrène une liste de noms. L'entendant appeler « Rose », j'entraîne Emerie vers lui, près de la porte de la salle d'audience.

– Salle 132, au fond du couloir et sur la droite, annonce-t-il en compulsant son bloc-notes. La substitut du procureur vous y retrouvera pour discuter de votre affaire avant que vous ne passiez devant le juge. Attendez devant. Elle vous appellera quand ce sera votre tour.

Sachant où se trouve la salle, j'entraîne Emerie dans le couloir et nous nous installons sur le banc devant. Elle reste silencieuse une minute avant de reprendre la parole. Dans sa voix, je perçois un léger tremblement, comme si elle retenait des larmes.

– Je suis vraiment désolée pour tout ça, Drew. Je vais vous devoir quelque chose comme cinq mille dollars pour le temps passé et je n'en ai même pas cinq cents à vous donner.

– Ne vous inquiétez pas pour ça.

Elle pose les doigts sur mon bras. J'avais ma main dans son dos quand on marchait et je l'ai aussi aidée à sortir de la voiture de police dans laquelle le sergent Caruso nous a conduits ici, mais c'est la première fois qu'elle me touche. J'aime bien. *Nom de Dieu.* Je ne la connais pas beaucoup, mais assez pour savoir qu'Oklahoma n'est pas le genre de femmes qu'on baise et qu'on jette. Il faut que j'en termine avec ce truc et que je me tire de là.

– Non, mais sincèrement. Je suis vraiment navrée et je ne sais pas comment vous remercier de m'avoir accompagnée aujourd'hui. Je serais dans tous mes états si vous n'étiez pas à mes côtés. Je vous rembourserai d'une façon ou d'une autre.

J'ai quelques idées en tête.

– C'est bon. Vraiment. Ne vous inquiétez pas pour ça. Tout va se passer comme sur des roulettes. Dans vingt minutes, on est sortis d'ici.

À cet instant, une voix retentit derrière la porte :

– Rose. Dossier numéro 18493094. Défenseur ?

Je suppose que c'est la substitut. Je ne suis pas beaucoup d'affaires criminelles, juste quelques amendes de circulation ou des accusations de violence domestiques pour un client dont je gère le divorce à six chiffres, à l'occasion. Pourtant, la voix de la femme m'est familière, même si je n'arrive pas à la remettre.

Jusqu'à ce que j'ouvre la porte.

Soudain, la raison pour laquelle je connais cette voix m'apparaît avec une clarté absolue.

Je l'ai déjà entendue, en effet.

La dernière fois, elle criait mon nom tandis que je la prenais par-derrière dans les toilettes du bureau d'une firme rivale.

De tous les avocats de la ville de New York, il fallait que je tombe sur la substitut Kierra Albright.

Bon, « comme sur des roulettes » n'est peut-être pas tout à fait l'expression idéale pour décrire la manière dont les choses vont se passer.

CHAPITRE 4

DREW

Et merde.

– Je ne comprends pas. Qu'est-ce qui se passe ?

La voix d'Emerie est empreinte de panique. Et je ne peux pas la blâmer. Tout le monde sait que les cobras, les tigres et les requins sont dangereux. Mais les dauphins à gros nez ? Si jolis et si mignons, dont les sifflements jouent des harmonies quand vous leur caressez le haut de la tête. Pourtant, blessez-en un par accident, et là, ils attaquent. C'est vrai. Mon passe-temps préféré, en plus de la baise et du travail, c'est regarder la chaîne National Geographic.

Kierra Albright est un dauphin à gros nez. Elle va recommander trente jours de prison au juge, plutôt que la simple amende dont on nous a parlé il y a moins d'une demi-heure.

– Donnez-moi une minute. Asseyez-vous dans le fond, je viendrai vous chercher. Je n'en ai pas pour longtemps, j'ai besoin d'échanger quelques mots avec la substitut. Seul.

Emerie hoche la tête, alors même qu'elle semble au bord des larmes, et je lui laisse un moment pour se ressaisir. Ensuite j'ouvre le portillon qui sépare le public des hommes et des femmes de loi dans la salle d'audience, puis je la conduis dans une pièce vide à l'arrière. En m'éloignant, je remarque une larme qui roule sur sa joue et cette vision me stoppe immédiatement.

Sans réfléchir, je lui soulève le menton afin que nos regards se croisent.

– Faites-moi confiance. Vous serez chez vous ce soir, OK ? Faites. Moi. Confiance.

***

Ma voix fait sursauter Kierra dans les toilettes pour dames, en face de la salle d'audience.

– C'était quoi, ce bordel ?

Je referme la porte à clé tandis qu'elle pivote pour me faire face.

– Tu n'as pas le droit d'entrer ici.

– Si quelqu'un te pose la question, réponds que c'est mon côté féminin qui domine, aujourd'hui.

– Tu es un connard.

– C'est moi, le connard ? Non, mais c'était quoi, sans déconner, ton « Ravie de te voir, Drew » de merde ? Et « Je recommande une amende de cinquante dollars et tu seras ressorti à temps pour ton parcours de golf » ?

Elle me tourne le dos et s'approche du miroir. Sortant un bâton de rouge à lèvres de la poche de son tailleur, elle se penche et peint ses lèvres en rouge sang, sans plus rien dire jusqu'à ce qu'elle ait terminé. Puis elle m'adresse le sourire le plus large, le plus étincelant que j'aie jamais vu.

– Je me suis dit que ton nouveau joujou avait besoin de s'habituer à ce qu'on lui dise blanc avant qu'elle se rende compte que, en fait, c'est noir qui se produira quand elle s'y attendra le moins.

– Elle n'est pas mon joujou. C'est... une amie à qui je donne un coup de main.

– J'ai vu la manière dont tu la regardais, celle dont tu lui posais la main dans le dos. Si tu ne la baises pas encore, ça ne tardera pas à arriver. Elle a peut-être besoin d'une nuit derrière les barreaux parce que tu n'es pas capable de te tenir en salle d'audience. Ça risque de la rendre moins réceptive à tes charmes. En y songeant, je lui rends service, à cette pauvre fille. Elle devrait me remercier.

– Tu es à côté de la plaque si tu t'imagines que je vais te laisser t'en tirer à si bon compte. Emerie n'a rien à voir avec ce qui s'est passé entre toi et moi. J'irai jusqu'à demander au juge Hawkins de se récuser, s'il le faut.

– De se récuser ? Sur quelle base ?

– Au motif que ton père joue au golf avec lui tous les vendredis et que tu m'as dit toi-même qu'il t'accorde tout ce que tu demandes. Tu as oublié comme tu aimais discuter boutique après qu'on avait baisé ?

– Tu n'oserais pas.

Jusque-là, je suis resté à une certaine distance, à peu près trois mètres, devant la porte verrouillée, mais je m'approche lentement vers l'endroit où elle se tient. Tout près.

– Tu en es certaine ?

Elle soutient mon regard un long moment.

– Bien. Mais faisons ça de la façon dont sont censés procéder des adversaires. Pas de menaces sous la ceinture. On va conclure un accord.

Je secoue la tête.

– Qu'est-ce que tu veux, Kierra ?

– Tu veux que ta cliente soit rentrée chez elle ce soir ? J'exige quelque chose en retour.

– Très bien. Tu veux quoi ?

Elle passe une langue humide sur sa lèvre supérieure, telle une affamée en train de contempler un bon gros steak.

– Toi. Et pas dans un placard ou sur la banquette arrière d'un Uber. Je te veux pour un vrai rendez-vous où tu m'emmèneras dîner et boire du vin dehors avant de rentrer m'offrir un soixante-neuf digne de ce nom.

***

– Oh, là, là, je ne vous dirai jamais assez merci.

– Allons payer votre amende et on s'en va d'ici.

Tandis que je la pousse hors de la salle d'audience, Emerie semble interpréter ma hâte comme de l'impatience parce qu'elle a déjà trop abusé de mon temps aujourd'hui. Sauf que ça n'a rien à voir. J'ai presque atteint la sortie quand Kierra nous interpelle.

– Drew, tu as un moment ?

– Pas maintenant. Je suis attendu quelque part.

N'importe où, à condition que ça soit ailleurs qu'ici.

Je garde la main dans le dos d'Emerie et continue d'avancer, mais ma cliente est d'un autre avis. Elle s'immobilise.

– Il faut qu'on y aille.

– Laissez-moi au moins remercier la substitut.

– Ce n'est pas nécessaire. La ville de New York la remercie un vendredi sur deux en lui remettant son chèque.

Emerie me jette un regard de reproche.

– Je ne vais pas me montrer malpolie sous prétexte que vous l'êtes.

Sur quoi, elle se retourne et attend que Kierra nous rattrape.

– Merci beaucoup pour tout, lui dit-elle, une main tendue. J'étais dans tous mes états, ce matin, quand j'ai cru que j'allais être envoyée en garde à vue.

Kierra baisse les yeux sur la main d'Emerie et la snobe. Elle pivote vers moi et c'est en me fixant du regard qu'elle lui répond :

– Ne me remerciez pas moi. Remerciez votre avocat.

– Oui, je vais le faire.

– Ne le remerciez pas trop non plus, n'allez pas me l'épuiser. (Sur quoi, elle tourne les talons et agite la main par-dessus son épaule.) Je t'appelle pour notre rendez-vous, Drew.

Emerie m'observe.

– C'était bizarre.

– Elle a dû oublier de prendre ses médocs. Venez, on file.

Le temps que l'on paie l'amende et qu'on récupère le double de l'attestation d'Emerie, il est presque seize heures.

Sur les marches du tribunal, elle se tourne vers moi.

– J'espère que vous n'êtes pas opposé aux démonstrations d'affection en public, parce que j'ai besoin de vous serrer dans mes bras.

En fait, je ne suis pas très démonstration d'affection en public, non, mais là… je ne serai pas payé pour cette journée fichue, alors autant en tirer quelque plaisir. Or ces jolis seins plaqués contre moi, c'est carrément mieux que rien. C'est peut-être même mieux qu'une journée complète à six cent soixante-quinze dollars de l'heure.

– Si vous insistez.

Le sourire qu'elle m'offre est proche de la perfection, je n'ai jamais vu un truc pareil. Et puis vient l'étreinte. Longue. Les seins et le petit corps menu m'enveloppent dans ce qui est bien plus qu'une étreinte de courtoisie. En plus, elle sent bon.

Quand elle s'écarte, elle garde les mains sur mes bras.

– Je vais vous rembourser, pour aujourd'hui. Même si ça doit me prendre des années.

– Ne vous tracassez pas là-dessus.

– Si, si, j'y tiens.

Nous passons quelques minutes de plus à parler, échangeons nos numéros au cas où des livraisons pour elle arrivent au bureau, et nous nous disons « au revoir ». Elle se dirige vers le nord de la ville, moi vers le sud, nous partons donc dans des directions opposées. Après quelques pas, je regarde par-dessus mon épaule le balancement de ses fesses. Cette fille est tout aussi chouette de dos que de face.

Ce qui me fait penser… Je parie qu'elle est encore plus magnifique sur le dos. Pile au moment où je vais reprendre mon chemin, Emerie se tourne vers moi et me surprend en train de la suivre du regard. Elle sourit jusqu'aux oreilles et agite la main une dernière fois avant de tourner à l'angle de la rue et de disparaître.

OK, si elle veut me rembourser pour aujourd'hui, je suis d'accord.

Et j'ai déjà plusieurs idées pour récupérer mon dû.

CHAPITRE 5

EMERIE

Je porte mon téléphone, qui vient de vibrer, à mon oreille, remarquant l'heure au passage. Presque vingt-trois heures. Ça fait tard, pour un appel.

– Allô ?

– Emerie ?

Cette voix. Pas besoin de demander qui c'est. Face à face, sa voix est profonde et rauque, mais au téléphone, elle est carrément rocailleuse.

– Drew ? Tout va bien ?

Oui. Pourquoi ?

– Eh bien, parce qu'il est tard, là.

J'entends l'appareil qui s'écarte et puis :

– Merde. Pardon. Je n'avais pas fait attention. Je viens de voir l'heure. Je croyais qu'il était dans les vingt et une heures.

– Le temps file quand on passe la majeure partie de sa journée au tribunal avec des criminels, pas vrai ?

– Il faut croire. Je suis rentré à la maison, j'ai rattrapé du travail en retard et puis je suis passé au bureau. J'ai dû perdre le fil.

– Et moi, je suis rentrée à la maison, j'ai bu quelques verres de vin et je me suis encore un peu apitoyée sur mon sort. Votre soirée me paraît largement plus productive. Vous êtes encore au bureau ?

– Ouais. C'est ce qui m'a poussé à vous appeler. Je suis assis là à me dire que, quand vous allez trouver un nouveau local, il sera très joli.

Quelle drôle de remarque.

– Merci. Mais qu'est-ce qui vous fait croire ça ?

– Verre et bois sombre. J'aime bien. Je vous aurais imaginée plus *girly* dans vos goûts, cela dit.

– De quoi est-ce que vous… Oh non ! Ils ont livré mes meubles de bureau aujourd'hui ?

– Effectivement.

– Comment ? Comment ont-ils pu entrer alors que vous étiez avec moi toute la journée ?

– Mon entrepreneur était ici pour les finitions et je n'avais pas eu l'occasion de lui expliquer votre mésaventure. Il a cru qu'il vous faisait une fleur en les laissant entrer.

Je laisse tomber ma tête contre le plan de travail de la cuisine et reste le front collé dessus pour ne pas m'assommer. Je ne parviens pas à réprimer le grognement qui monte de ma gorge, en revanche.

– Je suis désolée. Je vais m'en occuper sur-le-champ. Enfin, demain à la première heure.

– Prenez votre temps. Mes affaires sont encore en garde-meuble. Je peux garder ça ici un moment.

– Merci. Je suis vraiment navrée. Je vais les appeler demain matin et les envoyer tout récupérer. Ensuite je viendrai les attendre dans votre bureau afin que vous n'ayez pas à vous en occuper, si ça ne vous dérange pas.

– Non, pas de problème.

– Désolée.

– Arrêtez de répéter ça, Emerie. Les anciens criminels sont endurcis. Ils ne s'excusent pas. À demain.

Je ris, parce que ça m'évite de pleurer.

***

– Y a quelqu'un ?

Je frappe à la porte à moitié ouverte et écoute retentir l'écho de ma voix. La porte finit de s'ouvrir et, à ma grande surprise, je découvre l'entrée vide. J'aurais cru que mes meubles auraient été déposés là.

Au loin, une voix me parvient que je n'arrive pas à distinguer. J'avance d'un pas et crie un peu plus fort.

– Coucou ! Drew ?

Des pas rapides claquent sur le sol de marbre tout neuf, de plus en plus fort, jusqu'à ce que Drew émerge du couloir. Le téléphone coincé contre l'oreille, il lève un doigt en continuant son appel.

– Nous ne voulons pas de la maison de Breckenridge. Mon client déteste le froid. Elle peut la garder, mais ce sera la seule propriété qu'elle emportera de ce mariage. (Pause.) Non, je ne suis pas dingue. Sitôt que j'aurai raccroché, je vous envoie des photos de la propriété de Breckenridge. Je pense qu'elles vous convaincront que madame Hollister apprécie vraiment, vraiment cette maison.

À cet instant, un livreur de FedEx apparaît avec un diable chargé de cartons. Drew écarte le combiné de son oreille et demande au garçon d'empiler les cartons sur le comptoir d'accueil recouvert de plastique. Après un « merci » muet, il reprend sa conversation téléphonique.

Je profite de ce qu'il hurle ou presque sur celui ou celle qu'il a au bout du fil et je m'accorde une minute pour le reluquer. Si je me fie au tombé de son costume, Drew porte une tenue très onéreuse. La manche de son bras qui tient le téléphone est retroussée, révélant une grosse montre de luxe. Ses chaussures brillent et sa chemise sort manifestement tout droit du pressing. Il a les cheveux bruns et trop longs pour un homme qui cire ses chaussures. Quant à sa peau bronzée de ses récentes vacances, elle fait ressortir l'éclat de ses yeux d'un vert très clair.

Mais ce sont ses lèvres qu'il est impossible de ne pas admirer. Pleines et parfaitement dessinées. *Il est vraiment bel homme.* Je ne suis pas sûre d'avoir qualifié un homme de « beau » avant. Séduisant, oui. Sexy, soit. Mais beau, c'est exactement comme ça que je décrirais Drew Jagger. Aucun autre adjectif ne lui rendrait justice.

Il est en train de mettre un terme à son appel.

– Sérieusement, Max, dans combien d'affaires est-ce que tu t'es retrouvé de l'autre côté de la table à admirer ma belle gueule ? Tu ne sais toujours pas deviner quand je bluffe ? Regarde les photos, ensuite tiens-moi au courant de ta réponse concernant mon offre. Je pense que tu la jugeras plus qu'honnête, une fois que les choses auront été remises en perspective. Son moniteur de ski de vingt et un an lui enseignait une godille d'un tout nouveau genre. L'offre reste sur la table quarante-huit heures. Après ça, je serai obligé de te repasser un coup de fil, ce qui signifie que mon client recevra une autre facture et que ta proposition descendra d'un sacré paquet.

Il appuie sur un bouton pour couper la communication et lève les yeux vers moi, sur le point de parler, quand l'appareil se remet à vibrer dans sa paume.

– Merde.

Il soupire, baisse les yeux sur l'écran et les relève vers moi.

– Pardon, je dois décrocher aussi.

Un livreur arrive avec un diable chargé de packs de Perrier et frappe à la porte. Je m'adresse à Drew.

– Je m'en occupe. Allez prendre votre appel.

Sur les quinze minutes que dure la conversation téléphonique de Drew, je renvoie un avocat, je réponds au téléphone fixe enterré sous une bâche goudronnée (deux fois) et je signe le récépissé de documents officiels destinés au « Cabinet d'avocat de Drew M. Jagger ». Je suis en train d'embobiner un client potentiel au téléphone quand Drew reparaît.

– Nous remercierons monsieur Aiken de vous avoir recommandé à nous. (J'écoute, avant d'ajouter :) Nos tarifs sont de… (Je croise le regard de Drew.) sept cents dollars de l'heure.

Je vois la commissure de ses lèvres tressauter.

– Bien sûr. Et si je vous proposais un rendez-vous pour une prise de contact ? Je vous mets en attente une seconde, le temps de consulter le planning de M. Jagger.

J'appuie sur le bouton et tends la main, paume vers le haut.

– Votre planning est synchronisé avec votre téléphone ?

Drew sort son portable de sa poche et me le tend.

– Oui.

Ayant ouvert son calendrier sur Outlook, je le passe en revue, en quête de sa disponibilité la plus proche. Rien avant un bon mois.

– Vous pouvez repousser votre dîner avec une certaine Monica de dix-huit à vingt heures, que je place M. Patterson à seize heures trente, mercredi prochain ? Il dit que c'est urgent. Il a peut-être besoin d'une ordonnance restrictive afin de protéger ses biens, comme vous en avez obtenu une pour M. Aiken.

– OK.

Je reprends l'appel.

– Je vous propose seize heures trente mercredi prochain, le huit. Parfait ? Super. Nous prenons un acompte de… (Je relève les yeux vers Drew, qui me montre ses dix doigts.) Douze mille… OK, merci. Nous avons hâte de vous rencontrer. Au revoir.

Drew me regarde raccrocher d'un air amusé.

– Je viens d'augmenter mes émoluments de six cent soixante-quinze à sept cents dollars de l'heure ?

– Non, les vingt-cinq dollars en plus sont pour moi. Pour chaque heure que vous lui facturerez vous pourrez les déduire de ce que je vous dois. J'ai calculé que ma facture, pour huit heures de présence hier, se monte à cinq mille quatre cents dollars – je me compte au tarif standard, évidemment, pas au tarif gonflé de monsieur Patterson –, et donc, si vous pouviez facturer quelques centaines d'heures à monsieur Patterson, ce serait super.

Il s'esclaffe.

– Je retrouve bien la tigresse qui m'a attaqué à coup de krav-maga l'autre nuit. Votre manque de mordant m'inquiétait, hier.

– J'avais été arrêtée et j'ai failli finir en prison.

– Vous aviez donc si peu confiance en moi pour vous tirer de là ? Ça me brise le cœur.

– Cette bonne femme était prête à me sauter à la gorge, au début. Qu'est-ce que vous lui avez dit pour la faire changer d'avis, d'ailleurs ?

– On a passé un accord.

Je plisse les paupières.

– Et vous lui avez promis quoi, en échange de sa clémence à mon égard ?

Il soutient mon regard.

– Rien d'important.

Le téléphone fixe se remet à sonner derrière moi.

– Vous voulez que je… ?

Il agite la main.

– Le répondeur va s'en charger. Venez, que je vous montre vos meubles.

– Je pensais les trouver dans le hall.

– Tom croyait se rendre utile, du coup il les a fait déposer dans mon bureau.

Je le suis dans le couloir et il ouvre la porte d'une vaste pièce près de la salle d'archives où je travaillais il y a quelques jours. Je ne l'avais pas vu terminé, ce bureau ; les moulures et la décoration n'étaient pas installées et tout était recouvert de bâches. L'entrepreneur a dû travailler toute la journée d'hier pour avoir terminé.

– Waouh. C'est magnifique. Sauf… (Je me ravise et secoue la tête.) Non, rien. C'est superbe.

– Sauf quoi ? Qu'est-ce que vous alliez dire ?

– La pièce est belle. Vraiment belle, avec les hauts plafonds, les moulures en forme de couronne, sauf que… tout est blanc. Pourquoi n'avoir pas mis des couleurs ? Ce n'est pas un peu ennuyeux, tout en blanc ?

Il hausse les épaules.

– J'aime quand c'est simple. Noir et blanc.

Je ricane.

– Heureusement que vous êtes rentré à temps, alors, j'avais déjà choisi un jaune vif pour les murs. Et la salle de la photocopieuse allait être rouge.

Mon bureau est superbe, dans cette immense pièce, même sur le blanc si tristounet de ces murs. Le dessus en verre trempé, les pieds en acajou sombre. Je ne suis pas très fana des meubles modernes, en général, mais celui-ci est si beau, il dégage une telle sérénité que je n'ai pas pu résister.

– Le magasin de meubles n'a pas su m'indiquer d'heure, mais ils sont censés venir le récupérer aujourd'hui. Ils voulaient me prendre quarante pour cent de frais et me faire payer le retour. Il m'a fallu une heure au téléphone avec un responsable pour leur expliquer qu'ils avaient dénoncé leur propre contrat en laissant une personne non autorisée accepter la livraison.

– Vous êtes douée au téléphone.

– J'ai travaillé comme standardiste dans le service clientèle pour un imprimeur pendant toutes mes années d'université. Je me rappelle ce qui m'amenait à écouter vraiment et à contourner les règles pour un client après une longue journée à traiter des plaintes.

Le portable de Drew se remet à sonner. Il consulte l'écran et décide de ne pas décrocher.

– Répondez. Je vous laisse tranquille. J'ai déjà pris bien trop sur votre temps. Et vous avez l'air plutôt occupé.

– C'est bon. Je ne suis pas obligé de répondre.

– Vous êtes tout seul dans ce vaste espace ?

– Normalement, j'ai un auxiliaire juridique et une secrétaire. Mais depuis deux semaines, ma secrétaire est en congé maladie pour quelques mois et mon auxiliaire a décidé d'aller à la fac de droit dans un autre État.

– On dirait que vous allez être un peu débordé.

Nouvel appel et, cette fois, il me signifie qu'il doit décrocher. Il m'enjoint à faire comme chez moi, sauf que… il n'y a pas grand-chose à faire. Drew va s'asseoir à la table de la salle des archives, celle que j'utilisais comme bureau, et je retourne dans le hall d'accueil. Ayant retiré le reste des bâches de la zone de réception, je trouve des produits ménagers dans la salle de bains et entreprends de nettoyer le comptoir avant d'y installer mon ordinateur portable.

Entre deux mails en retard, je réponds au téléphone fixe et je prends les messages.

Quand Drew ressort une heure plus tard, il semble ennuyé.

– Mon portable est en panne de batterie. Je pourrais vous emprunter le vôtre quelques minutes ? Le sans-fil est au garde-meuble avec le reste de mes affaires et j'étais sur le point de parvenir enfin à un accord. Je ne veux pas donner à cet avocat le temps de réfléchir à deux fois à toutes les conneries qu'il vient d'accepter.

Je lui tends mon téléphone.

– Je vous en prie.

Il s'éloigne de quelques pas, avant de s'arrêter.

– Quel est le mot de passe ?

– Euh… Merde.

– Vous ne souhaitez pas que je connaisse votre mot de passe ?

– Non. « Merde », c'est le mot de passe.

Drew rigole.

– Une fille selon mon cœur.

Puis il tape le code et il repart.

Quand midi arrive, j'ai le ventre qui gargouille : m'étant réveillée en retard, je n'ai pas eu le temps de prendre un petit déjeuner. Mais je ne peux pas non plus quitter le bureau et risquer de rater une nouvelle fois la compagnie de livraison des meubles. En entendant Drew s'interrompre dans ses conversations téléphoniques, je m'aventure jusqu'à la salle des archives.

– Vous commandez le déjeuner sur place, en général ? J'ai peur de sortir et de rater la livraison.

– Parfois. Qu'est-ce qui vous tente ?

Je hausse les épaules.

– Peu m'importe. Je ne suis pas difficile.

– Un indien, ça vous va ? Le *Curry House* n'est qu'à quelques pâtés d'immeubles et ils livrent vite.

Je plisse le nez.

– Vous n'aimez pas la nourriture indienne ?

– Pas trop.

– OK. Chinois alors ?

– Trop de glutamate de sodium.

– Des sushis ?

– Je suis allergique au poisson.

– Mexicain ?

– Trop lourd pour le déjeuner.

– Vous comprenez la signification de la phrase : « Je ne suis pas difficile » ?

Je fronce les sourcils.

– Bien entendu. C'est vous qui ne proposez que des trucs bizarres.

– Qu'aimeriez-vous manger, Emerie ?

– Une pizza ?

Il hoche la tête.

– Va pour une pizza. Vous voyez ? Je ne suis pas difficile, moi.

***

Une fois le déjeuner terminé, Drew débranche son portable du chargeur.

– Je peux regarder vos photos ?

– Les photos de mon téléphone ? Pourquoi ?

– La meilleure manière de découvrir quelqu'un, c'est de regarder les photos qui sont dans son portable quand il ou elle s'y attend le moins.

– Je ne sais même pas trop ce que j'ai là-dedans.

– Justement, c'est le but. Si vous avez le temps de trier, je ne découvrirai pas la vraie vous. Je verrai seulement ce que vous voulez montrer.

J'essaie de me rappeler s'il n'y a pas quelques clichés embarrassants ou incriminants tandis que Drew fait glisser l'appareil de mon côté de la table vers le sien, un sourire moqueur aux lèvres. À la dernière seconde, je pose une main sur la sienne et l'arrête.

– Attendez. Si vous devez regarder les miennes, je veux voir les vôtres. Et vous avez intérêt à en avoir des honteuses, parce que je suis à peu près sûre que moi, oui.

– Mais je vous en prie. Je ne suis pas facile à embarrasser.

Il fait passer son téléphone de mon côté de la table pliante. Je le regarde entrer le mot de passe et commencer à consulter mes photos. Au bout d'un moment, il s'interrompt, les sourcils haussés.

– Celle-ci en dit long sur vous.

Je tends la main vers l'appareil, mais il est plus rapide.

– Quoi ? C'est quelle photo ?

Il tourne l'écran face à moi. *Oh non.* Vraiment gênant. Il s'agit d'un gros plan de moi, la semaine dernière, pendant que je travaillais. Ce lundi matin-là, j'avais passé la journée en séances de thérapie téléphonique et mon haut-parleur avait gentiment décidé de cesser de fonctionner de bonne heure. Je n'avais pas le temps de filer en acheter un nouveau pour le bureau, et dès le début de l'après-midi, j'étais frustrée de ne pouvoir effectuer plusieurs tâches en même temps, puisqu'une de mes mains était occupée à tenir le téléphone. Alors j'avais fait preuve de créativité. J'avais pris un rouleau de scotch orange, que j'avais déroulé autour de ma tête en y emprisonnant le téléphone. Très efficace, la technique maintenait l'appareil collé à mon oreille, si bien que je n'avais plus besoin de le tenir. Unc bande de scotch me passait sur le front, juste au-dessus des sourcils, et plissait ma peau d'une façon qui me donnait un drôle d'air mécontent. Une autre bande de scotch était collée à mon menton et y creusait une fossette tordue que je n'ai pas normalement.

– Mon haut-parleur ne fonctionnait pas et j'avais des tas de coups de fil prévus ce jour-là. J'avais besoin de pouvoir utiliser mes deux mains.

Il éclate de rire.

– Inventif. Il n'y a pas eu une seule mise à jour d'iPhone utile depuis la mort de Steve Jobs. Vous devriez envisager de leur vendre votre nouvelle innovation high-tech.

Je froisse ma serviette en papier et la lui jette au visage.

– Oh, taisez-vous.

Il fait encore défiler deux ou trois photos et s'immobilise à nouveau. Cette fois, je ne parviens pas à déchiffrer ce qu'il pense.

– Quoi ? Qu'est-ce que vous avez déniché, maintenant ?

Il contemple la photo un long moment et déglutit avant de tourner l'écran vers moi. Il s'agit d'un cliché en pied pris le soir où j'étais allée à un mariage avec Baldwin. C'est sans doute l'une de mes meilleures photos. Je m'étais fait coiffer et maquiller par une professionnelle et la robe que je portais m'allait comme un gant. Toute simple, noire, sans manches, avec un décolleté en V vertigineux qui révélait la naissance de mes seins. Une robe plus osée que ce que je porte en général, mais dans laquelle je me sentais à l'aise et jolie. Même si ce sentiment n'avait duré que le temps d'un petit quart d'heure après que Baldwin avait pris cette photo, car ensuite, j'avais ouvert la porte de son appartement et compris : ce mariage où nous avions été invités tous les deux, il y assisterait avec une cavalière, mais cette cavalière ne serait pas moi.

– Mariage, je lâche au souvenir de ma tristesse ce soir-là.

Drew hoche la tête et se replonge dans l'observation de la photo, avant de relever les yeux vers moi.

– Vous êtes sublime. Follement sexy.

Je sens le rouge me monter aux joues. C'est pour cette raison précise que je déteste avoir la peau claire.

– Merci.

Il reprend le défilé et s'arrête deux ou trois clichés plus loin.

– Petit ami ? demande-t-il en me montrant l'écran.

Celle-là, elle a été prise quelques minutes après que Baldwin m'avait complimentée sur ma beauté et qu'il avait pris l'autre photo, celle en pied. Il a un bras passé autour de ma taille et je souris, le regard fixé sur lui pendant qu'il prend le selfie. Sa cavalière avait sonné à la porte juste après. Le reste de la soirée n'a été que sourires forcés.

– Non.

– Ex-petit ami ?

– Non.

Il regarde le cliché, puis moi à nouveau.

– Il y a une histoire, là derrière, pas vrai ?

– Comment vous le savez ?

– À votre visage. À la manière dont vous le regardez.

C'est quand même assez triste qu'un quasi-étranger soit capable de deviner mes sentiments en quelques secondes, juste en observant une photo de nous, alors que Baldwin n'a jamais rien vu. Je pourrais mentir, mais pour une raison qui m'échappe, je ne le fais pas.

– On s'est rencontrés en licence. Il était chargé des TD de mon cours de psychologie tout en préparant son doctorat. C'est l'un de mes amis les plus proches. En fait, je vis dans l'appartement voisin du sien.

– Ça n'a pas marché ?

– Ça n'a jamais commencé, il n'éprouve pas la même chose que moi.

Drew semble sur le point d'ajouter quelque chose, mais il se ravise et se contente de hocher la tête, avant de reprendre son entreprise d'espionnage. Quand il a terminé, il a en effet beaucoup appris sur moi. Il a vu des photos de mes deux petites sœurs, notamment des selfies avec le chien datant d'avant mon emménagement à New York. Il est au courant de mes sentiments pour Baldwin et sait que je peux faire preuve d'une grande créativité en cas de besoin urgent.

– Bon… Vous avez dit que regarder les photos d'un inconnu vous en apprenait beaucoup sur la personne qu'il était, dis-je, quand il me refait passer le téléphone. Qu'est-ce que mes photos vous ont appris sur moi ?

– Très famille, cœur brisé et un petit peu foldingue.

J'ai envie de me vexer concernant ce dernier point, mais c'est difficile puisqu'il a tout à fait raison. Enfin, je ne vais pas non plus le lui avouer. À la place, je me saisis de son portable.

– Mot de passe ?

Il ricane.

– Pipe.

– Ne vous moquez pas de moi ! Vous venez de le changer.

Il secoue la tête.

– Non. C'est l'un de mes mots préférés, pour une multitude de raisons. « Casse ta pipe », que l'on peut marmonner au moins une fois par jour à l'intention de quelqu'un. Et, bien sûr, qui n'aime pas une bonne pipe ?

– Pervers.

– Venant de la femme dont le mot de passe est « merde »…

– J'ai choisi « merde » parce que je n'arrivais pas à me rappeler quel était mon mot de passe. Chaque fois que je me trompais, je grognais « merde ».

La dernière fois que je me suis retrouvée incapable d'entrer dans mon propre portable, Baldwin m'a suggéré de changer le mot de passe pour « merde ».

– Baldwin ?

Nos regards se retiennent.

– Le gars de la photo.

Drew hoche la tête.

Bizarrement, parler de Baldwin avec lui me met mal à l'aise. Alors je change de sujet.

– Voyons voir ce que je vais apprendre sur vous, monsieur l'avocat, j'annonce en tapant « pipe » sur son clavier.

Drew noue les mains derrière sa tête et se cale contre le dossier de sa chaise pour m'observer.

– Faites-vous plaisir.

Je trouve l'icône de la galerie photos et clique dessus. Ne voyant rien, je vais dans l'application de l'appareil photo et l'ouvre. Rien non plus.

– Vous n'avez aucune photo ? Je croyais que c'était un exercice destiné à apprendre à se connaître.

– Ça l'était.

– Et qu'est-ce que je suis censée apprendre de vous, avec un appareil rempli de vide ?

– Vous avez appris que je ne joue pas franc jeu.

CHAPITRE 6

DREW

Quel trou du cul.

Je parle de moi. Pas du joli petit cul qu'elle vient de me surprendre en train de mater. Même si… *Quel cul.*

Emerie est penchée par-dessus le comptoir d'accueil pour décrocher mon téléphone fixe qui sonne encore, quand elle me repère en train de me délecter de la savoureuse vue de derrière qu'elle m'offre. La politesse voudrait que je détourne les yeux, que je fasse celui qui ne la matait pas. Mais moi, qu'est-ce que je fais ? Je lui adresse un clin d'œil.

Encore. *Quel trou du cul.*

Et maintenant, Emerie me jette un regard noir tout en continuant à parler au téléphone. Quand une nana vous surprend en train de la reluquer, les choses peuvent aller dans deux directions. Soit elle saisit la perche et flirte aussi, soit…

Emerie raccroche et s'approche de moi d'un pas décidé. Son expression impassible ne me permet pas de deviner à quoi m'attendre.

Elle s'immobilise dans l'encadrement de la porte et croise les bras.

– Vous étiez en train de regarder mes fesses ?

OK, donc on prend l'autre direction, apparemment. Celle où l'objet du zieutage vous met le nez dans votre caca. Imitant sa posture, je croise les bras à mon tour.

– Vous voulez que je vous mente ?

– Non.

– C'est un très joli postérieur.

Ses joues s'embrasent.

– Vous êtes un trou du cul, vous le savez, ça ?

– Dans ce cas, je dois en être un beau. Entre beaux culs, on se reconnaît.

Son expression neutre se fissure et elle éclate de rire. J'aime bien l'idée qu'elle soit plus amusée qu'agacée.

– Les femmes trouvent votre comportement séduisant, en général ?

Je hausse les épaules.

– Vous seriez surprise de voir tout ce qu'on me passe.

– Vous êtes très imbu de vous-même.

– Peut-être. N'empêche que c'est vrai.

Je contourne le bureau derrière lequel je me tenais, pour ne laisser qu'environ cinquante à soixante centimètres entre nous.

– Avouez. Si j'étais petit, chauve, fauché et sans dents avec une bosse dans le dos, vous m'auriez envoyé sur les roses, à l'instant où vous m'auriez surpris en train de vous mater les fesses.

Elle ouvre la bouche. Elle est adorable, quand elle tente de trouver une réplique bien sentie, alors même que son visage m'a déjà dit que j'avais raison.

– Vous êtes un égocentrique.

– Peut-être, mais un égocentrique séduisant.

Elle lève les yeux au ciel et lâche un soupir, mais j'aperçois un léger sourire sur ses lèvres juste avant qu'elle ne sorte de mon bureau en balançant des hanches.

Quel cul.

Le reste de l'après-midi, je le passe pendu au téléphone. J'ai beau avoir libéré mon agenda de toute consultation au bureau jusqu'à la semaine prochaine, le mot est passé que je suis de retour et tous mes pauvres clients tiennent à me faire leur rapport sur les dernières manœuvres en date de leur future ex-épouse. Je travaille dans un domaine plutôt moche, mais je suis sacrément doué. La vengeance, c'est ce à quoi ils aspirent, alors chaque fois que je flanque un bon coup à une femme qui l'a mérité, dans ma tête, c'est avec mon ex, Alexa, que je règle mes comptes encore et encore. Je devrais sans doute consulter un psy, mais la vengeance par procuration, c'est moins cher et bien plus satisfaisant.

Je viens de raccrocher d'avec un client qui demande une ordonnance restrictive afin d'empêcher la femme dont il s'est séparé de brûler son stock de revues porno, quand j'entends Emerie, au téléphone, dans l'aire d'accueil. L'espace vide porte sa voix et je ne résiste pas à la curiosité.

– Le Queens ? C'est ce que vous pouvez me trouver de plus central pour moins de cinq cents dollars par mois ? Et si je prends plus petit ? Pas d'accueil, juste un bureau dans un immeuble. (Elle marque une pause.) Qu'est-ce qui vous fait rire ? Oui, oui, je souhaite en effet que vous me soumettiez des espaces où on peut entrer à plus d'une personne. (Nouvelle pause.) Non, je ne suis pas originaire de New York. Mais… mais… vous savez quoi ? Laissez tomber. Je vais m'adresser à un autre agent.

– Vous avez du mal à trouver un bureau ?

Elle fait volte-face. Et son visage exprime l'exaspération la plus totale.

– Qu'est-ce que je fiche à New York ?

– À vous de me le dire.

Elle lâche un soupir.

– C'est une longue histoire. Je…

Mon téléphone fixe sonne, elle lève un doigt et décroche avant que j'aie eu le temps d'essayer.

– Bureau de Drew Jagger… Puis-je savoir qui le demande ? Monsieur London…

Elle se tourne vers moi et j'agite les mains, geste universel pour indiquer : « Non, pas question. » Sans se démonter, elle reprend :

– Pour le moment, M. Jagger est occupé avec un client. Il a aussi un rendez-vous juste après qui attend déjà. Puis-je prendre un message détaillé à lui transmettre ?

Elle reste silencieuse une bonne minute, le téléphone écarté de son oreille, les sourcils haussés. J'entends cette grande gueule de Hal London d'où je me tiens, soit à cinquante centimètres environ. Profitant de ce qu'il reprend son souffle, elle parvient à se débarrasser de lui sans se départir de sa courtoisie.

– Vous avez tout entendu ? me demande-t-elle.

– Oui. Ce type est un connard. Je préférerais presque représenter sa salope de femme qui l'a trompé. Il me garde au téléphone une heure, chaque fois qu'il en a l'occasion. C'est son fric, certes, n'empêche que je n'ai pas envie de lui parler. Vous avez réussi l'exploit de lui clouer le bec vite fait.

– Essayez le super extra mielleux. Ça décontenance toujours les gens.

– Je vais tâcher de m'en souvenir.

Emerie jette un coup d'œil à sa montre.

– Il est presque seize heures. Je n'en reviens pas que les meubles ne soient pas encore arrivés. Je suis désolée, j'ai passé toute la journée ici.

– Pas de problème, j'ajouterai ça à votre loyer.

Elle sourit.

– Très bien. Mais dans ce cas, je vous facture mes services de secrétariat. Et je ne suis pas donnée.

Une image cochonne d'Emerie en train de jouer la secrétaire avec moi dans le rôle du patron s'affiche devant mes yeux et les mots sont sortis avant que je puisse les arrêter :

– Je serais prêt à payer cher pour vos services.

Elle rougit, mais ne lâche pas l'affaire.

– Vous devez être une sacrée tête de nœud comme patron, entre votre ego surdimensionné et vos sous-entendus pervers. Ça tombe bien que vous soyez avocat, c'est pratique quand vous êtes attaqué en justice.

– Vous venez de me traiter de « tête de nœud » ?

Elle mordille sa lèvre sensuelle.

– Effectivement.

– Vous avez vite deviné où se logent mes plus grosses qualités, dis-je en ricanant.

Une alarme se déclenche sur son portable, qu'elle éteint.

– J'ai un appel à seize heures avec un patient, je ne peux absolument pas le rater. Je vais sortir le prendre dehors. Comme ça, je ne raterai pas non plus les livreurs.

– Pourquoi n'utiliseriez-vous pas mon bureau ? Tant qu'à faire, vous profiteriez de ce beau meuble avant qu'ils le reprennent. Moi je suis un peu dur avec le mobilier, je ne voudrais pas taper dessus et ficher en l'air votre garantie. Et puis, ça vous donnera plus d'intimité avec votre patient.

– Mais je ne veux pas manquer les livreurs.

– Je garde un œil sur eux.

Elle hésite.

– Ça ne vous dérange pas ?

Je secoue la tête.

– Non. Allez-y. C'est moi qui joue le secrétaire pour vous, cette fois.

Il n'en faut pas plus pour la convaincre. Je la regarde s'éloigner dans le couloir… non, je regarde ses fesses s'éloigner dans le couloir. En atteignant mon bureau, elle s'arrête, jette un coup d'œil par-dessus son épaule et me surprend à nouveau. Alors je lui adresse un clin d'œil. On ne pourra pas m'accuser d'incohérence.

Il est un peu plus de seize heures trente quand les gars du magasin de meubles se pointent enfin. Emerie étant toujours dans mon bureau, je vais frapper à la porte entrouverte pour attirer son attention. Elle est en train d'écrire sur un bloc-notes, avec un casque sur les oreilles. Elle a remonté ses longs cheveux cuivrés en un vague chignon au sommet de son crâne et quand elle lève les yeux, c'est la première fois que je la vois avec des lunettes. Des montures sombres, rectangulaires, qui crient : « Bibliothécaire perverse ».

Du moins, c'est ce que j'entends, moi. Je la dévisage quelques secondes, pris dans mon fantasme, le temps qu'elle en termine avec son appel.

Les sourcils froncés, elle salue son interlocuteur et retire son casque.

– Tout va bien ?

Elle a toujours eu les yeux aussi bleus ? La monture noire doit rehausser la couleur de ses prunelles encore plus que ne le fait déjà sa peau claire.

– Euh… oui. Les gars sont là pour le meuble.

Elle m'adresse un drôle de regard mais sort néanmoins dans le couloir. Une fois qu'elle a signé des papiers, les types la suivent dans mon bureau. Ils emballent le meuble dans des couvertures de déménagement qu'ils maintiennent avec du scotch.

Emerie pousse un soupir en les observant.

– Elle est vraiment belle, cette table de travail.

Je la regarde les regarder préparer l'enlèvement.

– Magnifique.

En trois jours, elle a appris qu'elle s'était fait arnaquer de dix mille dollars, elle s'est fait arrêter et s'est rendu compte que son espace de bureau de rêve appartenait à quelqu'un d'autre. Et pourtant, c'est la première fois que je la vois vraiment triste. Comme si elle avait atteint sa limite. Quand ses yeux s'emplissent de larmes, je sens ma poitrine se serrer. Je suis plus affecté que je ne pourrais l'expliquer. Et bien entendu, je ne suis pas seulement affecté au niveau de la poitrine. Cette fille affecte aussi…

Mon cerveau.

Car la très mauvaise idée que je m'entends suggérer ne serait certainement pas sortie de ma bouche sans une défaillance momentanée de mes cellules grises.

– Restez. Vous et votre bureau. Restez. J'ai largement assez de place, ici.

CHAPITRE 7

DREW

Réveillon du 31 décembre,
huit ans plus tôt

Certains des meilleurs moments de la vie commencent par de mauvaises idées.

La grande blonde aux jambes aussi longues qu'une échelle vers le paradis, par exemple, c'était définitivement une mauvaise idée. Toute la soirée, je l'avais gardée en ligne de mire. Elle était venue avec deux amies et toutes les trois paraissaient n'avoir guère plus de dix-huit ans. Un gars du coin, l'ami d'un ami de l'un de mes potes de la fraternité, les avait amenées avec lui. Le gars en question avait l'œil sur la blonde, et parfois aussi les mains, mais elle semblait plus intéressée par la perspective de rencontrer des membres de Sigma Alpha.

Moi, j'aurais dû être en train de bosser mes cours de droit. J'aurais dû quitter Atlanta et rentrer à la maison pour les vacances comme je le faisais en général. Mais vu que c'était notre dernier semestre, tous les étudiants de dernière année de ma fraternité avaient décidé de rester pour les vacances d'hiver. Une fête en entraînait une autre, ça durait depuis dix jours non-stop. Bref, ce soir-là, puisque c'était le réveillon de la nouvelle année, la foule était mélangée. La plupart des étudiants étaient rentrés à la maison, ce qui laissait de la place pour les locaux. Et Daisy Duke[2] et ses longues jambes sentaient bon les vergers du Sud.

Nos regards se croisent alors que je prends une gorgée de ma bière. Elle m'offre un large sourire, et soudain, j'ai une folle envie de mordre dans un fruit. Elle vient vers moi, je n'ai même pas besoin de me lever.

– Ce siège est pris ?

Momentanément perplexe, je regarde sur ma droite, puis ma gauche. Je suis assis sur un fauteuil inclinable, dans un angle du salon, à regarder la fête se dérouler sous mes yeux. Le siège le plus proche est à l'autre bout de la pièce.

– Tu peux t'asseoir où tu veux, sans problème.

Ce qu'elle fait aussitôt, en posant son joli petit cul sur mes genoux.

– J'ai remarqué que tu me regardais.

– C'est difficile de ne pas te voir.

---

2. Daisy Duke est un personnage de fiction créé pour la série télévisée *Shérif, fais-moi peur*, interprété par Catherine Bach.

– Pareil pour toi. Tu es le plus beau garçon de la soirée.

– Ah oui ?

J'avale une nouvelle gorgée de ma bière et mademoiselle Longuesjambes me la prend des mains juste après. Elle la porte à ses lèvres et descend la moitié de la bouteille. À la suite de quoi, elle émet un long : « Aaaahhh ».

– C'est quoi ton petit nom, gambettes ?

– Alexa. Et toi ?

– Drew. (Je lui reprends ma bière et la vide.) C'est qui, le gars avec qui tu es venue ?

– Oh lui ? C'est Levi.

– C'est pas ton petit ami ou un truc du genre ?

Elle secoue la tête.

– Nan. C'est juste Levi. Il vit à Douglasville, pas loin de chez moi. Il est doué avec les voitures, il répare la mienne parfois.

À cet instant, le Levi en question repère Alexa depuis l'encadrement de la porte. Et il ne semble pas plus enthousiaste que ça de la trouver assise sur mes genoux.

Je lève le menton dans sa direction.

– Tu es sûre que Levi ne pense pas que vous êtes un peu plus que potes ? Il n'a pas l'air ravi, ravi, là.

Elle était assise en amazone sur mes genoux, mais elle pivote pour me faire face et me chevaucher, me bloquant par la même occasion la vue sur son mécano pas content.

– Voilà, comme ça tu ne le vois plus.

Je noue les mains derrière son dos.

– Ma vue vient de devenir bien plus jolie.

Moins d'une heure plus tard, elle me demande de lui montrer ma chambre. À quoi, évidemment, j'obtempère. On peut dire que je suis sympa avec les belles filles. Cela fait quatre ans que je vis sur le campus. Certaines sont plutôt directes et n'hésitent pas à dire clairement ce qu'elles veulent. Moi, je suis occupé et je ne cherche pas particulièrement une relation, alors j'apprécie les nanas qui ne minaudent pas, qui vont droit au but.

Les doigts d'Alexa ont saisi la braguette de mon short avant que j'aie refermé la porte de ma chambre. Je la plaque contre le battant pour mieux reléguer la fête au-dehors, ce qui a pour autre avantage de claquer la porte. Une pierre, deux coups.

– Tu t'inscris en école de droit, l'an prochain ? me demande-t-elle, tandis que je lui pelote les seins.

Une question qui aurait dû allumer une lumière rouge dans ma tête, vu que je n'ai pas mentionné mes projets d'avenir devant elle. Mais voilà… elle a une poitrine de rêve. Et des jambes à tomber. Qui se trouvent justement nouées autour de ma taille. Sans compter que je picole depuis le début de l'après-midi.

– Ouais. Je vais probablement aller à Emory. Mon père et mon grand-père y étaient, ils peuvent me coopter.

Sur quoi, nous accueillons la nouvelle année dans un grand coup de reins.

Super souvenirs.

Mauvaise idée.

CHAPITRE 8

DREW

– Tu as fait quoi ?

Roman Olivet me dévisage comme si je venais de lui avouer que j'avais tué la reine Élisabeth. Il secoue la tête.

– Mauvaise idée, mec.

Je plonge les yeux dans mon scotch et, une minute durant, je fais tourner le liquide ambré au fond de mon verre avant de le porter à mes lèvres.

– Elle va m'aider pendant les trois mois de congés de Tess en échange du loyer. Ça lui donnera le temps de se dégoter un espace dans ses moyens et de retomber sur ses pieds.

Roman sirote sa bière.

– Je t'ai demandé de me sous-louer de l'espace il y a deux ans et tu m'as répondu que tu ne pouvais partager avec personne.

– Exact. Sauf que là, c'est temporaire.

Il m'observe derrière ses paupières plissées.

– Elle est sexy, c'est ça ?

– Quel rapport ?

– Tu es vraiment une tête de nœud.

– Quoi ? Emerie m'a dit la même chose.

Roman hausse brusquement les sourcils.

– Elle t'a traité de tête de nœud et tu la laisses partager son espace de bureau avec toi ? Elle doit avoir un sacré cul.

Je tâche de conserver mon expression stoïque, mais Roman et moi sommes amis depuis toujours. Il repère le léger sourire qui se dessine à la commissure de mes lèvres.

– Une jolie paire de fesses, c'est ta kryptonite, mon pote, lâche-t-il en riant.

Pour être honnête, je ne suis pas encore revenu de ce qui m'est arrivé quelques heures plus tôt. Non content d'inviter cette femme qui, c'est vrai, a un fessier spectaculaire, à emménager dans mon bureau, j'ai dû la convaincre, tenez-vous bien, d'accepter mon offre. Je répète, j'ai déployé des trésors de persuasion pour qu'elle consente à emménager dans mon bureau de Park Avenue, ce même espace que je déteste partager avec quiconque. Et gratuitement, en plus.

Je descends le reste de mon scotch et lève la main pour commander son petit frère.

– Elle opère dans quel domaine du droit ?

– Elle n'est pas avocate. Elle est psychologue.

– Une psy ? Tu vas accueillir des dingos dans ton bureau ?

Je n'avais pas vraiment réfléchi à ça. Et si ses patients étaient des psychotiques aux multiples troubles de la personnalité ? Ou des anciens détenus qui ont tranché la gorge à des petites vieilles mais échappé à de lourdes peines de prison sous prétexte qu'ils sont malades mentaux ? *Je vais me faire assassiner à cause d'une belle paire de fesses. Aucun cul ne mérite ça.*

Cela dit… et mes clients, à moi, ils sont tous complètement sains d'esprit ? Ferdinand Armonk, soixante et onze ans, qui pèse cent millions de dollars, a été arrêté l'an dernier pour agression sur son épouse de vingt-trois ans à coups de canne, au motif qu'il l'avait surprise à genoux entre les jambes de son kiné. Voilà le genre de folie que je gère déjà au quotidien.

Je hausse les épaules.

– Ses dingos ne peuvent pas être bien pires que les miens.

Candice Armonk a fait arrêter son mari pour agression à la canne et tente de récupérer la moitié de sa fortune à l'issue du divorce. Roman n'est pas seulement mon meilleur ami, il est aussi mon détective privé et il a travaillé sur l'affaire Armonk. Il a déniché un vieux porno lesbien que Candice avait tourné à l'âge de dix-huit ans, alors qu'elle vivait encore en France. Intitulé *Candice aime la canne*, le film la montrait jouissant de femmes qui la bastonnaient. En revanche, un coup de son mari qui n'avait même pas laissé de marque, ça valait cinquante millions. Quand elle est venue à mon bureau avec son avocat pour la conciliation, elle a refusé de s'asseoir dans la salle de conférences en présence de Ferdinand tant que je n'aurais pas sorti la canne du bâtiment.

Le barman m'apporte mon verre que je déguste lentement.

– Les dingos d'Emerie auront tout à fait leur place chez moi.

***

Après une matinée de conférences en ville, je retourne au bureau et découvre Emerie en train de faire les cent pas dans son espace, un casque sur les oreilles, en pleine conversation téléphonique. Elle me tourne le dos quand j'entre dans le couloir, ce qui m'offre l'occasion de la contempler tout à loisir. Elle porte une jupe noire ajustée qui la moule à tous les bons endroits, et un chemisier de soie blanche. En entendant mes pas, elle se retourne et je remarque qu'elle est pieds nus. Le vernis rouge vif sur ses orteils est assorti à ses lèvres étirées sur un sourire. Un drôle de serrement dans la poitrine me pousse à lui rendre son sourire, et en même temps à me demander si j'ai besoin de prendre de l'oméprazole[3] ou quoi. Sur un signe de la main, j'entre dans mon bureau rempli de mes

3. Médicament pour le traitement des ulcères.

meubles bien que je n'aie pas encore demandé qu'on les rapporte.

Dix minutes plus tard, Emerie frappe doucement à ma porte même si elle est ouverte. Elle a remis ses chaussures, escarpins rouges, qui couvrent ses orteils carmin. *Joli.*

– Bonjour.

Je hoche la tête.

– Bonjour.

Elle me montre un bloc-notes et retire le crayon qu'elle avait derrière l'oreille.

– Vous avez eu une matinée chargée. Six appels : Jasper Mason, Marlin Appleton, Michael Goddman, Kurt Whaler, Alan Green et Arnold Schwartz. J'ai noté les messages sur un bloc que j'ai trouvé dans votre placard à fournitures. J'espère que ça ne vous dérange pas que je me sois servie.

– Je vous en prie, servez-vous. De toute façon, sans Tess, je n'ai aucune idée d'où se trouvent les choses.

Elle arrache le feuillet du bloc à papier carbone et vient les poser sur mon bureau.

– Voilà.

– Merci. Au fait, vous avez quelque chose à voir avec le fait que mes meubles soient revenus du garde-meuble ?

– Oh. Oui. J'espère que ça ne vous embête pas. L'entreprise de stockage a appelé ce matin et voulait programmer sa livraison pour aujourd'hui, alors j'ai pris le premier créneau disponible. L'entrepreneur était en train de nettoyer quand je suis arrivée ce matin, il a dit que les travaux salissants étaient terminés. Il va envoyer des gars à lui plus tard pour effectuer les dernières bricoles, comme poser les caches des interrupteurs électriques et raccrocher la plaque dans le hall. Les cartons contenant vos effets personnels sont par terre. J'allais y jeter un coup d'œil et les sortir pour vous, seulement je me suis dit que ce serait outrepasser mon rôle.

– Ça ne m'aurait pas gêné. Mais merci. Merci d'avoir tout pris en charge ce matin. Je pensais arriver ici et devoir m'asseoir à la table et sur la chaise pliante. Alors c'est une bonne surprise.

– Pas de problème. (Elle baisse les yeux sur sa montre.) J'ai une vidéoconférence dans quelques minutes, mais je suis dispo entre douze heures vingt et quatorze heures aujourd'hui, si vous voulez de l'aide pour organiser votre bureau. Je peux nous commander à manger sur place et on se fait un déjeuner de travail, si ça vous tente.

– Super idée. J'ai un appel à passer qui devrait être terminé avant douze heures trente.

– De quoi vous avez envie pour le déjeuner ?

– Surprenez-moi.

– N'importe quoi ?

– N'importe quoi. Contrairement à vous, je ne suis pas difficile.

Sur un sourire, elle retourne vers son bureau. Je l'interromps pour lui poser une question qui me trotte dans la tête depuis mon dîner avec Roman hier soir.

– Quel genre de psy êtes-vous ? Vous avez une spécialité ?

– Oui. Je croyais vous l'avoir dit. Je suis conseillère conjugale.

– Conseillère conjugale ?

– Oui. J'œuvre à sauver les mariages en péril.

– Non, c'est sûr qu'on n'en a pas parlé. Je m'en serais souvenu, sachant que je travaille aussi sur les mariages en péril… pour les dissoudre de manière permanente.

– Ça pose un problème ?

Je secoue la tête.

– A priori, non.

Je me souviendrai longtemps de ces derniers mots.

CHAPITRE 9

EMERIE

– Tenez, encore quelques messages.

Juste après avoir terminé son appel, Drew me fait signe d'entrer dans son bureau. Je dépose le sac contenant notre déjeuner sur sa table de travail et lui tends les feuillets. Il les compulse rapidement et en retire un.

– Si ce type rappelle, Jonathon Gates, vous avez la permission de lui raccrocher au nez.

– Je peux l'insulter avant ?

Il prend un air amusé.

– Vous le traiteriez de quoi ?

– Ça dépend. Qu'est-ce qu'il a fait de mal ?

– Il frappe sa femme.

– Oh, bon Dieu. OK. (Je grimace en réfléchissant à un nom d'oiseau pour monsieur Gates.) Je le traiterais de putain d'animal et puis je lui raccrocherais au nez.

Drew s'esclaffe.

– Vous ne jurez pas comme une New-Yorkaise.

– Comment ça ?

– Vous prononcez le mot en entier. P-U-T-A-I-N.

– Et je devrais prononcer comment ?

– 'Tain. Sans le « pu ».

– 'Tain.

– Encore un peu raide. Il faudra vous entraîner, avant que ça sonne naturel.

Je plonge la main dans le sac de courses et en sors la nourriture que j'ai achetée. Avec un sourire, je la lui tends.

– Prenez votre déjeuner, 'tain.

– Bien, commente-t-il, un sourire aux lèvres. Continuez comme ça. Vous ne tarderez pas à passer pour Tess.

– Tess ?

– Ma secrétaire qui est en congé après son opération de la hanche. Elle a soixante ans et ressemble à Mary Poppins, mais elle jure comme une charretière.

– Je vais m'entraîner dur.

Je nous ai commandé des sandwichs chez un traiteur que j'ai découvert le premier jour de ma fausse location. Comme Drew m'a l'air du genre à prendre soin de lui, j'ai choisi un club sandwich pain complet dinde et avocat et pareil pour moi, même si, en général, j'ai tendance à manger moins sainement. Drew a dévoré son sandwich en entier avant que j'aie mangé la moitié du mien, alors que je ne suis pourtant pas du genre à manger lentement.

– J'en déduis que vous avez aimé ? demandé-je en regardant son emballage vide.

– Je suis allé à la salle de sport à cinq heures du matin et n'ai pas eu le temps de petit-déjeuner avant une réunion de bonne heure dans le nord de la ville. C'est la première chose que j'avale de la journée.

– Cinq heures du matin ? Vous êtes allé au sport à cinq heures du matin ?

– Je suis un lève-tôt. À votre ton horrifié, j'en conclus que ce n'est pas votre cas ?

– J'essaie de me faire violence.

– Et ça fonctionne ?

– Pas super, j'admets en riant. J'ai du mal à m'endormir le soir, du coup, les réveils sont rudes.

– Vous faites du sport ?

– J'ai commencé les fameux cours de krav-maga quelques fois par semaine pour me fatiguer, en espérant que ça m'aiderait à dormir. Mais ça ne marche pas trop. Enfin, j'aime bien quand même.

– Et les boissons à base de mélatonine, vous avez essayé ?

– Oui. Aucun effet.

– Les somnifères ?

– Je suis encore groggy vingt-quatre heures après la prise. Même le paracétamol me fatigue.

– La prolactine alors.

– La prolactine ? C'est quoi ? Une vitamine ?

– C'est une hormone que l'on produit après l'orgasme. Ça donne envie de dormir. Vous avez essayé la masturbation juste avant de vous coucher ?

Je m'étrangle au milieu d'une bouchée de mon sandwich. Pas l'étranglement avec crachouillis et toux, genre c'est-passé-par-le-mauvais-tuyau. Non. Je m'étrangle. Littéralement. Un morceau de pain est resté coincé dans ma gorge, qui empêche le passage de l'air. Prise de panique, je me lève en renversant l'emballage, le reste de mon sandwich à la dinde et mon soda. Tout finit par terre. Et je désigne furieusement ma gorge.

Par chance, Drew comprend le message. Il se précipite de mon côté du bureau et m'assène quelques tapes dans le dos. Voyant que je reste incapable de respirer, il m'enveloppe de ses bras par-derrière et pratique la méthode de Heimlich. À la seconde forte poussée, le pain qui me bloquait la trachée est délogé et vole à travers le bureau. Bien que la scène n'ait sans doute pas duré plus de quinze secondes, je me plie en deux, aussi haletante que si j'avais été privée d'oxygène pendant plusieurs minutes. Mon cœur tambourine comme un fou dans ma poitrine, surexcité par l'afflux soudain d'adrénaline.

Drew ne me relâche pas. Il garde les bras étroitement noués autour de moi, juste sous ma poitrine, tandis que je prends de longues inspirations.

Enfin, une fois que ma respiration a retrouvé un rythme à peu près normal, il me demande d'une voix basse et hésitante :

– Ça va ?

Ma voix, à moi, est gutturale.

– Je pense que oui.

Son étreinte autour de moi se desserre, mais il ne bouge pas. Au lieu de quoi, il pose la tête sur le sommet de mon crâne.

– Vous m'avez flanqué une de ces trouilles.

Je porte une main à ma gorge.

– C'est une sensation terrifiante. Je ne m'étais jamais étouffée avant.

L'espace du bref instant de ma mort imminente, j'ai complètement oublié ce qui a causé cet étranglement à la base. Mais ça me revient très vite.

– Vous avez failli me tuer.

– Vous tuer ? On dirait que votre cerveau a été privé d'oxygène, ma belle, parce que je viens au contraire de vous sauver la vie.

– C'est à cause de vous si je me suis étranglée. Qui parle de masturbation avec une quasi-inconnue au beau milieu de son déjeuner ?

– Une quasi-inconnue ? Je vous ai vue en sous-vêtements, vous ai sortie de prison et donné un endroit où poser vos fesses toute la journée. Je trouve plutôt que je suis votre meilleur ami dans cette ville, à ce stade.

Je fais volte-face pour planter mes yeux dans les siens.

– Je n'ai peut-être pas besoin de me masturber, de toute façon. Qui vous dit que je n'ai pas un petit ami pour prendre soin de mes besoins ?

Drew ricane. Il ne sourit pas, il ricane.

– Si tel est le cas et que vous avez toujours des soucis d'endormissement une fois qu'il s'est occupé de vous le soir, eh bien, plaquez-le parce qu'il est nul au lit.

– Je suppose que toutes vos nanas s'endorment sur-le-champ, une fois que vous vous êtes chargé de leur cas ?

– Carrément. Je suis une sorte de superhéros. Prolactinator, on m'appelle.

Cet homme possède l'étrange capacité de me faire rire au beau milieu d'une dispute. Hilare, je me penche pour ramasser mon sandwich éparpillé au sol.

– OK, Prolactinator, et si vous utilisiez vos superpouvoirs pour m'aider à nettoyer ce bazar ?

Une fois la débâcle de ce déjeuner contenue, je propose à Drew de l'aider à déballer ses cartons. Il y a une perceuse sans fil dans le premier que nous ouvrons, et il accroche ses diplômes joliment encadrés pendant que je sors et nettoie des objets. La conversation est légère et fluide jusqu'à ce qu'il me pose une question que je redoute toujours.

– Vous ne m'avez jamais expliqué ce qui vous avait amenée à New York, tout compte fait ?

– C'est une longue histoire.

Il regarde sa montre.

– J'ai vingt minutes avant mon prochain rendez-vous. Allez-y.

L'idée me traverse brièvement d'inventer une réponse afin de m'éviter le récit de la vérité. Et puis je me dis que ce type m'a vue au plus mal, qu'il m'a aidée à ne pas atterrir en prison et qu'il a été le témoin privilégié de ma naïveté ; on pourrait me vendre le pont de Brooklyn, comme disent les New-Yorkais. Alors j'opte pour la franchise.

– Pendant ma première année de fac, je ne savais pas trop quels cours choisir. J'ai donc assisté à une heure de cours de psychologie et le prof était génial. Seulement, il était aussi alcoolique et ratait souvent ses cours ou arrivait alors qu'il ne restait plus que dix minutes. Il avait un assistant de New York, mais qui bossait pour son doctorat à l'université d'Oklahoma. C'est lui qui se retrouvait à enseigner la plupart des cours que le prof aurait dû donner lui-même. Cet assistant, c'était Baldwin.

Drew lâche une pile de dossiers dans un placard, qu'il referme, avant de se tourner vers moi.

– Alors vous avez déménagé à New York pour vous rapprocher de ce Baldwin ? Je croyais que vous aviez dit l'autre jour qu'il n'éprouvait pas les mêmes sentiments que vous ?

– C'est le cas. Baldwin et moi sommes devenus bons amis, au fil des quatre années suivantes. Il avait une petite amie, avec qui il vivait, une étudiante en histoire de l'art qui faisait aussi du mannequinat à côté. (Je lève les yeux au ciel au souvenir de Meredith, si imbue de sa personne.) Il est resté à la fac pour enseigner après avoir bouclé son doctorat, avant de décider de retourner à New York, d'ouvrir son propre cabinet et d'enseigner ici. On est restés en contact pendant que moi, je préparais mon diplôme, et il m'a beaucoup aidée à rédiger ma thèse pendant une année.

– On en vient bientôt aux scènes de sexe ou à quelque chose d'un peu excitant, dans cette histoire ? Parce qu'il commence à m'ennuyer profondément, ce bon vieux Baldwin.

Il se trouve près de moi, en train d'ouvrir le dernier carton. Je lui donne une petite tape sur le bras.

– C'est vous qui avez voulu l'entendre, cette histoire.

– Je croyais que ce serait plus intéressant, me taquine-t-il, sourire arrogant aux lèvres.

– Bon, je vais abréger pour ne pas vous endormir…

– Pas de souci, m'interrompt-il. Je n'ai pas sommeil. Je ne me suis pas masturbé, ce matin.

– Merci de me tenir au courant. Vous voulez entendre la fin ou quoi ?

– Bien sûr. J'ignore pourquoi, mais j'ai hâte de savoir ce qui cloche chez ce Baldwin.

– Pourquoi est-ce que vous présumez que quelque chose cloche chez lui ?

– Simple pressentiment.

– Eh bien, vous avez tort. Rien ne cloche chez Baldwin. C'est un type super, extrêmement intelligent et cultivé.

Drew pose les mains sur ses hanches et s'arrête de travailler pour m'accorder toute son attention.

– Vous avez dit qu'il « avait » une petite amie pendant quatre ans. J'en déduis qu'ils ont rompu ?

– Oui. Juste avant qu'il ne rentre à New York.

– Et il n'a rien tenté avec vous, sachant que vous étiez amoureuse de lui ?

– Comment vous savez que j'étais amoureuse de lui ?

Il me regarde, suggérant que la réponse était évidente.

– Vous l'étiez ?

– Oui. Mais... je ne vous l'ai pas dit.

– On lit en vous comme dans un livre ouvert.

Je lâche un soupir.

– Pourquoi est-ce si facile pour vous de le voir, alors que Baldwin ne s'en rend pas compte ?

– Il s'en rend compte. Il le sait. Mais pour une raison ou une autre, il vous le cache.

C'est assez dingue : Drew a mis le doigt sur un truc que je suspecte depuis longtemps. J'ai toujours eu l'impression que Baldwin connaissait mes sentiments pour lui, même si jamais je ne les ai exprimés en sa présence. Et une partie de moi a toujours espéré qu'il éprouvait au moins quelque chose pour moi, même s'il n'en a jamais rien montré. Raison pour laquelle j'ai décidé de faire le premier pas, au sens propre, en venant habiter à New York. Je ne sais pourquoi, je m'étais mis en tête que son célibat actuel rendait la période propice. Hélas, tout ce que j'ai réussi à faire, c'est me torturer un peu plus chaque fois qu'il ramenait ses rencards chez lui plusieurs fois par semaine. Et moi qui avais pensé qu'en emménageant à New York, ça déclencherait peut-être un début de relation…

– Il est célibataire, maintenant ?

– Il ne sort avec personne de façon régulière, en tout cas. Même si j'ai l'impression qu'il est passé sur la moitié des femmes de la ville en quelques mois. Il rentre avec une fille différente presque chaque semaine. La dernière en date s'appelle Rachel.

Je lève les yeux au ciel.

– Vous vivez avec lui ?!

– Non, je sous-loue l'appartement à côté du sien pendant que son voisin est parti enseigner en Afrique pour un an.

– Attendez un peu que je récapitule : il passe devant chez vous avec des femmes et n'a jamais admis être au courant de ce que vous ressentez pour lui.

– C'est ma faute. Je ne lui ai toujours pas avoué mes sentiments.

– Ce n'est pas votre faute. Ce type est un connard.

– Non, pas du tout.

– Ouvrez les yeux, Emerie.

– Vous ne savez pas de quoi vous parlez.

– Je vous souhaite d'avoir raison, mais je suis prêt à parier que non.

Je sens la colère qui me monte dans la gorge et envisage de retourner en trombe dans mon bureau en le laissant se débrouiller pour déballer ses cartons. Mais j'ai un espace sur Park Avenue gratuitement grâce à lui. Alors je me tais et je finis ce que nous avons commencé. Jusqu'à exhumer le dernier objet.

C'est un petit cadre photo enveloppé dans du papier bulle. Drew a emporté quelques cartons vides au composteur de papier dans la cave de l'immeuble. Il revient pile au moment où j'arrache la dernière couche de scotch. Le cliché représente un beau petit garçon en tenue de hockey. Il doit avoir six ou sept ans, et un golden retriever lui lèche le visage tandis qu'il rit.

Souriant, je me tourne face à Drew.

– Il est adorable. C'est votre fils ?

Il me prend la photo des mains.

– Non, répond-il sèchement.

Quand nos regards se croisent, je suis sur le point de le questionner encore, mais il me devance.

– Merci de votre aide. Je dois me préparer pour un rendez-vous.

CHAPITRE 10

DREW

Réveillon du 31 décembre,
sept ans plus tôt

Je suis dans la petite salle à l'arrière de l'église, le regard perdu par la fenêtre. Il pleut des cordes et le ciel est d'une teinte gris sombre. À l'image de mon humeur.

Très sombre.

Ce qui constitue sans doute le signe le plus encourageant de la justesse de mon choix.

Roman ouvre la porte.

– Ah, te voilà. Il a invité combien de personnes, ton père ? Ils doivent être au moins quatre cents, là-dedans. Ils ont déjà commencé à remplir le balcon.

– Aucune idée. Je n'ai pas demandé.

À la vérité, je me suis très peu renseigné sur l'organisation du mariage. J'ai d'abord mis mon manque d'intérêt sur le compte de mes études de droit qui m'occupent beaucoup. Mais récemment, je me suis rendu compte qu'il y avait autre chose. Je ne suis pas enthousiaste à l'idée de me marier.

Roman vient se poster près de moi et s'abîme lui aussi dans la contemplation du paysage. Il plonge la main dans la poche intérieure de son smoking et en sort une flasque, qu'il me tend. Je la prends, j'en ai besoin.

– Ma voiture est garée derrière, si tu veux t'enfuir.

Je lui jette un regard de travers en avalant une double gorgée de whisky à sa flasque.

– Je ne peux pas lui faire ça. Elle porte mon bébé, mec.

– Ton bébé, elle va l'avoir dans deux mois, quoi qu'il arrive.

– Je sais. Mais c'est mon devoir.

– Qu'il aille se faire foutre, le devoir.

Un sourire narquois aux lèvres, je rends la flasque à mon garçon d'honneur.

– Tu es au courant que tu te trouves dans une église.

Il boit à son tour.

– De toute façon, je suis en partance pour l'enfer, alors…

Je ris. Même s'il a tout juste vingt-quatre ans, on a déjà poliment « demandé » à mon meilleur ami de quitter la police de New York. « Demandé » entre guillemets, car en fait c'était « démissionne, sinon on te vire ». Il n'est pas vraiment ce que l'on pourrait appeler un ange.

– Je tiens à Alexa. On va faire en sorte que ça fonctionne.

– Je ne t'ai pas encore entendu prononcer le mot « amour ». Tu l'épouserais, si tu ne l'avais pas mise en cloque comme un imbécile, seulement quelques mois après l'avoir rencontrée ?

Je ne réponds pas.

– C'est bien ce que je pensais. On peut avoir un enfant sans être marié. On n'est plus en 1960, monsieur le Lâcheur.

– On va s'en sortir.

Roman m'assène une claque dans le dos.

– C'est ta vie. Mais les clés sont dans ma poche, si tu changes d'avis.

– Merci, mon pote.

CHAPITRE 11

EMERIE

– Ce n'est pas parce que vous êtes séparés par des milliers de kilomètres que vos cœurs le sont. Vous devriez, chacun, prendre le temps de signifier à l'autre ce que vous pensez de lui. Je vais vous poser une question, Jeff : vous avez dit que vous aviez pensé à Kami aujourd'hui, quand vous êtes allé courir, parce que vous étiez passé devant un magasin de lingerie du nom de « Kami-soles ». Vous en aviez parlé à Kami, avant notre séance de thérapie d'aujourd'hui ? Par exemple quand elle a mentionné le fait qu'elle trouvait que vous ne pensiez jamais à elle ?

Mon écran de quarante-deux pouces est divisé en deux : Jeff Scott à gauche et Kami Scott à droite. Tous les deux étaient mariés depuis moins d'un an quand Jeff a été muté sur la côte Ouest. Sachant qu'il est leur seule source de revenus, Kami effectuant sa deuxième année d'internat dentaire, il n'a guère eu d'autre choix que de déménager en attendant de pouvoir trouver un autre travail, plus près de leur résidence, dans le Connecticut.

– Non, je ne lui en avais jamais parlé. Je suis débordé. Elle sait que je pense à elle.

Le visage de Jeff se fige quelques secondes, alors que sa voix continue à se faire entendre. La fixation de l'image l'a pris au milieu d'un mot et dans une posture bizarre du visage. Un œil fermé, l'autre à demi, avec le blanc de l'œil qui apparaît. Il a la bouche ouverte et celle-ci semble comme tachée par le café. Il faut que je me dégote un meilleur logiciel vidéo pour mes séances de thérapie. Dieu sait à quoi je ressemble sur leurs écrans respectifs en ce moment.

Notre séance de quarante-cinq minutes de thérapie de couple touche à sa fin.

– Cette semaine, j'aimerais que vous fassiez un exercice. Au moins une fois par jour, quand quelque chose vous fait penser à l'autre, racontez-le-lui sur-le-champ. Si vous êtes en plein jogging et que vous repérez quelque chose, prenez une photo et envoyez-la par MMS, par exemple. Kami, si un patient enrhumé vient se faire soigner et éternue beaucoup, ce qui vous rappelle la propension de Jeff à éternuer cinq ou six fois d'affilée, dites-le-lui. Ces petits détails peuvent faire beaucoup pour rappeler à l'autre que votre cœur n'est jamais loin, même s'il y a tous ces kilomètres entre vous. La distance n'est qu'un test destiné à mesurer à quel point l'amour peut voyager.

Je perçois ce qui ressemble fort à un ricanement derrière ma porte presque fermée. Une fois ma séance terminée, la curiosité me pousse donc à aller trouver Drew. Il est dans la salle de reprographie, voisine du bureau que j'utilise, occupé à faire des photocopies.

– Vous m'avez dit quelque chose ?

Je lui accorde le bénéfice du doute, mais…

– Non. Mon père m'a toujours appris que si je n'avais rien de gentil à dire à une femme, mieux valait me taire.

Je n'ai donc pas rêvé.

– Vous écoutiez ma séance de thérapie. Vous avez ri du conseil que j'ai donné à mes clients, c'est ça ?

– Je n'écoutais pas. Votre porte était ouverte et vous parlez fort, au téléphone. Vous êtes au courant que vous n'avez pas besoin de hurler pour que votre interlocuteur vous entende pendant une visioconférence ?

– Je ne hurlais pas.

Il termine ses photocopies et retire une liasse de feuilles de la machine.

– Peu importe. Mais mieux vaut que vous fermiez la porte, dorénavant, si vous ne voulez pas que j'entende par hasard vos mauvais conseils.

Je sens mes yeux s'écarquiller comme des soucoupes.

– Des mauvais conseils ? De quoi vous parlez ? Je suis une psychologue assermentée qui a fait sa thèse sur « Surmonter les barrières dans les relations en ouvrant les lignes de communication lors des thérapies de couple ».

Drew ricane. Encore.

– C'est vous l'experte, dans ce cas. Je vous laisse vous débrouiller.

Sur ce, il retourne à son bureau.

Il ne sait pas du tout de quoi il parle. Mes conseils sont solides, fondés sur des années d'études de couples qui veulent vraiment résoudre leurs problèmes. Alors je ne peux pas m'en empêcher, je le suis et me plante dans l'encadrement de sa porte.

– Et quels conseils donneriez-vous à un couple obligé de vivre une relation à distance ?

– Un conseil plus réaliste que : « La distance n'est qu'un test destiné à mesurer à quel point l'amour peut voyager. » Quelle connerie ! Vous avez lu ça où ? Sur une carte de vœux ?

Alors là, j'en ai les yeux qui me sortent de la tête.

– J'écoute, c'est quoi votre idée d'un conseil « réaliste », alors ?

– Simple : « Offrez-vous les services d'un bon avocat spécialisé dans le divorce. » Les relations à distance NE FONCTIONNENT PAS.

– J'en déduis que vous avez essayé et que vous vous êtes brûlé les ailes, du coup vous en concluez que tout le monde va échouer aussi ?

– Pas du tout. Je n'ai jamais eu de relation à distance. Et vous savez pourquoi ? Parce qu'elles ne fonctionnent pas ! Je sais ça d'expérience. Quelle expérience vous avez, vous, des relations à distance ?

– J'étudie les couples depuis des années. Je pense avoir plus d'expérience que vous sur le sujet.

– Ah bon ?

Drew se dirige vers un classeur et en sort une grande chemise extensible entourée d'un élastique. Qu'il pose brutalement sur son bureau.

– Morrison. Mariage heureux pendant quatorze ans. Divorcé il y a deux ans. Trois ans avant le divorce, Dan Morrison a pris un boulot de représentant de commerce. Mieux payé : sa femme n'aurait plus besoin de travailler. Quatre nuits par semaine en déplacement, et pourtant Dan n'a pas raté un seul rendez-vous du vendredi soir avec son épouse, ni n'a rechigné à conduire soixante kilomètres tous les dimanches, son seul jour de repos, pour aller donner le bain à son vieux beau-père. En revanche, vous savez ce qu'il a raté ? Tous les mardis, mercredis et jeudis, jours où madame Morrison se tapait Laire, son prof de tennis.

Voyant que je continue à fixer sur lui un regard furieux, il ouvre un autre tiroir dont il tire un deuxième dossier qu'il pose d'un coup sec sur celui de Morrison.

– Loring. Marié et heureux pendant six ans quand son bureau a été transféré de New York dans le New Jersey. Cent vingt kilomètres. Pas énorme. Sauf qu'Al Loring travaillait seize heures par jour, plusieurs jours par semaine. Sa garce de femme, Mitsy, avait le sommeil léger, alors il passait les nuits où il travaillait trop tard sur le canapé de son bureau, afin de ne pas réveiller sa princesse d'épouse. Il est rentré chez lui un soir où il était censé rester au bureau parce que Mitsy lui manquait. Il a trouvé sa chère épouse dans le lit conjugal, avec leur voisin en train de l'honorer. Aujourd'hui, c'est le voisin en question qui a son chien et sa femme. Quant à Al, il est devenu alcoolique et il a perdu son boulot dans le New Jersey.

Du même tiroir, il sort un troisième dossier.

– McDune. Marié et heureux six ans. Erin est partie vivre à Dublin temporairement, pour s'occuper de sa mère tombée en dépression après le décès de son père. Elle a divorcé de Liam pour un type qui ressemble à un gnome, sous prétexte qu'elle aurait trouvé l'« âme sœur » sur sa « terre natale ». Au temps pour la relation à distance afin d'apaiser l'âme de maman.

Drew ouvre le tiroir du bas de son classeur. Cette fois, je l'interromps.

– Vous avez le droit de me raconter tout ça ? Le secret professionnel, ça vous dit quelque chose ?

– J'ai changé les noms pour protéger les pas-si-innocents-que-ça. Croyez-le ou pas, contrairement aux épouses de mes clients, j'ai une éthique. (Il désigne le tiroir.) Vous en voulez encore ? Il faut vraiment que vous écoutiez l'histoire du lieutenant O'Connor. Un vrai tire-larmes. Sa femme baisait avec son frère pendant qu'il se battait en Irak et elle…

De nouveau, je le coupe.

– OK, j'ai compris votre point de vue. Mais vous oubliez une chose : peut-être ces divorces n'auraient-ils pas eu lieu si les conjoints s'étaient fait conseiller. Vous voyez les gens quand ils ont touché le fond, quand ils ont abandonné l'idée de se battre pour leur mariage.

Il me dévisage, l'air incrédule.

– Vous pensez vraiment que tous les mariages peuvent être sauvés ?

Je réfléchis à sa question une minute avant de lui répondre.

– Non, pas tous. Mais la plupart, oui. Ouvrir les lignes de communication, ça peut réparer beaucoup de choses.

Drew secoue la tête.

– Quelle naïveté. J'ai un espace de bureau sur Park Avenue que vous pouvez louer pour deux mille balles par mois, au fait.

– Allez vous faire voir, je siffle, avant de retourner dans mon bureau comme une furie.

***

Je laisse la porte de mon bureau volontairement fermée tout le reste de l'après-midi. Un coup frappé peu avant dix-neuf heures me fait sursauter alors que je travaille sur la transcription des pattes de mouche que j'ai griffonnées pendant les séances de thérapie du jour. J'ai un dossier électronique sur chacun de mes patients.

– Entrez.

La porte s'ouvre, ou plutôt elle s'entrouvre, juste assez pour laisser passer un bras. Ce qui est exactement ce que je vois apparaître. Le bras de Drew, qui agite un tissu blanc.

C'est quoi ? Des… sous-vêtements ?!

Tout l'après-midi, j'ai gardé en moi la colère qu'a provoquée notre vive dispute et ça commence à me peser. Son geste apporte une légèreté dont j'avais bien besoin.

– Entrez, je répète.

Il pousse la porte, quelques centimètres de plus, et cette fois sa tête rejoint le bras au drapeau blanc.

– Vous n'êtes plus furax ? Vous n'allez pas me faire un coup de krav-maga ?

Je ris.

– Je devrais. Vous méritez une bonne fessée. Mais je vais me retenir.

Souriant, il ouvre la porte en grand mais reste sur le seuil.

– Je crois que je vous dois des excuses pour certaines des choses que j'ai dites, aujourd'hui.

Je me cale contre le dossier de mon fauteuil.

– Exact.

Il baisse la tête. Un geste qui me rappelle un petit garçon qui viendrait de baigner son chien… dans de la peinture rouge. C'est mignon. Il est mignon. Mais je vais quand même le laisser ramer. La tête toujours légèrement inclinée, il lève les yeux derrière ses cils noirs.

– Pardon pour tout à l'heure.

– Vous vous excusez de quoi, exactement ?

Il rabaisse la tête au maximum.

– Vous n'avez pas l'intention de me faciliter la tâche, c'est ça ?

– Non.

– Bien. Je m'excuse de vous avoir traitée de naïve.

– Autre chose ?

Je regarde son visage tandis que les rouages tournent dans son cerveau.

– D'avoir écouté votre conversation avec vos clients.

– C'est tout ?

– Il est censé y avoir autre chose ?

L'espace d'une fraction de seconde, il a l'air inquiet.

– Oui, il y a autre chose.

Après trente secondes de réflexion, il claque des doigts, comme s'il était fier de lui.

– Je m'excuse d'avoir regardé vos fesses.

Je fronce les sourcils.

– Quand est-ce que vous avez regardé mes fesses ?

Il hausse les épaules.

– Chaque fois que j'en ai eu l'occasion.

Je ne peux m'empêcher de rire.

– Excuses acceptées.

Ses épaules tombent imperceptiblement, il semble soulagé. Cet homme paraît sûr de lui, vu de l'extérieur, mais parfois ce sont ceux qui ont vécu des choses dures qui portent l'armure la plus épaisse.

– Et si je vous payais un burger de chez Joey pour le dîner, histoire de me faire pardonner ? demande-t-il avec un clin d'œil. Je choisirai le plus gros qu'ils aient, pour que vous soyez si rassasiée que vous serez obligée de dégrafer votre jupe devant moi.

CHAPITRE 12

EMERIE

– Je peux vous poser une question personnelle ?

La réponse de Drew ne tarde pas.

– Non.

Je grimace, perplexe.

– Non ? Vous savez, en général, quand les gens mangent ensemble en discutant, et que l'un d'eux demande à l'autre s'il peut lui poser une question personnelle, l'autre répond « oui ». Par politesse.

– Eh bien moi, j'ai une règle : quand on cherche à savoir si on peut me demander quelque chose, je réponds « non ».

– Pourquoi ?

– Parce que si vous posez la question, c'est probablement qu'il s'agit d'une chose à laquelle je n'ai pas envie de répondre.

– Comment le savez-vous, si vous n'entendez même pas la question ?

Drew s'adosse contre son fauteuil.

– Quelle est votre question, Emerie ?

– Ben maintenant, j'ai l'impression qu'il vaut mieux ne pas la poser.

Il hausse les épaules et finit sa bière.

– OK. Alors ne la posez pas.

– Il vous est arrivé quelque chose, pour vous rendre aussi amer concernant les relations ?

– Je croyais que vous n'osiez pas demander ?

– J'ai changé d'avis.

– Vous êtes une plaie. Vous le savez, je suppose ?

– Et vous êtes un salopard amer, du coup je suis curieuse de savoir ce qui vous a rendu ainsi.

Il s'efforce de le cacher, mais je vois une esquisse de sourire se dessiner à la commissure de ses lèvres.

– OK, je vous dis pourquoi je suis un salopard amer, si vous me révélez pourquoi vous êtes une plaie.

– Sauf que je ne pense pas en être une.

– Vous devriez peut-être consulter un psy, qui vous aiderait à le découvrir.

Je froisse ma serviette en papier et la lui jette au visage. Je l'atteins pile sur le nez.

– Très mature, commente-t-il.

– Je ne pense pas être chiante, de manière générale. Je dirais que c'est vous qui faites ressortir ce défaut en moi.

Sourire narquois.

– Eh bien, apparemment, je contribue à exposer pas mal de choses chez vous. À ce sujet, si vous avez assez mangé, je peux aider à vous dégrafer pour vous mettre plus à l'aise.

Bon sang, quelle arrogance !

– Vous allez perpétuellement me resservir la soirée où l'on s'est rencontrés, c'est ça ?

– Exact.

Je sirote mon merlot. Non que j'en aie très envie, tellement je suis remplie après l'énormissime burger que m'a commandé Drew, mais je n'aime pas gâcher… En toute honnêteté, j'ai hâte de rentrer à la maison et de défaire ma jupe. Évidemment, je ne risque pas de l'admettre devant lui.

– Revenons-en à ma question originelle. Pourquoi tant d'amertume quand il s'agit des relations ?

– Je m'occupe de divorces toute la journée. C'est un peu compliqué d'avoir une vision positive, quand on ne croise que tromperies, mensonges et vols, quand des personnes qui ont commencé par être amoureuses finissent par se déchirer.

– C'est donc à cause de votre travail. Vous n'avez pas eu de relation qui vous ait rendu amer ?

Drew me dévisage un long moment. Son pouce va et vient sur sa lèvre inférieure si sensuelle tandis qu'il choisit sa réponse, et mes yeux suivent son geste. *Merde, il a vraiment des super lèvres. Je parie qu'elles dévoreraient ma bouche.*

Heureusement, la serveuse arrive, interrompant ma contemplation.

– Je peux vous apporter autre chose ? demande-t-elle.

Drew se tourne vers moi.

– Un dessert ?

– J'ai déjà trop mangé.

– Juste l'addition, répond-il à la serveuse. Merci.

Elle ramasse nos assiettes et son départ nous plonge dans une minute de silence embarrassé. Il n'a toujours pas répondu à ma question, et je me dis qu'il va peut-être essayer de changer de sujet à nouveau ; d'où ma surprise lorsqu'il répond :

– Je suis divorcé. Mon mariage a duré cinq ans.

– Waouh. Je suis désolée.

– Ce n'est pas votre faute.

Je vois bien que cet aveu lui a déjà coûté un gros effort et je sais que je devrais sans doute en rester là, pourtant je ne peux m'en empêcher.

– C'était une relation à distance ?

– Pas au sens propre, non. L'amertume que vous avez perçue aujourd'hui était purement due à mon expérience des divorces. La raison numéro un pour laquelle les gens atterrissent dans mon bureau, c'est qu'ils ne passent pas assez de temps ensemble.

– J'admets que nombreux sont les couples que je conseille à être dans le même cas. Ce n'est pas forcément une relation à distance au sens de celles dont vous m'avez parlé aujourd'hui, mais dans la majorité de mes thérapies, les couples ne partagent pas grand-chose en matière de temps. Soit ils travaillent beaucoup et ne se ménagent pas de moments en commun, soit ils se raccrochent à la vie de célibataire qu'ils avaient avant de se marier.

– Je parie que nous traitons au fond des affaires très similaires. En y réfléchissant, vous pourriez peut-être distribuer mes cartes professionnelles, pour les cas où votre thérapie ne fonctionne pas.

J'écarquille les yeux.

– Vous plaisantez, là, j'espère ?

Un sourire paresseux s'étire sur son visage et il porte sa bière à ses lèvres.

– Oui.

La serveuse revient avec l'addition et Drew sort son portefeuille. Je vais pour chercher le mien, mais il m'interrompt.

– C'est moi qui offre. En guise de demande d'excuse pour avoir été une tête de nœud aujourd'hui, vous vous rappelez ?

– Bon, merci. J'espère que vous serez souvent une tête de nœud. J'ai dix mille dollars d'économies à refaire.

Il se lève et contourne ma chaise, qu'il tire quand je me mets debout.

– Oh, ça ne devrait pas poser de problème. Il se trouve que je suis une tête de nœud au quotidien.

***

La serrure de mon appartement est bizarre. Il faut l'agiter un peu, effectuer des mouvements circulaires et enfoncer puis retirer la clé à plusieurs reprises avant de trouver le point précis qui me permet de la tourner dans le pêne. Baldwin a dû entendre tinter mon trousseau, car sa porte, voisine de la mienne, s'ouvre.

– Salut. J'ai frappé, tout à l'heure, pour te proposer qu'on aille dîner, mais tu n'étais pas encore rentrée.

– Ah oui, j'ai dîné avec Drew.

Il me prend la clé des mains et, allez savoir comment, il débloque la serrure à la première tentative, comme chaque fois. La porte s'ouvre et il me suit à l'intérieur.

– Drew ?

– Le véritable locataire du bureau que j'avais cru louer. Celui qui me permet de rester quelques mois, tu vois ?

Baldwin hoche la tête.

– Tu sors aussi avec lui, maintenant ?

Je m'esclaffe.

– Non. Il s'est comporté comme un abruti aujourd'hui, alors il s'est fait pardonner en m'invitant à dîner.

– Pourquoi s'est-il mal comporté ?

Je me dirige vers ma chambre pour me changer, tout en continuant notre conversation à travers la porte entrouverte.

– En fait, il ne s'est pas vraiment mal comporté. Disons plutôt qu'on a des opinions très divergentes sur la thérapie de couple. Il m'a entendue au bout du fil et m'a fait savoir le fond de sa pensée, comme quoi les conseils que je prodiguais à mes patients ne fonctionneraient jamais.

Ayant enfilé un survêtement et un tee-shirt, je reviens dans le salon. Baldwin est assis à sa place habituelle quand on discute. Je prends le canapé, lui l'immense fauteuil en cuir. Parfois, ça me donne l'impression d'être sa patiente.

– Il ne devrait pas écouter tes séances de thérapie. C'est confidentiel.

– C'était ma faute. J'ai tendance à crier quand je fais une vidéoconférence, et j'avais laissé ma porte ouverte.

– Je ferais peut-être mieux de passer à ton bureau, non ?

– Pour quoi faire ?

– Je ne sais pas. Voir si tout se passe bien.

Baldwin est adorable. Entendre que quelqu'un s'est mal comporté avec moi, ça fait ressortir son côté protecteur. Même si l'idée d'un combat Baldwin *versus* Drew est plutôt comique.

Ils sont à l'opposé du système solaire, tous les deux. Baldwin est mince, de taille moyenne, doté de bonnes manières avec tous les traits typiques du professeur qu'il est. Il porte même des lunettes et des nœuds papillons qui lui donnent l'air plus vieux que ses trente-cinq ans. Drew en a vingt-neuf, il est grand, large d'épaules et costaud. Il jure quand l'envie l'en prend, sans se préoccuper de qui va l'entendre. Même si je ne le décrirais jamais comme quelqu'un d'aussi élégant que Baldwin, il y a chez lui un côté chevaleresque sous l'aspect rude de son apparence.

– Je ne pense pas que ce sera nécessaire. Tout va bien. Il est juste un peu brut de décoffrage, c'est tout.

Sachant que Baldwin aime bien prendre un verre de vin en fin de soirée, je me rends à la cuisine et sors du frigo la bouteille que je garde pour lui, sans attendre qu'il réponde à ma question.

– Tu veux un verre de vin ?

– Oui, merci.

Je lui en verse un, me contentant d'eau.

– Tu ne trinques pas avec moi ? me demande-t-il quand je lui tends son vin.

Je me laisse tomber sur le canapé.

– J'ai le ventre trop plein. J'ai mangé un hamburger au dîner. Drew m'avait commandé un maxi double cheeseburger.

– Il a commandé pour toi ? Difficile comme tu l'es ?

– Il sait que j'aime les hamburgers.

Je hausse les épaules et débouche ma bouteille d'eau.

– Et toi, tu as mangé quoi ? je lui demande.

– Je me suis fait livrer des sushis de chez *Zen*.

Je plisse le nez.

– Je ne suis pas fâchée d'avoir raté ça.

– J'aurais choisi autre chose, si on avait mangé ensemble.

Baldwin s'en remet toujours à moi, pour les commandes de repas. C'est l'une des choses que j'adore chez lui. Enfin, vu que les restaurants de sushis semblent être les choix qu'il privilégie pour ses rencards, ce n'est pas comme s'il risquait d'en manquer.

– Pas de rendez-vous, ce soir ?

En général, j'évite le sujet de sa vie amoureuse. C'est pénible de le voir avec des femmes, alors en entendre parler dans les détails, ça me tuerait. Ce soir, pourtant, j'éprouve moins de réticence à le questionner, sans que je sache trop pourquoi.

– Copies à corriger. Tu aurais apprécié la réponse que m'a faite l'une de mes étudiantes.

– Quelle était la question ?

– Je leur avais demandé de me donner un argument valable prouvant que les techniques de psychanalyse de Freud étaient défectueuses. Comme cela fait trois semaines que nous étudions Grünbaum et Colby, ça aurait dû être une question facile.

– Oui, je suis d'accord. Et donc, tu as obtenu quelle réponse ?

– Mademoiselle Balick a écrit : « Freud était un homme. »

J'éclate de rire.

– Je dirais que l'argument est probablement valide. Tu devrais lui accorder des points.

– Gentil. Mais je ne crois pas, non.

– Tu as toujours noté sévèrement.

– Je t'ai toujours donné de bonnes notes, à toi.

– Je les méritais. (Ce qui est vrai, pourtant ça m'amène à réfléchir.) Il t'est déjà arrivé d'attribuer des points à quelqu'un qui ne les avait pas mérités ? Disons à une jolie fille ou bien par pitié ?

– Jamais.

Sa réponse ne me surprend pas.

– Alors, où est-ce que tu veux aller, jeudi soir ? me demande-t-il en sirotant son vin.

– Jeudi ?

– Pour ton repas d'anniversaire.

– Oh, j'avais oublié.

J'ai été tellement débordée, ces derniers temps, que l'approche de mon anniversaire m'était complètement sortie de l'esprit.

– Eh bien, ça ne m'a pas échappé, à moi. Je pensais qu'on pourrait aller à Écru. C'est un nouveau restaurant français dans l'Upper East Side. La liste d'attente pour les réservations est de trois mois, mais un de mes collègues est ami avec le propriétaire, il a dit qu'il pourrait m'avoir une place.

– Super idée. Merci.

Pour être tout à fait honnête, j'aurais préféré retourner chez Joey déguster un bon gros burger bien gras, mais Baldwin est un fin gourmet et il cherche toujours à étendre mon horizon gustatif. À l'occasion, d'ailleurs, j'aime bien les plats un peu recherchés.

Baldwin reste un petit moment, on discute boutique. Il me parle d'un article qu'il espère faire publier et je lui raconte comme je suis nerveuse à l'idée de rencontrer au bureau deux de mes patients vidéo demain. Depuis que j'ai emménagé à New York, certains de mes patients téléphoniques ou vidéo qui habitent dans la région sont devenus des clients en face à face. C'est toujours étrange de les rencontrer en chair et en os la première fois, mais le rendez-vous de demain me stresse particulièrement parce que je soupçonne le mari d'abuser physiquement de sa femme.

Il se fait tard et, à un moment donné, je bâille et m'étire. Mon fin tee-shirt remonte, révélant un bout de ventre. Le regard de Baldwin zoome sur ma peau nue et je le vois déglutir. Ce genre d'instants me rend plus que perplexe. Je n'irais pas clamer que je suis une experte ès hommes, mais je suis tout de même sortie avec un certain nombre de garçons, j'ai même eu quelques relations plus ou moins longues. En temps normal, je devine assez bien quand un homme est attiré par moi, or, en cet instant, je pourrais jurer que c'est le cas de Baldwin. Ça n'est pas nouveau. J'ai ressenti la même chose en de nombreuses autres occasions. Ce qui est peut-être la raison pour laquelle je continue à m'accrocher à lui après toutes ces années.

Parfois une étincelle produit un grand feu.

Baldwin s'éclaircit la gorge et se lève.

– Bon, je vais devoir y aller. Il est tard.

– Tu es sûr ? Je vais peut-être me verser un verre de vin, si tu veux en prendre un deuxième…

– J'ai un cours de bonne heure, demain matin.

– D'accord.

Masquant ma déception, je l'accompagne à la porte.

Baldwin me dit « au revoir », puis il s'arrête et se retourne. L'espace d'une fraction de seconde, mon imagination prend le dessus et je me le figure qui rentre, referme la porte… et décide de rester.

Au lieu de quoi…

– J'attends un colis, demain. Si tu le vois dans le couloir, tu peux le récupérer pour moi ? Je vais rentrer tard.

– OK. C'est demain soir, le colloque « New York Psychology » dont tu m'as parlé ?

– Non. C'est la semaine prochaine. Demain, Rachel a des places pour une pièce de théâtre indépendant.

– Ah. Rachel.

– Tu l'as brièvement croisée la semaine dernière au café.

– Oui. Rachel.

Comme si je pouvais l'oublier. Elle portait en guise de robe la chemise dans laquelle j'avais aperçu Baldwin, la veille au soir, quand j'avais entendu sa porte s'ouvrir et que j'avais épié par le judas.

– Je ramasserai ce que je trouverai devant ta porte. Amuse-toi bien demain soir.

Une fois qu'il est parti, je me démaquille et me brosse les dents. Évidemment, alors que je bâillais il n'y a pas cinq minutes, je suis très éveillée, maintenant que je peux aller me coucher.

L'histoire de ma vie.

Je repense à ma conversation avec Drew de cet après-midi ; j'ai l'impression qu'elle a eu lieu il y a une semaine. Le capitaine Prolactinator m'a suggéré de me masturber avant de dormir, mais je ne suis pas d'humeur à penser à Baldwin, maintenant qu'il m'a parlé de son rencard de demain avec Rachel.

Même si…

Après tout, je ne suis pas obligée de penser à Baldwin, si ? Une image de Drew s'affiche soudain dans mon esprit. Oui, il est carrément assez beau pour faire l'affaire…

Mais je ne devrais pas.

Je me retourne dans mon lit et m'oblige à fermer les yeux. Une heure plus tard, je tends la main vers ma table de chevet. Après une longue, une épuisante journée, j'ai besoin de dormir. Je n'en peux plus.

J'actionne le vibromasseur et ferme les yeux, tâchant de me détendre à son bourdonnement.

Dix minutes plus tard, je suis profondément endormie, un sourire aux lèvres.

CHAPITRE 13

DREW

Pendant longtemps, Alexa a bousillé le plaisir que je prenais à mon boulot. Après mon divorce, je trouvais des morceaux de mon mariage ici et là, dans chaque bataille amère lancée par mes clients. Elles me rappelaient tout le temps gâché, comment, dès la première nuit, ma queue avait pris des décisions concernant Alexa à la place de ma tête. Bref, tout dans les dossiers de mes clients devenait personnel, c'était comme revivre les pires moments de ma vie au quotidien.

Au bout du compte, j'ai fini par apprendre à séparer les choses. Plus ou moins. Mais en chemin, j'ai perdu quelque chose. Mon job est devenu une source de revenus et plus l'activité que j'aimais. Si je ne redoutais plus de descendre au rez-de-chaussée pour gagner mon bureau, je n'avais plus d'enthousiasme non plus.

Jusqu'à aujourd'hui.

Je suis debout plus tôt qu'à mon habitude. Après la salle de sport, je suis au bureau à sept heures, à travailler sur un dossier. Henry Archer est l'un des rares clients que j'apprécie. Son divorce se passe même à l'amiable, parce que c'est un vrai bon gars. Sa réunion de conciliation est prévue aujourd'hui à onze heures. Tout le monde sera présent pour essayer d'arracher un accord final. Par miracle, je ne méprise pas sa future ex-femme non plus.

Je suis dans la salle de reprographie quand j'entends arriver Emerie. Ses talons claquent sur le sol lorsqu'elle entre dans le hall, chargée d'un gros carton marron. Je m'interromps dans ma tâche et vais le lui prendre des mains.

– Merci. Vous savez que personne ne m'a offert son siège dans le métro alors que je portais ce truc ?

– La plupart des gens sont des sales cons. Qu'est-ce que vous transportez là-dedans ? Ça pèse un âne mort.

Je dépose le carton sur son bureau et l'ouvre sans demander sa permission. Il contient un presse-papier en verre, mais au regard de son poids, il aurait tout aussi bien pu être en plomb.

– Ce truc pèse au moins cinq kilos. Vous craignez qu'un ouragan ne s'engouffre par la fenêtre et n'emporte tous vos papiers ?

Elle me prend l'objet des mains.

– C'est une récompense. Que j'ai gagnée pour un article que j'ai écrit et qui a été publié dans *Psychology Today*.

– C'est une arme. Je suis content que vous n'ayez pas eu cet objet sous la main quand je vous ai surprise dans mon bureau, le premier soir.

– Oui. J'aurais pu fendre votre joli crâne.

Je lui adresse un sourire satisfait.

– Je le savais. Vous me trouvez beau.

J'essaie de voir ce que le carton contient d'autre, mais elle me tape sur la main.

– Curieux.

– Vous avez bien déballé mes cartons.

– C'est vrai. Alors vous pouvez regarder.

– Ben oui, mais maintenant que vous m'en avez donné l'autorisation, je n'en ai plus envie.

– Vous êtes un vrai gamin, vous le savez, ça ?

J'ai laissé mon téléphone portable près de la photocopieuse, je l'entends sonner depuis l'entrée. Le temps que j'aille répondre, l'appelant a raccroché. Une fois mes photocopies terminées, je ramasse ma liasse de feuilles et m'arrête à nouveau devant le bureau d'Emerie.

– Vous êtes en avance, aujourd'hui, je la taquine depuis le seuil. Vous avez suivi mon conseil pour mieux dormir ?

– Non.

Sa réponse a été rapide… trop rapide. Des années à prendre des dépositions m'ont rompu à la détection des petits indices. Parfois un infime détail m'emmène sur un chemin que je n'avais pas envisagé et vers quelque chose d'intéressant. En l'occurrence, dans les trois lettres de sa réponse, j'ai détecté un indice et je m'apprête à suivre la piste.

– Vous n'avez donc pas eu de mal à vous endormir, hier soir ?

La voyant rougir et s'affairer sur son carton, j'ai ma confirmation : je tiens une piste. Curieux, j'entre dans son bureau et contourne sa table de travail afin de voir son visage qu'elle garde soigneusement baissé.

J'incline la tête pour intercepter son regard.

– Vous vous êtes masturbée hier soir, c'est ça ?

Sa rougeur s'intensifie.

– Et vous ? contre-attaque-t-elle.

Elle détourne le sujet. On sait tous ce que ça signifie.

– Oui, je lui réponds avec un large sourire. Et ce matin aussi. Ça vous intéresse de savoir à quoi je pensais en le faisant ?

– Non !

– Vous n'êtes même pas un tout petit peu curieuse ?

Malgré ses joues écarlates, j'adore le fait qu'elle n'ait pas peur de se confronter à moi.

– Vous n'avez pas des mariages à profaner, pervers ?

– Allez, admettez-le. Vous vous êtes masturbée hier soir et c'est pour ça que vous avez si bien dormi et que vous êtes arrivée au travail à l'heure pour une fois.

– Qu'est-ce que ça peut bien vous faire ?

– J'aime avoir raison.

– Vous êtes vraiment un énorme égocentrique.

– On le dit, oui.

– Vous promettez de lâcher le sujet si je vous avoue la vérité ?

Je hoche la tête.

– Promis.

Elle plonge les yeux droit dans les miens.

– Oui.

– Quoi ?

– Comment ça, « quoi » ? Vous m'avez très bien comprise.

Bien sûr que oui.

– Je n'en suis pas certain. Pourquoi ne m'expliquez-vous pas à quoi vous faites référence ?

– Sortez d'ici.

– Dites que vous vous êtes masturbée et je sors.

– Pourquoi ? Que vous puissiez vous caresser en m'imaginant en train de me masturber ?

– Je croyais que vous ne vouliez pas savoir à quoi je pensais ce matin, quand je me suis fait plaisir ?

Je ricane. Emerie tente de la jouer dure à cuire, mais je devine dans sa voix plus de gêne et d'amusement que de colère. D'humeur inhabituellement clémente, je décide de lâcher l'affaire avant de pousser un peu trop loin le bouchon.

– J'ai une conférence à dix heures, ce matin, qui va probablement se poursuivre avec un déjeuner en compagnie de mon client. Il y a des menus dans le tiroir du haut, à droite du bureau d'accueil, si vous voulez commander votre repas.

– Merci.

– De rien.

Je m'arrête juste après avoir franchi sa porte.

– Une dernière chose.

– Hmm ?

– Vous pensiez à moi quand vous vous êtes masturbée ?

J'ai posé la question pour le simple plaisir de jouer les têtes de nœud, mais la soudaine expression de petit lapin pris dans des phares de voiture m'indique que j'ai visé juste. *Eh bien, ça alors. Venir au travail va devenir de plus en plus intéressant.* Une partie de moi (une très grande partie de moi, évidemment) brûle de rester et d'approfondir ce tout petit bout d'information, mais je viens de me transformer en gamin de douze ans et je sens mon sexe enfler sous ma braguette.

Grâce à ses pensées cochonnes, miss Jolies-fesses-Oklahoma vient de gagner son répit.

***

– C'est pas ça, le problème, putain. Le problème, c'est ton incapacité à cuisiner un repas mangeable sans le cramer.

Ce genre de déclarations, de braillements, même, n'est pas étranger entre ces murs. Sauf que cette fois, ils ne proviennent pas de l'un de mes clients.

Je viens de rentrer au bureau après un déjeuner tardif avec Henry Archer, et la voix furieuse d'un homme résonne jusque dans le hall. La porte du bureau d'Emcrie est légèrement entrouverte et j'hésite à passer voir si tout va bien, au cas où. En écoutant plus attentivement, je l'entends qui demande au bonhomme de se calmer, puis une autre femme prend la parole. Alors je retourne à mon bureau pour m'occuper de mes propres affaires.

Quinze minutes plus tard, ça recommence. Je suis au téléphone quand la même voix masculine traverse le couloir pour me parvenir.

– J'étais déjà hésitant à t'épouser à la base. J'aurais dû annuler en voyant que tu n'étais même pas fichue de porter notre gosse.

Les poils se mettent au garde-à-vous dans ma nuque. Quelle horreur. J'en ai entendu, pourtant, des couples qui s'envoient des atrocités à la figure pendant un divorce. Plus grand-chose ne me choque aujourd'hui. Mais ce type-là… c'est moins ce qu'il dit que la manière dont il le dit. Sa voix est empreinte de colère, à la fois menaçante et insultante. Je n'ai pas vu son visage, néanmoins mon instinct me souffle qu'il n'agresse pas les femmes que verbalement. Hélas, j'en ai croisé aussi, des hommes physiquement violents, au fil des ans. Il y a quelque chose dans la façon qu'ont ces connards de hurler qui les démarque du conjoint « Je te déteste et je veux te faire du mal » ordinaire.

J'expédie le client avec qui je conversais au téléphone et me dirige vers le bureau d'Emerie. Avant que j'aie le temps de l'atteindre, un énorme craquement me fait accélérer le pas.

Quand j'arrive à la porte, le type est assis sur son siège et sa femme, à quatre pattes, nettoie quelque chose par terre. Emerie est debout.

– Qu'est-ce qui se passe ici ? Tout va bien ?

Emerie hésite et croise mon regard. Elle essaie de me transmettre un message sur la situation. Je le vois dans ses yeux, je l'entends dans sa voix.

– Monsieur Dawson s'est un peu emballé et il a renversé une récompense en verre que j'avais posée sur mon bureau.

Le lourd presse-papier qu'elle a trimballé avec difficulté dans le métro est en mille morceaux au sol.

– Sortez marcher un peu et vous calmer dehors, mon vieux.

Le connard tourne brusquement la tête.

– C'est à moi que vous parlez ?

– Exact.

– Vous êtes qui, vous, bon Dieu ?

– Je suis le type qui vous dit de sortir marcher et de vous calmer.

Il se lève.

– Et si je refuse ?

– Vous serez sorti d'ici *manu militari*.

– Vous allez appeler les flics sous prétexte que j'ai cassé un truc en verre ?

– Non, à moins qu'Emerie ne me le demande. En revanche, je vais vous virer à coups de pompe dans le cul moi-même.

Je croise les bras sans le quitter des yeux. Les hommes qui frappent leur femme sont des trouillards. Je lui botterais les fesses avec le plus grand plaisir.

Au bout de quelques secondes, il tourne la tête vers sa femme.

– C'est fini, ces conneries de psychothérapie. J'arrête.

Sur quoi il sort en trombe. Je m'écarte d'un pas pour le laisser passer.

Emerie et sa cliente restent muettes jusqu'à ce qu'on entende claquer la porte d'entrée.

– Ça va ? je lui demande.

Elle hoche la tête et, pour la première fois, la femme me fait face. Elle a une joue mauve et jaune, traces d'un vieil hématome. Ma mâchoire se crispe. J'aurais dû balancer mon poing dans la gueule de cet enfoiré quand j'en avais l'occasion.

– Il n'est pas comme ça, d'habitude. C'est juste compliqué à son travail, ces derniers temps.

Ben voyons.

Emerie et moi nous regardons fixement à nouveau, dans un échange muet. On est sur la même longueur d'onde.

– Je vous laisse discuter toutes les deux.

Et je referme la porte derrière moi.

Pendant la demi-heure qui suit, je travaille sur un dossier au bureau d'accueil vide, dans le hall d'entrée, pour le cas où l'autre trouduc aurait la mauvaise idée de revenir en douce. Au bout d'un moment, j'aperçois sa trogne par la fenêtre. Il fume une cigarette en attendant sa femme dehors. *Malin.*

Emerie raccompagne madame Dawson à l'accueil.

– Je vous propose de nous appeler au téléphone demain. Même juste un quart d'heure, d'accord ? J'aimerais vraiment avoir de vos nouvelles, après la séance d'aujourd'hui.

Sa cliente acquiesce.

– OK.

– Vers dix heures, ça vous conviendrait ?

– Oui, c'est bien. Bill part au travail à huit heures.

Emerie hoche la tête.

– Vous savez quoi ? Je ne vous ai pas donné de carte de rendez-vous pour la semaine prochaine. Ne bougez pas, je vais en chercher une dans mon bureau. Je reviens.

Pendant son absence, je m'adresse à madame Dawson. D'une voix basse, sans jugement et avec précaution.

– Ça va aller ?

Elle croise rapidement mon regard, mais baisse aussitôt le sien.

– Oui. Bill n'est pas une mauvaise personne. C'est vrai, vous l'avez juste rencontré à un mauvais moment.

– Hum.

Emerie est de retour avec une petite carte, qu'elle tend à sa cliente.

– On se parle demain, alors ?

L'autre hoche la tête et s'en va.

Sitôt la porte refermée, Emerie lâche un bruyant soupir.

– Je suis vraiment désolée.

– Il n'y a pas de quoi. Ce n'est pas votre faute si votre client est un connard. J'en ai moi-même pas mal dans ce genre.

– Je pense qu'il est physiquement violent avec elle.

– J'ai tendance à être d'accord avec vous.

– Et je ne pense pas que je vais la revoir ni avoir de ses nouvelles. Elle va m'éviter parce que je l'ai mise face à la réalité de ce que je soupçonne.

– Vous ne pensez pas qu'elle va vous appeler demain ou qu'elle viendra à son rendez-vous de la semaine prochaine ?

– Non. Il ne la laissera pas continuer. Maintenant que je le connais un peu mieux, je suis même surprise qu'il ait accepté de venir à la base. Mes séances de conseil n'étaient censées se dérouler qu'avec elle, au départ.

– C'est rude.

Elle pousse un nouveau soupir.

– J'espère qu'elle vous appellera.

– Qui, moi ?

– La carte de rendez-vous que je lui ai donnée était votre carte professionnelle, en fait. Je me suis dit qu'elle avait plus besoin d'un avocat que d'un conseiller matrimonial.

Je hausse les sourcils.

– Sympa.

Nous nous engageons dans le couloir côte à côte.

– Je prendrais bien un verre.

– Votre bureau ou le mien ?

Elle me jette un regard étonné.

– Vous avez de l'alcool au bureau ?

– J'ai souvent des journées de merde.

Elle sourit.

– Mon bureau.

***

– Ça a un goût d'essence de térébenthine, commente Emerie, les sourcils froncés.

Je sirote.

– C'est un Glenmorangie de vingt-cinq ans d'âge que vous buvez, là. Soit un diluant à six cents dollars la bouteille.

– À ce prix, ils auraient pu ajouter un peu de saveur.

Je m'esclaffe. Je suis assis dans le siège du client, Emerie derrière son bureau. Elle a dû déballer le reste de ses cartons, car je découvre de nouveaux objets personnels ici et là. Je soulève la base plane qui supportait sa récompense que ce connard de Dawson a cassée.

– Vous allez avoir besoin d'une nouvelle arme.

– Je ne pense pas, avec vous dans les parages pour menacer mes clients.

– Il l'avait mérité. J'aurais dû lui flanquer un bon coup de poing dans la figure, comme il aime le faire à sa femme.

– Oui, vous auriez dû. Ce type est vraiment un connard. Un 'tain de connard.

Elle est trop mignonne, quand elle s'entraîne à prendre l'accent new-yorkais. Même si ça ressemble plus à celui de l'Oklahoma qui imite New York.

Il y a deux cadres sur son bureau. J'en saisis un. La photo représente un couple entre deux âges.

– Ne vous gênez pas ! dit-elle, mi-ironique, mi-amusée.

J'observe son visage, puis le couple sur la photo, puis elle à nouveau.

– Ce sont vos parents ?

– Oui.

– À qui est-ce que vous ressemblez ?

– Ma mère, d'après ce qu'on me dit.

Je contemple plus attentivement les traits de sa mère. Rien à voir.

– Je ne trouve pas.

Elle tend la main et me prend le cadre des mains.

– J'ai été adoptée. Je ressemble à ma mère biologique.

– Oh. Pardon.

– Pas de problème. Ce n'est pas un sujet que je rechigne à aborder.

Je me cale contre le dossier de mon siège et la regarde regarder sa photo. Je perçois une forme de révérence dans le ton, quand elle reprend la parole.

– Je ne ressemble peut-être pas à ma mère, mais il n'empêche que nous avons beaucoup de points communs.

– Ah oui ? Elle est chiante aussi ?

Elle fait mine de s'offusquer.

– Je ne suis pas chiante.

– Cela fait à peine une semaine que je vous connais. Le premier jour, vous m'avez volé mon espace de bureau et avez menacé de me frapper quand je vous ai prise la main dans le sac. Quelques jours plus tard, vous avez déclenché une dispute à cause d'un commentaire innocent que j'ai eu le malheur de faire sur un mauvais conseil que vous prodiguiez à des clients, et aujourd'hui, j'ai failli me battre avec un type à cause de vous.

– Mes conseils n'étaient pas mauvais, corrige-t-elle dans un soupir. Pour le reste, en revanche, je crains que ce ne soit vrai. Bon, j'ai été passablement chiante, alors ?

Je vide mon verre et me verse deux doigts supplémentaires, avant de remplir le verre d'Emerie.

– Vous avez de la chance. Il se trouve que j'aime bien les chieuses.

Nous discutons encore un peu. Emerie me parle de la quincaillerie de ses parents, dans l'Oklahoma. Elle est en train de me raconter l'histoire du jour où ils ont vendu du matériel à un type qui a fini par être arrêté pour avoir enfermé sa femme dans un bunker en sous-sol pendant deux semaines, quand mon téléphone fixe sonne. Je vais pour décrocher, mais elle est plus rapide.

– Bureau de M. Jagger, que puis-je faire pour vous ? demande-t-elle d'une voix sexy.

Les deux verres d'alcool l'ont désinhibée, la rendant joueuse. J'aime bien.

– Puis-je savoir qui est à l'appareil ?

Elle prend un stylo bille et s'immobilise pour écouter, passant machinalement la pointe sur sa lèvre inférieure. Mes yeux suivent son mouvement. *Je parie qu'elles ont un goût délicieux.* L'envie irrépressible me saisit soudain de me pencher par-dessus le bureau pour en mordre une. *Merde.* C'est pas bon, ça, comme pensée.

Pourtant j'ai toujours les yeux rivés sur ses lèvres quand elle relève les siens vers moi. Je devrais arrêter, mais la manière dont elles bougent quand elle se remet à parler me captive.

– OK, madame Logan. Je vais voir s'il est disponible.

Voilà qui détourne mon regard *illico*. Agitant les deux mains devant elle, je lui fais signe que non, je ne suis pas disponible. Elle met l'appel en attente cinq secondes, puis reprend le combiné.

– Je suis navrée, madame Logan, apparemment il est sorti. (Pause.) Non, je suis désolée, mais je n'ai pas l'autorisation de transmettre le numéro de portable de M. Jagger. En revanche, je l'informerai de votre appel.

Une fois qu'elle a raccroché, elle me dit :

– Vous savez ce dont je viens de me rendre compte ?

– Que votre voix est plus sexy après quelques verres ?

Elle cille.

– Ma voix est plus sexy ?

J'avale quelques gorgées de mon deuxième whisky.

– Oui. Vous flirtiez au téléphone.

– Je ne flirtais pas.

Je hausse les épaules.

– Peu importe. J'ai bien aimé. Qu'est-ce que vous alliez me dire ? À propos de ce que vous aviez réalisé ?

– Je ne me rappelle même plus, maintenant. Je pense que ces deux petits verres me sont montés directement à la tête.

– Et aux lèvres, je marmonne.

– Quoi ?

– Rien.

– Oh, ça y est, je me souviens de ce que j'allais dire, reprend-elle, un doigt pointé vers moi. J'ai répondu au moins à vingt coups de fil en trois jours et vu des tonnes de rendez-vous dans votre agenda. C'était la première « madame » qui ait appelé. Vous n'avez pas de clientes du nom de Jane, Jessica ou Julie.

– Parce que je ne prends que les clients hommes.

– Quoi ?

Elle me dévisage comme si je venais de lui affirmer que le ciel est violet.

– Les clients hommes. Vous savez, un peu comme femmes, mais avec moins de cris et de larmes, et un se… (Je me tais en entendant s'ouvrir la porte d'entrée.) Vous attendez quelqu'un ?

– Non, pourquoi ?

– Je viens d'entendre la porte. (Je me lève et m'avance dans le couloir.) Bonjour ?

Un type que je n'ai jamais vu passe la tête à l'angle de la zone d'accueil.

– Bonjour, je cherche Emerie Rose.

Je fronce les sourcils.

– Qui êtes-vous ?

Ce ne serait pas ce connard de Dawson qui serait revenu causer des problèmes, au moins ? Sauf que ce gars-là n'a pas l'air du mec qui cause des problèmes : la dernière fois que ça a dû lui arriver, c'était sans doute quand les autres gamins se moquaient de lui à l'école élémentaire.

Je me retourne vers Emerie, qui s'approche déjà. Elle me rejoint dans l'encadrement de la porte.

– Baldwin ? Il me semblait bien avoir reconnu ta voix. Qu'est-ce que tu fais ici ?

– J'ai eu envie de te faire une surprise.

Sur quoi le gars lui tend un bouquet de fleurs que je n'avais pas remarqué contre son flanc, dont la couleur est assortie à son nœud papillon froissé.

Nazes, les fleurs, on croirait qu'il les a achetées au Chinois du bas de la rue pour 7,99 dollars.

– C'est adorable.

Emerie s'écarte de la porte où nous étions bien, tous les deux, presque collés, et se dirige vers le type, afin de l'enlacer et l'embrasser sur les deux joues. Pour une raison qui m'échappe, je ne bouge pas et j'observe la scène.

Ayant récupéré ses fleurs, elle se rappelle enfin que je suis derrière elle.

– Baldwin, je te présente Drew. Drew, voici Baldwin, l'ami dont je vous ai parlé l'autre jour.

Je suis perplexe et elle le voit sur mon visage.

– C'était mon chargé de cours à la fac. Rappelez-vous, je vous ai raconté.

Vraiment ? Ce gars-là ?

– Ah oui ! (Je tends la main.) Enchanté. Drew Jagger.

– Pareil. Baldwin Marcum.

S'ensuit un drôle de silence gêné, qu'Emerie finit par briser.

– Tu ne trouves pas le bureau magnifique ?

– Très sympa.

– Tu es en chemin pour retrouver Rachel ?

– La représentation ne commence pas avant une heure et demie. Du coup, je me suis dit que j'allais passer voir si tu allais bien.

Baldwin balaie les lieux du regard, quand il remarque la bouteille de Glenmorangie et les deux verres vides sur le bureau d'Emerie.

Il repose les yeux sur elle.

– C'est du scotch ? À dix-sept heures ?

Soit Emerie ne perçoit pas la touche de dédain dans sa voix, soit elle est très douée pour l'ignorer.

– On a eu une rude journée, explique-t-elle.

– Je vois.

– Je vous sers un verre ? je propose, certain qu'il va décliner au regard de ce que je perçois de lui au bout de soixante secondes d'observation. C'est un vingt-cinq ans d'âge très doux.

– Non, merci.

Bon, j'en ai assez vu.

– J'ai du travail à rattraper. Content d'avoir fait votre connaissance, Baldwin.

Il hoche la tête.

Une heure plus tard, je suis en train de ramasser mes affaires dans mon bureau quand je les entends rire. Les événements de la journée ont laissé des résidus de testostérone bouillonnante dans mes veines. Raison pour laquelle, probablement, je ressens une envie sortie de nulle part de flanquer mon poing dans la figure de ce type. J'ai besoin d'un exutoire. *Une bonne partie de jambes en l'air pour évacuer la colère. Oui, j'ai besoin d'une nana.*

Je frappe un coup léger à la porte d'Emerie avant de l'ouvrir.

– Je file. Ce soir, vous devriez réutiliser la technique d'endormissement que je vous ai conseillée, comme ça vous arriverez aussi à l'heure demain matin.

Emerie écarquille les yeux tout en tentant de masquer un sourire entendu.

– Oui. Je vais peut-être faire ça.

Baldwin observe attentivement notre échange.

– Allez, bonne nuit, je lance avec un salut de la main.

Je m'éloigne d'un pas avant qu'Emerie ne me rappelle.

– Drew ?

Je me retourne.

– Oui ?

Elle se tord les mains.

– Merci, pour aujourd'hui. Je ne vous l'ai pas dit, mais j'ai apprécié tout ce que vous avez fait.

– Avec plaisir, Oklahoma. (Je tapote l'encadrement de sa porte du dos de la main.) Ne restez pas trop tard, OK ?

– Non. Je vais y aller d'ici quelques minutes. Baldwin a des projets pour ce soir, du coup je partirai en même temps que lui.

– Vous voulez que je vous attende ? On pourrait retourner manger un hamburger chez Joey.

Emerie s'apprête à répondre quand monsieur Nœudpap l'interrompt.

– En fait, j'ai eu un changement de projet de dernière minute. Ça te dirait que je t'emmène dîner ?

– Tu ne vas pas au spectacle avec Rachel ?

– On pourra le voir une autre fois. Je ne savais pas que tu avais eu une mauvaise journée. Tu me raconteras tout ça au cours du repas.

Emerie me regarde, déchirée. Alors je décide de lui faciliter la tâche. Après tout, qui suis-je pour briser un couple si heureux ?

– Eh bien, passez une bonne soirée, dans ce cas.

C'est peut-être arrogant de ma part, on m'a répété à plusieurs reprises récemment que mon ego était surdimensionné, n'empêche que je suis prêt à en jurer : le changement de programme du petit copain d'Emerie a quelque chose à voir avec moi.

CHAPITRE 14

DREW

Réveillon du 31 décembre,
cinq ans plus tôt

– Joyeux anniversaire de mariage.

Alexa est assise sur le canapé, à feuilleter un *People*. Je me penche pour lui donner un baiser sur la joue, puis un peu plus pour effleurer le front de mon fils de presque deux ans, qui dort, la tête sur une cuisse de sa mère. Il bave. Il y en a plein sur la cuisse de ma femme.

– Il y a quelques années, ce n'est pas ainsi que tu mouillais le soir du réveillon, je plaisante en désignant sa jambe.

Elle lâche un soupir.

– J'aimerais tant qu'on puisse sortir. C'est le premier réveillon que je passe à la maison depuis mon enfance.

Les fêtes de fin d'année, c'est important pour mon épouse. Elle les attend avec l'impatience d'une gamine qui guette le père Noël. Or, hier, quelqu'un a annoncé à Alexa que le père Noël n'existait pas. On avait prévu de sortir ce soir, une fête dans le centre-ville d'Atlanta, organisée par une amie à elle que je n'apprécie pas spécialement. Mais la baby-sitter s'est décommandée. Alexa était au trente-sixième dessous. Pour ma part, je me suis réjoui en secret. C'est le premier jour de repos que j'ai depuis un mois, et rester à la maison à regarder des films, voire fêter les douze coups de minuit par une partie de jambes en l'air avec ma femme, ça me convient parfaitement, en matière de réjouissances.

Mais Alexa boude depuis vingt-quatre heures. Elle a encore du mal à s'adapter au nouveau style de vie induit par la maternité. Après tout, elle n'a que vingt-deux ans et toutes ses copines s'éclatent comme les filles insouciantes de leur âge.

J'avais espéré qu'elle se fasse de nouvelles amies aux cours de « La mère et l'enfant » qu'elle a intégré le mois dernier, genre des amies mariées, mamans, et qui ne pensent pas que se montrer responsable en matière de boisson signifie juste ne pas renverser son shot de Goldschläger.

– Pourquoi tu ne sortirais pas ? Je peux rester à la maison avec Beck.

Ses prunelles s'allument.

– C'est vrai ?

Ce n'est pas exactement comme ça que j'avais envisagé de passer notre anniversaire de mariage, mais Alexa en a besoin.

– Bien sûr. Je suis crevé. On va passer la soirée ici, mon petit bonhomme et moi. Ça tombe bien, on n'a pas assez l'occasion de passer du temps ensemble.

Alexa soulève délicatement la tête de Beck de sa cuisse, la pose sur un coussin et bondit pour m'enlacer.

– J'ai trop hâte de porter ma nouvelle robe. Lauren et Allison vont être vertes de jalousie que j'aie les moyens de faire mon shopping chez Neiman Marcus.

Je m'oblige à sourire.

– J'ai trop hâte de t'aider à l'enlever quand tu rentreras à la maison.

***

On a déposé Alexa chez sa copine Lauren hier soir et j'ai proposé de repasser la chercher, mais elle a refusé ; elle prendrait un taxi pour rentrer afin que je n'aie pas à réveiller le bébé. En l'occurrence, ça n'aurait pas posé problème. Car le bébé en question est bien réveillé… vu qu'il est huit heures du matin et que ma femme n'est toujours pas rentrée.

Beck est assis dans sa chaise, occupé à suçoter des Cheerios. Il lâche un couinement de canard bruyant alors que je me verse ma deuxième tasse de café. Je gonfle mes joues d'air et l'expulse d'un coup en m'asseyant, imitant son coin-coin. L'espace d'un instant, il a l'air surpris par le son et je le crois sur le point de pleurer. Puis il éclate d'un rire qui déclenche mon hilarité à mon tour.

– Tu aimes ça, mon petit bonhomme, hein ? (Je me penche vers lui et remplis mes joues à nouveau.) Coin-coin.

Mon fils observe mon visage comme si j'étais un extraterrestre, avant d'éclater de rire à nouveau. Au bout de la troisième ou quatrième fois, il comprend et je le vois essayer d'émettre le même bruit. Ses petites joues se gonflent, mais il ne sort qu'un filet d'air et de bave de sa bouche. Pas de coin-coin. Il ne se décourage pas pour autant.

Après chacune de ses tentatives, je reproduis le son et il m'observe attentivement avant de réessayer. À un moment donné, c'est à son tour et je crois qu'il va enfin avoir son instant de gloire. Il aspire une grande goulée d'air et… retient son souffle. Ses joues potelées virent au rouge et son expression se fait extrêmement concentrée. C'est bien mon fiston, ça. *Si tu ne réussis pas du premier coup, essaie encore. Plus fort.* Je fais l'expérience d'un moment d'intense fierté paternelle. Mon fils sera un travailleur acharné.

Il recommence le coup du visage-tout-rouge-qui-retient-sa-respiration plusieurs fois et se remet à rigoler. Alors je me repenche vers lui pour faire le canard et, quand j'inspire, je me rends compte qu'en fait, depuis quelques secondes, il a cessé de s'entraîner à couiner. En fait, il est en train de remplir sa couche.

Nous passons les dix minutes durant lesquelles je le change à nous marrer. Même si je le soupçonne de rire de moi et pas avec moi.

Peu après, ma petite machine à caca baisse le rideau. Je le contemple un long moment, émerveillé. Ce n'est pas exactement comme ça que j'envisageais ma vie il y a trois ans, pourtant je ne l'échangerais pour rien au monde aujourd'hui. Mon fils représente tout à mes yeux.

À l'approche de dix heures, mon agacement qu'Alexa ne soit toujours pas rentrée à la maison commence à virer à l'inquiétude. Et si quelque chose lui était arrivé ? Je ramasse mon téléphone sur le plan de travail de la cuisine et vérifie mes SMS. Toujours rien. Alors je compose son numéro. Et tombe directement sur sa boîte vocale.

La fenêtre du salon de notre appart au troisième étage donne sur Broad Street, une rue paisible bordée d'arbres, dans la proche banlieue d'Atlanta. Le monde entier ou presque a fait la fête hier soir, en conséquence, la rue est particulièrement calme ce matin. Je ne peux donc pas rater la Dodge Charger jaune vif suréquipée, ornée du chiffre « 9 » peint sur un flanc, qui tourne à l'angle de la rue. Malgré les fenêtres fermées, j'entends le rugissement du pot d'échappement sans silencieux et le crissement des pneus quand le chauffeur prend le virage trop vite.

Quel connard. Ce coin, il est à angle mort. Alexa aurait pu être en train de traverser avec la poussette et ce crétin ne les aurait vus que trop tard. Je secoue la tête et suis des yeux le véhicule qui stoppe à plusieurs pâtés d'immeubles de ma fenêtre. Il reste à l'arrêt quelques minutes. Et puis la portière côté passager s'ouvre et une paire de jambes à tomber par terre apparaît.

Je suis marié, je ne suis pas mort. J'ai le droit de regarder.

Sur quoi la propriétaire des gambettes descend de la voiture et je me rends compte que, en effet, j'ai totalement le droit de regarder.

Parce que la femme qui sort d'une voiture de sport à quelques immeubles de celui où nous vivons se révèle être *ma* femme.

CHAPITRE 15

EMERIE

Je suis arrivée au bureau avant Drew. Quand il fait son entrée à près de dix heures, je l'accueille sur un mode sarcastique.

– Panne de réveil ? Je pourrais peut-être vous recommander un truc qui vous aiderait à vous endormir.

Je m'attends à une réplique capable de me faire rougir, mais je ne suis même pas sûre qu'il m'ait entendue.

– Bonjour.

Il disparaît dans son bureau et décroche aussitôt son téléphone, partant dans ce qui ressemble à une dispute violente. L'ayant entendu raccrocher, je lui laisse quelques minutes pour se remettre et prends avec moi les messages de la matinée, pour les lui apporter.

Je le trouve debout derrière son bureau, qui regarde par la fenêtre tout en sirotant un grand café. Il a l'air à des années-lumière d'ici. Je suis sur le point de lui demander si tout va bien, quand il fait volte-face. Et j'ai ma réponse. Il n'est pas rasé, sa chemise habituellement impeccable ressemble à un chiffon dans lequel il aurait dormi et il a des cernes noirs sous ses yeux habituellement vifs.

– Vous avez une sale tête.

Il m'adresse une ombre de sourire forcé.

– Merci.

– Tout va bien ?

Il se frotte la nuque pendant un moment, avant de hocher la tête.

– Problèmes personnels, ça va aller.

– Vous voulez en parler ? Je sais écouter.

– Parler, c'est bien la dernière chose dont j'ai besoin. J'ai passé deux heures au téléphone hier soir. J'en ai ma dose, de parler.

– D'accord. Bon… qu'est-ce que je peux faire d'autre ? De quoi avez-vous besoin ?

Malgré sa tête de déterré, une lueur du vrai Drew s'allume dans le fond de ses prunelles et il hausse un sourcil canaille en guise de réponse.

– Je ne sais pas pourquoi, mais je doute que vous ayez besoin de moi, pour ça, je lui indique.

À quoi il sourit. Vraiment.

– Pourtant, ça m'aurait sans aucun doute aidé à m'endormir hier soir.

Au bout de quelques minutes de conversation, je désigne mon bureau.

– J'ai une vidéoconférence dans une poignée de minutes, je ne pourrai pas répondre au téléphone pendant une heure. Mais ensuite, je serai disponible jusqu'à une réunion en fin d'après-midi ici, dans mon bureau.

– Pas de problème, je m'occupe des appels.

– Merci. (Je m'apprête à partir quand je me rappelle ce que je souhaitais lui demander ce matin avant qu'il n'arrive.) Cela vous dérange si je fixe un petit panneau blanc sur ma porte ? J'ai des gommes bleues pour le coller, il ne l'abîmera pas.

– Je vous en prie.

Après avoir transmis encore un message à Drew, je parviens à trouver le temps, avant mon appel vidéo, de coller le tableau effaçable blanc sur ma porte, sans qu'il penche de côté. Mon projet, c'est d'y inscrire une phrase qui prête à réflexion et d'en changer chaque jour, comme je l'ai toujours fait sur mon site web, quand je ne prodiguais mes conseils que via des appels et des vidéoconférences. À présent que les gens viennent sur place, je tiens à poursuivre cette pratique.

Vu que mon rendez-vous ne m'a pas encore bipée sur l'ordinateur, j'attrape mes lunettes de lecture, compulse le journal où je conserve les pensées et autres citations en rapport avec les relations et le feuillette jusqu'à tomber sur celle qu'il me faut. Je l'inscris proprement sur le tableau.

Éteindre la bougie d'autrui
ne fera pas briller la mienne pour autant.

Aujourd'hui, je vais faire briller
ma compagne/mon compagnon
en ______________________________.

Un pas en arrière, je souris en relisant ma citation. *Dieu, ce que j'aime aider les gens.*

***

– Fouille son courrier. Je me fous de savoir comment tu obtiens l'info. J'ai besoin de savoir si elle baise avec ce type avant demain quatorze heures.

Je n'ai pas revu Drew depuis ce matin, même si je distingue parfaitement ses paroles tandis que je rince ma tasse à café dans l'évier de la petite cuisine attenante à son bureau.

– Roman, je te file cinq mille balles si tu me dégotes une photo intime d'eux ensemble. Dépose un panier de pique-nique devant sa porte d'entrée, s'il le faut. N'importe quoi pour qu'ils apparaissent en public dans une situation de couple amoureux.

La voix de Drew tonne à travers le couloir, suivie d'un gros éclat de rire. Et puis :

– Ouais, ouais. Je t'emmerde aussi, mon grand… À plus.

Drew entre dans la cuisine alors que j'essuie ma tasse.

– Je n'ai pas pu m'empêcher d'entendre votre conversation.

– Ah oui ? Quelle partie ?

Je souris.

– À peu près toutes. J'en déduis que vous êtes assez proche de votre détective privé ?

Il sort une bouteille d'eau du réfrigérateur et dévisse le bouchon.

– Roman est mon meilleur ami depuis que je lui ai volé sa petite copine en sixième.

– Vous lui avez volé sa fiancée et ça vous a rendu amis ?

– Ouais. Il lui avait filé la varicelle, qu'elle m'a ensuite passée. Roman et moi, on a eu la version sévère de la maladie et on a manqué l'école pendant deux semaines. On s'est retrouvés à jouer à des jeux vidéo chez lui pendant dix jours d'affilée.

– Qu'est-ce qui est arrivé à la petite copine ? Elle ne s'est pas interposée entre vous ?

– Roman et moi avons passé un pacte : plus jamais on ne courrait après la même fille. Je l'ai larguée le jour de notre retour en classe, et depuis, Roman et moi sommes potes.

– C'est bizarre, mais je trouve ça plutôt mignon.

Il éclate de rire.

– C'est tout nous. Roman, c'est le gars qui fouille dans les poubelles d'une bonne femme sur le trottoir en plein milieu de la nuit pour dénicher des préservatifs usagés, et moi je suis celui qui glisse ses découvertes à l'avocat de la partie adverse au milieu d'un jugement de divorce. On est tous les deux « mignons ».

Je plisse le nez.

– C’est vrai, cette histoire ? C’est dégoûtant. Du point de vue de l’hygiène comme de la morale.

– Comment pouvez-vous affirmer ça sans savoir ce que mon client a subi ? La vengeance peut être très savoureuse.

– Ah oui ? Et quelle partie est savoureuse ? Celle où vous vous sentez mal tous les deux au lieu qu’il n’y en ait qu’un seul qui souffre ?

Drew boit une longue goulée d’eau et appuie une hanche contre le plan de travail.

– J’avais oublié que vous étiez une incorrigible optimiste en matière de relations. En parlant de ça, comment s’est passé votre rencard d’hier soir ?

– Mon rencard ?

– Avec monsieur Nœudpap.

– Ah, le dîner. Sympa, mais je n’appellerais pas exactement ça un rendez-vous.

– Pas de passage à l’acte à la fin de la soirée, c’est ça ?

– Ce ne sont pas vos affaires, mais non. Il ne s’est rien passé entre nous de physique. On a partagé un bon dîner et on a beaucoup parlé de travail. Baldwin essaie de m’obtenir un poste de vacataire à l’Université de New York, où il enseigne. Je ne pense pas avoir envie d’enseigner un jour à plein temps, mais j’adorerais donner des cours à temps partiel et recevoir mes patients le reste du temps. Bref, après le dîner, on s’est dit « au revoir » devant ma porte.

– Il veut quoi, en fait, ce type ? Sortir avec vous ou pas ?

– Je n'en sais rien. Il m'envoie des signaux contradictoires. Comme hier soir. Il devait sortir avec Rachel, une fille qu'il fréquente, et le voilà qui se pointe ici sans prévenir, change d'avis et m'emmène dîner à la dernière minute.

– Il vous arrive de lui parler de vos sentiments, à vous ?

– L'occasion ne s'est jamais présentée.

Drew lève le menton.

– L'occasion ? Et hier soir, ça n'allait pas ?

– Il voit quelqu'un.

– Et ?

– Je ne veux pas m'immiscer dans sa relation.

– Je ne vous dis pas d'aller coucher avec lui. Juste de lui exprimer ce que vous ressentez.

– C'est ce que vous feriez, à ma place ?

Il ricane.

– En fait, moi, j'ai plutôt pour habitude de baiser avec mes rencards sans parler de sentiments. Mais ça, ce n'est pas votre style.

Je lâche un soupir.

– Je le regrette.

– Sur ce point, je peux vous aider, fait-il en agitant les sourcils. Si l'envie vous vient d'essayer quelque chose de nouveau.

– Comme c'est généreux de votre part.

– Oh, je saurais me montrer trèèèès généreux. Faites-moi confiance.

À la vue de son sourire coquin, mon cœur effectue un petit saut dans ma poitrine, mais je secoue la tête.

– Ma vie en est donc rendue à ça ? Je suis conseillère matrimoniale et je prends mes conseils en matière de relations auprès d'un avocat spécialisé dans les divorces ?

– Vous êtes idéaliste. Je suis réaliste.

Je redresse les épaules.

– Puis-je savoir quel est votre statut à vous, du point de vue personnel ? Puisque vous êtes un expert ?

– J'ai des tas de relations.

– Vous parlez de relations sexuelles ?

– Oui. J'aime le sexe. En fait, j'adore ça. C'est le reste, tout ce merdier, que je n'aime pas.

– La partie relationnelle, vous voulez dire ?

– Je veux dire la partie où deux personnes se mettent ensemble et commencent à compter l'une sur l'autre, à partager leur vie, jusqu'à ce que l'une des deux entube l'autre.

– Toutes les relations ne tournent pas comme ça.

– Dans toute relation, l'un des deux finit par entuber l'autre à un moment donné. À moins justement qu'on s'en tienne à la baise. Dans ce cas, il n'y a pas de fausses attentes.

– Je pense que votre divorce et votre travail ont entaché votre vision des choses.

Il hausse les épaules.

– Entaché, ça me va.

***

Sarah et Ben Aster sont l'exemple parfait de la raison pour laquelle j'adore le conseil matrimonial. J'ai commencé à voir Sarah après la naissance de leur fils et, très vite, je me suis rendu compte que leurs problèmes de couple allaient bien au-delà du stress additionnel de l'arrivée d'un enfant. Le couple était ensemble depuis seulement quatre mois quand Sarah est tombée enceinte, ce qui a conduit à un mariage ultra rapide et à une interruption prématurée de la période normale dite de la « lune de miel » dans la relation, à cause de la survenue du bébé.

Après un départ pour le moins chaotique, le couple a fini par s'installer, pour découvrir assez vite que les espoirs et les rêves de chacun étaient très différents. Ben aspire à une maison pleine d'enfants, en banlieue, avec un grand jardin et une femme qui resterait à la maison. Sarah, pour sa part, souhaite rester vivre dans leur minuscule appartement de l'Upper East Side, reprendre le travail et embaucher une nounou.

Le plus drôle, c'est que chacun affirme avoir dit à l'autre comment il envisageait l'avenir. D'ailleurs, je pense qu'ils l'ont fait. Le problème réside dans leur mode de communication. En conséquence, même si au cours des mois écoulés ils ont réussi à trouver un compromis en cherchant une maison à Brooklyn avec une petite cour et un temps de trajet raisonnable jusqu'à Manhattan, il leur reste à travailler sur la communication. Ce qui m'a conduite à l'exercice de cette semaine.

J'ai demandé à Sarah et à Ben de dresser la liste de cinq choses qu'ils veulent accomplir au cours de l'année à venir. Aujourd'hui, nous avons passé la majeure partie de l'heure à compulser la liste de Sarah. Elle a lu à Ben ce qu'elle envisage de faire et il devait lui expliquer en retour ce que signifiait ce projet. C'est inouï ce qu'un couple pourtant marié depuis dix-huit mois peut encore mal interpréter les choses.

– Je veux faire un voyage en Caroline du Sud pour rendre visite à Beth, ma meilleure amie, annonce Sarah.

Je me tourne vers Ben.

– Ben, expliquez-moi ce que Sarah vient de dire.

– Eh bien, elle veut partir en Caroline du Sud pour voir Beth, son amie célibataire.

– Sarah n'a pas mentionné le fait que Beth soit célibataire, mais apparemment vous avez entendu ce détail qui est important à vos yeux. En quoi le fait que Beth soit célibataire est-il significatif ?

– Elle veut partir. Je le comprends et elle a bien besoin de faire un break. Seulement, elle veut aller passer du temps avec Beth pour retrouver la vie qu'elle avait avant que nous soyons ensemble. Une existence de célibataire insouciante. Après, elle va revenir et elle nous en voudra.

Sarah exprime ensuite qu'elle souffre de ne plus avoir son amie auprès d'elle et explique comment elle envisage d'occuper son temps quand elle lui rendra visite. Il est clair qu'il y a une grande différence entre ce qu'elle souhaite à travers ce voyage et la manière dont Ben l'avait interprété. Au bout de quinze minutes de conversation sur le sujet, elle a réussi à l'apaiser. Entre ces deux-là, la communication et la confiance s'améliorent de semaine en semaine et, à la fin de l'heure, je suggère que nous passions à une séance toutes les deux semaines au lieu d'un rendez-vous hebdomadaire.

– Vous savez ce que je viens de remarquer ? me dit Sarah tandis que Ben l'aide à enfiler son manteau.

– Quoi donc ?

– Après la fin de nos séances de vidéoconférence, il y avait toujours une petite citation sympathique sur votre page d'accueil, que je ne manquais pas de lire. Qui me rappelait de faire quelque chose de gentil pour Ben. On n'en aura plus, c'est dommage.

Je lui souris.

– Eh bien, si. D'abord, les citations sont toujours mises à jour sur mon site web, mais j'en écrirai aussi sur ma porte. Elle était ouverte quand vous êtes arrivés, vous ne l'avez probablement pas remarquée. Mais vous pourrez lire celle du jour en sortant.

Sarah arrête Ben et ensemble ils lisent l'ardoise après avoir ouvert ma porte. Sarah tourne la tête vers moi, une drôle d'expression sur le visage, tandis que Ben sourit de toutes ses dents.

Une fois qu'ils sont partis, je saisis mes lunettes de vue et m'approche de la porte en me demandant si j'ai fait une faute d'orthographe.

Ce n'est pas le cas, mais apparemment Drew a trouvé amusant de modifier ma citation. Là où j'avais écrit :

> Souffler la bougie d'autrui ne fera pas pour autant
> briller la mienne.
> Aujourd'hui, je vais faire briller ma compagne/mon compagnon en ______________________

L'ardoise affiche désormais :

> Souffler la bougie d'autrui fait encore plus briller la mienne.
> Aujourd'hui, je vais faire briller ma compagne/mon compagnon en lui soufflant dans les bronches.

Je vais le tuer.

CHAPITRE 16

DREW

– Quel gros con !

– Steve, je te rappelle. Je crois qu'il y a une dispute en demande d'arbitrage dans la salle de conférences d'à côté.

Je raccroche pile au moment où Emerie débarque dans mon bureau pour poursuivre sa diatribe.

– Ce genre de plaisanteries, c'est peut-être drôle avec vos clients masculins qui embauchent des gens pour fouiller dans les poubelles de leur femme, mais pas pour les miens !

– C'est quoi, votre problème, merde ?

Elle a l'air sacrément furax, mais… elle porte aussi ses lunettes tout en me hurlant dessus. *Elles ont quelque chose, ces lunettes.* Et puis, je ne l'avais pas remarqué ce matin, mais sa jupe est un peu serrée aux entournures. Le rouge lui va bien.

Elle incline la tête.

– Vous faites quoi, là ?

– Quoi ? Comment ça, je fais quoi ?

Elle lève les mains au ciel.

– Vous me reluquez. Je vous ai vu. Je suis entrée ici pour vous enguirlander et vous, vous me reluquez.

– J'admirais votre tenue. Ça n'a rien à voir avec « reluquer ».

– Ah oui ? (Ses mains se posent sur ses hanches.) Et en quoi c'est différent ?

– En quoi c'est différent ?

– Ne répétez pas la question pour vous donner le temps d'inventer une réponse. En quoi est-ce qu'admirer ma tenue et me reluquer sont deux choses différentes ?

Il n'y a qu'une issue.

– J'aime bien, quand vous portez vos lunettes.

– Mes lunettes ?

– Oui, vos lunettes. Vous les mettez juste pour lire ?

Elle se tait pour évaluer mon degré de crédibilité ; ou d'incrédibilité. Au bout du compte, elle secoue la tête.

– Vous pensez pouvoir vous en tirer par un compliment ?

J'espère.

– Je pense que vous êtes un peu folle.

– Moi, je suis folle ?

Le ton a monté d'un cran.

Je me cale contre le dossier de mon fauteuil, amusé. C'est marrant de jouer avec elle. Ça m'évite de penser à d'autres choses.

– Je ne croyais pas que les rousses pouvaient se permettre de porter du rouge.

Elle baisse les yeux vers sa jupe, les relève vers moi, prise de court, mais se ressaisit vite.

– Arrêtez ça tout de suite, m'ordonne-t-elle, les sourcils froncés.

– Quoi ?

– D'essayer de me radoucir en me balançant des trucs gentils.

– Vous n'aimez pas les compliments ?

– Quand ils sont sincères, si. Je les aime. Mais quand il s'agit de conneries destinées à détourner mon attention, non, je ne les aime pas du tout.

– Je ne donne pas dans le faux compliment.

Elle m'adresse une expression qui m'indique clairement qu'elle n'en croit pas un mot.

– Donc vous aimez vraiment mes lunettes de vue ?

– Elles vous donnent un look de bibliothécaire sexy.

Elle secoue la tête.

– Et ma jupe rouge ?

– Pour être honnête, je me fous de la couleur. Mais elle est serrée. Et elle moule joliment tous les bons endroits.

Les joues d'Emerie rosissent. Ce qui me pousse à me demander quelle couleur prendrait sa peau laiteuse si je la suçotais.

– Ne vous avisez plus de jouer avec mon ardoise ! Mes clients la lisent. J'ai de la chance qu'ils soient contents de moi, autrement votre petite blague les ferait douter de mon professionnalisme.

– Bien m'dame.

Je porte deux doigts à mon front en une imitation moqueuse du salut scout.

– Merci.

Quand elle fait demi-tour pour sortir, je ne résiste pas.

– Je parie que le gars va se faire souffler dans les bronches, ce soir.

– Eh bien, comme ça, vous serez deux.

***

Pour une fois, je quitte le boulot à dix-huit heures.

– Vous voulez vous joindre à Roman et à moi pour une bière au *Fat Cat ?*

Emerie est assise à son bureau et se regarde dans un petit miroir tout en peignant ses lèvres d'un rouge vif accordé à sa jupe. En suivant des yeux sa main qui dessine la courbe de sa lèvre supérieure, je songe que, sur le fond blanc immaculé du mur, elle ressemble à une éclaboussure d'art vivant sur une toile.

Non, mais tu t'écoutes, Jagger ? De l'art vivant ?

– Merci, mais j'ai des projets pour ce soir.

– Un rencard ?

– Baldwin m'invite dans un restaurant français.

Une soudaine tension mêlée à une bonne dose de jalousie me vrillent l'estomac de manière inattendue.

– De la nourriture française ? Bof, je ne suis pas très fan.

– Moi non plus. Mais Baldwin adore les *escargots*[4].

– Les limaces, oui, j'ironise, avant de marmonner : Tu m'étonnes.

– Pardon ?

– Non, rien.

Ben oui, quoi, les escargots, ça me fait penser aux limaces. Or manger ces trucs, ça revient à du cannibalisme, pour monsieur Nœudpap. Ce type *est* une limace. Au lieu de lui expliquer tout ça, je me contente de :

– Passez une bonne soirée.

---

4. En français, dans le texte.

CHAPITRE 17

DREW

– C'est quoi, ta position préférée ?

Emily grimpe sur mes genoux, qu'elle chevauche.

– J'aime bien celle-ci.

Il va falloir que j'envoie une bouteille de Gran Patrón Platinum à Roman pour l'idée de génie qu'il a eue ce soir. On s'est retrouvés pour boire des verres à notre pub habituel, mais ensuite il a insisté pour qu'on aille à côté, chez *Maya*, histoire d'essayer leurs *empanadas ;* il est obsédé par la nourriture mexicaine, ce gars. Emily DeLuca et sa copine Allison y étaient déjà, à déguster des *margaritas* au bar. Emily est avocate dans un cabinet à l'autre bout de la ville, auquel je transfère souvent du boulot de planification successorale. On a flirté quelques fois et il y a même eu une étincelle, sauf que chez moi, les étincelles n'ont jamais engendré le souhait d'allumer une autre étincelle à un certain doigt de la main gauche d'une fille. Or la pierre énorme qu'elle arbore est difficile à rater.

Tout aussi difficile à rater, le fait qu'elle ne la porte pas ce soir, d'autant qu'elle m'a agité sa main gauche sous le nez, juste avant de me demander si elle pouvait me payer un verre. Malgré son geste évident, je lui ai quand même fait confirmer sa rupture avant qu'on s'en aille ensemble. Une femme a beau être hyper entreprenante, je ne touche pas à celles qui trompent leur mec.

Emily se frotte sur mon sexe en train de durcir et je passe la main sous sa jupe relevée pour lui empoigner les fesses. Puis je tire sur le morceau de dentelle qui court le long de sa fente pour augmenter la friction. Elle lâche un grognement, alors je tire plus fort.

Punaise, j'adore les strings.

Elle entreprend de défaire les boutons de ma chemise tandis que je lui lèche le cou.

– À l'instant où je t'ai vu, la première fois, j'ai su qu'on prendrait du plaisir ensemble. J'espère que tu as une boîte de préservatifs pleine. Parce qu'après t'avoir chevauché, je veux que tu me prennes en levrette.

La pensée d'Emily, les fesses en l'air, c'est exactement ce dont j'ai besoin. D'autant que je viens de passer la semaine à fantasmer sur le derrière d'une autre… une femme à qui je ne devrais pas penser maintenant. Cela dit, la vision répétée du postérieur laiteux et rond d'Emerie, orné de la marque rouge de ma main tandis que je l'assaille par-derrière, c'est l'un de mes fantasmes les plus efficaces. Je rêve de jouir en elle et de recueillir mon sperme qui dégoulinerait d'elle pour l'étaler, tel un onguent, sur l'empreinte que j'aurai laissée sur sa peau.

Les yeux fermés, je dois serrer plus fort encore les paupières afin de chasser l'image d'une autre. Parce que songer à une femme pendant qu'une autre vous chevauche, c'est vraiment un truc de connard, même pour un type comme moi.

Emily se soulève suffisamment pour glisser une main entre nous et agrippe mon érection, qu'elle empoigne avec vigueur.

– Je te veux. Maintenant.

D'un geste frénétique, elle se met à déboutonner mon pantalon et, par réflexe, j'attrape mon portefeuille. Avant de me rappeler que je n'ai pas de préservatif là-dedans. *Merde.*

– Tu n'aurais pas une capote, par hasard ? je lui demande, en lui mordillant le lobe.

Sa voix est crispée quand elle me répond.

– Non. Et j'ai merdé avec ma pilule, ce mois-ci, alors je t'en supplie, dis-moi que tu en as quelque part dans cet appartement.

Merde. Non. J'ai épuisé la grosse boîte de ma table de chevet le mois dernier et n'ai pas eu l'occasion de la remplacer. Ensuite, à Hawaï, j'ai utilisé celui que je gardais dans mon portefeuille en cas d'urgence.

Mais… j'en ai quelques-uns dans un tiroir de mon bureau, en haut, à droite. Au moins, je n'aurai pas à sortir me les geler. Avec un grognement, je m'écarte.

– J'en ai pour deux minutes, j'annonce à Emily, dont je prends le visage entre mes mains. Désolé, les préservatifs sont dans mon bureau, en bas.

– Tu veux que je vienne avec toi ? Je n'aurais rien contre un petit coup sur le bureau. Et puis, ça nous fera gagner du temps.

Petite maligne. Mais… ce n'est sans doute pas une bonne idée de l'entraîner dans un endroit rempli de trucs qui me rappellent la femme que je m'efforce justement de m'ôter de la tête.

Je lui donne un chaste baiser et la soulève de mes genoux.

– Reste là. Mon bureau est au rez-de-chaussée. Il est doté d'un système de sécurité qui fonctionne vingt-quatre heures sur vingt-quatre. Je ne veux pas avoir à te couvrir la bouche quand tu hurleras mon nom.

Ce fichu ascenseur met une éternité à monter me rejoindre, laps de temps dont je profite au moins pour reboutonner mon pantalon. Une fois en bas, je cours vers Ted, le portier de nuit. J'aurais dû renfiler mes chaussures, parce que le sol de marbre est glacial – il serait dommage que je fasse descendre ma température corporelle.

À l'intérieur du bureau, en traversant le couloir, je prends bien garde à ne pas tourner la tête vers la porte close d'Emerie. Pas besoin d'un élément supplémentaire pour me la remémorer. Surtout pas l'ardoise blanche où elle avait inscrit sa citation sentimentalo-nunuche, avant de débarquer comme une balle dans mon bureau, furax et si sexy.

Non. Je ne regarderai pas. Tel un gosse de deux ans, je porte ma main contre mon visage pour bloquer ma vision périphérique et m'empêcher de voir le bureau qui fait face au mien tandis que j'ouvre ma porte.

À force de fouiller dans mon tiroir, je déniche trois préservatifs esseulés. *Putain, merci.* Je les fourre dans ma poche et ressors dans le couloir, en direction du hall. J'ai presque atteint le bout du couloir quand j'entends un bruit.

Je devrais aller voir.

Et merde. Ils n'ont qu'à entrer, les cambrioleurs, et voler ce qui leur chante. Je m'en chargerai demain. J'ai plus important qui m'attend là-haut.

Et puis je l'entends à nouveau, ce bruit. On dirait presque… un reniflement.

Emerie est encore là ? J'essaie de passer mon chemin, mais je sais que je ne réussirai jamais à me concentrer si je l'imagine blessée ou autre. Supposons qu'elle soit tombée en partant et qu'elle se vide de son sang dans son bureau fermé ? Je cours vers sa porte et l'ouvre.

Emerie sursaute sur son siège et porte les mains à sa poitrine.

– Drew ! Vous m'avez flanqué la trouille de ma vie.

– Qu'est-ce que vous faites encore ici ? Je croyais que vous aviez un rencard avec monsieur Escargot ?

– Effectivement.

Après une observation plus attentive, je vois qu'elle a pleuré. Elle a un mouchoir en boule dans la paume et sa peau pâle est constellée de taches rouges.

– Qu'est-ce qu'il a fait ?

J'éprouve soudain l'envie irrépressible d'étrangler ce pauvre blaireau avec son nœud papillon.

Elle renifle.

– Rien de précis. Il a juste annulé notre dîner.

– Pour quelle raison ?

– Aujourd'hui, c'est mon anniversaire et…

– C'est votre anniversaire ? Pourquoi vous ne m'en avez rien dit ?

– Je n'ai jamais fait tout un plat des anniversaires. Quand j'étais petite, j'ai pris l'habitude de fêter les « Bienvenue chez nous » comme d'autres fêtent leurs anniversaires.

– Les « Bienvenue chez nous » ?

– Le jour où mes parents adoptifs m'ont ramenée à la maison. Ils disaient toujours que tout le monde a un anniversaire, et que le jour où ils m'avaient eue, c'était le plus beau cadeau qu'ils aient jamais reçu. Alors ils se sont mis à fêter les « Bienvenue chez nous » avec moi au lieu des anniversaires. Ça craint, en fait. Pour moi, les anniversaires, ce ne sont que des chiffres.

– C'est incroyable. Enfin, bon, vous auriez quand même dû me dire que c'était votre anniversaire.

L'ironie ne m'échappe pas : Emerie parle à peine de son anniversaire, alors que mon ex-femme pense que le sien doit être célébré comme une fête nationale. Ça m'a toujours tapé sur les nerfs, même avant que la situation ne dégénère grave.

Elle hausse les épaules.

– Non, mais je me comporte comme un gros bébé, là. Baldwin avait réservé dans ce fameux restaurant français si branché où il est impossible d'obtenir une table et j'étais censée le retrouver à vingt heures.

– Qu'est-ce qui s'est passé ?

– Il m'a envoyé un SMS disant que Rachel était furieuse qu'il l'ait lâchée pour m'emmener dîner, l'autre soir, et quand il lui a annoncé qu'il sortait à nouveau avec moi, elle s'est tellement énervée qu'il a dû annuler ce soir.

Ce type est vraiment un connard fini. Et il embobine Emerie, je n'ai plus aucun doute là-dessus, maintenant qu'elle m'a expliqué, et vu la manière dont il a réagi l'autre fois, quand j'ai proposé qu'elle et moi sortions manger ensemble. Il est possessif avec elle, d'une façon qui est plus qu'amicale. Et pourtant, il veut pouvoir manger à tous les râteliers.

– Je sais que vous éprouvez des sentiments pour lui. Mais ce type m'a l'air d'être un sacré trouduc.

– Il faut juste que j'arrête de m'accrocher à lui et que je passe à autre chose.

– Je pense en effet que c'est une bonne idée.

– Je devrais sortir fêter mon anniversaire moi-même. Draguer quelqu'un dans un bar et le ramener à la maison.

– Non, ça, ce n'est pas une bonne idée.

Elle pousse un soupir.

– Je sais. En plus, je ne suis pas du genre à coucher au hasard avec le premier venu. J'ai essayé et ensuite je me déteste pendant des semaines. Ça n'en vaut pas la peine.

Dieu merci. L'idée d'Emerie qui ramène un inconnu chez elle me donne littéralement la nausée. En parlant de ça… mon coup d'un soir m'attend à l'étage.

– Qu'est-ce que vous allez faire, alors ?

– Je termine ce dossier et je rentre chez moi. Je suis fatiguée, de toute façon.

– OK. Ne restez pas trop tard. On fêtera ça demain. Je vous emmène déjeuner chez *Joey*.

Elle esquisse un sourire forcé et triste.

– Super. (Ses yeux tombent sur mes pieds.) Pas de chaussures ?

– Je suis descendu en vitesse.

– Vous travaillez tard et vous avez oublié quelque chose ?

– Non… je… euh… j'ai de la compagnie.

– Ah…

Son visage, déjà triste, prend l'expression de qui vient d'apprendre la mort de son petit chien. Cette fois, elle ne parvient même pas à afficher un sourire.

– Ne traînez pas à cause de moi. Je ne vais pas tarder à partir, ne vous inquiétez pas.

Je lui souhaite une bonne soirée, mais je me fais l'effet d'être une grosse merde en m'éloignant. Pourquoi ai-je l'impression d'avoir cent kilos de poids supplémentaire sur les épaules tandis que je remonte chez moi en ascenseur ? Ce n'est pourtant pas moi qui me suis fichu d'elle. Je ne savais même pas que c'était son anniversaire.

Je rentre dans mon appartement, complètement perdu dans mes pensées, et suis accueilli par Emily, plantée dans l'encadrement de la porte du salon. Elle n'est plus vêtue que de ses escarpins à talons aiguilles sexy en diable et de son string de dentelle noire.

Rien de tel qu'un excitant bonnet D pour te requinquer quand tu n'as pas le moral.

Elle incline la tête et croise les jambes au niveau des chevilles. Ses chaussures, pas question qu'elle les quitte. Je vois déjà les talons qui s'enfoncent dans mon dos.

– Le spectacle te plaît ?

Ma réponse se passe de mots. Je me dirige vers elle à grandes enjambées et la soulève pour nouer ses jambes autour de ma taille.

– Tu pourras t'asseoir sur moi plus tard. D'abord, je vais te baiser sur la table de ma cuisine. Ça te dit, Emerie ?

Elle pouffe.

– Emily. On dirait que tout le sang a déserté ton cerveau et gêne un peu tes capacités oratoires.

Merde. Je viens de l'appeler Emerie et je ne m'en étais même pas rendu compte.

– Oui, ça doit venir de là.

Je nous transporte jusqu'à la table et lui écarte les cuisses afin de défaire rapidement ma braguette, mais quand je baisse les yeux vers son visage souriant, je vois Emerie.

Emerie.

Et pas Emily, que je suis sur le point de baiser.

Je cille et mes yeux refont la focale. Cheveux châtain, peau mate à l'italienne, grands yeux marron. Rien à voir. Penché au-dessus d'elle, je prends le temps de retirer mon caleçon et en profite pour me clarifier l'esprit et replonger dans l'instant présent. Puis je fonds sur sa bouche.

Nous nous embrassons, et pourtant je n'arrive pas à effacer l'image d'Emerie en train de pleurer, toute seule dans son bureau. Ses grands yeux bleus rougis, sa peau claire rougie aussi, triste à cause d'un connard qui mange probablement des escargots et va la réveiller à deux heures du matin en faisant trembler ses murs.

Merde.

Merde.

– Meeeeeerde !

Je me redresse et me passe une main dans les cheveux, que j'ai envie de m'arracher tant je suis frustré.

– Quoi ? Qu'est-ce qui ne va pas ?

Je remonte mon pantalon.

– C'est une cliente. Elle a appelé pendant que j'étais en bas et je l'ai envoyée balader. Seulement, je dois aller bosser sur un truc.

– Tu plaisantes, là ? Maintenant ?

– Je suis désolé, Emerie.

– Emily.

Elle se couvre la poitrine et se rassoit sur la table.

– Emily. Oui. Pardon. J'ai l'esprit ailleurs.

Auprès d'Emerie, et pas d'Emily, où je devrais être.

– Pas de souci, marmonne-t-elle.

Je vois bien que si, il y a un souci. Normal, je ne la blâme pas. Je serais en rage si une femme me balançait l'excuse minable que je viens de lui servir. Sauf que je ne peux rien y faire. Hormis m'excuser.

– Je suis vraiment navré. Le temps est compté, autrement je ne te lâcherais pas comme ça.

– Je comprends.

Elle se rhabille et, moins de cinq minutes après être revenu dans mon appartement pour y trouver une femme super sexy qui m'y attendait nue, je la raccompagne à l'ascenseur.

La descente se déroule dans une atmosphère tendue. Dans le hall, elle m'embrasse sur la joue et sort sans un regard en arrière. Je devrais me sentir mal, mais à la place, je n'éprouve que de l'anxiété en me demandant si Emerie est encore là.

Elle a intérêt à n'être pas déjà partie.

CHAPITRE 18

DREW

– Oh, bon Dieu !

Emerie est juste derrière la porte d'entrée du bureau quand je l'ouvre à la volée. Un pas de plus et je la lui aurais envoyée dans la figure.

Elle serre les mains contre sa poitrine.

– Vous essayez de me donner une crise cardiaque ou quoi ?

– Ah, vous êtes encore là.

– Je me préparais à partir. Qu'est-ce qui se passe ? Tout va bien ?

– Tout va très bien. Mais je vous invite à sortir pour votre anniversaire.

– Vous n'êtes pas obligé de faire ça.

– Je le sais bien. Mais j'en ai envie.

Elle fronce les sourcils.

– Je croyais que vous aviez de la compagnie.

– Je m'en suis débarrassé.

– Pourquoi ?

– Pourquoi quoi ?

– Pourquoi vous avez planté votre rencard ? (Son expression confuse se change en autre chose, comme si une idée venait de la frapper.) Oh.

– Quoi, « oh » ?

– Vous en avez terminé avec votre rencard.

– J'étais loin d'en avoir terminé, je marmonne, avant de désigner la rue d'un geste du menton. Allez, vous méritez une agréable soirée d'anniversaire. Ce crétin n'a pas la moindre idée de ce qu'il rate. Allons nous mettre minable.

Son sourire lui remonte jusqu'aux oreilles.

– J'adore cette idée.

***

– Je ne vais même pas avoir l'occasion de manier la queue.

– C'est peut-être pour ça que vous êtes aussi tendue. Ça fait tellement longtemps que vous n'avez pas couché avec un homme que vous en avez oublié que ce sont eux qui ont une queue.

Avec un sourire narquois à l'attention d'Emerie, j'envoie la boule numéro cinq dans le trou de gauche. C'est notre première partie de billard et je viens de rentrer ma cinquième boule d'affilée. Elle a raison, je pourrais avoir nettoyé le tapis avant qu'elle ait fini d'enduire la pointe de sa queue de craie bleue.

Elle plisse les paupières.

– Qu'est-ce que vous en savez, de ma période d'abstinence ?

– Je vous trouve un tout petit peu à cran.

Je m'attends à ce qu'elle s'énerve contre moi, au lieu de quoi elle me surprend. Au sens propre du terme. Pile au moment où je vais pour taper mon sixième coup, elle hurle :

– Attention !

Ma main dérape en plein geste et la boule numéro deux atterrit à des lieues du trou que je visais.

Elle lâche un petit gloussement, toute fière.

– OK, vous voulez jouer à ce petit jeu ?

– À quel jeu ? Je suis tellement crispée que je ne peux pas m'en empêcher. Parfois les mots restent coincés et ils sortent de ma bouche d'un coup, comme un bouchon de champagne.

– À vous.

Je tends la main vers la gauche. Pendant qu'elle se positionne, je contourne la table et m'approche jusqu'à me retrouver juste derrière son dos. Elle tente de faire comme si cela ne la dérangeait pas, mais elle finit par se retourner.

– Vous faites quoi ?

– Je vous regarde jouer.

– De derrière ?

Je lui adresse un large sourire.

– J'ai une meilleure vue.

– Retournez à votre place, m'ordonne-t-elle, en agitant la main en direction de l'autre côté de la table de billard. Je pense que la vue est plus dégagée de là-bas.

Puis elle se penche à nouveau et essaie d'aligner la queue avec la boule. Mon regard tombe sur son magnifique postérieur.

– Ça dépend de ce que je regarde.

Quand enfin elle lâche son coup, la pointe frotte le feutre et rate complètement la boule.

– Je croyais que vous saviez jouer.

– Je sais jouer.

– On ne dirait pas.

– Vous me déconcentrez, à rester planté derrière moi.

Je me penche vers elle pour lui montrer comment placer sa main afin de tenir la queue et qu'au minimum elle entre plus facilement en contact avec la boule. Une fois qu'elle a pigé, je vais de l'autre côté de la table. Mes intentions sont purement altruistes, cette fois, du moins jusqu'à ce que son chemisier bâille et m'offre une vue plongeante sur ses seins.

Je n'arrive pas à me convaincre de bouger. Elle doit porter l'un de ces soutiens-gorge qui ne couvrent que la moitié du sein, car moi, je ne vois que deux globes parfaitement ronds de peau laiteuse et appétissante, avec juste une touche de dentelle noire.

Une superbe poitrine, en parfait accord avec un superbe postérieur.

Je porte ma bière à mes lèvres en attendant qu'elle ajuste son coup, sans toutefois cesser de la zieuter par-dessus ma bouteille pendant que je bois une longue goulée. La seule chose qui finit par détourner mon attention, c'est le mouvement d'avant en arrière de la queue entre ses doigts.

Car alors j'imagine mon sexe à la place de la queue.

M'obligeant à fermer les yeux au moment où elle tire enfin, je vide le contenu de ma Stella. Emerie parvient à toucher une boule, cette fois, sauf qu'elle rentre dans l'une des miennes au lieu de la sienne. Mais elle est si ravie que je n'ai pas le cœur de la détromper.

– Ça veut dire que j'ai le droit de tirer à nouveau ?

– Absolument. Je vais me chercher une autre bière. Vous en voulez une ?

– Je veux bien un verre, mais pas encore une bière. C'est trop de liquide.

– OK. Vous voulez quoi ?

– Surprenez-moi. Je boirai ce que vous me donnerez.

Bon, il faut vraiment que je m'éloigne quelques minutes.

Au bar, l'attente pour être servi est longue, seulement moi, je suis un habitué des lieux. Roman et moi nous retrouvons au *Fat Cat* tous les week-ends pour jouer au billard et discuter boulot. Alors quand Tiny, le barman qui doit mesurer quelque chose comme deux mètres, me voit, il prend ma commande avant la plupart des autres clients.

– Je vais prendre une autre Stella et puis un de ces trucs.

Je désigne une *margarita*. Tiny se fend d'un sourire.

– Roman se met en contact avec son côté féminin, ce soir ?

– Non. Il est probablement à la maison à se mettre en contact avec lui-même. Je suis venu avec…

Elle est quoi, d'ailleurs ? Pas un rencard. Pas une collègue, même si on travaille dans le même bureau. Je ne peux même pas la désigner comme une employée. Faute de trouver le mot adéquat, je finis par opter pour le plus simple.

– … une femme.

Oui, Emerie est une femme, aucun doute là-dessus.

Pendant que j'attends mes verres, je songe au fait que pas une fois je n'ai eu l'idée d'emmener un rencard ici, même si, je le répète, ma sortie de ce soir n'est pas un rencard. C'est le genre d'endroit où l'on vient traîner entre mecs et où l'on peut être soi-même. Pourtant, je n'ai pas eu la moindre inquiétude à y entraîner Emerie. C'est agréable de passer du temps avec une femme avec qui je sais que je serai à l'aise dans un bar-salle de billard underground. Et cerise sur le gâteau, il se trouve qu'elle est sexy en diable.

Je ne me suis absenté que quelques minutes, pourtant, quand je retourne à notre table, un type est déjà en train de parler avec Emerie. Une pique de bonne vieille jalousie masculine s'éveille en moi. Résistant à l'envie brûlante de lui ordonner de se casser, je choisis de mettre le gars mal à l'aise au point qu'il décidera de s'éclipser par lui-même.

Je m'approche d'Emerie, lui tends son verre tout en dévisageant le serpent.

– Tenez, voilà. C'est qui, votre ami ?

– Will. Il a proposé de me montrer quelques coups.

– Ah oui ?

Will a un verre dans la main gauche. Le doigt dont il a retiré son alliance porte encore la trace de l'anneau. J'attends que nos regards se croisent, puis je guide le sien vers son doigt.

– Nous avons la table encore une vingtaine de minutes. Votre femme et vous souhaitez la prendre une fois qu'on aura terminé ?

Rien de tel qu'une conversation silencieuse d'homme à homme. Il désigne le bar du menton.

– Peut-être une autre fois. Mes amis m'attendent. *Ravi d'avoir discuté avec toi, Will.*

Après cette interruption, Emerie et moi finissons notre partie et allons nous asseoir dans une zone du bar moins bruyante. Elle a bu sa première *margarita* assez vite et la serveuse vient de lui en apporter une deuxième. La dépression causée par le connard au nœud papillon s'est changée en gaieté alcoolisée.

– C'est quoi le meilleur cadeau d'anniversaire que vous ayez reçu ? me demande-t-elle.

– Moi ? Je ne sais pas. Grandir avec mon père m'a valu pas mal de cadeaux nuls. Alors je dirais une voiture pour mes dix-sept ans, sans doute.

– Quel ennui…

Elle boit une gorgée de sa *margarita* et une ligne de sel reste collée à sa lèvre.

– Vous avez… (Je montre, sur ma bouche, l'endroit où le sel s'est attardé sur la sienne.) Du sel.

Elle s'essuie, mais du mauvais côté. En riant, je tends la main par-dessus la table.

– Attendez.

Machinalement, je récupère le sel sur ses lèvres et porte mon pouce aux miennes. Je me la raconte peut-être, gros ego et tout ça, mais je jurerais qu'elle entrouvre les lèvres et que si je m'étais penché un peu, j'aurais entendu un léger soupir.

Merde. Je parie qu'elle est du genre très réceptive au lit.

Je m'éclaircis la gorge.

– Et vous ? Le meilleur cadeau de toute votre vie ?

– Mes parents m'ont offert un chèque-cadeau pour une opération des yeux au laser, le jour de mes dix-huit ans.

– Au laser ? Mais vous portez des lunettes.

– Parce que je n'ai pas gardé le cadeau. Je suis allée voir le chirurgien et lui ai expliqué que mes parents s'étaient trompés et que je ne souhaitais pas être opérée.

– Donc vous ne vouliez pas de cette opération. Pourtant c'était le plus beau cadeau de votre vie ?

De nouveau, elle boit une gorgée de sa *margarita*. Hélas, il ne reste pas de sel, cette fois. J'envisage de faire semblant que si, mais elle reprend la parole trop vite.

– Si, si, je la voulais bien, cette opération. En primaire, Missy Robinson m'appelait « mémé » parce que j'avais besoin de deux paires de lunettes : une pour voir au tableau et une pour lire. Le surnom m'a collé aux basques pendant toute mon école élémentaire. Je détestais mes lunettes. Pendant longtemps, j'ai refusé de les porter, même si je devais plisser les paupières et que j'avais des migraines en permanence.

– Je ne comprends pas, du coup. Vos parents vous ont offert un cadeau que vous vouliez vraiment, donc vous l'avez refusé ?

– Mes parents n'avaient pas les moyens de payer cette opération. Ça coûtait six mille dollars et mon père se trimballait dans une voiture vieille de vingt ans. N'empêche, c'était le plus gentil cadeau qu'ils auraient pu m'offrir.

Ajoutez « bon cœur » à un décolleté remarquable, un cul très appétissant et une langue bien pendue. *La langue en question se trouvant d'ailleurs dans une bouche très appétissante aussi, si je puis me permettre.*

– Et aujourd'hui ? Si vous pouviez avoir n'importe quoi pour votre anniversaire, que choisiriez-vous ?

Un doigt sur les lèvres, elle réfléchit.

– Un bain.

– Un bain ? Du genre de ces traitements en spa avec bain de boue ?

– Non. Juste un bon bain dans une grande baignoire. Dans mon appartement, je n'ai qu'une douche et ça me manque beaucoup, de pouvoir prendre un bain. Avant, je m'en offrais un tous les samedis matin. Je mettais mes écouteurs et je trempais jusqu'à avoir la peau fripée. C'était mon moment de bonheur.

Je prends une longue gorgée de ma bière en l'observant.

– Vous êtes facile à contenter.

Elle hausse les épaules.

– Et vous ? Si c'était votre anniversaire et que vous puissiez choisir un cadeau, ce serait quoi ?

Je ravale ma première pensée. *Beck.* Pour ne pas jouer les rabat-joie et déprimer à nouveau Emerie le jour de son anniversaire, je lui avoue mon deuxième choix de cadeau.

– Une pipe, ce serait sympa.

Au milieu de sa gorgée, elle éclate de rire et m'éclabousse de sa *margarita.*

Je m'essuie le visage à l'aide d'une serviette en papier.

– Eh bien, maintenant, j'ai le sel et la *margarita.*

Elle continue à glousser.

– Pardon.

***

Il est deux heures du matin passées quand nous rentrons à l'appartement d'Emerie d'un pas mal assuré. J'ai insisté pour la raccompagner chez elle. Moi, j'ai vaguement la tête qui tourne et je pense qu'elle est plus proche d'être saoule.

– Chuuuut, fait-elle, un doigt sur la bouche, pour m'enjoindre au silence, alors qu'elle-même fait beaucoup de bruit. C'est l'appartement de Baldwin, ajoute-t-elle en fouillant son sac à main en quête de ses clés.

Oui. Elle est bel et bien saoule. Je lui prends les clés des mains.

– Ça pourrait lui faire du bien de vous voir avec un autre homme.

Emerie s'écarte pour me laisser déverrouiller sa porte. Avec un profond soupir, elle pose la tête contre mon bras pendant que je bataille avec la serrure. Cette saleté est bloquée ou quoi ?

– Il ne serait pas jaloux, bredouille-t-elle. Il ne veut pas de moi.

J'agite encore un peu la clé dans la serrure et elle cède enfin.

– Eh bien, dans ce cas, c'est un idiot.

Je pousse la porte et lui tends les clés. Au dernier moment, elles lui échappent des mains et elle pouffe encore quand nous nous cognons la tête en nous baissant pour les ramasser par terre. Par-dessus le son de son rire, j'entends la porte voisine s'ouvrir. Emerie ne s'en rend pas compte.

Quand Baldwin sort dans le couloir et nous dévisage, un soudain accès de possessivité s'empare de moi. De dos, Emerie n'a toujours pas remarqué que nous avons du public. Elle lève vers moi ses grands yeux bleus, tout sourire, et je suis comme possédé. Je me penche et lui dépose un doux baiser sur les lèvres ; comme on plonge un orteil dans l'eau pour prendre la température.

Ce petit baiser, c'est de la testostérone pure, c'est moi qui joue les gros cons devant le trouduc d'à côté. Ma façon de pisser contre la porte, d'une certaine manière. Mais quand je recule la tête et que je vois ses pupilles dilatées et ses lèvres entrouvertes, dans l'attente de la suite, ma réaction n'a plus rien à voir avec celui qui nous observe.

Là, c'est du désir pur. Je perds les pédales. J'écrase ma bouche sur la sienne et elle s'ouvre à moi. Je glisse la langue et la goûte longuement pour la première fois. Elle est salée et poivrée par la tequila, pourtant c'est ce que j'ai goûté de plus délicieux de ma vie. Et soudain, je suis affamé.

Je l'attire contre moi et l'enlace étroitement. Oublié le type dont elle est amoureuse et qui nous regarde, il n'y a plus qu'Emerie et moi. Tout le reste disparaît tandis que j'approfondis le baiser et qu'elle plaque ses seins contre mon torse avec ardeur. Le son qu'elle émet quand je pose une main sur son cul phénoménal m'encourage à continuer. Je n'ai qu'une envie : la pousser contre la porte et frotter mon sexe érigé contre elle. D'ailleurs, je m'y serais peut-être autorisé, si le connard d'à côté n'était pas venu tout gâcher.

Baldwin se racle la gorge. Emerie l'entend et met un terme à notre étreinte, se tournant pour découvrir que l'homme qu'elle aime vient d'assister à toute la scène. Elle a l'air surprise et je déteste la lueur de regret qui s'allume déjà dans ses yeux.

Je lui prends les joues dans mes mains et lui chuchote à l'oreille.

– Ça va peut-être le réveiller. (Puis je lui donne un baiser sur la joue.) À demain au bureau, et joyeux anniversaire.

CHAPITRE 19

DREW

Réveillon du 31 décembre,
quatre ans plus tôt

– Putain, mais c'est qui, tous ces gens ?

Quand je sors sur le balcon de mon appartement pour m'échapper quelques minutes, Roman est assis là, dans le noir, qui fume une cigarette roulée.

– Tu le saurais peut-être, si tu étais dedans au lieu d'ici. (Je m'assieds à côté de lui et m'abîme dans la contemplation de l'océan de lumière qu'est New York.) Il fait un froid de gueux.

– T'as vu les nichons de la blonde au pull bleu ?

– Elle s'appelle Sage, c'est l'une des nouvelles amies d'Alexa.

– Elle n'est pas très finaude. En déconnant, je lui ai affirmé que je pouvais deviner son âge rien qu'en la touchant.

– Ne me dis pas qu'elle t'a laissé la peloter ?

La pointe de la cigarette de Roman s'allume en rouge vif quand il tire une longue taffe.

– Si. Et une fois que je l'aie eu bien tripotée, elle m'a demandé quand elle était née. (Il souffle un chapelet d'anneaux de fumée.) Je lui ai répondu « hier » et je suis sorti m'asseoir ici.

Je lâche un rire. Sacré Roman. Soit il se prend une baffe, soit il a de la chance. Parfois je me demande laquelle des deux options il préfère, en fait.

– Ouais, Alexa a le don pour choisir ses copines.

– Au moins, elle a l'air de s'être bien acclimatée à New York.

Vu de l'extérieur, en tout cas, on aurait pu le croire, ce soir. Enfin, la soirée se passe mieux que celle de l'année passée, où elle était sortie seule et où on avait eu une énorme dispute pour fêter le passage à la nouvelle année quand je l'avais questionnée sur le type qui l'avait raccompagnée à la maison. Cette année, notre maison est remplie de tous les amis qu'elle s'est faits au cours des quatre mois écoulés, soit depuis notre déménagement d'Atlanta à New York. Mais à la vérité, elle continue de se plaindre tous les jours au motif qu'elle a dû abandonner ses potes.

– Elle a fait des connaissances. Surtout dans le cours de comédie qu'elle prend et à la salle de sport. J'espérais qu'elle trouverait des amies qui auraient plus de points communs avec elle, genre des femmes de « La mère et l'enfant », mais elle prétend que ce ne sont que des garces vieux jeu mal habillées.

– Si leurs pulls ressemblent à celui de la blonde, je vais t'emprunter ton gosse pour assister au cours de « La mère et l'enfant ».

Nous restons muets quelques minutes, à profiter du calme d'une nuit claire. Quand il reprend la parole, Roman le fait d'une voix sérieuse.

– Comment va AJ ?

AJ, c'est le surnom de mon père, Andrew Jagger. Ni lui ni moi n'utilisons notre nom de naissance : moi, on m'appelle toujours Drew et lui, AJ.

– Pas bien. Ça s'est étendu à un poumon, maintenant. Apparemment, ils vont devoir lui en retirer un morceau.

– Merde. Désolé, mon pote. AJ est trop jeune pour cette saloperie.

Quatre mois plus tôt, mon père était allé consulter son médecin pour son check-up annuel et ses analyses de sang ont révélé un souci avec ses enzymes hépatiques. Deux jours plus tard, on lui a diagnostiqué un cancer du foie. Même si les statistiques ne sont pas favorables, quinze pour cent de chances de survie à partir du diagnostic, il reste optimiste. Il a enduré des mois de chimio à haute dose qui l'ont rendu malade comme un chien, pour s'entendre expliquer le lendemain de sa dernière série de piqûres que le cancer avait métastasé sur le poumon.

– Oui. Je suis content d'avoir pu être là pour lui. Il a une palanquée d'amis et d'associés de boulot, mais sans une femme pour prendre soin de lui, il fallait que je revienne à New York.

– Je commençais à craindre que tu ne reviennes jamais.

– Je pense que c'était le plan d'Alexa.

Moi, j'ai toujours eu l'intention de revenir à New York pour travailler dans le cabinet de mon père. Mais quand j'ai passé le barreau, Alexa m'a supplié de rester à Atlanta une année supplémentaire. Ce qui impliquait de passer une seconde fois le barreau, mais je m'efforçais de la rendre heureuse, d'autant qu'elle peinait à s'ajuster à son rôle de mère. Alors on est tombés d'accord pour rester un an de plus à Atlanta. Un an qui s'est changé en deux et, jusqu'à ce que mon père tombe malade, je crois qu'Alexa prévoyait de renouveler sa demande chaque année.

– Elle s'adapte. Ici, elle aime faire du shopping et elle a décidé de prendre des cours de comédie. Apparemment, c'est un truc dont elle avait toujours rêvé, même si elle n'en avait jamais parlé avant son inscription. (Je hausse les épaules.) Peu importe, ça la rend heureuse.

Roman me regarde.

– Et toi ? Elle te rend heureux ?

– C'est une bonne mère.

– Ma mère aussi. Ce qui ne signifie pas que j'aie envie de la baiser et de passer le reste de ma vie à ses côtés.

– Tu as une façon unique d'envisager les trucs, toi.

– Je me tape une prof de yoga, elle est à fond dans ces conneries sur l'introspection et tout ça.

– Et bien sûr, c'est pour ça que tu sors avec elle. Pas parce qu'elle est capable de lever la jambe par-dessus son épaule.

– Les seuls moments où elle la ferme et cesse de tenter de m'inculquer ses grandes théories de sagesse inutile, c'est justement quand elle a les jambes écartées. Ma queue agit comme une bonde dans une baignoire remplie d'aphorismes à la noix.

Je me lève en ricanant et assène une tape dans le dos de mon pote.

– Allez, viens, revenons à la fête. Je me les gèle ici, et puis je veux aller voir si Beck dort. Ça devient plutôt bruyant, là-dedans.

En naviguant à travers la fête qui bat son plein, je me dirige vers la chambre de mon petit garçon. Il est si mignon qu'il sourit même dans son sommeil. OK, bon, c'est peut-être juste un réflexe, mais ensuite sa bouche se détend, pour sourire à nouveau à intervalles réguliers. Il doit rêver à ses voitures de course ou à du raisin, les deux trucs qu'il préfère ces derniers mois. Je remonte la couverture sous son menton et effleure ses joues si douces du bout des doigts. Bon Dieu, jamais je n'aurais pensé pouvoir aimer quelqu'un autant. Mon cœur se serre dans ma poitrine quand je me demande si mon père me regardait comme ça, il y a vingt et quelques années. Il faut vraiment qu'il guérisse, je veux qu'il apprenne à connaître mon fils et m'aide à devenir le genre de père qu'il a été pour moi.

Je n'ai pas la foi ; la dernière fois que je suis entré dans une église, c'était pour mon mariage précipité avec Alexa. Et avant ça, sans doute pour un enterrement. Pourtant, une petite croix est suspendue au-dessus du berceau de mon fils. Je la regarde tous les jours, sans jamais la voir autrement que comme un objet de décoration.

Ça ne peut pas faire de mal d'essayer.

Debout auprès du berceau de Beck, je lance une prière à Dieu, qu'il veille sur mon père et sur mon fils.

Cela fait quatre mois qu'on est revenus à New York, et cette croix n'a pas bougé de sa place depuis, accrochée au mur près du berceau. Mais quand j'ouvre la porte pour retourner à la fête, elle tombe au sol.

Pourvu que ce ne soit pas un signe de mauvais augure.

CHAPITRE 20

EMERIE

J'ai la tête comme si je venais de me faire rouler dessus par un car rempli de membres en colère des Alcooliques anonymes. J'ai si soif que ma bouche a été remplacée par un désert, et pourtant chaque gorgée d'eau me donne la nausée. *Bon Dieu, pas étonnant que je ne boive pas souvent.*

Le seul avantage de cette gueule de bois, c'est que je suis tellement occupée à me sentir mal que je n'ai pas la capacité de repenser à la soirée de la veille.

Drew.

Ce baiser.

Ce baiser.

Baldwin.

Retenant mon souffle, j'entre dans le bureau encore plus tard que d'habitude, même selon mes standards. Je n'ai pas de séance avant cet après-midi, mais j'ai des notes à rentrer dans les dossiers de mes patients.

La pensée de me retrouver face à Drew me suggère soudain que ma nausée alcoolisée n'est en réalité qu'un échauffement pour ce qui m'attend. En tournant à l'angle du couloir, je suis soulagée de constater que sa porte est fermée. La situation avec lui va être embarrassante, c'est inévitable, mais ce sera moins compliqué à gérer quand je me sentirai mieux. Repousser l'inévitable le plus loin possible m'apparaît comme la solution idéale, pour le moment.

À l'intérieur de mon bureau, j'accroche mon manteau au crochet derrière la porte et allume mon ordinateur portable. Ce n'est qu'une fois assise à mon bureau face à l'écran allumé de mon ordinateur fixe que je vois le message. C'est l'écriture de Drew.

En déposition toute la journée à Jersey. Ne serai pas rentré avant ce soir. Besoin que tu me rendes un service : monte à mon appartement, j'ai laissé un mot avec les instructions dans la cuisine. Loft Est. Carte-clé pour l'ascenseur et clé de la porte dans ton tiroir du haut. Merci, D.

Bizarre. J'essaie de m'installer et réponds à quelques mails, mais ma curiosité n'attendra pas beaucoup plus longtemps. Moins de cinq minutes plus tard, je ramasse les clés et la carte pour l'ascenseur et me dirige dans le hall. Pendant la montée, j'observe les néons comme à travers un brouillard. Je savais que Drew vivait dans l'immeuble, mais il n'avait jamais mentionné que son appartement était le loft. Qu'est-ce qu'il peut bien avoir besoin que je fasse chez lui ? Il a un chat ?

Les portes brillantes de l'ascenseur s'ouvrent dès qu'il arrive au dernier étage. Je sors, et il n'y a que deux portes sur le palier : LO et LE. Contrairement à chez moi, la clé tourne facilement dans la serrure du loft est. Drew m'a écrit qu'il ne serait pas rentré avant ce soir, pourtant je me sens obligée d'appeler sitôt que j'entrouvre sa porte.

– Coucou !… Coucou ? Il y a quelqu'un ?

Silence. Pas de petites créatures à poils pour m'accueillir à la porte non plus. Je la referme derrière moi et pars en quête de la cuisine.

Punaise !

L'appartement de Drew Jagger est inouï.

Bouche bée, je passe devant la cuisine rutilante, descends deux marches jusqu'au salon en contrebas et m'approche du mur de vitres. Des fenêtres du sol au plafond encadrent une vue sur Central Park qui aurait pu être tirée d'un film. Ayant admiré le paysage pendant quelques minutes, je me décolle de la fenêtre et retourne à la cuisine. Sur le plan de travail en granite se trouve effectivement un message :

Dans le couloir, première porte à droite.

Qu'est-ce que… ?

Il n'y a qu'un couloir. Je tends une paume moite vers la poignée de la porte indiquée. Pourquoi suis-je aussi stressée ?

Sans la moindre idée de ce qui m'attend, je pousse très, très lentement. Pour découvrir… une salle de bains vide ! J'ai toujours le morceau de papier à la main, alors je revérifie les instructions. « Première porte à droite. » Songeant qu'il a dû faire une erreur, je m'apprête à refermer la porte quand j'aperçois un post-it sur le miroir au-dessus du lavabo. J'allume et balaie soigneusement la pièce des yeux avant de lire. C'est une sacrée belle salle de bains. Plus grande que ma chambre. Je me tourne face à mon reflet et décolle le post-it.

Sac sur le comptoir. Avec des trucs de bain
pour fille. La télécommande pour les jets
de la baignoire est dans le sac aussi.
Joyeux anniversaire en retard. Bonne journée.
PS : ibuprofène dans l'armoire de toilette.

Inopinément, mes yeux se gonflent de larmes. Alors comme ça, le dur à cuire spécialisé dans la destruction des mariages a donc un cœur.

***

Ma peau commence à ressembler à celle d'un pruneau. Cela fait une vingtaine de minutes que je me suis endormie dans l'eau tranquille de mon bain en écoutant Norah Jones. Drew m'a choisi des sels de bain, du bain moussant à la lavande et deux petites bougies à la lavande aussi. La drôle de sensation que j'ai éprouvée à me déshabiller et à faire couler un bain dans un appartement étranger a vite disparu quand je suis entrée dans l'eau chaude.

Ça fait à présent plus de trente minutes que je me prélasse et l'eau commence à refroidir, mais je n'ai pas encore essayé les jets tourbillonnants. Je soulève la bonde quelques secondes, puis j'ajoute de l'eau brûlante pour remplir à nouveau la baignoire. Sur la petite télécommande, j'enfonce quelques touches et l'eau se met à bouillonner.

Hum, c'est paradisiaque.

J'augmente la pression des jets dans mon dos et place la plante de mon pied droit sur une sortie d'eau qui se trouve à l'autre bout, simulant un massage de pied.

Oui, ça fait vraiment l'effet d'un massage. C'était quand, la dernière fois où on m'a fait un vrai massage ? Où un homme m'a fait un massage ? Il y a longtemps. *Trop longtemps*. C'est probablement pour ça qu'en fermant les yeux afin de mieux en profiter, je me mets à penser à la sensation que me procurerait ce massage en d'autres endroits de mon corps…

Ce qui me ramène automatiquement à Drew.

Ce baiser.

Ce baiser.

Soupir : je ne me suis même pas rendu compte de la présence de Baldwin sur le palier et Drew m'a embrassée dans l'unique objectif de le rendre jaloux. Ça paraissait si réel, pourtant. Si ardent. La façon dont il s'est collé contre moi, si fort, dont il m'a enlacée, si étroitement. J'ai vraiment cru que c'était le désir qui animait son baiser. Et même si j'ai été surprise au départ, mon corps y a réagi immédiatement. Raison pour laquelle, en comprenant qu'il avait fait ça dans l'unique intention d'attiser la jalousie de Baldwin qui nous regardait, j'ai été envahie par un tas d'émotions contradictoires.

Aujourd'hui s'est ajouté un élément supplémentaire à ma confusion : il semblerait que je sois plus inquiète que les choses virent au bizarre entre Drew et moi que de ce que Baldwin a dû penser.

Vu qu'il occupe mes pensées, je décide d'envoyer un SMS à Drew. Je ne sais même pas s'il est du genre « textoteur », je ne l'ai jamais vu prêter attention à son téléphone autrement que pour y répondre.

Emerie : C'est probablement le plus
beau cadeau d'anniversaire de ma vie.
Merci.

Mon cœur pitoyable s'emballe quand les points de suspension s'affichent, indiquant qu'il est en train de rédiger sa réponse.

Drew : Un cadeau qui fait suite
à un autre, destiné à t'ouvrir les yeux,

et que tu m'as rendu.
Décidément, tu es facile à contenter.

En riant, j'ôte mon pied du jet pour sentir le bouillonnement entre mes jambes que j'écarte.

Emerie : C'était très mignon de ta part.
Cette baignoire est un vrai paradis.

Drew : Est ?
Tu m'écris de la baignoire, là ?

Emerie : Oui.

Drew : Tu ne peux pas me dire
des trucs pareils. Je suis en pleine
déposition, maintenant je vais avoir
toutes les peines du monde
à me concentrer, avec l'image
de toi nue dans ma baignoire.

J'entame ma réponse, avant de m'interrompre. Drew m'imagine nue. Ma peau se couvre de chair de poule, alors même que je suis engloutie par l'eau chaude. Je sais qu'il me taquine, n'empêche qu'il y a quelque chose d'excitant là-dedans et j'ai envie de jouer aussi.

Emerie : Tu aimes ce que
tu imagines ?

Drew : Je viens d'ajuster mon pantalon
sous la table. À ton avis ?

Mon avis… c'est que j'aime bien l'idée que Drew Jagger soit excité en pensant à moi. Mon corps réagit à ses messages de la même manière qu'il a réagi à son baiser hier soir. J'essaie de réfléchir à une réponse sexy, mais avant que quelque chose de spirituel me vienne à l'esprit, les points de suspension se remettent en action.

Drew : Comment ça s'est passé
avec le professeur Crétin,
après mon départ ?

À la mention de Baldwin, la même *autre* sensation que la veille me frappe à nouveau comme un seau d'eau glacée : en fait, Drew se comporte uniquement comme le type grossier qu'il est. Et pourtant, l'espace d'une minute, j'avais cru qu'il était sincère.

Emerie : Pas grand-chose à raconter.

Pour une raison que je ne m'explique pas, j'omets de lui préciser que Baldwin m'a demandé s'il pouvait m'inviter ce soir, histoire de se faire pardonner d'avoir annulé le rencard précédent.

Les messages de Drew me sont arrivés en rafale jusqu'à présent, mais là il reste silencieux plusieurs minutes. Jusqu'à ce que les pointillés s'agitent de nouveau.

Drew : Amuse-toi bien. Je dois
retourner à mon affaire.

Je ne reçois plus de message après celui-là. Je trempe encore quelques minutes dans mon bain, puis je retourne au bureau. Mes rendez-vous de l'après-midi se passent sans accroc et le reste de la journée aussi. Pendant que je continuais à mettre mes dossiers à jour, Baldwin m'a prévenue par message qu'il a pris une réservation pour dix-neuf heures dans un endroit dont je ne me risquerais pas à prononcer le nom, alors je quitte le bureau à dix-sept heures trente, afin de me rafraîchir avant le dîner.

Je change ma jupe et mon chemisier de travail pour une petite robe noire. Inutile de chercher sur Internet le restaurant où nous allons, je sais que ce sera un endroit chic. Contrairement à Drew, Baldwin ne fréquente pas les salles de billard underground, pas plus qu'il ne mange des burgers en provenance de chez *Joey*. Le plus drôle, c'est que je n'ai pas du tout envie d'aller dans un restaurant prétentieux, ce soir. En mettant mes boucles d'oreille en perle, je commence à m'en vouloir de faire semblant d'aimer aller dans ce genre d'endroits avec Baldwin. À dire vrai, je fais semblant d'apprécier les mêmes choses que lui, juste pour me donner des prétextes pour passer du temps avec lui.

Quand Baldwin frappe à ma porte à dix-neuf heures pile, je ne suis toujours pas redevenue moi-même. Mon enthousiasme habituel a été remplacé par l'agacement. Je suis agacée qu'il m'ait posé un lapin la veille au profit de la dernière nana qu'il a levée, et je suis agacée d'avoir fait mine d'apprécier des choses pour lui faire plaisir, quand lui n'a manifestement jamais fait aucun effort envers moi. J'ouvre la porte et l'invite à entrer le temps que j'attrape mon téléphone sur le chargeur et change de sac à main. Pendant que je suis dans la chambre, j'entends sonner un portable dans le salon et Baldwin y répondre.

J'écoute sa moitié de la conversation en revenant au salon.

– Sans doute vers vingt-trois heures.

Je me rends à la cuisine et ouvre le sac à main que j'avais pris au bureau aujourd'hui, entamant le transfert de quelques objets dans ma petite pochette noire.

– OK, oui. Il sera tard, mais on pourra en discuter à ce moment-là.

Je fais défiler mes messages pendant que Baldwin termine sa conversation. Un SMS de Drew est arrivé il y a une dizaine de minutes.

Drew : Suis sur le retour.
Tu es toujours au bureau ?
Je dois rédiger une motion en arrivant,
la nuit va être longue pour moi.
Je commande du chinois à livrer.
Tu veux quelque chose ?

Je commence à rédiger ma réponse quand Baldwin raccroche et me demande :

– Tu es prête ?

– Oui, oui.

Je saisis mon sac à main et vais décrocher mon manteau dans le placard. Baldwin, éternel gentleman, me le prend des mains et se place derrière moi pour m'aider à le passer.

– Tu dois travailler après le dîner ?

– Hum ?

– Ton coup de fil. Je t'ai entendu dire à quelqu'un que vous parleriez plus tard.

– Ah. C'était Rachel. On a tous les deux une sortie de travail à laquelle on doit assister ce week-end. Elle veut que je l'accompagne à la sienne après la mienne. Je lui ai dit qu'on en discuterait quand je vais rentrer ce soir.

La petite bulle de colère qui menaçait d'éclater finit par exploser en moi. Bizarrement, je ne suis pas vraiment en colère contre Baldwin. Je suis furieuse contre moi. Je me tourne face à lui.

– Tu sais quoi ? Je suis désolée de faire ça à la dernière minute, mais j'ai eu la migraine toute la journée et ça empire. Je crains de ne pas être de très bonne compagnie ce soir.

Baldwin est pris de court, il fronce les sourcils.

– Tu ne veux pas sortir dîner ?

– Pas ce soir. Désolée. On peut remettre à une autre fois ?

Je ne l'ai pas fait intentionnellement, mais sitôt les mots sortis de ma bouche, je me rends compte que j'ai utilisé les mêmes que lui quand il a annulé hier soir. « On peut remettre à une autre fois ? »

Quand il est parti, je me rappelle que je n'ai pas envoyé à Drew le SMS que j'avais commencé à taper. Mon doigt reste suspendu au-dessus de mon :

Suis déjà partie,
mais merci quand même.

Finalement, j'efface la phrase.

Et merde.

Je tape, sans me laisser le temps de réfléchir à deux fois.

Emerie : Je vais prendre
le porc moo shu.

CHAPITRE 21

DREW

– Eh bien, j'ai mal choisi ma journée pour m'absenter du bureau…

Emerie vient de retirer son manteau, pour révéler une petite robe noire moulante. Elle me sourit. *Waouh.* Hier soir, j'ai passé mon trajet retour en taxi à me convaincre que ce baiser, je le lui avais donné pour son bien. Pour l'aider. Et pas parce qu'elle est belle et intelligente et incapable de jouer au billard mais ne s'est pas pour autant plainte une seule fois quand je l'ai entraînée dans une salle de billard. Je l'ai fait parce que le professeur Crétin avait besoin d'être un peu motivé pour agir. Et j'ai presque fini par m'en persuader moi-même.

N'empêche, ça m'a rongé toute la journée. Et si j'avais enfin trouvé le courage d'agir et suscité par la même occasion l'envie de passer à l'acte chez lui ? Emerie a fondu pendant ce baiser, j'ai senti son corps s'abandonner à moi, entendu le petit gémissement qu'elle a émis. Bref, je sais qu'elle a ressenti la même chose que moi. Le moteur était démarré et prêt à rugir. *Pour ce connard.*

Ma motion aurait dû être bouclée en quatre heures, aujourd'hui. Pourtant elle m'a pris presque le double du temps à cause de mon manque de concentration. Et puis ce soir, j'ai appelé Yvette pour annuler le rencard qu'on avait fixé un mois plus tôt. *Yvette, l'hôtesse de l'air qui ne veut pas s'engager et me chante une délicieuse mélodie en me taillant une pipe.* Cette nana, c'est de l'or en barre pour un célibataire.

– J'étais censée sortir et j'ai eu un changement de programme, m'explique Emerie.

Je hoche la tête.

– Viens manger. Ton *moo shu* va refroidir.

Elle s'assied dans l'un des fauteuils en face du bureau.

– Ça fait beaucoup à manger, on attend quelqu'un ?

– Comme tu as mis un moment à répondre, j'ai commandé des trucs en plus au cas où tu serais encore là. Je ne savais pas trop si tu aimais le poulet, le bœuf ou les crevettes, du coup j'ai pris un peu de tout. Le type au bout du fil parlait à peine anglais. Quand j'ai rappelé pour ton porc, j'ai pensé qu'il serait plus simple de le faire ajouter à la commande existante au lieu de tout modifier. (Je lui fais passer une boîte sur le bureau.) Pas d'assiettes. Pas de fourchettes. J'espère que tu sais manger avec des baguettes.

– Je suis assez nulle, en fait.

Je désigne le plafond d'un geste du pouce.

– Tu peux monter chercher une fourchette là-haut dans mon appart, si tu veux. Mais moi, je n'ai rien mangé depuis six heures du matin, alors je te laisse faire.

En souriant, elle déchire l'emballage de ses baguettes.

– Je vais me débrouiller. Mais tu ne te moques pas, hein ?

Pas facile. Cette fille a deux baguettes gauches. Elle fait tomber plus de nourriture qu'elle n'arrive à s'en fourrer dans la bouche. Mais rapidement, nous mettons tous les deux en place un système tacite : chaque fois qu'elle laisser échapper un morceau de porc en chemin vers ses lèvres, je ricane et elle louche dans ma direction. C'est aussi amusant que de lui lancer des moqueries, et moitié moins fatigant.

– Alors, qu'est-ce qui s'est passé avec le professeur Crétin, la nuit dernière ?

Avec un soupir, elle se cale contre le dossier de son siège.

– Rien. Il m'a invitée à dîner ce soir pour se faire pardonner d'avoir annulé.

Je me fige, les baguettes à mi-chemin de ma bouche.

– Et il t'a encore posé un lapin ce soir ?

– Pas cette fois. C'est moi, qui lui en ai posé un.

J'enfourne une crevette.

– Bien joué. Égalité. Et ça t'a fait quel effet ?

Un sourire s'étire sur son beau visage.

– Super agréable, j'avoue.

– C'est donc pour ça que tu es sur ton trente-et-un ?

Elle hoche la tête.

– On était censés aller dans un restaurant chic pour mon dîner d'anniversaire en retard. Il est passé me chercher chez moi et je l'ai entendu parler à Rachel au téléphone, disant qu'il la rejoindrait après le dîner.

– Du coup tu as été jalouse et tu as annulé ?

– Pas exactement. J'étais agacée contre moi-même. Ça fait trois ans que je passe mon temps à accepter les miettes que m'offre un homme qui ne me verra jamais autrement que comme une amie ou une voisine. Je mérite mieux que ça.

– Tu as tout à fait raison.

Elle lâche un soupir.

– Il faut que je passe à autre chose.

Je saisis une crevette au bout de mes baguettes et la lui offre.

– Crevette ?

– OK, mais c'est toi qui me la mets dans la bouche, sinon tu vas avoir une traînée de sauce sur ton bureau, d'ici à ce que je réussisse à l'avaler.

Je hausse un sourcil.

– Je te la mets dans la bouche avec plaisir. Ouvre grand.

Elle éclate de rire.

– Tu es capable de tourner n'importe quel propos anodin en truc salace, y compris la remarque la plus innocente.

– C'est un don.

J'approche mon offrande et sa belle bouche s'ouvre afin que je puisse la nourrir. Quand ses lèvres se referment sur mes baguettes, je ressens leur effet directement autour de mon sexe. J'imagine mon érection à leur place, avalée par ses lèvres parfaitement maquillées. Le goût délicieux de la crevette atteint ses papilles et elle ferme les yeux pour mieux l'apprécier. À ce stade, j'ai besoin de rajuster ma braguette. Encore.

Je déglutis en la regardant déglutir.

– C'était quand, la dernière fois que tu as fait l'amour ?

Elle tousse, s'étranglant presque sur un morceau de crevette, cette fois.

– Pardon ?

– Tu m'as très bien entendu. Le sexe. C'était quand, la dernière fois ?

– Tu connais déjà mon histoire. Je n'ai pas eu de relation depuis presque un an.

– Tu parles de relation sexuelle ? Quand tu m'as dit ça, je pensais que tu parlais de fréquenter quelqu'un de manière récurrente.

– Ben non.

– Tu es au courant que toute relation ne doit pas forcément aller au-delà du sexe ?

– Bien sûr que je le sais. Mais j'ai besoin de plus qu'une aventure d'une nuit.

– Genre quoi ?

– Je ne sais pas. Quelque part dans un coin de ma tête, j'ai besoin de me sentir en sécurité avec mon partenaire. D'être attirée physiquement par lui. Il faut qu'on puisse s'entendre bien après l'acte et j'ai besoin de sentir qu'on ne profite pas de moi, que notre relation, quelle qu'elle soit, ne va pas que dans un sens. Si c'est juste du sexe, OK, mais il faut qu'on soit tous les deux d'accord sur ce point.

Je hoche la tête.

– Tout ça me semble logique.

À ce moment-là de la soirée, j'ai déjà plus ou moins perdu l'esprit. Ce qui explique sans doute comment la pensée suivante fait son chemin depuis mon cerveau et franchit directement mes lèvres.

– Et moi, je corresponds au profil ?

– Au profil ?

Elle a l'air vraiment perplexe. Pourtant, je croyais avoir été plutôt clair.

– De partenaire sexuel. Je pense qu'on devrait coucher ensemble.

CHAPITRE 22

EMERIE

– Tu es dingue !

– Parce que je pense qu'on devrait coucher ensemble ? En quoi est-ce que ça fait de moi un dingue ?

– Nous sommes à l'opposé. Tu estimes qu'une relation, c'est la période de temps que deux personnes passent ensemble avant qu'une des deux ne fasse une crasse à l'autre.

– Et alors ?

– Je crois dans l'amour et le mariage, dans la possibilité de faire en sorte que les choses marchent.

– Je ne parle pas de tout ça. Je te parle de sexe. Je sais que ça fait un moment, mais tu vois, c'est quand un homme et une femme…

Je le coupe.

– Je sais ce qu'est une relation sexuelle.

– Bien. Moi aussi. Alors ayons-en une ensemble.

– C'est n'importe quoi.

– Tu te sens en sécurité avec moi ?

– En sécurité ? Oui. Je pense. Je sais que tu ne laisserais rien de mal m'arriver.

– Tu es physiquement attirée par moi ?

– Tu sais bien que tu es bel homme.

– Et si nous nous mettions tous les deux d'accord sur le but de la relation ? Tu n'aurais pas l'impression que je profite de toi. (Drew incline sa chaise en arrière.) Conclusion : je corresponds à tes critères. (Il m'adresse une œillade.) En plus, j'ai une grande baignoire. Ce qui est un bonus. En y songeant, je devrais peut-être te faire passer un test. Je suis une sacrée bonne prise.

Je ne peux m'empêcher de rire face à autant d'absurdité.

– Tu vois. Encore un point bonus : je te fais rire.

Là, il n'a pas tort. Honnêtement, au cours des deux semaines écoulées, Drew Jagger a éveillé des tas de sensations en moi que je n'avais plus éprouvées depuis longtemps. Je me mords la lèvre. Mon estomac me fait l'impression d'être un sèche-linge à moitié rempli : ça bouge un peu dans tous les sens et ça s'échauffe. Je n'en reviens même pas d'être seulement en train de réfléchir à ce qu'il me suggère.

– C'était quand, la dernière fois où tu as couché avec une femme ?

– La veille de notre rencontre.

– Donc juste quelques semaines. Tu sortais avec elle ?

– Non. Je l'avais rencontrée pendant mes vacances à Hawaï.

– Vous avez pris le temps de faire connaissance, avant de coucher ensemble ?

Ne me demandez pas pourquoi je lui pose la question, je n'en sais rien du tout. Drew repose sa boîte de nourriture sur la table.

– Elle m'a taillé une pipe dans les toilettes moins d'une demi-heure après qu'on s'est rencontrés au bar du restaurant.

Je plisse le nez.

– Quoi ? Tu préfères que je te mente ?

– Non, sans doute pas. Cela dit, j'aurais préféré que ce ne soit pas ta réponse.

Il hoche la tête.

– Tu voulais croire qu'il y avait eu une amourette dans un décor romantique. Bref, que c'était plus que ça n'était. Non, c'était juste du sexe entre deux adultes consentants. Il n'y a pas toujours besoin de plus.

Je finis mon plat chinois et me cale contre mon dossier, croisant les mains sur mon ventre plein.

– C'est très tentant… (Je lui adresse un large sourire.) Surtout à cause de ta baignoire. Mais je ne pense pas que ce soit une bonne idée. On passe trop de temps ensemble pour que ça reste purement sexuel.

Drew porte un pouce à sa bouche et il frotte sa lèvre inférieure si sensuelle.

– Je pourrais te mettre dehors.

– Et du coup, je mourrais d'envie de coucher avec toi. Parce que rien ne me met plus d'humeur coquine que de me faire jeter à la rue, je le taquine.

Drew contourne le bureau pour prendre ma boîte vide et, avec la sienne, tout jeter à la poubelle. Une fois l'opération effectuée, je le sens venir se poster derrière moi. Il se penche, tête par-dessus mon épaule, et son souffle me chatouille le cou quand il parle.

– Si tu changes d'avis, tu sais où me trouver.

Même si je n'ai pas très envie de me retrouver seule, peu après que nous avons terminé notre repas, je lui annonce que je dois rentrer chez moi pour travailler. Son SMS, plus tôt, disait qu'il avait des heures de travail qui l'attendaient en rentrant au bureau et je ne souhaite pas l'en détourner. En plus, j'ai besoin de temps pour digérer notre discussion de ce soir. Si bizarre que soit sa proposition, je mentirais si je ne reconnaissais pas que l'idée d'avoir une relation sexuelle avec Drew est très attrayante.

***

Au cours des jours suivants, les choses reviennent à la normale entre Drew et moi au bureau. Par normale, j'entends qu'il se moque des conseils qu'il m'entend prodiguer à mes patients, et que je lui suggère d'aller voir ailleurs s'il n'y retrouverait pas son éthique après avoir surpris certaines suggestions qu'il fait à ses clients. Avec

Baldwin, la tension reste palpable. Je l'ai entendu ouvrir et refermer sa porte hier matin, puis il a frappé à la mienne, à quoi j'ai réagi de façon très mature en faisant semblant que je n'étais pas à la maison.

J'ignore pourquoi je l'évite, il n'a rien fait de mal, au fond. Du coup, le lendemain, quand il frappe de nouveau, je prends une profonde inspiration et je me montre plus mûre.

– Je m'inquiétais pour toi, me dit-il.

– Ah bon ? Je ne voulais pas te donner de soucis, j'étais juste très occupée au travail.

– Ce qui est une bonne nouvelle, je suppose. Je suis content que les choses tournent comme tu le projetais en emménageant ici.

Pas toutes les choses, mais bref.

– Oui, je suis ravie de la manière dont évolue mon cabinet.

– Tu es libre pour le petit déjeuner ? J'aurais bien aimé que nous parlions un peu. Histoire de se mettre à jour sur tout ce qui se passe.

Je suis libre, mais je lui mens. Baissant les yeux vers ma montre, je constate qu'il est sept heures trente.

– En fait, j'ai une séance de conseil à huit heures trente. Et je n'ai pas fini de me préparer.

– À dîner alors ?

– Ma journée est complètement bouclée, je lui réponds avec un pauvre sourire. Je vais travailler tard à transférer mes notes dans mes dossiers électroniques.

Baldwin fronce les sourcils.

– Déjeunons. On peut manger à ton bureau, si tu préfères.

Il ne va pas me lâcher tant que je n'aurai pas dit « oui ».

– Euh… d'accord.

Une fois qu'il est parti, je me ravise quant au fait qu'il vienne au bureau pour déjeuner et lui envoie un SMS pour qu'on se rejoigne dans un restaurant pas loin. Non que mettre Drew mal à l'aise ou quoi que ce soit me tracasse, mais qui sait ce qui peut sortir de la bouche de cet homme…

***

Ce n'est pas ce que l'on dit qui compte,
c'est la manière dont on le dit.
Aujourd'hui, j'aimerais te dire ____________
et te montrer que je le pense.

Ayant inscrit ma citation quotidienne sur mon ardoise, je la tape sur mon site web et puis j'entreprends de passer mes dossiers en revue. Mon planning est totalement rempli cet après-midi par des séances de thérapie, et je veux être préparée au cas où je rentrerais tard de mon déjeuner. Baldwin m'a envoyé un SMS pour m'annoncer qu'il avait réservé au *Seventh Street Café*, un restaurant du type nappe et serviettes en tissu où ils mettront peut-être un certain temps à préparer leurs plats élaborés. Ils ne font pas dans le hamburger, là-bas. Ils servent du bœuf de Kobe aux graines de fenouil cuit à la graisse de canard fermier ; bref, des intitulés exotiques sur le menu, qui servent à justifier les plats à vingt-cinq dollars.

Une demi-heure avant le déjeuner, je suis surprise de voir Baldwin débarquer au bureau au lieu de me retrouver au restaurant, comme convenu.

– Je croyais qu'on avait rendez-vous au *Seventh Street Café* ?

– Comme j'étais dans le quartier, je me suis dit que j'allais passer te prendre sur le chemin.

Je l'invite à me suivre dans mon bureau, où je vais chercher mon manteau et éteindre mon ordinateur portable. Drew a passé toute la matinée en conférence téléphonique et, comme de bien entendu, il termine pile à ce moment. Il entre dans mon bureau, sans savoir que j'ai de la visite.

– De quoi tu as envie ? Je pensais à un hot-dog. Ça te dit de marcher jusqu'à… (Il se fige sur place en voyant Baldwin.) Je n'avais pas vu que tu avais de la compagnie.

Je remarque la légère crispation de sa mâchoire. Décidément, il n'est pas fan de Baldwin. Bien entendu, celui-ci ne sert pas sa propre cause quand il réplique sur un ton narquois :

– Oui, on a rendez-vous pour le déjeuner dans un endroit où on sert de la vraie nourriture.

Drew me regarde et ses yeux me transmettent le message qu'il n'exprime pas tout haut. Puis il fait demi-tour et regagne son bureau, non sans avoir lancé par-dessus son épaule :

– Profitez bien de votre « vraie nourriture ».

Je suis presque sortie du bureau quand Baldwin remarque ma citation du jour. Il se tourne vers moi.

– Tes clients apprécient ce genre de choses ?

Je suis aussitôt sur la défensive.

– Oui. J'inscris la même citation quotidienne sur mon site, où les gens se connectent et se déconnectent pour les séances de conseil vidéo. Offrir une phrase inspirante et une suggestion pour qu'ils donnent plus à leur relation, c'est un plus pour mes séances.

– Sans doute, mais cela dépend de ce que tu leur suggères.

Je ne comprends pas bien ce qui ne lui plaît pas là-dedans, car cette idée de citations quotidiennes, je la tiens de ses TD à la fac. Alors, qu'est-ce qui peut bien le perturber dans le fait que je l'utilise ?

En franchissant ma porte, je m'arrête pour relire ma citation.

Drew.

Je vais le tuer.

Il l'a modifiée.

Encore.

J'avais inscrit :

Ce n'est pas ce que l'on dit qui compte,
c'est la manière dont on le dit.

Aujourd'hui, j'aimerais te dire ____________
et te montrer que je le pense.

Il a dû la changer pendant que la porte était fermée, car désormais on peut lire :

Ce n'est pas ce que l'on fait qui compte,
c'est la manière dont on le fait.
Aujourd'hui, j'aimerais te faire jouir.
Et je le pense vraiment.

CHAPITRE 23

EMERIE

– J'ai un cadeau d'anniversaire en retard, m'annonce Baldwin, tandis qu'on attend dans l'entrée du restaurant que la serveuse ait fini d'installer les clients devant nous.

– Ah bon ?

Tout sourire, il opine du chef.

– Tu as un entretien pour un poste de vacataire dans deux semaines. C'est seulement pour enseigner à une classe, mais ça te permettra de mettre un pied à l'université.

– Oh, là, là, Baldwin ! (Sans réfléchir, je me jette à son cou et lui fais un câlin géant.) Merci beaucoup. C'est le… (Je m'apprêtais à dire « meilleur cadeau que j'aurais pu demander cette année », mais je me rappelle celui de Drew et me corrige :) C'est génial. Merci beaucoup.

L'hôtesse d'accueil revient nous placer et nous passons l'heure qui suit à discuter du travail et du professeur qui va me faire passer mon entretien. C'est agréable de reprendre contact avec Baldwin, j'apprécie vraiment sa compagnie. Je me suis rendu compte, le mois écoulé, que la frustration causée par mes sentiments pour lui a commencé à dégrader notre relation. Il est temps que je passe à autre chose et que j'apprécie ce que nous partageons à sa juste valeur.

Une fois le repas terminé, le serveur débarrasse et Baldwin commande un expresso. Il croise les mains sur la table et détourne la conversation du sujet « travail ».

– Alors tu fréquentes l'avocat dont tu partages l'espace de bureau ?

– Non. Ce baiser auquel tu as assisté, c'était le résultat d'un excès de *margaritas*.

Baldwin fronce les sourcils, mais il hoche la tête.

– Bon, tant mieux. Je ne suis pas sûr qu'il soit le genre de personne à qui il faut trop s'attacher.

– C'est-à-dire ?

OK, je suis furax contre Drew et je prévois de lui botter les fesses dès mon retour au bureau, mais Baldwin n'a pas le droit de le critiquer alors qu'il ne le connaît même pas.

– Il a l'air… Je ne sais pas. Maladroit.

– Il est direct. Oui. Et parfois même un peu lourd. Mais il est plutôt attentionné, une fois qu'on le connaît.

Baldwin scrute mon visage.

– En tout cas, je suis content qu'il n'y ait rien entre vous. Je suis protecteur envers toi. Tu le sais.

C'est marrant, ces derniers temps, c'est plutôt Drew qui m'a donné l'impression d'avoir été protecteur envers moi.

***

La porte de Drew est close quand je retourne au bureau. J'écoute afin de m'assurer qu'il n'est pas en ligne, puis je l'ouvre d'un coup sec.

– Tu es vraiment un gros con !

– Oui, on me l'a dit. Comment s'est passé ton déjeuner avec le professeur Pompeux ?

– C'était délicieux. (Je mens, mon burger sophistiqué n'était pas si bon que ça.) Baldwin a lu ce que tu as écrit sur mon ardoise. Il faut que tu arrêtes de te foutre de moi.

Il m'adresse un large sourire.

– Mais c'est si drôle de me moquer de toi. Et comme tu refuses de me laisser te faire jouir, il faut bien que je compense d'une autre manière.

– Maintenant, il doit penser que je n'ai pas une attitude professionnelle avec mes patients.

Drew hausse les épaules.

– Pourquoi tu ne lui as pas dit que c'était ma prose ?

– Déjà qu'il ne t'aime pas trop. Je n'ai pas voulu empirer ton cas.

– Je me fous complètement de son opinion à mon sujet. Pourquoi ça t'importe, ce qu'il peut bien penser de moi ?

Excellente question. Dont je n'ai pas la réponse.

– Ça m'importe, c'est tout.

Il me dévisage. Et puis il se met à frotter de son pouce sa fichue lèvre inférieure si alléchante.

– Tu veux savoir ce que je pense ?

– J'ai le choix ?

Drew contourne son bureau et vient appuyer une hanche contre l'avant.

– Je pense que tu m'aimes bien. C'est pour ça que l'opinion de ce connard t'importe.

– Là, tout de suite, je ne t'aime pas bien du tout.

Son regard tombe sur ma poitrine.

– Une partie de toi m'aime bien, pourtant.

Je baisse les yeux à mon tour, pour découvrir mes tétons durs et pointés. Bon sang, ils percent presque la soie de mon chemisier, ces imbéciles. *Les traîtres.*

Je croise les bras.

– Il fait froid, ici.

Drew se redresse et avance encore de quelques pas vers moi.

– Il ne fait pas froid du tout. Au contraire, je trouve qu'il fait assez chaud.

Il attrape le nœud de sa cravate et le desserre.

Merde, pourquoi est-ce que je trouve ça sexy ?

Mon cœur bat comme un fou dans ma poitrine.

Il s'approche d'un pas supplémentaire. Il ne doit plus y avoir qu'une cinquantaine de centimètres entre nous, à présent.

– Je pense que ton corps m'apprécie et que ta tête lutte contre cette attirance. Or ils devraient régler ça de manière adulte : en te mettant nue dans une chambre avec moi.

– Et moi, je pense que tu es fou. Or je suis psychologue, donc mon diagnostic est sans doute plus conforme à la vérité.

Il fait encore un pas.

– Donc si je remontais ta jupe et que je glissais une main entre tes cuisses, tu ne serais pas mouillée ?

Ma peau s'échauffe, sans que je sache si c'est dû aux paroles de Drew ou au besoin que j'éprouve de les voir mises à exécution. Je n'arrive plus à le regarder dans les yeux, pourtant je suis tout aussi incapable de m'en aller. Je garde le regard planté droit devant, et comme il est bien plus grand que moi, je contemple son torse qui se soulève et redescend. Chaque respiration est plus profonde, et la mienne se cale sur son rythme.

– Regarde-moi, Emerie.

Sa voix est grave et pleine d'assurance. Il attend que mon regard rejoigne le sien avant de franchir l'espace qui nous séparait encore d'un seul petit pas.

– Tu as trois secondes pour sortir de mon bureau. Autrement, tu me donnes la permission de faire de toi ce que je veux.

Je déglutis. D'une voix étranglée, les yeux toujours plantés dans les siens, je lâche :

– Je suis venue te crier dessus.

– J'aime bien quand tu es en colère. (Il marque une pause.) Un.

– Tu aimes quand je suis en colère ?

– J'ai découvert que ça m'excitait. Deux.

– Tu ne feras rien à trois, si je te dis d'arrêter.

Encore quelques centimètres vers moi.

– Bien sûr que non. Tu me fais confiance. Mais tu ne me demanderas pas d'arrêter. (Nouvelle pause.) Dernière chance.

Je reste pétrifiée tandis qu'il prononce le dernier chiffre.

– Trois.

Avant que j'aie pu objecter, la bouche de Drew s'écrase sur la mienne. Sa lèvre inférieure est si douce et si pleine, elle est parfaite. Ça fait des semaines que je l'observe et soudain ce zieutage intensif prend le contrôle de mon cerveau. Je l'attrape par la cravate et l'attire encore plus près tout en suçotant sa lèvre inférieure de rêve. Il répond par un grognement et passe les deux bras derrière moi, pour saisir mes fesses à pleines mains et me soulever du sol.

Ma jupe se retrousse quand je noue les jambes autour de sa taille. Il avance ainsi de quelques pas, jusqu'à ce que mon dos cogne contre le mur, puis il m'y plaque de son bassin afin de libérer ses mains.

Merde, il connaît tous les trucs. Sa bouche descend dans mon cou, qu'il suce, et j'entends le sifflement de sa ceinture quand il la sort des passants de son pantalon d'un geste sec.

Ce bruit.

Si puissant et pressé. Si je n'étais pas déjà trempée, je le serais, après avoir entendu ce bruit.

– Tu as des rendez-vous prévus, aujourd'hui ?

– Non. Juste des séances vidéo. Et toi ?

– Tant mieux.

Il attrape mon chemisier, une main de chaque côté, et tire un coup sec. Les boutons de nacre s'éparpillent au sol. Du pouce, il écarte un bonnet de mon soutien-gorge et se penche pour aspirer un téton dans sa bouche. *Fort.*

– Oh oui…

Je cambre le dos. Ça fait mal, pourtant j'en veux plus. J'essaie de saisir son pantalon, seulement en raison de la manière dont il me tient prisonnière, je n'y arrive pas. J'ai besoin de m'agripper à quelque chose. Alors j'enfonce mes doigts dans ses cheveux et je tire tandis qu'il augmente ses succions. Jamais de ma vie je n'ai ressenti pareil désir. C'est si puissant que j'ai envie de lui infliger une forme de douleur. Ce qui ne me ressemble absolument pas. J'aime le sexe en douceur, tendre. Là, c'est du besoin à l'état pur, un désir sauvage et charnel.

Mon corps est à vif, tellement palpitant et avide de jouir que je manque de perdre les pédales quand sa main glisse entre mes jambes pour écarter ma culotte. Il lâche un grognement en rencontrant mon humidité.

– Je savais que tu étais trempée.

Il insère deux doigts en moi et, à mon tour, j'émets un gémissement bruyant.

Ça fait trop longtemps.

Bien trop longtemps. S'il ne ralentit pas, je vais jouir.

– Drew…, je souffle, en guise de mise en garde. Doucement.

– Pas question, grommelle-t-il. Je ralentirai après t'avoir regardée jouir sur mes doigts. Je prendrai tout mon temps pour lécher chaque goutte du miel écoulé de ta petite chatte étroite. En attendant, je ne compte pas y aller doucement.

Il effectue des va-et-vient avec ses doigts, puis il en replie un pour stimuler pile la bonne zone et ça me rend complètement folle de plaisir. Je jouis dans un grognement, même pas gênée qu'il ait mis moins de cinq minutes à m'emmener au sommet.

– Oh merde, Emerie. C'est le truc le plus sexy que j'aie jamais vu.

Je suis sur le point de lui suggérer de faire en sorte que ça recommence, quand une voix résonne à travers le couloir.

– UPS. Drew Jagger, c'est bien ici ?

***

Drew a quelques chemises de rechange accrochées au dos de la porte de son bureau. J'en enfile une pendant qu'il va à la rencontre du livreur d'UPS. On est d'abord restés immobiles et muets, en espérant qu'il s'en aille, mais il avait dû entendre du bruit, parce qu'il se dirigeait vers nos bureaux, ce qui a obligé Drew à partir à sa rencontre à contrecœur.

Voilà comment je me retrouve à boutonner frénétiquement une chemise d'homme dix tailles trop grande pour moi afin de me couvrir, comme si Drew risquait de ramener le gars d'UPS ici pour dire « bonjour ». Il y a deux minutes, j'étais tout là-haut, là-haut, du coup la chute est d'autant plus rude. *Qu'est-ce que je suis en train de faire ?*

OK, Drew est sexy et je suis physiquement attirée par lui. Impossible de le nier. Mais c'est une erreur. Lui et moi, nous avons des attentes différentes. Le fait que j'apprécie sa compagnie et que je passe toutes mes journées avec lui rendrait difficile de séparer le sexe et les sentiments. Il est comme une drogue : je sais que je ne devrais pas, seulement l'addiction est prompte à me saisir.

J'en suis au bouton du bas quand il revient dans le bureau.

– Le livreur d'UPS pense m'avoir interrompu en pleine séance de masturbation.

– Quoi ? Pourquoi ?

– Il avait un paquet pour toi et m'a demandé si tu étais là. Je ne voulais pas qu'il exige que tu le signes, alors j'ai répondu que non, que j'étais seul ici aujourd'hui.

– Et alors ? Comment il en serait arrivé à la conclusion que tu te masturbais ?

– Quand il m'a tendu sa tablette électronique afin que j'appose ma signature, j'ai remarqué son regard braqué là.

Il désigne son bas-ventre. Il a en effet un énorme renflement, on distingue même les contours de son érection à travers son pantalon. Sans compter que sa braguette est ouverte et qu'un pan de sa chemise s'en échappe.

Je porte une main à ma bouche pour pouffer.

– Oh non !

Puis je jette un second coup d'œil à son entre-jambe.

Oh non… Le sexe de Drew est si large, si long qu'on le croirait armé d'une batte de base-ball.

Le temps a dû m'échapper pendant mon observation, car je l'entends qui ricane.

– Arrête de le regarder comme ça, sinon je n'aurai pas la patience de te laisser prendre ton temps pour l'introduire petit à petit dans ta bouche quand tu me suceras, tout à l'heure.

Bon sang, ce qu'il peut être vulgaire.

Bon sang, ce que j'ai envie de le sucer.

Je secoue la tête et m'oblige à relever les yeux vers son visage. Dans ses prunelles danse une lueur amusée.

– Tu as besoin de quelque chose, avant qu'on monte à l'étage ?

– À l'étage ?

– Chez moi. Je veux m'assurer que nous ne soyons pas interrompus, la première fois où je plongerai en toi.

– Mais… je ne pense pas…

Il me fait taire avant que je puisse terminer ma phrase, en plaquant ses lèvres sur les miennes. Quand nous reprenons notre respiration, j'en ai la tête qui tourne. Il me regarde droit dans les yeux.

– Ne pense pas. Pas aujourd'hui. Tu penseras demain. Si tu préfères que ça reste une seule fois, je l'accepterai. Mais aujourd'hui, on va le faire.

Mon cerveau hurle « non », mais ma tête dit oui.

Il sourit.

– OK ?

– OK.

Il fourre la main dans sa poche et en tire ses clés.

– Prends ton ordinateur et ton téléphone portable. Monte chez moi et annule tout ce que tu as prévu pour le reste de la journée. Je vais en faire autant et je te rejoins dans un quart d'heure.

– Pourquoi est-ce qu'on ne peut pas le faire tous les deux ici ?

– Parce que j'ai une érection de malade et que te voir dans ma chemise ne va pas me calmer. C'est déjà assez difficile de t'avoir vue jouir, t'abandonner à moi comme ça, l'image va rester gravée sur ma rétine. Je dois reprendre un minimum de contrôle, sinon je vais me ridiculiser.

– Oh.

Il m'adresse un large sourire.

– Ouais, « oh ». (Il dépose un chaste baiser sur mes lèvres et me chasse d'une tape sur les fesses.) File.

CHAPITRE 24

EMERIE

Je n'ai rien de sexy à mettre, alors je fais avec les moyens du bord. Je repousse mes appels professionnels, le temps de recoiffer d'abord mes cheveux ébouriffés et de retoucher mon maquillage. Coup de chance, je porte un joli soutien-gorge en dentelle noire et un string assorti. J'ôte donc ma jupe et choisis d'attendre Drew seulement dans sa chemise, que je déboutonne un peu pour révéler la dentelle de mon dessous. Satisfaite du résultat, je me rends au salon pour ouvrir mon agenda sur mon ordinateur et j'entreprends d'annuler mes patients de l'après-midi.

Je suis devant la fenêtre, au milieu de mon dernier appel, quand j'entends du bruit à la porte d'entrée. Le calme dans lequel j'ai réussi à me glisser pendant que je travaillais à reprogrammer mes patients disparaît aussitôt, avec l'arrivée d'une nuée de papillons au creux de mon ventre.

Tess McArdle est en train de me relater son récent rendez-vous médical, sans rapport avec notre thérapie, et je juge préférable de ne pas me tourner vers Drew. J'ai déjà bien assez de mal à prendre ma part dans l'échange, maintenant que la serrure a tourné.

En revanche, je n'arrive pas à détacher le regard du reflet de Drew dans la vitre. Il dépose ses clés sur la console, vide ses poches, sort ce que je soupçonne être un préservatif de son portefeuille et vient se poster derrière moi. Sans jamais lâcher la vitre des yeux pendant tout ce temps.

Je bataille pour me débarrasser de madame McArdle, mais elle ne saisit pas mes insinuations. Drew est assez proche maintenant pour que je sente dans mon dos la chaleur émanant de son corps, pourtant il ne me touche pas. Au lieu de quoi, il commence à se déshabiller.

D'abord la chemise. Son torse sculpté est magnifique. Je vois chaque ligne ciselée de ses abdominaux. S'il est si beau dans le reflet de la vitre, je n'ose même pas imaginer comme il doit être follement sexy quand on le regarde en direct.

C'est ensuite le tour des chaussures et des chaussettes. Et puis… le pantalon. Mes yeux sont rivés aux mouvements de ses doigts tandis qu'il baisse rapidement la braguette. Son pantalon fluide tombe au sol. Il fait un pas de côté et s'en débarrasse d'un coup de pied. Je retiens mon souffle quand il porte les mains à la ceinture de son boxer et je lâche un halètement audible lorsqu'il le descend d'un geste sec.

– Emerie ? Vous êtes là ? Tout va bien ?

Merde. Merde. Ça fait une bonne minute que je n'ai pas écouté un mot de ce que me raconte madame McArdle, et elle m'a entendue hoqueter.

– Oui, pardon madame McArdle, je lui réponds, au comble du trouble. Une… une araignée géante vient de grimper sur mon bureau et m'a fait sursauter.

Drew sourit, narquois, dans le reflet. Il s'amuse comme un petit fou. Peut-être même un peu trop. Il prend son érection dans son poing et commence à se caresser tout en me fixant des yeux.

– Madame McArdle, je suis navrée. Je dois vraiment filer. J'attends quelqu'un d'un instant à l'autre.

Drew se penche pour m'embrasser dans le cou, tout en chuchotant dans mon oreille, celle qui n'est pas déjà collée à l'appareil :

– Ah oui ? Tu m'attends ?

Il passe une main sous ma chemise et me serre les fesses à pleines mains.

– Je vais te prendre là, contre cette fenêtre.

Je serre les cuisses, ce qui ne change en rien les pulsations entre mes jambes. Quand la main qu'il a sur mes fesses se déplace vers mon entrejambe et qu'il recueille mon humidité pour la déposer entre mes fesses, mes jambes se mettent à trembler. Il ne prévoit quand même pas d'enfoncer ce truc à cet endroit ? Je n'ai jamais fait ça et ne suis pas certaine d'avoir envie de commencer avec lui, tant son érection est impressionnante.

Il continue son massage et à étaler mon suc partout. Quand enfin je réussis à raccrocher d'avec madame McArdle, je suis plus lubrifiée que lorsque je me caresse moi-même et que j'utilise du vrai lubrifiant.

Je lâche mon portable au sol, peu m'importe s'il se casse, et m'appuie contre Drew tandis qu'il insinue deux doigts en moi.

– Tellement mouillée, tellement prête.

Sa voix est rauque, gutturale, si sexy qu'elle pourrait suffire à me faire jouir. Ses mots. Le ton. Sa manière de ne pas demander, mais de m'annoncer ce qu'il va me faire.

– J'adore ton corps.

J'adore les sensations qu'il me donne.

– Les gens… les gens peuvent voir à l'intérieur ?

Mes paroles sont à peine cohérentes, mais quand je me force à rouvrir les yeux, je vois des passants dans la rue. OK, ils sont loin, mais n'empêche.

Drew continue le va-et-vient de ses doigts en moi.

– C'est important ? S'il y avait la moindre chance qu'on nous voie, est-ce que tu me demanderais d'arrêter sur-le-champ ?

La réponse que je lui fais est honnête.

– Non.

Non, je ne lui demanderais pas d'arrêter si nous avions un public entier pour nous observer, prêt à lever le carton sur lequel il aurait affiché la note de notre prestation. Je suis beaucoup trop excitée pour ça.

– Bien.

Ses doigts quittent momentanément mon intimité et, avant que j'aie compris ce qui m'arrive, il m'arrache ma chemise. Enfin, pour être exacte, ce sont les boutons de sa chemise qui cognent contre la vitre.

– Tu as quelque chose contre les boutons ?

– J'ai quelque chose contre le fait que tu portes des vêtements.

Je ne sais comment, il parvient à me retirer sa chemise, mon soutien-gorge et ma culotte en un temps record. Et soudain mon corps chaud se retrouve collé contre le verre froid.

– Il se peut qu'on te voie, d'en bas. (Il glisse une main entre mes seins et la vitre et me pince un téton.) Il y a peut-être un homme, dans ces immeubles, là-bas. (Du menton, il désigne les bâtiments en bord de parc, qui sont légèrement de biais.) Il nous observe aux jumelles tout en se caressant, il s'imagine qu'il est devant toi pendant que moi, je te prends par-derrière.

– Oh…

La fenêtre est si froide, et mon corps est en feu.

Drew me lèche l'épaule, remonte vers mon cou, pour atteindre mon oreille.

– Écarte les jambes pour moi, Em.

À ce stade, j'aurais sauté par la fenêtre s'il m'en avait donné l'ordre. J'écarte donc les jambes et Drew me passe un bras autour de la taille, cambre mes fesses vers lui en m'obligeant à arquer le dos tandis que mes seins restent collés au verre. Puis il saisit son sexe, enfile le préservatif et plie légèrement les jambes afin de s'insinuer doucement en moi.

Il entre et sort à quelques reprises, chaque assaut allant un peu plus loin, jusqu'à ce qu'il soit entièrement fiché en moi. Jamais je n'ai été avec un homme aussi solidement constitué, chacun de ses passages caresse mes parois internes, force mon corps à l'envelopper comme un gant.

– Oh putain, c'est si bon d'être en toi. Tu es très étroite, tu me serres si fort. Tu veux que je te remplisse, hein ? Tu veux aspirer tout mon sperme.

Oh, là, là, j'adore quand il me parle comme ça. Dans un gémissement, je me pousse contre lui pour le prendre plus profondément encore.

– Oui, Drew. Oui, encore.

L'appartement est plongé dans le silence, à l'exception du son de nos peaux humides qui entrent en contact. Les claquements semblent tourner tels des échos tout autour de nous. Ce son exquis doit l'exciter autant que moi, car Drew se met à m'assaillir de plus belle. Plus fort, plus profond. Chacun des grognements qu'il émet avec ses coups de boutoir m'envoie plus près du précipice. J'avais fermé les yeux pour mieux me perdre dans le plaisir de mon corps, mais quand je les rouvre, ils sont aussitôt happés par ceux de Drew dans le reflet. Ce lien me fait basculer. Je jouis longuement et intensément, sans jamais rompre le contact visuel avec lui malgré mes gémissements.

– Putain ce que tu es belle.

Et dans un dernier assaut, tout au fond de moi, je sens une pulsation chaude, tandis qu'il me répète encore et encore combien je suis belle.

Après quoi il ralentit jusqu'à une cadence alanguie, avant de se retirer pour se débarrasser du préservatif. Quand il revient, je suis toujours collée à la fenêtre et il me surprend en me soulevant dans ses bras.

– Qu'est-ce que tu fais ?

– Je t'emmène au lit.

Je pose la tête contre son épaule.

– Je suis épuisée.

Il m'adresse un sourire canaille.

– Je ne parle pas de dormir. Je parle de te prendre avec la manière, la prochaine fois.

– Avec la manière ? je croasse.

– Oui. J'ai besoin d'une dizaine de minutes, mais j'ai hâte de prendre tout mon temps et de contempler ton visage quand tu jouiras dans mon lit.

– Dix minutes ?

Pour ma part, j'aurais plutôt besoin de quelques heures.

Drew s'esclaffe et me dépose un baiser sur le front.

– On prendra un bain après le deuxième round. Ça te dit ?

Et comment.

– Tu vas me priver de bain, si je suis trop fatiguée pour le deuxième round ?

– Ne t'inquiète pas. Je ferai tout le travail. Tu n'auras qu'à rester allongée à profiter de ma langue, en rêvant à la baignoire.

– Et à penser que j'avais dit « non » à tout ça, pas plus tard qu'hier.

– C'était la dernière fois que tu me disais « non ».

– Ah oui ?

– Oh que oui. Maintenant que je sais comme c'est bon, toi et moi, tu pourras toujours dire « non », je ne te croirai pas.

***

– Je t'ai laissé une marque.

Drew prend de l'eau chaude dans ses paumes et la laisse tomber en grosses gouttes sur mon téton érigé. Je suis bien installée entre ses jambes et nous trempons tous les deux dans le bain.

– Où ?

– Là.

Il désigne une trace rouge sur mon sein que je n'avais pas remarquée.

– Pas grave. Il y a peu de chances que quelqu'un la voie.

Il se raidit.

– Peu de chances ?

– J'entends par là qu'elle sera couverte par mon soutien-gorge, donc même si je me déshabille devant quelqu'un, genre dans une cabine d'essayage ou chez le docteur, elle ne se verra probablement pas.

– Tu ne prévois donc pas de coucher avec quelqu'un d'autre avant qu'elle disparaisse ?

J'incline la tête pour lever les yeux vers lui.

– C'est plus qu'une histoire d'une nuit ?

Il fouille mon regard.

– Oui.

– OK, alors non, personne ne verra ma peau marquée. Pas besoin de te tracasser pour ça.

Sa mâchoire se détend.

– Bien. Parce que ce n'est pas la seule marque que j'ai laissée.

– Quoi ? Où encore ?

– Ici. (Il touche ma clavicule.) Ici. (Il montre un point juste sous mon oreille.) Et je suis à peu près sûr que tu vas en trouver quelques-unes à l'intérieur de tes cuisses.

J'éclate de rire.

– Celles-là, elles ne me dérangent pas du tout. Mais tu ne peux pas me faire des suçons dans le cou, où mes patients risquent de les voir. La plupart d'entre eux traversent une période difficile dans leur relation, je n'ai pas envie de leur infliger la preuve que moi, je passe du bon temps la nuit.

– Promis. Je limiterai mon marquage à tes seins, tes cuisses, ta chatte et ton joli cul.

– Tu sais que tu es un grossier personnage ?

Il me pince un téton.

– Tu ne semblais pas t'en offusquer quand j'étais en toi.

– Oui, eh bien…

Je n'ai rien à répondre, vu qu'il a raison. Je sens mes joues s'échauffer. Drew ricane.

– Tu t'es assise sur mon visage, et le fait que je dise « chatte » et « cul » te fait rougir ?

– La ferme.

Je l'éclabousse.

Il actionne les jets et je me détends dans ses bras, profitant du massage de l'eau. Le bruit des tourbillons est sourd, il a sur moi un effet calmant. Pourtant, j'ai quelque chose en tête depuis une heure et je n'arrive pas à m'en défaire.

Au bout d'un moment, les jets s'apaisent et je finis par rassembler mon courage.

– Je peux te demander quelque chose ?

– Tes fesses sont collées contre mes testicules. Je suppose que ce n'est pas une question à laquelle je vais avoir envie de répondre, si tu as attendu jusqu'à maintenant pour la poser.

Gros malin. Je ne me démonte pas pour autant.

– Qu'est-ce qui s'est passé pendant ton mariage pour que tu finisses par divorcer ?

Il lâche un soupir.

– Tu as déjà la peau toute fripée. Tu es sûre de vouloir entendre la réponse ? Tu risques de faire quatre-vingt-dix ans, le temps que je finisse de déverser toutes les merdes qui se sont passées avec Alexa.

Alexa. Je la hais déjà, rien que pour son prénom.

– Fais-moi la version courte.

– Je l'ai rencontrée pendant ma dernière année de fac. Elle est tombée enceinte au bout de trois mois.

Il a un enfant ?!

– Waouh. Donc vous vous êtes mariés ?

– Ouais. Pas la meilleure décision de ma vie, avec le recul. Mais elle m'avait l'air gentille et elle portait mon enfant. En plus, elle n'avait pas eu le style de vie dont j'avais bénéficié quand j'étais gosse, alors je voulais les mettre à l'abri du besoin, elle et mon fils.

– C'est très noble.

– Je pense que tu confonds noble et naïf.

– Pas du tout. Je trouve incroyable que tu aies tenu à t'assurer qu'ils aient une belle vie.

– Ouais… pour te la faire courte, elle n'était pas la gentille fille qu'elle avait montrée au départ. Pourtant, j'ai continué à faire des efforts longtemps.

– Qu'est-ce qui a fini par te pousser à y mettre un terme ?

Drew reste silencieux un long moment. Quand il reprend la parole, sa voix est rauque.

– Ça s'est terminé la nuit où elle a eu un accident de voiture avec mon fils.

CHAPITRE 25

DREW

Réveillon du 31 décembre,
trois ans plus tôt

J'ai les yeux rivés sur la croix au mur de la chambre de mon fils. Elle m'a inspiré une prière il y a pile un an. Le berceau au-dessus duquel je l'avais suspendue a disparu, au profit d'un petit lit de bébé en plastique en forme de voiture de course. Pourtant, je l'ai raccrochée, après que Dieu m'a laissé entendre, quand j'espérais la guérison de mon père, que je n'étais pas un veinard. Il est mort il y a trois jours.

Au sortir du service funéraire, ce matin, quelques personnes sont venues à la maison pour déjeuner. Je ne suis pas fâché qu'elles soient toutes reparties, maintenant. J'ai besoin de silence. Et puis, j'ai aussi besoin de boire quelques verres en paix. Je fais tournoyer le liquide ambré au fond de mon verre.

La porte s'entrouvre, mais je ne prends même pas la peine de me retourner. Des bras m'enlacent par-derrière, dont les mains se nouent à ma taille, sur la boucle de ma ceinture.

– Qu'est-ce que tu fais là ? Beck est au bac à sable avec la baby-sitter. Il ne va pas rentrer avant une heure ou deux.

– Rien.

– Viens dans le salon. Que je te masse les épaules.

L'année écoulée a été rude, entre Alexa et moi. Non qu'on se soit disputés tant que ça, mais l'excitation de la nouveauté a depuis longtemps disparu, dans notre relation. On a trois trucs en commun : on aime tous les deux le sexe, l'argent (je le gagne, elle le dépense) et notre fils. Mais quand tu travailles dix heures par jour et que les nuits et les week-ends tu t'occupes de ton père qui est littéralement en train de mourir sous tes yeux, même le sexe passe au second plan.

Avant que mon père ne commence à décliner à vue d'œil, j'ai essayé de m'intéresser aux nouveaux passe-temps de ma femme, histoire de nous donner quelque chose en commun. Sauf qu'en dehors d'assister à une des pièces que son école avait montées, ça n'était pas très facile. Je lui ai fait répéter son texte, mais elle me reprochait de ne pas mettre assez de cœur dans mon jeu. Sans doute parce que *je ne suis pas un putain d'acteur !* Je suis allé assister à ses répétitions et elle m'a dit que ma présence gênait la spontanéité de son interprétation. Au bout du compte, j'ai cessé de faire des efforts. Ces derniers jours, en revanche, elle a été absolument géniale.

Je pivote sur moi-même et étreins ma femme, je dépose un baiser au sommet de son crâne.

– Oui, allons-y. J'ai les épaules nouées, ça me fera du bien.

Après une quinzaine de minutes, je commence à me détendre… jusqu'à ce qu'Alexa ne provoque une nouvelle tension dans mon cou.

– On devrait aller à la fête de Sage, ce soir.

– J'ai enterré mon père il y a deux heures. Le seul parent que j'avais, vu que ma mère s'est barrée avec son mec quand j'étais à peine plus vieux que notre fils. Je ne suis pas vraiment d'humeur à faire la fête.

– Mais c'est notre anniversaire. Et puis, c'est le Nouvel An.

– Alexa, il n'est pas question que j'aille à une putain de fête ce soir, OK ?

Elle interrompt son massage.

– Pas la peine de t'énerver.

Je me redresse.

– De m'énerver ? Tu attends de moi que j'assiste à une fête le jour des obsèques de mon père ! Je pense que j'ai des raisons de m'énerver.

Ma femme souffle bruyamment. Nos cinq ans de différence d'âge me donnent parfois l'impression que vingt ans nous séparent.

– J'ai besoin de faire la fête. Ces derniers mois ont été déprimants.

Ce n'est pourtant pas comme si elle m'avait aidé avec mon père. Tous les week-ends, pendant que je m'occupais de lui, elle sortait avec ses amies, la plupart du temps pour des virées shopping ou des déjeuners ou Dieu sait quoi. Son égoïsme me dégoûte.

– Quelle partie des derniers mois a bien pu te déprimer ? L'appart sur Park Avenue et les milliers de dollars dépensés en shopping chaque semaine ? Ou peut-être la nounou qui garde notre fils afin que tu puisses prendre des cours de comédie et sortir déjeuner ? Ou non, les séjours de trois semaines que tu as faits à Atlanta pour rendre visite à tes amis immatures ; ceux où tu as voyagé en première classe et séjourné au *St. Regis*, en centre-ville, au lieu de coucher chez ton frère dans la cambrousse ? Ouais, ça a dû être carrément déprimant.

– Mes amis ne sont pas immatures.

Je renifle avec mépris et m'apprête à répliquer, avant d'opter pour un autre verre plutôt que de poursuivre cette conversation. Parmi tout ce que je lui ai balancé au visage, ce qui l'a vexée, c'est l'affirmation que ses amis sont immatures ? C'est tordu, comme sens des priorités. Je me dirige vers la cuisine, ouverte sur le salon, où elle est toujours assise, et me verse un autre verre.

– Va à ta fête toute seule, Alexa.

***

Le soleil se couche quand j'ouvre les yeux. Alexa a emmené Beck au centre commercial, où elle compte s'acheter une énième robe, et moi je me suis endormi sur le canapé après avoir fini mon verre et ma dispute avec elle. Je m'assieds et me passe les doigts dans les cheveux. Je ne devrais pas être surpris qu'Alexa ait prévu de se rendre à une fête ce soir. Elle n'en rate pas une, surtout pas le soir du Nouvel An. Apparemment, je lui ai accordé plus de crédit qu'elle n'en mérite dans le domaine de la générosité.

Mon estomac gargouille. Je ne me rappelle pas la dernière fois où j'ai vraiment mangé. Hier, peut-être ? Le repas dans un resto italien entre la veillée mortuaire du matin et l'après-midi au funérarium, je pense. En fouillant dans le frigo, je tombe sur le plateau qu'on avait commandé pour ce matin et picore des antipasti avec les doigts. Alors que je suis occupé à me goinfrer, mon portable sonne et, au début, je n'y prête pas attention. Mais constatant qu'il recommence à sonner aussitôt, je vérifie l'identité de l'appelant. C'est un numéro local. Et très familier. À la troisième sonnerie, mon cerveau a passé en revue mon annuaire interne et fini par retrouver pourquoi je le connais.

Je l'ai composé mille fois, au cours des mois écoulés, chaque fois que la santé de mon père empirait. C'est l'hôpital de Lenox Hill qui m'appelle.

***

Le chauffeur de taxi me hurle dessus quand je bondis en direction de l'entrée des urgences. Apparemment, je suis sorti si vite que j'ai oublié de fermer la portière.

– Ma femme et mon fils ont eu un accident de voiture. Ils ont été amenés en ambulance, je crie à la femme derrière le Plexiglas de son guichet.

– Quel nom de famille ?

– Jagger.

Elle lève les yeux et hausse un sourcil.

– Ces lèvres… Je ne résiste pas à l'envie de vous poser la question : vous êtes parent avec Mick ?

– Non.

Elle grimace, mais désigne une porte sur ma gauche.

– Chambre 1A. Je vous ouvre.

***

Traumatisme abdominal. C'est ce que nous a indiqué le docteur il y a deux heures. Alexa n'a eu besoin que de deux ou trois points de suture, mais Beck n'a pas eu autant de chance. Son siège bébé a encaissé tout l'impact de la collision, quand les freins d'une camionnette de livraison de fleurs ont lâché et que le véhicule a grillé un feu rouge en plein milieu de la circulation du centre-ville. Son conducteur a braqué pour éviter l'accident, mais il a fini sa course dans la portière arrière, côté chauffeur, de la voiture d'Alexa. Pile où Beck était assis.

Les médecins nous ont assurés que ses blessures ne semblent pas engager son pronostic vital, mais une radio a montré que son rein gauche était endommagé, au minimum une petite lésion qui nécessite d'être réparée sur-le-champ. Alors, au chevet de mon fils, j'attends que les infirmières m'apportent les formulaires de consentement pour l'opération. Beck est paisiblement endormi dans son lit. Alexa, quant à elle, subit un autre examen neurologique dans la pièce attenante.

Une fois que les médecins sont venus m'expliquer les risques de l'intervention, l'infirmière m'apporte une liasse de formulaires à remplir. Consentement médical, protection des renseignements personnels, autorisations d'assurance… Le dernier papier concerne les transfusions sanguines.

L'infirmière m'explique qu'ils n'ont pas le temps de nous prendre notre sang avant l'opération de Beck et que si par hasard il avait besoin de sang, on lui transfuserait celui de la banque de sang. Cependant, nous pouvons le faire prélever et il sera stocké pour l'avenir, en cas de besoin. Je remplis le formulaire qui sera ensuite entré dans leur base de données et vérifié pendant que nous attendons, puis je demande à l'infirmière de tout faire signer à Alexa dans la chambre à côté. Je ne veux pas laisser Beck tout seul, au cas où il se réveillerait.

Les heures qui suivent, celles où mon fils est en salle d'opération, sont un véritable enfer. Il s'écoule deux heures avant que le chirurgien assistant sorte et vienne nous parler. Il abaisse son masque de papier.

– Ça n'est pas aussi simple que nous l'avions pensé au départ. Les dégâts causés au rein de votre fils étaient plus importants que ne le montrait la radio. En ce moment, nous essayons de suturer la lésion, mais elle entoure le pédoncule vasculaire, qui contient les artères et les veines qui le connectent à l'aorte. Vous devez comprendre qu'il y a une chance que nous ne puissions pas réparer suffisamment bien la blessure pour sauver son organe. Que le risque pour sa santé soit trop important. Si tel était le cas, il devrait subir une néphrectomie partielle ou totale.

Sur quoi, il tente de nous convaincre qu'on vit très bien avec un seul rein. Je connais des tas de gens qui n'en ont qu'un, mais si on naît avec deux, je veux que mon fils ait les bénéfices de ses deux reins, dans la mesure du possible.

Alexa et moi nous sommes à peine parlé, en dehors du moment où je lui ai demandé si elle allait bien. Je suis focalisé sur Beck et une partie de moi lui reproche l'accident. Non que ce soit sa faute, mais si elle n'avait pas été aussi obsédée par ce besoin de s'acheter encore une putain de robe pour sortir ce soir, rien de tout ça ne serait arrivé.

– J'ai vu un distributeur près des ascenseurs, en bas. Tu veux un café ?

Elle hoche la tête.

Quand je reviens avec les cafés, l'infirmière est déjà en train de parler avec Alexa.

– Ah, monsieur Jagger. Voici votre carte de groupe sanguin. Elle indique votre rhésus, si jamais vous en avez besoin un jour. On la transmet à tous les gens qui donnent leur sang.

– Merci. Je suis un donneur compatible avec Beck ?

– Laissez-moi regarder son dossier.

Elle va au pied du lit de mon fils, où ils ont accroché un bloc à pince métallique.

– Vous êtes O négatif, lit-elle en tournant les pages. Ça signifie que vous pouvez donner votre sang à n'importe qui. (Elle s'arrête sur une feuille rose.) Vous avez de la chance. Ce n'est pas souvent qu'un beau-père est donneur universel.

– Je suis son père, pas son beau-père.

L'infirmière raccroche le dossier de Beck au rail et reporte son attention sur le bloc qu'elle a apporté. Un air stupéfait passe sur son visage.

– Vous êtes de groupe sanguin O. Beckett est AB. (Elle fronce les sourcils.) Vous me dites que Beckett est votre fils biologique ?

– Oui.

Elle regarde Alexa, puis moi de nouveau et secoue la tête.

– Ce n'est pas possible. Génétiquement, un O ne peut pas produire un enfant de groupe AB.

Je suis épuisé après une journée infernale, entre l'enterrement de mon père et l'accident de ma femme et de mon fils. J'ai dû mal comprendre.

– Le labo a fait une erreur, alors ?

L'infirmière secoue la tête.

– Ils sont très fiables, en règle générale… (Elle nous dévisage tour à tour à nouveau, ma femme et moi.) Mais je vais les envoyer vous refaire une prise de sang.

Sur quoi, elle quitte la chambre pour ainsi dire au pas de course. Je me tourne vers ma femme, qui a la tête baissée.

– C'est une erreur du labo, hein, Alexa ?

Je manque de vomir quand elle relève les yeux. Elle n'a pas besoin de dire un mot, j'ai compris.

Il n'y a pas eu d'erreur.

Pas de putain d'erreur.

Beck n'est pas mon fils.

CHAPITRE 26

EMERIE

– Tu as un fils ?

Je me tords le cou pour regarder Drew. Nous sommes toujours dans la baignoire et je n'ai pas beaucoup de marge de manœuvre, assise entre ses jambes.

Les yeux fermés, il hoche la tête avant de les rouvrir et de me contempler. Il y a tant de douleur dans son expression que mon ventre se serre rien qu'à imaginer ce qui va suivre.

– C'est une longue histoire. Et si on sortait, que je te prépare quelque chose à manger pendant que je t'explique ?

– D'accord.

Il sort le premier pour nous attraper des serviettes. Une fois séché, y compris trois secondes à se frotter les cheveux, il noue la serviette autour de sa taille et me tend la main.

Il a toujours l'air pensif et j'ai envie de détendre l'atmosphère. Quoi qu'il s'apprête à me raconter sur son fils, ça n'est manifestement pas une histoire facile.

Je prends sa main et enjambe le bord de la baignoire.

– Tu ressembles à un mannequin pour une pub de mousse à raser, là, et moi je dois avoir l'air d'un rat mouillé.

J'ai les cheveux collés au visage et je remercie la buée sur le miroir, qui m'empêche de bien m'observer dedans.

Drew m'enveloppe dans une serviette moelleuse et entreprend de me sécher.

– On est bien bichonné, dans ton établissement, je le taquine, tandis qu'il s'agenouille pour m'essuyer une jambe, puis l'autre.

Il m'adresse une œillade.

– Ça va avec la fouille au corps.

– Ta fouille au corps était très spectaculaire aussi.

– Je fournis tout le package.

Quand il a fini de m'essuyer (mes seins et mon entrejambe sont extra-secs, avec tout le temps qu'il y a passé), il me glisse la serviette autour de la poitrine et coince une extrémité dedans. Toujours adorable, il entremêle nos doigts pour m'entraîner hors de la salle de bains.

Dans la cuisine, il tire un tabouret de sous l'îlot en granite et tapote dessus.

– Assieds-toi.

Je tournicote un peu dessus pendant qu'il sort des choses de ses placards et de son frigo. Au souvenir de ce qu'on a fait contre la vitre quelques heures plus tôt, j'interromps mes rotations et regarde par la fenêtre. Il fait sombre, dehors, à présent, je vois les lumières de la ville illuminée.

– On peut… Les gens peuvent vraiment voir à l'intérieur ?

Un mélange de panique et de gêne me monte aux joues tandis que je me remémore la manière dont mes seins étaient collés à la vitre. Sur le moment, l'idée qu'on me voie était excitante, elle ajoutait à l'érotisme. Sauf que je n'ai absolument pas envie de finir sur YouTube parce qu'un pervers nous aura filmés à travers son télescope.

Drew s'esclaffe.

– Non. C'est une vitre teintée. Je ne te ferais pas prendre ce genre de risques. (Il tend le bras par-dessus ma tête pour attraper une poêle et m'embrasse sur le front au passage.) En plus, je ne partage pas ce qui m'appartient.

La première moitié de sa réponse suscite un soupir de soulagement dans la partie rationnelle de mon être, mais la seconde agite mon bas-ventre de délicieuses crispations.

Drew aussi ne porte qu'une serviette, nouée autour de sa taille étroite, et je profite de la vue de ses dorsaux qui roulent sous sa peau tandis qu'il émince un oignon. Soudain, je remarque une cicatrice qui traverse en diagonale le côté de son torse, passant de devant à derrière. Elle n'est plus qu'une bande de peau plus claire que le reste, pas nouvelle, donc, mais quand même le vestige d'une sérieuse blessure.

– Tu as été opéré ?

– Hmm ?

Il jette du beurre dans la poêle, qu'il touille en haussant les sourcils.

– Ta cicatrice, je précise, en la montrant du doigt.

Une lueur passe sur son visage. De la tristesse, il me semble. Il se retourne.

– Ouais. Je suis passé sur le billard il y a quelques années.

J'analyse peut-être trop, à scruter tout ce qu'il fait, mais je ne peux pas m'en empêcher. Mon cerveau essaie de reconstituer un puzzle sans savoir à quoi ressemble l'image de départ.

Drew tranche encore des légumes, refusant de me laisser l'aider. Quand il nous sert deux magnifiques omelettes, elles pourraient tout aussi bien sortir de l'un des restaurants chics que Baldwin affectionne tant.

Baldwin.

Je ne peux pas perdre encore trois ans à me languir pour un homme qui ne m'aimera jamais en retour. Je dois aussi me rappeler que Drew n'est intéressé que par une relation sexuelle. M'attacher à cet homme-là et développer des sentiments pour lui n'est pas une option.

Pourtant… Je ne peux nier l'espèce de connexion qui nous unit. Comme s'il y avait une raison pour que je me sois fait arnaquer et que j'aie atterri dans son bureau un soir de Nouvel An. C'est idiot, je sais. Je n'ai pas la moindre idée de ce qu'elle est, cette connexion entre nous, mais je suis déterminée à le découvrir.

Pendant le repas, nous discutons de tout et de rien et une fois nos agapes terminées, je nettoie. Comme il n'y a pas de quoi faire tourner le lave-vaisselle, je lave moi-même les assiettes et autres couverts pendant que Drew essuie. Je me surprends à songer qu'on travaille bien, ensemble. C'est drôle comme au bureau nos opinions et nos conseils sont totalement opposés, alors que nous sommes si synchrones sur le plan physique.

– Tu veux un verre ? me demande-t-il une fois la cuisine remise en ordre.

– Non, merci, je ne peux plus rien avaler.

Il hoche la tête.

– Viens, allons nous asseoir au salon.

Il déplace les coussins sur le canapé, en dispose un au bout, pour que j'y appuie ma tête, et tend le doigt.

– Allonge-toi.

Il attend que je sois confortablement installée, ensuite il me soulève les jambes et pose mes pieds sur ses genoux.

– Tu es chatouilleuse ?

– Tu vas en faire un défi si je te réponds que non ?

Il esquisse un sourire en coin.

– Non, j'allais te masser les pieds.

Ravie, j'en lève un en l'air, que je lui présente.

– Je ne suis pas chatouilleuse. Le problème, c'est que quand on dit ça aux gens, ils se sentent obligés de t'enfoncer les doigts dans les côtes jusqu'à te donner des hématomes pour te prouver que tu te trompes.

Drew saisit mon pied et commence son massage. Il a les doigts puissants et quand il appuie habilement la pulpe du pouce sur un point situé dans la partie antérieure de ma plante de pied, celle où, à cause de mes talons, pèse l'essentiel du poids de mon corps, je lâche un petit miaulement.

– C'est bon ?

– Mieux que bon, j'avoue dans un soupir.

Au bout de quelques minutes de ce traitement, mon corps tout entier se détend et Drew commence à parler à voix basse.

– Beck avait cinq ans quand il a eu un accident de voiture avec mon ex-femme.

Oh, bon Dieu !

– Je suis désolée, désolée, désolée.

Drew fronce les sourcils, puis semble rapidement comprendre à quoi j'ai pensé.

– Oh, merde. Non. Je ne voulais pas te faire croire… Il va bien. Beck va bien.

Je porte une main à ma poitrine.

– Punaise. Tu m'as flanqué une de ces trouilles. J'ai cru…

– Oui, je viens de comprendre. Pardon. Il va bien. On a eu très peur, après l'accident, mais maintenant on n'imaginerait même pas qu'il a subi trois opérations.

– Trois opérations ? Qu'est-ce qui lui est arrivé ?

– Une fourgonnette de livraison a percuté la voiture d'Alexa, qui a été pliée en deux.

– C'est horrible.

– Le siège bébé de Beck et une partie de la portière lui ont perforé le flanc, ce qui lui a lacéré le rein. Les chirurgiens ont essayé de le réparer, mais à cause de la localisation et de la taille de la lésion, ils ont dû lui retirer une partie du rein. Le jour de son accident, il a eu une néphrectomie partielle du rein gauche.

– Waouh. Le pauvre.

– Merci de ta sollicitude. (Il prend une minute avant de poursuivre.) Pendant qu'il était en salle d'opération, les infirmières nous ont proposé de donner notre sang. Je me sentais impuissant, j'avais besoin de me sentir utile.

– Bien sûr.

– Bref, ils ont fait des tests de compatibilité sur Alexa et moi, pour voir si on pouvait donner du sang à stocker pour Beck. Il s'est révélé qu'aucun de nous n'était compatible.

– Je ne savais pas que deux parents pouvaient avoir un enfant à qui ils ne pouvaient pas donner leur sang.

Drew plonge les yeux dans les miens.

– C'est impossible, en effet.

Il me faut quelques battements de cœur pour comprendre ce qu'il est en train de m'expliquer.

– Tu as découvert que Beck n'était pas ton fils.

Il hoche la tête.

– J'étais là pour l'accouchement, du coup j'étais sûr et certain qu'il était le fils biologique d'Alexa.

– Je ne sais pas quoi dire. C'est affreux. Elle savait que tu n'étais pas le père ?

– Elle savait. Elle refuse de l'admettre, mais elle le savait depuis le début. Beck est né avec quelques semaines d'avance. Je n'ai pas trouvé ça bizarre, sur le moment. (Il secoue la tête.) S'il n'y avait pas eu l'opération, je ne l'aurais peut-être jamais su.

– Bon sang, Drew, tu as appris ça pendant qu'on l'opérait. Tu parles d'un stress supplémentaire.

– Ouais, ce n'était pas une bonne journée. En fait, c'était la première d'une série de journées pas bien sympas à venir. Les semaines suivantes ont été pires encore.

– Qu'est-ce qui s'est passé ?

– Entre Alexa et moi, c'était fini avant que je quitte l'hôpital cette nuit-là. En vérité, c'était fini bien avant l'accident. Mais Beck…

Il détourne la tête quelques secondes et je le vois déglutir. Il ravale ses larmes, je le sais. Il a toujours mon pied entre ses mains, mais il a cessé de bouger. Je n'ai pas la moindre idée de ce que je suis censée dire ou faire, mais j'ai envie de lui offrir le peu de réconfort qui est dans mes cordes. Alors je me redresse et rampe sur ses genoux. Je m'enroule autour de son corps et lui donne le plus gros câlin que je peux.

Au bout de quelques minutes, je le relâche et lui chuchote :

– Tu n'es pas obligé de m'en dire plus. Peut-être une autre fois ?

Il m'offre une esquisse de sourire.

– Ce jour-là a radicalement modifié mes sentiments envers Alexa, mais il n'a rien changé de ce que j'éprouve pour Beck. Il restait mon fils.

– Bien entendu.

– Bref, quelques jours après son opération, le petit a eu une soudaine poussée de fièvre. Sa blessure guérissait, pourtant il était de plus en plus malade. Ils l'ont mis sous antibiotiques en intraveineuse, afin de traiter une éventuelle infection liée à l'intervention, mais sans succès. Les docteurs ont fini par se résoudre à le réopérer pour retirer le morceau de rein qu'ils lui avaient laissé. Sauf qu'entre-temps l'autre rein avait commencé à montrer des signes de dysfonctionnement. Ce n'est pas inhabituel, après l'amputation d'un rein, même partielle, que l'autre connaisse des difficultés à se comporter correctement pendant un moment.

– Pauvre bébé. Il a dû tellement souffrir. Un accident de voiture, l'opération, le début de guérison et encore une opération.

Drew lâche un profond soupir.

– Les jours où il piquait des crises étaient finalement plus réconfortants que ceux où il était trop faible pour faire quoi que ce soit. Voir ton enfant allongé sur un lit d'hôpital sans être capable de l'aider, c'est la pire sensation qui soit.

– Je n'arrive même pas à me l'imaginer.

– Une semaine supplémentaire s'est écoulée sans que la situation s'améliore vraiment. L'infection était réduite, mais l'autre rein ne fonctionnait toujours pas super bien. Ils l'ont mis sous dialyse, ce qui l'a soulagé, il allait mieux, mais ils ont commencé à parler de l'inscrire sur une liste de transplantation si ses tests se dégradaient encore. Les gens passent des années sur ces listes d'attente. Et traîner un gamin de cinq ans, qui se sent par ailleurs en forme, pour des heures de dialyse un jour sur deux, ça promettait d'être pénible. Alors je leur ai demandé de me faire passer des tests pour voir si j'étais donneur compatible. Et si incroyable que ça paraisse, alors que je n'étais pas son père biologique, mon rein était compatible. Une fois qu'il a été suffisamment remis pour une troisième opération, je lui ai donné un rein. Ils le lui ont transplanté à gauche, là où ils avaient retiré le sien qui était endommagé. Comme ça, il aurait deux reins entiers et si l'autre ne reprenait jamais un rythme normal, il conservait deux fois plus de chances qu'au moins un des deux fonctionne.

L'image du dos de Drew me revient en mémoire.

– C'est de là que tu tiens ta cicatrice ?

Il hoche la tête.

– Pour la faire courte, la transplantation a été un succès et finalement son autre rein s'est réveillé et a recommencé à fonctionner quelques semaines plus tard. Aujourd'hui, il est fort comme un bœuf. Mais ça a été une période sacrément flippante.

Toute cette histoire, c'est trop d'informations à ingérer. Des milliers de pensées me traversent, mais l'une d'elles ressort du lot.

– Tu es une belle personne, Drew Jagger. Et je ne parle pas de l'enveloppe extérieure.

Je me penche pour déposer une ligne de baisers d'une extrémité de sa cicatrice à l'autre.

– Oui, tu dis ça parce que j'ai omis le passage où j'ai fait les bagages d'Alexa et où j'ai viré toutes ses affaires pendant qu'elle n'était pas à la maison.

Le ton est taquin, pourtant je devine qu'il ne plaisante pas.

– Elle l'avait mérité. J'aurais découpé des trous dans l'entrejambe de tous ses pantalons, moi, à cette garce.

Drew recule la tête pour me regarder d'un air amusé.

– C'est le conseil relationncl que tu m'aurais donné si je m'étais pointé à ton cabinet en quête de suivi psychologique ?

Je réfléchis un instant. *Qu'est-ce que j'aurais fait ?*

– Je travaille seulement avec les couples qui cherchent sincèrement à faire fonctionner leur relation. Si j'avais entendu ton histoire, vu l'expression dans tes yeux, je ne t'aurais pas pris comme client. Parce que dans ce cas précis, ce serait revenu à donner de faux espoirs à la partie qui voulait que ça fonctionne. Sans compter que j'estime incorrect de prendre de l'argent pour parvenir à un but auquel je ne crois pas.

– Ça t'est déjà arrivé ? D'avoir des clients dont l'un veut que ça marche et l'autre non ?

– Oui. En fait, c'est loin d'être rare. J'organise des séances individuelles, au départ, afin que les parties puissent s'exprimer librement sans se soucier de heurter les sentiments de l'autre. Je me suis rendu compte que j'obtenais plus de vérités durant ces séances-là. À mes débuts, j'ai eu un couple marié depuis vingt-sept ans, un couple aisé, avec une vie sociale saine et deux grandes filles. L'homme était homosexuel et vivait la vie qu'il pensait devoir vivre, ayant grandi dans une famille ultra-conservatrice avec des parents très religieux. Ça lui a pris jusqu'à ses cinquante-deux ans, mais il a fini par faire son coming-out. Il a tout avoué à sa femme et lui a dit qu'ils devaient se séparer. Il se sentait très coupable, il était resté parce qu'il l'aimait, simplement pas de la manière qu'un mari est censé aimer sa femme.

Je me suis retrouvée à leur conseiller la séparation et à les aider à traverser cette épreuve.

– Merde. Dommage qu'on n'ait pas partagé nos bureaux à l'époque, j'aurais obtenu un bel accord à la dame, ironise Drew.

Je lui donne une tape sur le torse.

– Je croyais que tu représentais seulement les hommes.

– Ils étaient riches comment ? J'aurais peut-être fait une exception.

J'éclate de rire.

– Pourquoi d'ailleurs est-ce que tu ne représentes que des hommes ? À cause de ce que t'a fait ton ex-femme ?

Il secoue la tête.

– Non. Je m'entends mieux avec les mecs, c'est tout.

La réponse est vague et j'ai l'impression qu'il élude.

– Dis-moi la véritable raison, Jagger, j'insiste, sourcils froncés.

Il fouille mon regard.

– Tu n'as peut-être pas envie de l'entendre.

– Eh bien, tu as éveillé ma curiosité, alors que je veuille l'entendre ou pas, tu dois me le dire.

Il serre les mâchoires.

– La baise de compensation.

– Pardon ?

– Quand je représentais des femmes furieuses et vexées, elles avaient à cœur de se venger.

– Elles étaient amères. C'est normal, dans un divorce.

Drew a l'air embarrassé.

– Elles voulaient se venger de leur mari… avec moi.

– Tu couchais avec tes clientes ?

– Je n'en suis pas fier, mais oui. J'étais fraîchement divorcé et en colère moi-même. La baise de compensation, ça peut aider beaucoup à évacuer cette rage, du moins de manière temporaire.

– Les relations sexuelles avec les clients, ça ne va pas à l'encontre d'une règle de base chez les avocats ?

– Comme je te l'ai dit, ce n'est pas la période dont je suis le plus fier.

Je devine qu'il n'est pas simplement en train de m'avouer qu'il a honte. Il regrette vraiment ses actes et il a été honnête avec moi quand il aurait pu mentir. Qui suis-je pour juger son passé ? Je préfère le juger sur la franchise qu'il m'a montrée aujourd'hui.

– La baise de compensation, donc ?

J'essaie de masquer mon sourire. Il hoche la tête en m'observant attentivement.

– Eh bien, je pense que tu es un salopard égocentrique et égotique doublé d'un coureur de jupons.

Il se recule.

– P… Quoi ? Tu voulais que je te dise la vérité.

– Je ne pensais pas que la vérité serait que tu es un trouduc.

Il s'apprête à répliquer autre chose, quand je me colle à lui, un sourire moqueur aux lèvres.

– Je t'ai énervé ?

– Tu essaies de m'énerver ?

– J'ai entendu dire que la baise de compensation pouvait faire beaucoup pour aider à évacuer la rage, du moins de manière temporaire.

Avant que je comprenne ce qui m'arrive, Drew m'a soulevée dans les airs et allongée sur le dos, en travers du canapé.

Il se penche au-dessus de moi.

– Bien joué. Dans ce cas, je suis ravi de t'énerver tous les jours. On va avoir besoin de travailler beaucoup sur nos problèmes de colère.

CHAPITRE 27

DREW

Réveillon du 31 décembre,
deux ans plus tôt

Les juges détestent les affaires qui tombent le 31 décembre. Mais je sais ce qu'a prémédité mon ex-femme. Elle croit qu'en me traînant devant la cour le jour de notre anniversaire de mariage, sous un vague prétexte d'urgence, ça va me perturber. Elle me connaît vraiment si mal que ça ? Elle croit vraiment que je reste assis à la maison à me lamenter, trois mois après que notre divorce a été finalisé ? J'ai obtenu d'elle ce que je voulais à l'issue de la procédure : ma liberté et la garde partagée de notre fils. Qu'il soit mon enfant biologique ou pas ne change rien à ce que je ressens pour lui. C'est mon fils. Et ce n'est pas un test de paternité qui va me dire le contraire.

La réaction la plus intelligente d'Alexa a été de ne pas me disputer la garde partagée. Une fois que j'ai offert de lui verser une confortable pension alimentaire tous les mois, même si j'avais certainement en main des arguments pour ne rien payer, elle est soudain devenue très favorable à cet arrangement. Mon ex-femme n'a jamais été intéressée que par l'argent. Même quand on était mariés, je pense que je le savais, au fond de moi.

Je l'ai appelée au moins une demi-douzaine de fois pour savoir ce qu'elle mijotait, mais bien sûr elle n'a pas décroché. Son côté manipulateur a montré son vilain visage dès le jour où j'ai emballé ses affaires et les ai fait déménager dans un appartement de location à quelques rues de chez moi ; appartement que je continue à payer. S'il n'y avait pas eu Beck, j'aurais balancé ses merdes par la fenêtre quand j'ai changé les serrures. Mais je voulais avoir mon fils près de moi et il mérite de vivre dans un bel immeuble qu'Alexa n'aurait pas eu les moyens de se payer.

– Un 31 décembre. Quel pauvre bougre est-ce que tu vas dépouiller pour bien commencer la nouvelle année ? plaisante George, l'auxiliaire de justice posté à l'entrée du tribunal, tout en vérifiant ma pièce d'identité.

Il lui arrive de faire des heures supplémentaires pour Roman, par exemple en tenant des planques la nuit, et nous sommes devenus amis au fil des années.

– C'est moi, le pauvre bougre. Mon ex-femme continue à jouer les garces.

Il hoche la tête, au courant de ma situation merdique que Roman lui a racontée devant quelques bières, un soir.

– Tu vas à la fête de Roman, ce soir ? me demande-t-il en me rendant ma carte d'identité.

– J'ai hâte d'y être.

– On s'y verra alors. Bonne chance pour aujourd'hui.

Alexa et son ordure d'avocat, Wade Garrison, sont déjà assis dans la salle d'audience quand j'y entre. Difficile de ne pas rire de sa jupe jusqu'aux genoux et de son col si serré qu'il donne l'impression de l'étrangler. Surtout quand j'ai en ma possession un millier de photos d'elle pendant des fêtes ou des week-ends, en jupes ultra moulantes qui lui couvrent à peine les fesses et avec des décolletés très loin d'être pudiques. Cadeau de Roman, qui me les a procurées après qu'elle et moi avons rompu… au cas où j'en aurais besoin un jour.

Mon ex-femme regarde droit devant elle, refusant de tourner la tête vers moi. S'il est bien une chose que je sais sur Alexa, c'est que quand elle évite mon regard, elle la joue super salope.

L'officier du tribunal appelle notre numéro de dossier et je fais en sorte de m'approcher avant eux, histoire de pousser le portillon et d'obliger Alexa à établir le contact visuel.

– Tu vas t'habiller comme ça à ta fête de fraternité, ce soir ? je lui chuchote. Tu devrais mettre un soutien-gorge plus gainant, parce que tu as les seins qui tombent. Sans doute à cause de l'allaitement.

Elle me jette un regard glacial. Auquel je réponds par un large sourire.

– Alors, qu'avons-nous là, messieurs-dames ? J'ai lu la motion, mais je n'ai pas la moindre idée de ce qui vous amène devant moi aujourd'hui, si ce n'est me faire perdre mon temps précieux, lance le juge Hixton.

– J'aimerais moi aussi savoir pourquoi nous sommes là, j'ajoute.

Le juge Hixton tourne son attention vers l'autre côté de sa salle d'audience.

– Vous voulez bien nous éclairer tous les deux, maître ?

Garrison s'éclaircit la gorge, un raclement bien gras. Comment il fait pour parler, avec son col boutonné aussi serré ? Je dirais qu'il aurait besoin de passer d'une taille vingt-trois à une taille vingt-quatre, en tour de cou.

– Votre honneur, nous souhaiterions soumettre un avenant au contrat, ainsi qu'une déclaration sur l'honneur de New York Laboratory.

Le juge fait signe à l'assistant juridique de collecter les documents.

– Tout cela a-t-il été transmis à la partie adverse ?

– Non, votre honneur, nous avons reçu la déclaration sous serment hier soir. Nous en tenons une copie à disposition pour M. Jagger, ici.

L'assistant juridique me distribue les documents, ainsi qu'au juge Hixton, et nous prenons un moment pour les parcourir. Je saute l'avenant et les résultats du test de paternité, pour passer directement à la déclaration sous serment du tiers. Dont je n'ai besoin de lire que la moitié de la première page.

Nous, Alexa Thompson Jagger et Levi Archer Bodine, avons lu et comprenons les conséquences, alternatives, droits et responsabilités afférents à cette déclaration sur l'honneur. Nous déposons sous serment en toute conscience et disons :

Moi, Alexa Thompson Jagger, je suis la mère biologique de Beckett Archer Jagger, comme stipulé par le certificat de naissance n° NYC2839992 délivré par la Ville de New York.

Moi, Levi Archer Bodine, je suis le père biologique de Beckett Archer Jagger, comme certifié par le dossier n° 80499F fourni par New York Laboratory. D'où il apparaît que la paternité a été attribuée à Levi Archer Bodine avec une certitude scientifique de 99,99 %.

En conséquence, nous demandons tous deux une correction du certificat de naissance afin d'identifier Levi Bodine comme le père de l'enfant. Nous souhaitons aussi obtenir les droits parentaux complets, y compris la garde partagée et les droits de visite.

Il y a de la compassion dans la voix du juge Hixton quand il me demande :

– Monsieur Jagger, souhaitez-vous quelques jours pour répondre à cette motion ?

J'ai le cœur lourd de colère et de chagrin. J'ai l'impression que mon univers tout entier vient de s'écrouler. Je déglutis afin de ravaler mes larmes.

– S'il vous plaît, oui, Votre Honneur.

Tout ce qui se produit ensuite est enveloppé d'un brouillard. Garrison demande un droit de visite temporaire pour Bodine, que le juge décline le temps que j'aie vérifié la légitimité des tests présentés. Une date est arrêtée pour une nouvelle convocation, dans deux semaines à compter de mardi, et puis le marteau tombe.

Je suis encore pétrifié quand Alexa et son avocat quittent la salle.

Levi Archer Bodine. Ce type a le même deuxième prénom que notre fils. C'est Alexa qui l'a choisi, ce putain de deuxième prénom. J'avais suggéré qu'on lui donne les prénoms de nos pères respectifs, mais elle avait insisté, arguant qu'elle adorait ce prénom. *Elle avait toujours rêvé de donner à son petit garçon le deuxième prénom Archer.*

Sale menteuse.

Mais pourquoi son nom m'est aussi familier ?

Levi Archer Bodine.

Levi Archer Bodine.

Levi Bodine.

Bon sang, pourquoi ce nom m'est-il aussi familier, merde ?

Je le connais de quelque part.

Enfin, l'assistant juridique vient vers moi et me demande gentiment de partir afin qu'il appelle le cas suivant.

Sidéré, je me dirige vers la sortie. Je passe devant une poignée de gens que je connais sans leur prêter la moindre attention. J'entends leurs voix, mais je suis incapable de distinguer ce qu'ils disent. Ce n'est qu'une fois dehors, à l'air frais, que mon brouillard se lève. Pile au moment où je vois Alexa monter dans une Dodge Charger jaune vif avec le numéro « 9 » peint sur son flanc.

CHAPITRE 28

DREW

– Ta cliente devrait s'inquiéter de perdre son autorisation d'exercer, plutôt qu'un appartement en multipropriété aux îles Vierges. Son patient l'a filmée penchée sur la table d'examen alors qu'il était en train de pratiquer sur elle un toucher rectal avec sa bite, Alan. Quand on va se répartir les biens, considère cette vidéo comme l'un des miens. Mon client a dépensé vingt mille dollars pour se l'approprier, mais je dirais que sa valeur réelle est de cent fois celle-là, dans cette pièce.

Je suis assis dans ma salle de conférences, à discuter d'un accord avec l'avocat de la partie adverse, Alan Avery. Nous avons soutenu assez de cas ensemble pour qu'il sache que je ne bluffe pas. Roman avait découvert l'existence d'une *sex tape* avant mêmc que le bon docteur Appleton ne soit au courant. Et maintenant, monsieur Appleton réclame une pension alimentaire ainsi que tous les biens conjugaux.

Pourtant, Alan n'est pas focalisé sur les répercussions possibles de cet enregistrement. Il a l'air complètement ailleurs. Quand je me retourne pour vérifier par-dessus mon épaule ce qu'il est en train de regarder, je deviens encore plus furax que s'il me faisait juste perdre mon temps.

– C'est ta nouvelle secrétaire ? me demande-t-il.

Emerie se tient au bout du couloir, en train de signer le formulaire de remise d'un paquet par UPS. Dans sa jupe marron clair moulante, ses fesses sont encore plus phénoménales.

– Non, c'est ma sous-locataire temporaire, je réponds sèchement.

– Mariée ?

Je referme mon dossier dans un claquement.

– On peut revenir à notre accord ? Mon client n'accordera pas un centime au Dr BiteDansLeCul.

– C'est ridicule. Son mari vit à ses crochets depuis des années. C'est elle qui a financé tous les achats effectués en commun durant le mariage, grâce aux bénéfices réalisés par son cabinet médical.

– Ouais, eh bien tu n'as qu'à lui dire qu'on la remercie du cadeau de séparation. Elle regagnera tout ça. Je suis sûre qu'elle est une proctologue très réputée.

– Elle est ORL.

– Ah bon ? Sur la vidéo, on croirait qu'elle se spécialise plutôt dans les examens rectaux, pourtant.

– En parlant de trou du cul, quelle mouche t'a piqué ce matin ? Tu es d'une humeur massacrante.

– Écoute, finissons-en avec ces conneries, je marmonne. J'ai un après-midi chargé.

Quelques minutes plus tard, Emerie frappe à ma porte ouverte.

– Désolée de vous interrompre, mais j'ai un appel pour toi, Drew. Elle affirme que c'est urgent.

– C'est qui ?

Emerie hésite.

– Je ne sais pas, elle a refusé de me donner son nom.

– Dis-lui que je la rappellerai. Manifestement, ce n'est pas si important que ça, puisqu'elle ne veut pas te donner son nom.

Emerie soutient mon regard.

– L'appelante a un fort accent du Sud. De Géorgie, peut-être.

Super. Merde. Alexa.

– Excuse-moi une minute, j'indique à Alan, en me levant.

– Prends ton temps. Ta nouvelle locataire et moi allons profiter de ton absence pour faire connaissance.

Encore mieux. Parfait.

Je n'empêche pas la porte de claquer derrière moi tandis que je m'enferme dans mon bureau et me saisis de l'appareil.

– Drew Jagger.

– La femme qui a répondu à mon appel est pénible.

Je lâche un soupir irrité.

– Qu'est-ce que tu veux, Alexa ? Je suis au beau milieu d'une conférence.

– Je reste encore deux semaines à Atlanta.

– Pas question. Ma garde commence vendredi et tu as déjà prolongé ton séjour là-bas d'une semaine par rapport aux deux semaines sur lesquelles on s'était accordés. Ça fait plus de trois semaines que je n'ai pas vu mon fils.

– Tu peux venir la faire ici, ta garde.

– Je ne peux pas tout lâcher et m'envoler pour Atlanta une semaine sur deux parce que tu as envie de faire mumuse avec tes copines. Beck a besoin d'être à la maison, de retourner à l'école et à ses petites habitudes.

– Il a aussi besoin d'apprendre à connaître son père.

Je sais exactement ce qu'elle entend par là.

– Va te faire foutre, Alexa. Il le connaît, son père !

– Son père biologique. Levi veut le rencontrer, c'est important.

Je sens augmenter ma tension sanguine.

– Ah ouais ? Si c'est tellement important, putain, pourquoi tu ne le lui as pas dit il y a sept ans, quand tu as découvert que tu étais enceinte ? Et pourquoi est-ce qu'il n'a fait aucune tentative pour le connaître, notre fils, quand il a appris la vérité, il y a plus de deux ans maintenant ? D'ailleurs, il a commencé à te verser la pension ?

Je perds encore dix minutes de ma vie à argumenter en vain avec Alexa. Pour le bien de Beck, je tire sur le fil de ma patience aussi loin que possible sans qu'il casse, et je parviens à ne pas lui raccrocher au nez. Je ne fais pas confiance à mon ex-femme, elle est capable de jouer la toute dernière carte de son jeu déjà bien réduit en me traînant à nouveau devant un tribunal pour diminuer mon droit de visite. Même après que sa paternité a été prouvée et que le nom de Levi a remplacé le mien sur le certificat de naissance de mon fils, son péquenaud d'ex-petit ami n'a jamais essayé de se rapprocher de Beck. Devant le juge, on s'est mis d'accord sur les droits de garde et j'ai accepté de payer une coquette pension alimentaire alors même que j'aurais pu déposer une motion pour interrompre tout soutien financier dès que ma paternité a été infirmée. Mais dans un coin de ma tête, j'attends toujours que le couperet tombe, surtout maintenant qu'apparemment elle reparle avec Levi. Mon fils n'a toujours pas la moindre idée de qui est ce type.

Sachant combien Alexa peut se montrer vindicative, je me retiens de faire toutes les choses qui me passent par la tête pour lui rendre la vie dure, à commencer par lui raccrocher au nez aujourd'hui.

Au bout d'une minute de silence, elle en arrive enfin à la véritable raison de son appel. Je me botterais les fesses d'avoir avalé l'hameçon qu'elle me tendait avec sa discussion préalable.

– Si tu es tellement pressé que Beck revienne à New York, je pense qu'on pourrait organiser quelque chose.

– Qu'est-ce que tu veux, Alexa ?

– Eh bien, Levi a une grosse course la semaine prochaine et je veux être ici pour y assister.

Pour une raison qui m'échappe, je ne ressens pas la même colère à l'égard de Levi que contre Alexa. Une partie de moi a même pitié de ce crétin. Elle l'avait envoyé balader, traité de « mécano crado », si je me rappelle bien, préférant se raccrocher à un mari doté d'un compte en banque plus garni. Maintenant que le mécano est devenu pilote sponsorisé sur le circuit NASCAR, il est soudain devenu assez bien pour qu'elle daigne lui reparler.

– Tu veux en venir où, avec ton histoire, au juste ?

– Il y a beaucoup de bruit, lors des courses. Alors si tu voulais venir et emmener Beck avec toi pour la semaine, je pourrais rester seule ici avant de rentrer à New York. Et puis, je suis un peu limite niveau financier en ce moment, donc je vais avoir besoin d'un peu plus d'argent de poche pour assister à la course.

Ça me démange de lui suggérer d'aller se faire foutre, au lieu de quoi je lui réponds :

– Je m'occupe des billets d'avion pour Beck et moi. Je t'enverrai par SMS l'horaire d'atterrissage de mon vol et tu me l'amèneras à l'aéroport. Quant à l'argent, je te vire mille dollars, ne m'appelle pas pour en réclamer plus.

– OK.

Après avoir raccroché, je reste assis à mon bureau quelques secondes pour me ressaisir. Cette femme me donne envie de boire de l'alcool fort avant le déjeuner. Au bout d'une minute ou deux, je me sens légèrement mieux, mais la colère que j'avais vaguement réussi à calmer remonte à la surface quand je retourne à la salle de conférences pour trouver Alan encore en train de discuter avec Emerie. Elle rigole d'un truc qu'il vient de lui dire.

– Déjà terminé ? Tu n'as pas d'autres appels urgents à passer ? Emerie et moi, on commençait tout juste à faire connaissance.

– Tu aurais peut-être mieux fait de passer les quinze minutes écoulées à réfléchir à la manière dont ta cliente allait te payer ta note, une fois que je l'aurai dépouillée de tout, à l'exception de son autorisation d'exercer.

– Ravi de constater que ton coup de fil a amélioré ton humeur, Jagger.

Je grommelle quelque chose visant à lui suggérer de se carrer ses réflexions où je pense, puis je vais me rasseoir.

– Drew ? intervient Emerie. Avant que tu ne te remettes au travail, est-ce que je peux te parler une minute ?

Je hoche la tête et la suis dans son bureau. Dont elle referme la porte derrière nous.

– Il a l'air sympa, Alan.

– C'est un coureur de jupons.

Je n'en ai aucune idée, en réalité. C'est sorti comme ça.

– Je vois bien pourquoi, répond-elle avec un sourire. Il est bel homme.

Je lui jette un regard furibond.

– Tu as envie de te le taper ?

– Ça te mettrait en colère ?

– Tu te fiches de moi, là ? Sache que je viens juste de raccrocher d'avec mon ex-femme et je suis déjà d'une humeur de dogue, alors pas besoin de t'entendre me dire que tu es intéressée par le premier type que tu croises. Tu étais encore dans mon lit pas plus tard que ce matin, je te rappelle.

Elle se dirige vers son bureau et s'y appuie d'une hanche.

– Conserve ce sentiment. On en fera bon usage plus tard.

Je suis sur elle en moins d'une fraction de seconde. Les doigts enfoncés dans sa taille, je la coince entre mon corps et son bureau.

– C'est mignon. Tu veux qu'on essaie la baise compensatoire ? Je suis plus que volontaire pour répondre à tes desiderata, là, maintenant.

– Alan t'attend.

– Alan peut bien t'écouter hurler mon nom quand j'enfoncerai ma queue en toi.

L'envie irrépressible me frappe aussi violemment qu'un coup dans le bide, et soudain ma bouche s'écrase sur la sienne. J'avale le son de son hoquet tandis que, d'une main, je remonte de sa taille à son sein que j'empaume à travers son chemisier. Quand elle passe les bras autour de moi pour agripper mes fesses, mon autre main vole à son cou afin de lui incliner la tête, pile à l'angle qui convient pour qu'elle s'ouvre plus grand à moi. Elle sent divinement bon, sa peau se hérisse de chair de poule sous mes doigts et sa bouche brûlante a un goût de paradis.

Quand on interrompt le baiser, on est tous les deux hors d'haleine. Emerie a l'air un peu étourdie et moi, je me sens comme enivré.

– C'est quoi, ton planning de l'après-midi ?

Elle réfléchit.

– Mon dernier rendez-vous, c'est une séance vidéo de quinze à seize. Et toi ?

– Sois dans mon bureau à seize heures une.

Notre baiser a étalé son rouge à lèvres. De la pulpe du pouce, je lui essuie le visage et rapporte mon butin sur sa lèvre inférieure.

– Remets du rouge à lèvres avant de venir. Je veux baiser cette bouche peinte en rouge.

Elle semble encore sous le choc quand je rajuste ses vêtements, puis les miens. Un coup d'œil vers le bas m'apprend qu'il n'est pas grand-chose que je puisse faire pour cacher le renflement de mon pantalon. Avec un peu de chance, mon adversaire ne portera pas les yeux dans les parages de mon entrejambe quand je vais le rejoindre. Cela dit… après réflexion, j'espère que si.

Une fois que nous sommes à nouveau présentables, je donne un rapide baiser à Emerie.

– Seize heures une, je lui rappelle.

Elle déglutit et hoche la tête. Au moment où je pose la main sur la poignée, elle finit par recouvrer l'usage de la parole.

– Drew ?

Je me retourne. Elle désigne la commissure de mes lèvres.

– Tu as un peu de… rouge à lèvres. Juste là.

Je me fends d'un large sourire.

– Bien.

***

Drew : Vol American Airlines n° 302, atterrissage à 17 h 05 vendredi. Vol retour à 18 h 15. Vérifie la porte d'embarquement et retrouve-moi là.

Alexa : Ils n'ont pas quelque chose un peu plus tard ? La circulation depuis l'aéroport va être atroce pour mon retour à la maison.

Comme si j'en avais quelque chose à foutre qu'elle soit prise dans les embouteillages.

Drew : Non.

Je m'attends à recevoir un SMS bien énervé en retour, au lieu de quoi son prénom s'affiche à l'écran. À contrecœur, je décroche.

– Je ne change pas les vols.

La porte de mon bureau est à moitié ouverte et mon attention est rapidement détournée vers Emerie, qui vient de se glisser à l'intérieur et referme derrière elle. J'ai perdu le fil du temps, mais un coup d'œil dans l'angle supérieur droit de mon ordinateur me le rappelle : seize heures une.

Alexa est partie dans des explications confuses, comme quoi elle a commencé à regarder le planning des vols pour la semaine suivante, pour son vol retour à elle, et que les prix sont trop élevés. Mais impossible de me concentrer. Je parviens seulement à regarder Emerie, qui verrouille la porte et s'approche de moi. Une lueur espiègle dans les yeux, elle entreprend de déboutonner son chemisier tout en avançant.

En atteignant mon fauteuil, elle pose les mains en haut du grand dossier à l'ancienne et me fait pivoter face à elle. Je manque de laisser échapper le téléphone quand elle se passe la langue sur les lèvres et s'agenouille lentement devant moi.

Oh nom de Dieu de nom de Dieu.

Emerie s'attaque au déboutonnage de ma braguette, et ce n'est qu'en entendant le cri strident d'Alexa au bout du fil que je me rappelle que je n'en suis toujours pas débarrassé.

– Tu es là ? s'écrie-t-elle de sa voix de garce.

– Il te faut combien ?

– Mille de plus.

Si seulement elle savait : je lui donnerais cent mille, là, pour qu'elle me lâche la grappe et que je puisse tout entier me consacrer à la sublime vue qui s'offre à moi.

— Parfait. Je te donnerai ça. Ne me rappelle pas.

Je coupe la communication et jette mon téléphone sur le bureau. Emerie lève les yeux vers moi derrière ses longs cils et je me rends compte qu'elle a peint ses lèvres de rouge vif.

Oh waouh.

Ayant défait ma braguette, elle me pousse sur les fesses afin que je les soulève et qu'elle puisse ôter mon pantalon. À quoi j'obéis avec joie, l'aidant même à retirer mon boxer par la même occasion. Mon érection est libérée. D'une de ses petites mains délicates, elle enveloppe mon membre et le caresse lentement de bas en haut, jusqu'à ce qu'une petite goutte de plaisir brille à la pointe.

J'ai les yeux rivés sur elle qui se penche pour la lécher. Les paupières closes, elle ramène sa langue à l'intérieur de sa jolie bouche et se pourlèche les lèvres.

– Oh putain, je grogne.

Elle m'adresse un sourire canaille.

– Toujours en colère ?

– Ma fureur se dissipe à toute vitesse.

Je ne sais pas trop si elle prend volontairement son temps, ou si c'est mon esprit qui me joue des tours, en tout cas elle ouvre grand la bouche et tout semble se dérouler au ralenti. La façon dont elle s'approche de mon sexe, la langue tendue, dont ses magnifiques lèvres si rouges et si sensuelles se posent autour de mon gland et se referment dessus. Elle aspire toute ma longueur en un long mouvement profond.

– Oh, Em. Hmm.

Très bizarrement, au lieu du soulagement de sentir sa bouche sur moi, tout en sachant que mon orgasme ne tardera pas à m'apaiser, je suis soudain tendu, crispé, même. En fait, je suis en colère de découvrir qu'elle est douée pour ce genre de gâteries, furieux à l'idée qu'elle a dû apprendre ces astuces avec un autre bonhomme.

Elle remonte sans se presser, tout en maintenant ses lèvres étroitement serrées autour de ma longueur tandis que le plat de sa langue est collé à ma veine qui pulse au rythme de mon cœur. Puis, elle me relâche presque entièrement, pour mieux me reprendre tout entier. À chaque mouvement de sa tête, vers le haut, vers le bas, j'éprouve une émotion différente, oscillant entre la colère qu'elle se débrouille aussi bien et le ravissement pour exactement la même raison.

Elle alterne entre les va-et-vient où elle m'engloutit tout entier et les caresses avec sa main pendant que sa petite langue mouillée s'enroule autour de mon gland. Si j'étais en elle, là, le temps d'arriver à la jouissance serait d'une brièveté embarrassante.

En l'occurrence, il s'écoule moins de cinq minutes avant que je doive déjà me retenir et l'avertir que je suis sur le point d'exploser.

– Em, je vais…

Je grogne plus que je ne parle, mais elle a bien dû comprendre.

– Em…

Dernier avertissement. Pourtant, au lieu de s'écarter et de me retirer de sa bouche, elle fiche son regard dans le mien et le retient pendant qu'elle m'engloutit jusqu'au fond de sa gorge.

Magnifique. Ses yeux bleus levés vers moi, ses joues laiteuses gonflées par mon sexe et ses lèvres rouges serrées autant que possible. J'enfouis les doigts dans ses cheveux et souffle son prénom une dernière fois avant de jouir dans sa gorge. Elle émet un gémissement en fermant les yeux et avale jusqu'à la dernière goutte de mon sperme.

Incapable de parler, je l'attrape et la relève pour l'installer sur mes genoux afin de pouvoir enfouir mon visage dans son épaule. Une fois que ma respiration est calmée, je l'embrasse dans le cou.

– C'était… inouï. C'est étrange de dire « merci » après ça, mais merde : merci.

Elle pouffe. Un son qui me donne l'impression d'être un idiot.

– De rien.

Je la garde un long moment sur mes genoux. Quand le sang remonte enfin à mon cerveau, je me rappelle que j'étais en train de parler avec Alexa, juste avant.

– Reste avec moi ce soir encore. Je dois prendre un vol pour Atlanta demain après-midi, je vais donc quitter le bureau de bonne heure.

– Ah bon ? Tu seras absent combien de temps ?

– Juste la nuit. C'est une longue histoire, mais je vais chercher mon fils et je rentre dans la foulée avec lui, une heure plus tard. Alexa reste là-bas une semaine supplémentaire et je ne veux pas qu'il voyage seul.

– C'est sympa. Alors tu vas l'avoir toute la semaine pour toi tout seul ?

– Oui. Il va t'adorer, j'ajoute sans réfléchir. C'est un vrai petit homme à femmes.

Elle sourit.

– Je serai ravie de rester avec toi cette nuit, et j'ai hâte de rencontrer ton fils.

Je n'ai jamais présenté aucune femme à Beck. Pourtant, ne me demandez pas pourquoi, j'ai envie qu'il rencontre Emerie. C'est peut-être la meilleure pipe de ma vie qui me donne des idées bizarres, mais j'ai la sensation qu'il doit la rencontrer.

CHAPITRE 29

EMERIE

Je me réveille la première. Même si c'est généralement moi, la lève-tard, aujourd'hui c'est Drew qui dort encore à presque sept heures trente. Allongé sur le ventre, il a le drap entortillé autour de la taille et son fessier ferme bien en vue. Les deux bras relevés au-dessus de sa tête, coincés sous l'oreiller, il dort paisiblement, le visage tourné vers moi. Ses mâchoires sont couvertes d'un début de barbe et ses cheveux en bataille. Il s'est endormi il y a seulement quatre heures, et pourtant, si c'est possible, il est encore plus sexy qu'hier.

Comment cela se peut-il ? En fait, il est probable que ce soit moi qui sois devenue plus fan de lui, qui l'apprécie plus. Finalement, c'est sans doute aussi bien que le fils de Drew doive passer la semaine prochaine avec lui. Car il serait facile pour moi de m'attacher, or la dernière chose dont j'aie besoin, c'est de passer d'un homme qui n'est pas intéressé par moi à un autre qui n'est pas intéressé par une relation.

Mon téléphone vibre sur la table de chevet et je me dépêche de l'attraper avant qu'il ne réveille Drew. Ayant entré mon mot de passe, je découvre le SMS qui vient d'arriver.

Baldwin : *Casablanca* ce soir ?
Je rapporte des boulettes de viande marocaines de chez *Marrak*, sur la 53e.

Je lâche un soupir. C'est notre truc. On adore louer des films et transformer ça en dîner à thème. À la fac, on choisissait le film chacun notre tour, et l'autre devait rapporter le dîner qui allait avec. Par exemple, je louais *Sweet Home Alabama* et il apportait le poulet frit à la mode du Sud. Il choisissait *Les Évadés* et moi j'apportais des sandwichs à la bolognaise.

Il y a encore deux semaines, j'aurais sauté de joie à la pensée d'une soirée film avec Baldwin, mais aujourd'hui, pour une raison qui m'échappe, je me sens écartelée. Ce n'est pourtant pas comme si Drew et moi sortions vraiment ensemble, et même si c'était le cas, Baldwin ne nourrit de toute façon à mon endroit qu'un intérêt amical. Alors pourquoi est-ce que je me sens mal d'accepter ? Peut-être parce que je suis allongée nue à côté d'un homme, en train d'envisager la proposition d'un autre. Oui, c'est sûrement ça qui ne passe pas bien. Je referme le message et décide de réfléchir et de répondre à l'invitation de Baldwin plus tard.

Ma vessie me rappelant à l'ordre, je vais aller aux toilettes, et puis je préparerai du café avant de filer sans bruit. J'ai besoin de retourner chez moi chercher des vêtements propres et de prendre une douche rapide avant mon rendez-vous de neuf heures au rez-de-chaussée.

Une fois prête, je glisse un mot sous une tasse de café vide sur le plan de travail de la cuisine et vais prendre le métro.

Vers le deuxième arrêt, je me rends compte que j'ai oublié mon téléphone sur la table de chevet de Drew. Au moins, je n'aurai pas à aller bien loin pour le récupérer quand j'arriverai au travail tout à l'heure.

***

Le téléphone fixe du bureau sonne quand j'y arrive, à peine quelques minutes avant l'heure de mon rendez-vous. Je tends le bras par-dessus le bureau d'accueil et décroche.

– Bureau de Drew Jagger. Que puis-je faire pour vous ?

– Je dois à parler à Drew.

Je n'ai entendu la voix d'Alexa qu'une seule fois, pourtant je la reconnais. Drew n'a pas beaucoup d'amis qui aient cet accent du Sud et cette arrogance.

– Puis-je savoir qui l'appelle ? je demande d'une voix trop mielleuse.

– Non, vous ne pouvez pas.

Garce.

Je jette un coup d'œil sur la base du téléphone et constate que la ligne du bureau de Drew clignote en rouge : il est déjà au téléphone.

Un sourire aux lèvres, je reprends l'appareil.

– M. Jagger n'est pas disponible pour le moment. Souhaitez-vous laisser un message ?

Elle soupire bruyamment.

– Dites-lui d'appeler Alexa.

Sur ce, elle me raccroche au nez.

En passant devant le bureau de Drew, je l'entends discuter, alors je décide de lui noter le message sur mon bloc, dont je déposerai la feuille sur son bureau, avant l'arrivée de mon rendez-vous. Mais quand j'y retourne, il est en train de raccrocher.

– Bonjour, je lui lance, souriante. Je viens de prendre un message pendant que tu étais sur l'autre ligne.

Je m'approche et il s'adosse contre son fauteuil, regard impassible.

– Moi aussi, j'ai pris un message pour toi.

– Ah ?

Il pousse mon portable au bord de son bureau.

– J'ai d'abord cru que c'était toi qui appelais, pour vérifier si tu n'avais pas oublié ton téléphone chez moi, alors j'ai répondu.

Il n'y a que deux personnes susceptibles de me téléphoner si tôt le matin. Voyant la manière étrange dont se comporte Drew, j'en déduis que ce n'était pas ma mère.

– C'était qui ?

Un muscle tressaute dans sa mâchoire.

– Baldwin. Il voulait savoir s'il devait commander les boulettes de viande pour ce soir.

Merde. C'est encore plus bizarre que ce matin. Je ressens le besoin de lui expliquer.

– Il m'a envoyé un SMS ce matin, en demandant si je voulais louer un film et dîner avec lui. J'aime bien accorder la nourriture au thème du film. Je n'avais pas encore répondu.

L'expression de Drew reste indéchiffrable.

– Eh bien, il attend ta réponse.

Nous nous dévisageons et mon esprit cavale dans tous les sens, essayant de deviner ce que Drew attend de moi, parole ou réaction. Par chance, la sonnette de la porte d'entrée retentit. Je baisse les yeux vers ma montre, soulagée que mon rendez-vous de ce matin ait quelques minutes d'avance.

Drew se lève.

– C'est pour toi ?

– Je crois. J'ai une séance à neuf heures. Je vais leur ouvrir.

– Non, j'y vais. J'ai une conférence téléphonique, ma porte sera donc fermée, mais je n'aime pas que les gens te croient seule ici.

Il me tend mon portable en passant près de moi.
– Ne fais pas attendre le professeur Têtedenœud.

***

Ironie du sort, le problème du couple qui vient de quitter mon bureau, c'est qu'ils ne se disent pas ce qu'ils ont vraiment en tête. Ils ne sont pas honnêtes l'un avec l'autre. Lauren veut plus de cunnilingus et n'ose pas le demander. Son fiancé, Tim, veut qu'elle soit plus souvent à l'origine de leurs ébats amoureux. Si Drew et moi n'avons pas encore rencontré de soucis au lit, je n'ai en revanche pas la moindre idée de ce qu'il attend de moi. Et me voilà, qui conseille les gens en prônant la communication comme outil clé de toute relation épanouie, pourtant je me cache de Drew en restant dans mon bureau pour éviter de terminer une conversation dont je sais bien qu'elle est restée en suspens.

Je m'attarde à mon bureau encore une demi-heure, frustrée et en colère contre moi-même. Sans compter que Drew est le genre d'homme à dire exactement ce qu'il a en tête, lui, alors pourquoi ne m'explique-t-il pas ce qu'il pense de mon potentiel dîner avec Baldwin ? Et pourquoi suis-je aussi attentive à ce que pense Drew si notre relation n'est que sexuelle ?

Plus je demeure assise à mon bureau, plus je bouillonne. J'ai besoin de clarifier ce qui se passe entre nous. Si je ne règle pas ça avant son départ cet après-midi, ça va m'empoisonner. Alors je décide de suivre le conseil que je ne cesse de donner à mes clients. Mieux vaut en finir tant que je suis agacée.

Je me lève, prends une profonde inspiration et me dirige vers le bureau de Drew d'un pas ferme. Il est au téléphone quand j'entre.

– Je vais y réfléchir, dit-il à son interlocuteur après avoir jeté un coup d'œil vers moi. Je vous rappelle la semaine prochaine, d'accord, Frank ?

Une fois l'appareil raccroché, il se cale contre le dossier de son fauteuil dans la même posture que ce matin et hoche la tête.

– Emerie.

– Drew.

Nos regards s'affrontent. Voyant qu'il ne dit rien, je lève les yeux au ciel.

– On fait quoi ?

– Là, tout de suite ? Tu es plantée dans mon bureau, l'air un peu furax.

Je plisse les paupières.

– Tu sais très bien ce que je veux dire.

Pas sûr, non.

– Est-ce qu'on… (J'agite la main entre lui et moi.) couche juste ensemble ?

– On passe la plupart de nos journées ensemble, on partage presque tous nos repas et pour ce qui est de coucher… on ne dort pas beaucoup quand on est dans le même lit.

Il a l'air amusé. Pas moi.

– Est-ce qu'on… fait toutes ces choses ensemble de façon exclusive ?

Il se met debout et contourne son bureau. L'espièglerie a soudain disparu de sa voix quand il reprend la parole :

– Tu es en train de me demander si tu peux aller baiser avec quelqu'un d'autre ?

– Non !

Oui ? Non ? Peut-être ? Je n'ai envie d'être avec personne d'autre. Bizarrement, l'idée de coucher avec Baldwin n'est même plus séduisante. En revanche, je souhaite savoir s'il serait déplacé que je passe du temps avec un autre homme.

– Donc quelle est ta question, exactement ?

– Je… je ne sais pas.

Un silence s'installe entre nous. Je vois les rouages tourner derrière ses yeux tandis qu'il me dévisage, tout en se frottant la lèvre inférieure du pouce. Au bout d'une minute, il s'écarte de son bureau et le pouce en question trouve son chemin jusqu'à mon menton, qu'il soulève.

– Je ne projette pas de coucher avec qui que ce soit d'autre, m'affirme-t-il, droit dans les yeux. Et j'espère que toi non plus. Je pensais qu'on avait discuté de ça dans la baignoire, hier.

Ma voix sort dans un souffle, faiblarde.

– OK.

– Je suppose que ça a à voir avec le message que je t'ai transmis tout à l'heure ?

Je hoche la tête.

– Tu veux savoir ce que m'inspire la soirée que tu projettes de passer dans ton appartement à dîner et regarder un film avec le crétin ?

Je hoche de nouveau la tête.

– D'accord. (Il détourne les yeux, comme pour réfléchir une seconde à sa réponse, avant de reprendre :) Je t'apprécie. J'aime ta façon d'écouter les problèmes merdiques des gens toute la journée tout en continuant à penser qu'il y a moyen de sauver les choses. J'aime que tu sois partante pour tout, qu'il s'agisse de rester à la maison pour regarder de vieux films ou de sortir dans un bar jouer au billard. J'aime la façon dont tes yeux s'allument quand tu parles de tes parents. J'aime beaucoup la sensation d'être en toi et la manière dont tu gémis mon nom quand tu vas jouir. J'ai bien aimé que tu me prépares du café avant de partir ce matin, et j'aime même que tu te soucies de ce que je vais penser de ton dîner avec le professeur Chochotte.

Il marque une pause.

– Je pense que tout ça doit t'indiquer que, pour moi, il y a plus entre nous que le sexe. Cela dit, je vais ajouter que je déteste t'imaginer en train de te blottir contre un connard sur ton canapé pour regarder un film ; connard dont tu es amoureuse depuis trois ans. Mais je ne compte pas te demander de cesser de le voir. C'est une décision que tu dois prendre seule et je verrai la manière dont j'accepterai ton choix, parce que je suis conscient que mes problèmes de confiance émanent d'un passé qui n'a rien à voir avec toi.

Je déglutis. Ça fait beaucoup à avaler d'un coup. Et c'est bien plus que je n'en attendais de lui en matière d'engagement.

– D'accord.

– On est bons ? Parce que j'ai besoin de quatre heures pour effectuer l'équivalent de huit heures de travail avant de sauter dans un avion afin que ma feignasse d'ex-femme puisse se plaindre de la circulation jusqu'à l'aéroport, pendant que moi je parcourrai plus de mille quatre cents kilomètres pour récupérer mon fils avant de rentrer directement et de me retaper les mille quatre cents kilomètres retour. Et j'ai besoin d'au moins une demi-heure de libre sur ces quatre pour pouvoir te prendre sur ton bureau. Parce que tu m'as peut-être préparé mon café ce matin, mais tu n'es pas restée assez longtemps pour qu'on baise, un manque auquel je prévois de remédier avant mon départ pour l'aéroport.

J'ai peut-être la tête qui tourne, en revanche, je sais une chose de façon certaine. Il n'est rien que je veuille plus que de voir Drew terminer son travail et s'en tenir à ses plans.

Je me hausse sur la pointe des pieds et lui dépose un baiser sur les lèvres.

– Vas-y, qu'est-ce que tu fais encore planté là ? Tu as du boulot qui t'attend.

CHAPITRE 30

DREW

– Regarde comme elle a de longues jambes.

La biologie peut aller se rhabiller, ce gamin est bel et bien mon fils. Beck contemple une hôtesse de l'air effectivement dotée des jambes les plus longues que j'aie jamais vues. Elle lève les bras pour caler des bagages dans le compartiment au-dessus du siège devant nous et surprend Beck penché vers l'allée pour l'observer.

– Tu t'appelles comment ? lui demande-t-elle avec un sourire.

– Becket Archer Jagger.

Il a répondu avec une telle fierté que je n'ai pas le cœur de lui signaler que, normalement, on ne récite pas son premier et son deuxième prénoms, plus le patronyme, à des inconnus. L'hôtesse referme le porte-bagage dans un claquement et s'agenouille auprès de lui.

– Eh bien, bonjour Beckett Archer Jagger. Je suis Danielle Marie Warren, et tu es adorable. Quel âge as-tu, mon grand ?

– Six ans trois quarts.

– Six ans trois quarts, hein ? Moi, j'en ai trente et un et demi. (Elle m'adresse un clin d'œil tout en continuant sa conversation avec Beck.) Sauf qu'en général, j'arrondis de trente et un et demi à… vingt-sept. Puis-je t'apporter quelque chose à boire, Beckett Archer Jagger de six ans trois quarts ? Un jus de fruits, peut-être ?

Il hoche la tête, avant d'ajouter :

– Tu as des jambes de girafe.

– Beck…, je le gronde.

L'hôtesse éclate de rire.

– Non, laissez, j'ai l'habitude. Quand j'avais ton âge, les autres enfants se moquaient de moi à cause de mes longues jambes. (Elle désigne son badge nominatif, qui indique : « Danny ».) Je m'appelle Danielle, mais tout le monde m'appelle Danny. Et quand j'étais à l'école élémentaire, les garçons me surnommaient Danny-longues-jambes. Tu vois, explique-t-elle en agitant les doigts, comme ces araignées à longues jambes qu'on appelle les Daddy-longues-jambes ?

Beckett s'esclaffe.

– Maman aussi, elle a un surnom pour papa.

– Ah bon ? Je parie que c'est mieux que Daddy-longues-jambes.

– Je ne suis pas sûr qu'il soit très judicieux de répéter les surnoms que maman donne à papa, ces temps-ci, j'interviens, avant d'expliquer à l'hôtesse : Divorcés.

Elle m'adresse un sourire et un clin d'œil.

– Bon, et si j'allais te chercher un jus avant le décollage ? Et un petit quelque chose pour ton papa aussi ?

Quelques minutes plus tard, elle revient chargée d'un jus de pomme dans un gobelet en plastique avec un couvercle et une paille, plus un verre contenant deux doigts d'un liquide clair sur des glaçons.

– Nous allons avoir un peu de retard à cause des conditions météorologiques, nous informe-t-elle en passant les boissons. J'espère que vous n'aviez pas de projets pour ce soir. Tu n'as pas un rendez-vous galant, au moins ? ajoute-t-elle à l'intention de Beck.

Il fait la grimace, comme si elle venait de lui signifier qu'il devait manger tous ses brocolis et toutes ses betteraves. *Pourvu que ça dure comme ça longtemps, fiston. Je n'ai pas encore réussi à comprendre les femmes moi-même, alors je suis loin d'être en mesure de te donner des conseils.*

Même si ni Beckett ni moi n'avions de projets spéciaux pour ce soir, le commentaire de Danny-longues-jambes me pousse à me demander pour quelle soirée Emerie s'est finalement décidée. Après notre conversation de ce matin, elle n'en a pas reparlé. Peut-être parce que les seuls mots que nous ayons échangés cet après-midi, c'étaient ceux que je lui ai susurrés à l'oreille pendant qu'elle était courbée sur son bureau, sa jupe retroussée, vingt minutes avant mon départ programmé. *Jouis sur mon sexe*, c'est largement mieux que de discuter du professeur Crétin.

Sauf que maintenant, ça me fait gamberger. Est-ce qu'elle est assise à côté de ce connard sur qui elle bave depuis plus de trois ans ? Il se comporte peut-être avec un poil plus de raffinement que moi, cet enfoiré, mais au bout du compte, on est tous les deux des hommes et Emerie est une femme superbe. J'ai bien vu comment il a réagi quand il a soupçonné que quelque chose se passait entre elle et moi. Il s'est montré possessif mais pas jaloux. Ce qui en dit fort long sur ce qu'il pense. Les gens sont jaloux quand ils veulent quelque chose que possède quelqu'un d'autre. Ils sont possessifs quand ils protègent quelque chose qu'ils ont déjà. Cet enfoiré sait qu'il l'a dans sa poche depuis le début.

Mon instinct me dit qu'il évite d'entamer une relation avec Emerie parce qu'il a envie de passer du bon temps, genre baiser à droite et à gauche à la fac et parmi ses étudiantes, sans s'engager dans aucune relation sérieuse. Et comment exactement est-ce que je sais ça sur lui alors que je ne l'ai vu que deux fois ? Parce que je reconnais la tronche de ces gars-là. J'en vois une dans le miroir tous les jours depuis deux ans, depuis ce putain de divorce.

Beck a sorti son livre de coloriages, où il dessine une girafe. Je rigole en songeant au nombre de fois où je griffonne pendant que je suis au téléphone. L'acquis l'emporte souvent sur l'inné. Je me vois complètement en train de dessiner une girafe, en ce moment même, si j'avais un crayon à la main.

Sauf que ma girafe à moi aurait sans doute des seins, parce que depuis mes dix ans, tous mes gribouillis comportent des seins d'une manière ou d'une autre.

Si, pendant mon enfance, à peu près tout me faisait penser à des seins, cette semaine, tout me fait penser à Emerie. Une pub pour du rouge à lèvres rouge vif à l'aéroport. *Les lèvres peintes de rouge d'Emerie autour de mon érection.* L'hôtesse qui annonce que nos projets risquent d'être ruinés à cause de la météo et du retard. *Les projets d'Emerie : est-elle installée sur le canapé avec le crétin ?* Mon fils qui dessine une girafe. *Si je dessinais une girafe, elle aurait des seins. Les seins d'Emerie sont magnifiques.* Bref, tous les chemins de mon cerveau ont été déviés pour ne plus mener que vers une seule destination.

Je descends d'un trait la moitié de mon verre et pêche mon téléphone dans ma poche.

Drew : Tu as fait quoi, ce soir,
du coup ?

Puis j'attends la vibration qui m'informera de l'arrivée de sa réponse. Et j'attends encore.

***

Je suis en train de me transformer en fillette. C'est la troisième fois que je vérifie mon portable ce matin. *Rien.* Douze heures se sont écoulées.

Ayant préparé des pancakes aux pépites de chocolat qui comprennent plus de chocolat que de pancake, j'ai demandé à Beck ce qu'il voulait faire. Et reçu la même réponse que toujours : aller à la patinoire. Ce gamin est obsédé par le hockey. Alors j'ai enveloppé le petit monstre dans trois épaisseurs de vêtements, attaché nos patins par les lacets et jeté une paire de chaque sur mon épaule avant de nous mettre en route.

Dans l'entrée, j'ai prétendu devoir faire un arrêt express dans mon bureau. Comme je n'ai toujours pas eu de nouvelles d'Emerie, je commence à me demander si je devrais m'inquiéter de son silence au lieu de m'énerver à l'idée de ce qu'elle a bien pu faire.

Dans le bureau, j'entends une douce musique. Une version instrumentale quelconque. Mon cœur s'emballe à l'idée qu'Emerie se trouve donc au bout du couloir. Je ne saurais dire si c'est d'impatience ou de colère, en tout cas j'ai le sang qui me bat dans les oreilles alors que je me dirige vers son bureau.

La porte est entrouverte, mais comme elle ne semble pas m'avoir entendu entrer, je frappe pour ne pas l'effrayer. À en juger par son saut sur sa chaise, il faut croire que ma précaution a été vaine. Par instinct, je lève les mains dans un geste de reddition. Encore.

– Ce n'est que moi.

– Tu m'as fichu la trouille, merde.

Sur quoi Beck, qui se tenait derrière moi, passe la tête derrière mes jambes.

Emerie se couvre la bouche.

– Oh, là, là, pardon. Je parle très mal.

C'est Beck qui répond à ma place.

– Mon papa dit bien pire.

Je souris et lui ébouriffe les cheveux, songeant que je vais quand même devoir l'avoir avec lui, la conversation au sujet des secrets qu'il ne faut pas nécessairement révéler.

Emerie redescend de sa chaise, traverse la pièce et se penche, la main tendue.

– Tu dois être Beck.

– Beckett Archer Jagger.

La lèvre d'Emerie frémit et elle lève les yeux vers moi. Je hausse les épaules.

– Eh bien, enchantée de te rencontrer, Beckett Archer Jagger. Moi, c'est Emerie Rose.

– Rose, c'est ton deuxième prénom ou ton nom de famille ?

Elle sourit, avant de se mettre à rire. C'est exactement la question que je lui ai posée la première fois qu'on s'est rencontrés.

– C'est mon nom de famille. Je n'ai pas de deuxième prénom.

Sa phrase semble plonger Beckett dans une profonde réflexion, alors j'interviens.

– Pardon, on ne voulait pas t'effrayer. Beck et moi, on part faire du patin à glace. Je m'inquiétais juste que tu n'aies pas répondu à mon SMS hier soir.

Je plonge les yeux dans ceux d'Emerie. Elle se retourne et s'approche de son bureau, sur lequel elle ramasse son portable cassé, qu'elle balance entre son pouce et son index.

– Je l'ai fait tomber hier soir. Je viens d'aller m'en acheter un neuf et j'essaie de voir s'il y a moyen de récupérer mes contacts dans le *Cloud*. Je ne connais plus aucun numéro de téléphone par cœur.

Je lâche un soupir. Bon, elle ne me largue pas. Ça me taraudait vraiment. Sans doute bien plus que ça n'aurait dû, d'ailleurs.

En temps normal, si je suis intéressé par une femme et qu'elle ne réagit pas favorablement… « *Suivante !* » Une de perdue, dix de retrouvées. Sauf qu'avec Emerie, non seulement ça m'a rendu anxieux qu'elle ne réponde pas à mon SMS, mais l'idée de chercher dans ma liste de contacts un autre numéro à appeler ne m'a même pas effleuré.

– Tu veux un coup de main ? J'en casse un tous les mois, de téléphone.

Elle regarde les patins accrochés à mes épaules.

– Je m'en voudrais de vous retarder quand vous êtes partis pour vous amuser, les garçons.

– Ça ne dérange pas Beck. Hein, mon grand ?

Mon fils est vraiment facile à vivre. Il hausse les épaules.

– Non. Je peux aller dessiner dans ton bureau, papa ?

– Bien sûr. Tiroir du bas, à droite.

Il part en courant. Il adore s'asseoir derrière mon grand bureau et dessiner. Il pourrait y passer des heures. Je contourne le bureau d'Emerie.

– Il est adorable, commente-t-elle.

– Merci. Oui, c'est un bon gamin, je confirme en tirant son siège. Assieds-toi. Je vais te montrer comment charger ton nouveau téléphone.

Bien évidemment, je pourrais m'installer et le faire à sa place en deux secondes chrono, mais je préfère me pencher par-dessus son épaule et l'emprisonner entre mon corps et le bureau. Je lui parle volontairement bas et laisse mon souffle lui chatouiller le cou.

– Tu cliques sur ce dossier. (Je pose ma main sur la sienne, qui tient la souris et clique.) Ensuite, celui-ci. Et puis tu utilises le menu déroulant, ici, et tu cliques sur « restaurer ».

Voyant sa peau se couvrir de chair de poule, je penche la tête plus près encore de son oreille.

– Tu as froid ?

– Non, ça va.

Je souris *in petto* en me déplaçant dans quelques écrans supplémentaires. Et alors, le nouveau téléphone, qu'elle a déjà branché à son ordinateur portable, s'allume et entame son chargement via le *Cloud*.

– Waouh. Ça fait au moins une heure que j'essayais de faire ça.

– Comment tu as cassé l'autre ?

– Tu dois d'abord me promettre de ne pas rire.

– Mais je pourrai quand même me moquer de toi ?

– Non, non plus.

Je me redresse.

– Quel est l'intérêt d'entendre toute cette histoire, dans ce cas ?

Emerie pouffe.

– Comment s'est passé ton voyage à Atlanta, idiot ?

– Le vol a été retardé de quelques heures à cause des conditions météo, mais autrement, très bien. Au moins, Alexa ne m'a pas cassé les pieds.

Emerie vient de m'offrir l'ouverture idéale. Je déteste ce besoin qui me pousse à savoir, mais tant pis, c'est comme ça et point barre. J'essaie quand même de prendre un ton détaché.

– Comment s'est passé ton dîner d'hier soir ?

Elle commence par froncer les sourcils, avant de comprendre ce que je lui demande.

– Oh, je me suis juste commandé chinois toute seule.

– Tu n'as pas dîné avec Crétin ?

Elle se mord la lèvre inférieure et secoue la tête. Je m'avance d'un pas vers elle.

– Pourquoi ?

– Je… Ça ne me semblait pas bien.

Nous sommes tombés d'accord pour avoir une relation sexuelle exclusive et je lui ai dit à mots à peine couverts que j'espérais partager avec elle plus qu'une super alchimie, pourtant je ne peux décemment pas lui interdire de dîner avec un ami homme. Ne me faites pas dire ce que je n'ai pas dit, c'est exactement ce que j'ai envie de lui signifier, mais vu que cette pensée me fait peur, même à moi, je préfère garder ces conneries pour moi.

Au lieu de révéler ma chochotte intérieure, je me dirige vers la porte de son bureau. Sans la quitter des yeux, j'appelle mon fils.

– Tout va bien, Beck ?

– Oui ! crie-t-il en retour.

– OK, je te rejoins d'ici quelques minutes, bonhomme.

Sur quoi, je ferme doucement la porte.

– Tu viens ?

– Qu'est-ce que tu fais ?

– Viens ici.

Emerie s'exécute et vient se poster à portée de mes mains.

– Quoi ?

– Je n'ai pas arrêté de penser à toi durant tout le vol de retour.

Elle déglutit.

– Ah oui ?

– Et ce matin, sous la douche. J'ai dû me rincer à l'eau glacée pour me calmer, parce que chaque fois que je fermais les yeux, je revoyais tes fesses et toi à plat ventre sur mon bureau.

Elle écarquille les yeux.

– Ton fils est dans la pièce voisine.

– Je sais. C'est pourquoi tu n'es pas déjà sur ce bureau, à l'heure qu'il est. Je vais me contenter d'un petit échantillon.

Elle se lèche les lèvres. Décrétant que Beck ne va pas venir me chercher d'une seconde à l'autre, j'en ai fini de perdre du temps. Je prends sa nuque dans ma paume et l'attire à moi pour me coller à sa bouche dans un baiser avide. Je passe mon bras libre autour de sa taille et elle geint quand je plaque son corps contre le mien. Punaise ce qu'elle sent bon. Une fragrance sucrée mêlée à son odeur féminine si sexy. Enivrant. Il me faut faire appel à toute la maîtrise qui me reste pour ne pas la faire pivoter et la plaquer contre la porte. Lorsque je saisis ses fesses à pleines mains et qu'elle gémit dans ma bouche, je manque de la perdre, cette dernière bribe de contrôle.

Enfin je libère sa bouche, parce que mon érection pulse. Je m'apprête à recommencer quand j'entends mon fils appeler.

– Merde, je grommelle, en appuyant mon front contre celui d'Emerie. Je vais devoir cacher mon érection, sinon il pourrait me poser des questions auxquelles je ne suis pas prêt à répondre.

Heureusement, je porte un jean sombre et parviens à le rajuster avant d'aller voir Beck.

– Qu'est-ce qui se passe, fiston ?

– On peut boire un chocolat chaud avant d'aller patiner ?

– Tu viens de manger des pancakes aux pépites de chocolat pour le petit déjeuner. Tu ne trouves pas que ça fait assez de chocolat pour la matinée ?

Mon fils est un petit rusé.

– Mais il va faire froid, dehors, ça me tiendra chaud à l'intérieur.

Emerie vient se planter à côté de moi, tout sourire.

– Il marque un point.

– Tu vas venir à la patinoire avec nous ? lui demande Beck.

– Je ne pense pas que ce soit une bonne idée. Je ne sais pas faire de patin à glace.

– Mon papa peut t'apprendre. Il sait tout faire.

Bien dit, fiston.

Emerie cherche mon aide du regard. Je hausse les épaules.

– Le petit marque un autre point. Je suis doué dans tout ce que je fais.

Elle lève les yeux au ciel, avant de s'adresser à Beck.

– Ton papa et toi, vous n'avez pas besoin de moi pour vous ralentir.

– On n'est jamais allés patiner avec quelqu'un d'autre avant. Je pourrai te montrer comment faire les bons mouvements.

Emerie se tourne vers moi, un sourcil haussé.

– Ah, il a des « mouvements » ? Comme son papa ?

– Allez, je lui souffle à voix basse. Laisse-le te les montrer et je te montrerai les miens plus tard.

CHAPITRE 31

EMERIE

– Je ne pense pas qu'elle soit cassée. Mais on va faire une radio pour s'en assurer.

Le médecin des urgences manipule ma cheville. Qui vire déjà au bleu.

– Merci.

– L'infirmière va venir d'ici quelques minutes remplir votre dossier, puis elle appellera un radiologue.

– D'accord. (Je me tourne vers Drew.) Tout ça, c'est ta faute.

– Ma faute ?

– Oui. Tu me faisais aller trop vite.

– Trop vite ? Une grand-mère qui poussait un chariot nous a dépassés sur la glace. Tu n'aurais pas dû lâcher ma main.

– J'ai eu peur.

Ça faisait plus de deux heures qu'on patinait, et moi je n'arrivais toujours pas à acquérir les bases.

Parce que j'étais trop instable sur mes pieds, que mes chevilles tremblotaient sans cesse d'avant en arrière, ce qui a fini par desserrer mes patins. La dernière fois que je suis tombée, ma cheville n'était plus maintenue et je me la suis tordue. Bon sang, ça m'a fait mal, mais je n'aurais jamais cru qu'elle puisse être cassée.

Contrairement à Drew qui, après un regard sur mon pied gonflé, a décidé qu'on devait aller aux urgences. Impossible de l'en dissuader. Son copain, Roman, nous a rejoints devant l'hôpital pour prendre Beck chez lui afin que Drew puisse rester avec moi.

L'infirmière arrive avec son bloc-notes.

– Je dois vous poser quelques questions. Votre mari peut rester s'il le veut, mais il devra sortir quand le technicien viendra prendre la radio.

– Ce n'est pas… (Je nous désigne tour à tour, Drew et moi.) On n'est pas mariés.

L'infirmière sourit. Pas à moi, à Drew. Elle bat des cils, en plus.

Je rêve.

– Dans ce cas, je vais devoir vous demander de sortir, lui indique-t-elle. Je viendrai vous chercher une fois que j'en aurai terminé avec votre…

Elle attend que Drew complète.

– Petite amie.

– Ah. Oui. Eh bien, je viendrai vous chercher quand j'en aurai terminé avec votre petite amie.

C'est un effet de mon imagination, ou est-ce qu'elle a posé la question pour savoir si on était ensemble ?

Drew m'embrasse sur le front en promettant de revenir. Dès qu'il est sorti, l'infirmière entame sa liste de questions médicales. C'est juste à ce moment-là que je me rends compte que Drew m'a appelée sa petite amie.

***

– Je peux marcher.

Drew vient de me soulever dans ses bras pour la dixième fois. Il m'a portée de la patinoire au taxi, du taxi à l'hôpital, de l'hôpital au taxi et du taxi jusqu'à son appartement, où il m'a installée sur son canapé, en surélevant mon pied. *Comme le docteur l'a stipulé.*

Maintenant, il a fait livrer à manger et il me porte jusqu'à la table.

– Le docteur a dit qu'il ne fallait pas t'appuyer dessus.

– Ça va. C'est juste une entorse. L'attelle va m'empêcher de trop y mettre mon poids, de toute façon.

Beck tire la chaise tandis que son père approche avec moi dans ses bras. Roman, qui est en train de sortir les emballages de nourriture d'un grand sac de livraison, nous regarde bizarrement. C'est la première fois que je le rencontre, il doit me prendre pour une comédienne.

– Je suis gênée. Je te jure que je ne suis pas aussi empotée, en temps normal.

Roman continue à observer la scène qui se déroule sous ses yeux : Drew qui me repose et entreprend de remplir l'assiette devant moi. J'ai la sensation que Roman n'est pas homme à rater beaucoup de détails.

– Pas de souci, me rassure-t-il. Notre Florence Nightingale[5] n'aurait pas dû te laisser tomber.

– Je ne l'ai pas laissée tomber. Elle a lâché ma main.

J'adresse un clin d'œil à Roman, afin de lui signifier que nous sommes sur la même longueur d'onde, puis je conclus :

– Il m'a laissée tomber.

– N'importe quoi.

Drew s'immobilise, un plateau de *ziti* à la main. Il a déjà largement trop chargé mon assiette.

– Je ne l'ai pas lâchée, insiste-t-il en nous regardant tour à tour. Mais toi, je ne vais pas tarder à te lâcher, si tu continues à raconter des conneries, fait-il à Roman.

– Soigne ton langage, je le réprimande.

Roman se contente de ricaner.

Le dîner est loin d'être paisible. D'abord, Drew et moi sommes en désaccord sur la politique, puis Roman, Drew et Beck ont une discussion animée sur le nom des équipes qui vont arriver aux playoffs de hockey cette saison. Nous parlons fort, parfois

5. Florence Nightingale est considérée comme la première infirmière professionnelle et a joué un rôle majeur dans la création des soins infirmiers modernes.

en même temps, pourtant je ne me rappelle pas la dernière fois où j'ai autant apprécié un repas.

Une fois nos agapes terminées, Drew est implacable : non, je ne peux pas aider à débarrasser. Il me porte donc au salon. Roman, à qui il a ordonné de participer au nettoyage, préfère s'ouvrir une bière et me rejoindre.

– Tu en veux une ?

– Non, merci, je lui réponds, affalée sur le canapé, les mains jointes sur le ventre. Je suis déjà trop remplie par les dix kilos de pâtes et de poulet à la parmesane que Drew avait empilés dans mon assiette.

Roman prend une gorgée de sa bière en m'observant par-dessus la bouteille.

– Vous vous disputez beaucoup, tous les deux ?

Je souris.

– Pas mal, oui.

– C'est son truc.

Ma perplexité doit se voir sur mon visage, car il appuie sa bouteille sur sa cuisse et précise sa pensée :

– Drew et moi, on s'est rencontrés en première. Je lui ai piqué sa petite amie…

Je l'interromps.

– Quand Drew raconte l'histoire, c'est lui qui t'a volé ta petite amie avant que vous ne deveniez copains pendant une varicelle commune.

– Il t'a raconté ça ?

Je fais « oui » de la tête.

– Tout à fait. Et je l'ai trouvée étrangement mignonne, votre histoire. Il la raconte avec beaucoup d'émotion.

– Bref, lui et moi, on se dispute depuis la classe de première. Mais c'est aussi mon meilleur ami. Son père et lui étaient plus proches qu'aucun père et aucun fils de ma connaissance. Ils se disputaient tous les jours. Ce n'est pas une coïncidence que son métier consiste à argumenter avec les gens, d'ailleurs. (Roman reprend une gorgée de bière et semble réfléchir à ce qu'il s'apprête à ajouter.) Tu veux savoir pourquoi je savais depuis le début que ça ne fonctionnerait pas avec Alexa ?

– Vas-y.

– Ils ne se disputaient jamais. Du moins pas avant la fin, quand elle a commencé à montrer sa vraie nature de garce égoïste. Mais ça, c'est une forme de dispute différente de celle qu'il pratique quand il aime.

– On n'est pas…

Roman se cale contre le dossier du canapé, un sourire entendu aux lèvres.

– Je sais, je sais. Je vois bien que ni toi ni lui ne l'avez encore compris. On en reparle d'ici un mois ou deux.

***

– Il y a des travaux de voirie la nuit sur la 49e, tu devrais passer par la 51e.

– C'est pas vrai, quelle plaie cette fille ! marmonne Drew, en tournant brusquement à gauche.

On se dispute depuis une demi-heure sur mon retour à la maison. Il voulait que je reste chez lui afin de m'aider dans mes déplacements. Mais avec son fils qui est là, ça ne m'a pas paru correct. Il a fini par céder, à condition qu'on attende que Beck s'endorme pour nous mettre en route. Puis Roman est resté chez Drew afin que ce dernier puisse me raccompagner.

En arrivant devant mon immeuble, j'effectue une piètre tentative de protestation quand il va pour me porter, mais je lâche vite l'affaire. Je noue les bras autour de son cou et me laisse aller au plaisir de son contact.

– Tu devrais peut-être envisager de ralentir sur les burgers, me taquine-t-il.

– Hé, méfie-toi. Encore une blague sur mon poids et j'arrête *toutes* les gâteries.

– Je n'y crois pas une seconde. Tu aimes trop ça.

– Quelle arrogance.

– Peut-être. Pourtant c'est ce qui fait une partie de mon charme incommensurable. D'ailleurs je m'en vais t'en montrer une autre sur-le-champ.

La porte de l'ascenseur s'ouvre.

– On n'a pas le temps pour les galipettes. Tu dois rentrer libérer Roman.

– On s'en fout de Roman. (Une des paumes qui me soutient glisse vers mes fesses et les serre fort.) J'ai eu tes fesses entre les mains toute la journée. Alors je vais te déshabiller, que tu le veuilles ou non.

– Et si je ne t'invite pas à entrer ?

– Bonne question. Eh bien, je vais peut-être te prendre juste ici dans l'ascenseur, alors. (Il désigne d'un geste du menton la caméra placée dans un angle de la cabine.) Quelqu'un doit regarder. Offrons-lui un joli spectacle.

J'avais la tête posée contre son torse, je la relève pour le regarder dans les yeux. Je les découvre brûlants. Si nous n'atteignons pas l'intimité de mon appartement, il y a effectivement un risque que quelqu'un ait droit à un show torride. Mais pourquoi est-ce que l'ascenseur ne s'est pas encore mis en branle ?

– Tu as appuyé sur le bouton ?

– Merde.

Avec un ricanement, il se penche pour presser le bouton de mon étage. Juste avant que les portes se referment, un bras s'immisce qui les retient.

Évidemment, il fallait que ce soit Baldwin.

Il me contemple dans les bras de Drew, puis voit l'attelle strappée à ma jambe.

– Emerie ? Qu'est-ce qui s'est passé ?

Je sens l'étreinte se resserrer autour de moi.

– Je suis tombée en faisant du patin à glace. C'est juste une entorse.

Baldwin jette un regard noir à Drew.

Quoi ? Il a besoin d'une confirmation ?

– On a vérifié. La cheville n'est pas cassée, explique sèchement Drew.

Sa mâchoire est si crispée que je vois les muscles se tendre.

La porte de l'ascenseur se ferme enfin et l'atmosphère de la cabine devient pire que gênante. Elle est… suffocante. Les deux hommes se tiennent côte à côte. Je me prends à regretter de n'avoir pas plus insisté pour que Drew me repose au sol. Quand nous atteignons le troisième étage, je suis certaine qu'il ne reste quasi plus d'oxygène à l'intérieur de l'espace réduit. Baldwin tend le bras pour nous permettre de sortir en premier.

Je tente de trouver mes clés dans mon sac, mais ce n'est pas facile, vu ma position.

– Tu veux bien me reposer afin que je cherche mes clés ? je demande à Drew quand il s'immobilise devant ma porte.

Il se baisse délicatement, tout en gardant un bras passé autour de moi afin de réduire au minimum le poids sur mon pied.

Baldwin s'arrête devant ma porte aussi.

– Je peux faire quelque chose pour t'aider ?

J'ouvre la bouche pour répondre, mais Drew est plus rapide.

– Je m'occupe de tout.

– Je peux te déposer au bureau demain matin et repasser te prendre le soir, propose Baldwin, sans prêter la moindre attention à lui.

– J'ai une voiture, gronde Drew, qui me prend les clés des mains pour déverrouiller ma porte.

– Vous n'avez pas besoin de vous donner cette peine. Emerie et moi partons du même endroit, je peux faire un petit détour pour la déposer sur mon chemin pour l'université.

Ignorant le regard qui me brûle, je me tourne vers Baldwin.

– Ce serait super, merci. Sinon, je peux prendre un taxi. Je ne veux pas obliger Drew à traverser toute la ville le matin, surtout avec son fils.

– Dans ce cas, c'est décidé. Envoie-moi un SMS demain matin, si tu as besoin d'aide pour te préparer ou autre.

– Merci.

Baldwin adresse un hochement de tête à Drew et rentre enfin chez lui. La scène n'a pas dû durer plus de trois minutes en tout, pourtant elle m'a paru s'étirer pendant des heures.

À l'intérieur, j'allume les lumières et m'affaire à ôter mon manteau. Drew restant silencieux, je sens venir un commentaire. Au bout d'une minute, je commence à me détendre en songeant que, peut-être, j'ai tout imaginé et mal évalué la situation, que la gêne n'était qu'une vue de mon esprit.

À tort.

– Ce type est un connard.

– Qu'est-ce qu'il a fait ?

Drew a dû prendre ma question pour une manière de défendre Baldwin. Son comportement change du tout au tout.

– Tu as envie de baiser avec lui ?

– Quoi ? Non ! D'où ça sort, ça ?

Il se passe une main dans les cheveux.

– Faut que j'y aille. Je ne veux pas être absent si Beck se réveille.

Ça, je peux le comprendre, pourtant il y a cinq minutes, il n'avait pas l'air pressé. En moins de cinq minutes, montre en main, il est passé de pressé de se retrouver seul avec moi à pressé de s'en aller.

– C'est quoi le problème ?

– Tu veux que je t'enlève ton attelle ou que je fasse autre chose pour toi avant de partir ?

– Non, je réponds sèchement, frustrée. Vas-y.

Je presse la tête contre la porte derrière lui. Dans mon esprit, ça tourbillonne, mais c'est la même question qui tourne en boucle.

Est-ce que j'ai envie de coucher avec Baldwin ?

CHAPITRE 32

DREW

Dans la nuit, à une demi-douzaine de reprises, je m'interroge sur l'idée d'aller chez Emerie, avant de décider que je vais aggraver la situation si je m'y rends. Pas question qu'elle pense que mes excuses sont en fait un prétexte pour empêcher que Crétin la conduise au travail. Évidemment, je ne veux pas que ce connard lui serve de chauffeur. Enfin, vers deux heures du matin, après avoir longuement frappé mon oreiller, j'ai retrouvé mon bon sens.

Mon attitude agressive n'a rien à voir avec Emerie. Entre mon ex-femme malhonnête et ma dose quotidienne de clients qui ont été trompés ou ont trompé leur conjoint, je ne suis pas le type le plus confiant du monde. Je continue à penser que j'ai raison concernant Baldwin : ce mec est une tête de nœud et mon instinct me souffle que quelque chose va se produire quand il se rendra compte qu'Emerie ne se contente plus de rester sur la touche à l'attendre patiemment. Mais ce n'est pas sa faute à elle non plus.

Il est presque dix heures quand enfin elle montre le bout de son nez au bureau. Beck n'ayant école que le matin, j'espère qu'elle n'a pas un rendez-vous à assurer sitôt arrivée. Je suis en mode alerte rouge, à l'affût de tous les bruits me signalant son entrée, alors dès qu'elle a franchi la porte, je suis déjà dans la zone d'accueil.

Et l'autre enfoiré est avec elle. Un bras passé autour de sa taille, il tente de l'aider à marcher. Je vois sur le visage d'Emerie que la situation la met mal à l'aise.

– Salut.

– Bonjour, me répond-elle avec un sourire forcé. J'ai dit à Baldwin qu'il n'avait pas besoin de m'accompagner jusqu'à l'intérieur. Mais il a insisté.

Je parviens à lui répondre avec une pointe de sincérité.

– Tu as effectivement besoin d'aide. Le docteur a dit : « Pas de poids sur cette cheville. »

Pour tester ma résolution, je recule et le laisse l'accompagner sur tout le trajet jusqu'à son bureau et je retourne au mien. Je mentirais en affirmant que je ne tends pas l'oreille, cela dit. Il lui demande à quelle heure il doit repasser la prendre, à quoi elle répond qu'elle a des projets après le travail et qu'on la ramènera.

Une fois Crétin parti, je prends une profonde inspiration et m'en vais la trouver dans son bureau.

Elle est en train d'installer son ordinateur portable sur sa station d'accueil.

– Tu as un patient maintenant ?

– Non.

Elle ne lève pas les yeux.

– Donc on peut discuter ?

Elle me regarde.

– Oh. Tu es d'humeur à discuter, maintenant ?

Réplique méritée.

– Je devrais peut-être commencer par te présenter mes excuses.

Son expression s'adoucit, mais elle croise les bras, résolue à ne pas céder trop vite.

– Ce serait un bon début, oui.

– Excuse-moi pour la façon dont j'ai agi hier soir.

– Tu veux dire quand tu m'as accusée de vouloir baiser un autre homme alors qu'on s'était déjà mis d'accord tous les deux sur le fait qu'on avait une relation sexuelle exclusive, toi et moi ?

– Oui, ça.

Elle pousse un soupir.

– Je ne suis pas ce genre de personne, Drew. Même si j'avais envie de coucher avec un autre, je ne le ferais pas si je me suis engagée auprès de quelqu'un.

Elle vient sans le savoir de mettre le doigt pile sur mon point sensible. J'ai passé la moitié de la nuit et de la matinée à admettre que mes problèmes de confiance viennent de moi. Il est facile d'en attribuer la faute à d'autres. *C'est à cause d'Alexa.*

Mon boulot a tué ma foi dans la race humaine. Mais quand j'y réfléchis mieux, je vois bien que j'apprécie cette femme, peut-être plus que je ne le devrais après si peu de temps, et ça me file une trouille de dingue. Elle a passé les dernières années de sa vie à attendre qu'un autre type la remarque, et je ne suis pas sûr de ce qui arrivera quand enfin ça se produira.

Bien sûr que je suis jaloux. Mais j'ai aussi une frousse de malade. Et je n'aime pas, mais alors pas du tout ressentir ça.

Je m'approche d'elle, pas vraiment parce que je dois lui parler mais parce que je déteste rester à l'autre bout de la pièce quand je peux être près d'elle.

Il fait particulièrement frais dehors, aujourd'hui, et ses joues ont rosi, tout comme la pointe de son nez. Je prends son visage froid entre mes paumes, me penche et dépose délicatement un baiser sur ses lèvres.

Puis je m'écarte afin que nous soyons les yeux dans les yeux.

– Je suis désolé de m'être comporté comme un connard jaloux. J'avais prévu de t'expliquer pourquoi ça n'est pas ma faute si je suis jaloux, que mon histoire et mon boulot m'ont rendu comme ça, et peut-être que ça en fait partie. Mais ça n'est pas tout. Pour être honnête, la vérité m'a frappé il y a quelques minutes seulement.

– Et quelle est-elle ?

– J'ai besoin d'entendre où tu en es avec ce type, dans ta tête. Tu as traversé la moitié du pays pour le rejoindre, il y a quelques mois. Je sais que tu éprouvais des sentiments forts à son égard. Et si tu m'affirmes que tu me le diras, si jamais tu souhaites un jour t'extraire de cette exclusivité qu'on a décidée, je te croirai. Mais ce que j'ai besoin de savoir, c'est s'il t'avouait aujourd'hui qu'il a des sentiments pour toi, est-ce que tu me quitterais, moi ?

Emerie se fige, une lueur de quelque chose passe sur son visage avant que nos regards se nouent.

– Assieds-toi.

CHAPITRE 33

EMERIE

Fais ce que tu prônes.

Facile à dire, quand Drew Jagger a les yeux rivés sur vous, dans l'attente d'une réponse. Il veut savoir ce qui se passerait si l'homme dont je suis folle amoureuse depuis plusieurs années, l'homme pour qui j'ai emménagé à New York pour tenter ma chance auprès de lui, décidait soudain qu'il veut être avec moi. C'est la question que je me pose depuis que ces deux hommes m'ont laissée seule avec mes pensées, hier soir.

Je dois à Drew d'être franche avec lui. Mieux, je me le dois à moi-même.

– Ça fait si longtemps que j'ai des sentiments pour Baldwin que je ne me rappelle même plus quel effet cela fait de ne pas en avoir.

Drew s'appuie au bord de mon bureau, les jambes écartées dans une posture intuitivement dominante et mâle, une attitude très simple qui pourtant me confirme la vérité de ce que je m'apprête à ajouter.

– Mais ce que j'ai pu ressentir pour Baldwin est très différent de ce qui se passe entre toi et moi.

Son regard s'allume et je dois serrer les cuisses pour réprimer l'excitation qui me cueille à la pensée qu'il est en train de se mettre en colère. Pas de doute, s'énerver l'un l'autre constitue une forme de préliminaires un peu tordus entre nous, mais le moment est mal choisi pour ça.

– Baldwin est intelligent et courtois. Nous partageons la même passion pour la psychologie et la sociologie. Il n'emploie jamais de gros mots, m'emmène dans des restaurants chics, et pas une seule fois il n'a levé la voix sur moi.

Drew fait la grimace.

– T'as intérêt à ajouter un « mais » très bientôt.

Je réprime un sourire. Je dois absolument me dépêtrer de la partie pénible avant de lui donner son « mais ».

– Il y en a un. Sauf que je tiens à être parfaitement honnête.

L'expression de ses yeux m'enjoint d'en venir au fait. Et il hoche la tête dans le même objectif.

– Je mentirais si j'affirmais que je n'ai pas de sentiments pour lui. *Mais* il y a toi. Tu me chamboules, tu me fais perdre tous mes repères et je n'ai pas la moindre idée d'où ça va atterrir, ce qui se passe entre nous. En revanche, il y a une chose dont je suis certaine.

– Quoi ?

– Quand je te regarde, je comprends pourquoi ça n'aurait jamais fonctionné avec lui.

Son regard s'adoucit.

– Je suis nul en confiance.

– Je sais.

– Je vais continuer à crier, à dire « putain, merde et connard » à tout bout de champ.

Je lui adresse un sourire canaille.

– J'ai appris qu'il y a des moments où ton vilain langage me fait vraiment de l'effet.

Il me passe deux doigts sur le menton, le cou et descend vers ma clavicule, avant de glisser dans mon décolleté.

– Ah oui ?

Il ne m'en faut pas plus. Le son rauque de son « ah oui » et un simple effleurement. Je ne sais pas expliquer pourquoi j'éprouve des choses pour Drew, pas plus que je ne sais expliquer le goût de l'eau. Et pourtant, il est devenu une nécessité pour moi et je ne suis aucunement disposée à cesser de boire.

– Où est Beck ? je susurre.

Les yeux de Drew suivent ses doigts qui plongent sous mon pull.

– À l'école. J'ai une heure avant d'aller le chercher.

Mon corps tout entier me picote à l'idée de la manière dont on peut occuper l'heure en question.

– Des clients prévus d'ici là ?

Il commence à déboutonner les petits boutons de nacre qui ferment l'avant de mon gilet.

– Non. Et toi ?

Je secoue la tête.

La patience dont Drew a fait montre jusque-là s'envole par la fenêtre à partir de cet instant. Dans la minute qui suit, il me soulève du sol, m'arrache ma culotte et me hisse sur mon bureau, face à mon fauteuil, ma jupe remontée autour de ma taille. Tout en prenant soin de ne pas heurter ma jambe blessée.

Ensuite il s'assied sur le fauteuil, devant mon sexe nu, et desserre sa cravate.

– Qu'est-ce que tu fais ?

– Je te montre comme je suis désolé. Écarte les cuisses.

Oh là là.

J'ouvre les jambes pour lui en frissonnant sous son regard intense sur mon intimité. Quand il se lèche les lèvres, qu'il approche le siège et me tire jusqu'à amener mes fesses tout au bord de la table de travail, je suis déjà à mi-chemin vers l'orgasme alors qu'il n'a pas encore posé un doigt sur moi.

– Je n'aime peut-être pas dîner dans les restaurants chics, mais je te donnerai toujours à manger et je te dévorerai tant et si bien que ce sera toi qui crieras des obscénités.

Voilà typiquement le genre de propos qui fonctionnent sur moi.

***

Les choses ont changé depuis notre discussion de ce matin. Il y a une intimité, un lien qui n'existait pas avant. Drew est allé récupérer Beck à l'école et je nous ai apporté à déjeuner pour tous les trois avant qu'ils partent à la bibliothèque et encore une fois à la patinoire. J'aime beaucoup que Drew divise ses après-midis avec son fils entre travail et jeux. Beck lit une histoire sur le tapis destiné aux enfants pendant que Drew travaille sur une affaire dans la pièce adjacente. Une fois qu'ils ont terminé, le petit lit un livre à son père et, en récompense, ils vont à la patinoire.

Moi, j'ai un après-midi chargé en patients, et même à presque dix-huit heures trente, je conserve l'espoir toujours renouvelé qu'il existe une solution pour tous les problèmes des couples. Mon optimisme déteint sur mes séances de manière positive.

Je suis en train de ranger mon ordinateur portable quand j'entends s'ouvrir la porte d'entrée et des petits pieds courir vers mon bureau.

– On a tout ce qu'il faut pour une soirée film ! hurle Beck.

Ses joues potelées sont rougies par le froid et il est emmitouflé comme un petit bonhomme de neige.

– Ah oui ? Et vous prévoyez de regarder quoi ?

Beck lève deux doigts.

– On a deux films. Un pour le repas et l'autre pour le dessert.

Je ne comprends pas trop ce qu'il m'explique, mais son enthousiasme est contagieux.

– Super. Et quel film vous allez regarder en premier ?

Drew apparaît derrière son fils.

– Il m'a obligé à le déposer sur le trottoir au lieu de descendre au parking souterrain pour pouvoir courir t'annoncer la nouvelle le premier.

Le sourire de Beck est si large que je peux presque compter ses petites dents. Il agite un boîtier de DVD.

– Pour le dîner, on a pris *Tempête de boulettes géantes*.

Puis il tend le doigt vers son père, qui me montre un sac de nourriture à emporter.

– Mamma Theresa prépare les meilleures boulettes de viande de toute la ville.

Beck hoche vivement la tête, avant de me tendre un second DVD.

– Et pour le dessert, on a pris *Blanche-Neige et les Sept Nains*.

À nouveau, il désigne son père. On croirait qu'ils jouent un sketch. Drew tend un autre sachet.

– Tarte aux groseilles à maquereau de la *Pâtisserie Française*.

Je souris.

– C'est quoi, ça, les groseilles à maquereau ?

Drew hausse les épaules.

– Si je le savais… En tout cas, on a dû faire trois pâtisseries pour en trouver et ça coûte vingt dollars, le bazar, alors ça a intérêt à être bon.

– Je vais manger ma part avec de la glace à la vanille, précise Beck. Même si ça fait pas partie de ta soirée cinéma.

– « Ma » soirée cinéma ?

– Papa a dit que tu aimes bien les soirées avec un thème autour d'un film. Tu viendras, dis ?

Un nouveau petit pan du mur que j'ai construit autour de mon cœur par peur de tomber amoureuse de cet homme s'effrite.

Drew m'observe, jaugeant ma réaction. Je ne pourrais pas la masquer même si je le voulais.

Je porte une main à ma poitrine.

– Vous êtes adorables. Je suis très touchée que vous ayez organisé une soirée film pour moi. Je viendrai avec grand plaisir.

Pressé de commencer, Beck se lance en courant dans le couloir en criant :

– Je vais appeler l'ascenseur.

– Tu ne montes pas dedans avant que je sois là, le prévient Drew.

Je finis de ramasser mes affaires et le rejoins dans le couloir. Là, je me hisse sur la pointe des pieds et dépose un léger baiser sur ses lèvres.

– Merci.

Il m'adresse un clin d'œil.

– Avec plaisir.

Sur quoi il me soulève (apparemment je ne serai pas autorisée à remarcher avant qu'on m'enlève cette attelle) et me porte vers l'ascenseur.

– Je crois que je vais bien aimer cette idée de soirées cinéma à thème : ça va enfin me permettre d'utiliser ma collection de pornos à bon escient, me chuchote-t-il.

CHAPITRE 34

EMERIE

Le reste de la semaine a été tout aussi merveilleux que la soirée film. Passer du temps à la maison avec Drew et Beck m'en dévoile bien plus sur l'homme qu'il est que je n'en aurais appris en une dizaine de rendez-vous galants. En y songeant, d'ailleurs, on devrait inclure ça au rituel de la découverte en début de relation. Au deuxième ou troisième rendez-vous, l'homme devrait amener un enfant, nièce ou neveu s'il n'en a pas à lui, afin que la femme puisse constater quelle relation il a avec eux en général. Ça en dirait plus long que six mois de fréquentation classique.

Que ce soit au moment du petit déjeuner ou du dîner, Drew s'arrange toujours pour libérer du temps à partager tous les trois et aussi rien qu'avec son fils. Je commence à me sentir en famille. Pourtant, dans un coin de ma tête, je suis bien consciente que ça ne durera pas éternellement. Alexa rentre à New York demain et je ne sais pas trop comment ça va s'ajouter au tableau. En tout cas, je suis très curieuse au sujet de cette femme.

Cet après-midi, j'avais proposé de m'occuper de Beck seule quelques heures pendant que Drew participe à une déposition qu'il n'a pas pu reprogrammer. Il avait prévu de demander à l'une des assistantes scolaires qui le surveille parfois à l'école, mais j'ai insisté : je peux m'en charger.

Drew a une pile de films qu'on peut regarder dans son appartement et j'avais apporté du bon vieux pop-corn, de celui qu'on prépare à l'ancienne, à la poêle. Cette séance de baby-sitting s'annonçait comme une vraie partie de plaisir.

Du moins le pensais-je.

Parce qu'en réalité j'ai dû appeler Drew et l'interrompre en pleine déposition, dix minutes après qu'elle avait commencé. En l'informant qu'on devait aller à l'hôpital.

***

– Je suis tellement désolée.

C'est la millionième fois que je le répète. Nous sommes dans une petite chambre divisée par un rideau, au sein du service d'urgence où nous sommes venus pour ma cheville tordue, pile une semaine plus tôt. Sauf que cette fois, c'est Beck que l'on soigne.

– Ça arrive. C'était un accident. Maintenant, il saura qu'il ne faut pas toucher la cuisinière.

– C'est moi qui aurais dû me méfier.

Beck et moi étions en train de cuire le pop-corn ensemble. Il n'avait jamais vu faire du pop-corn comme ça. Ses grands yeux chocolat étaient ronds comme des soucoupes, quand il observait le sachet argenté gonfler à chaque explosion de grain de maïs. Une fois que les « pop » ont ralenti et que l'emballage m'a semblé sur le point d'exploser lui-même, j'ai déplacé la poêle du brûleur chaud sur un froid et j'ai percé un trou au sommet du sachet pour permettre à la vapeur de s'échapper. Beck s'est alors éloigné pour passer en revue la collection de films au salon, et j'ai cru pouvoir me rendre tranquillement à la salle de bains. Je me suis absentée moins de trois minutes, songeant au bel après-midi qu'on passait pendant que je me lavais les mains quand… le hurlement a retenti.

Le pauvre petit bonhomme était retourné auprès de la cuisinière, sans imaginer que le brûleur était encore chaud puisqu'il n'était plus orange. En voulant sauter pour regarder sortir la vapeur du sachet de pop-corn, il a posé la main tout entière sur le brûleur encore chaud.

– Chez sa mère, la cuisinière est au gaz. J'aurais dû lui expliquer que la plaque reste chaude, quand j'ai fait installer ma nouvelle cuisinière il y a un an. Ce n'est pas ta faute, c'est la mienne.

Beck hausse les épaules.

– Ça ne fait même plus très mal.

Ce petit gars-là est un vaillant. Le docteur a dit qu'il s'agissait d'une simple brûlure au premier degré et lui a appliqué de la pommade, avant d'envelopper sa petite main dans de la gaze d'abord et une bande Velpeau par-dessus.

Je pose une main sur le genou du petit.

– Je suis désolée, mon chéri. J'aurais dû t'avertir que ça restait chaud même quand ça changeait de couleur.

Peu après, une infirmière est venue pour nous montrer comment refaire le bandage, nous donner un tube de crème et de la gaze à utiliser demain, afin qu'on n'ait pas besoin d'aller tout de suite à la pharmacie. Tout le monde a beau se comporter comme si c'était on ne peut plus banal, n'empêche que moi, je me sens vraiment hyper mal.

***

– Je ressemble à un boxeur ! annonce Beck sur le trajet de retour à la maison. Papa, tu pourras me bander l'autre main ? Et aussi acheter ce truc en rouge ?

Il désigne la bande Velpeau.

– Bien sûr, mon grand.

Ils sont tous les deux revenus à leur attitude normale, mais moi, je me sens encore super mal. Drew lâche le volant d'une main, qu'il vient me poser sur le genou.

– Les gens vont commencer à me regarder de travers.

Je fronce les sourcils.

– Toi avec ton attelle et lui avec sa main bandée.

Je me couvre la bouche.

– Oh là là. Imagine… ils te regardent toi de travers, alors que les deux blessures sont complètement ma faute.

Drew baisse la voix.

– Arrête. Je te vois bien, qui essaie par tous les moyens de ramener la culpabilité à toi d'une manière ou d'une autre. C'était un accident. Ç'aurait pu être moi qui préparais du pop-corn et la même chose serait arrivée.

– Sauf que ce n'était pas toi.

– Ça suffit de te flageller. Il y a deux mois, il s'est fait un œil au beurre noir en fonçant dans une commode alors qu'il était sous la surveillance de sa mère. C'est un petit garçon. Il agit sans réfléchir et il se fait mal.

– Oh non.

– Quoi ?

– Je n'avais même pas pensé à sa mère. Elle va me détester.

– Ne t'inquiète pas pour ça. Il n'y avait pas beaucoup de chances qu'elle t'apprécie, de toute manière.

Super. Su-per.

CHAPITRE 35

EMERIE

– Vous êtes qui ?

Trois mots m'ont suffi pour deviner que la femme qui entre dans le bureau le lendemain matin est une garce.

Jean ultramoulant, bottes en cuir marron à hauts talons sur de longues jambes minces et une taille toute menue dans un haut à travers lequel on voit la peau alors même qu'on est fin janvier et qu'il fait un froid de canard à New York. Je n'ai pas envie de lever les yeux. J'ai envie de rentrer à la maison et d'enfiler une tenue moins professionnelle et plus sexy. Dans ma tête, aucun doute sur son identité.

Redoutant ce que je vais découvrir encore, je poursuis mon observation et tombe sur un visage tout aussi beau que le corps. *Évidemment.*

– Je suis Emerie Rose. Et vous êtes ?

– Alexa Jagger. La femme de Drew.

Ce dernier se matérialise soudain à côté de moi dans le hall d'entrée.

– Mon ex-femme.

Ses paupières plissées s'accordent au ton sec de sa réplique.

Alexa lève les yeux au ciel.

– Peu importe. Il faut qu'on parle.

– Prends rendez-vous. Je suis occupé, ce matin.

Sans prêter la moindre attention à ce qu'il vient de dire, elle le frôle en se dirigeant d'un pas assuré vers son bureau.

Drew et moi restons plantés là un moment. Puis je lui dis à voix basse :

– Eh bien, elle est charmante.

Drew prend une profonde inspiration.

– Tu devrais peut-être mettre des boules Quiès.

***

– On s'en va !

– Pas question que tu l'emmènes sur les routes pour suivre une troupe de pilotes de course à travers le pays en lui faisant l'école toi-même ! Si tu veux y aller, fais-toi plaisir, mais Beck reste ici.

– Qu'est-ce qu'il va faire, ici avec toi ? Tu bosses soixante heures par semaine.

– Je me débrouillerai. Au moins, ici, il a son école, ses habitudes, sa maison.

– Tu ne te débrouilles pas. Tu le refiles à une baby-sitter. Ce matin, j'en ai plus entendu sur la nouvelle que sur toi. En plus, elle n'est apparemment même pas capable de le surveiller, vu qu'il s'est brûlé la main.

Merde.

Les hurlements se taisent et je devine que Drew est en train d'essayer de se maîtriser. Je visualise sa mâchoire crispée tandis qu'il inspire du feu et tâche d'expirer de la glace.

Quand enfin il reprend la parole, le ton est plus que furieux, à deux doigts d'être assassin.

– Tu parles sans rien savoir du tout. Je ne « refile » pas mon fils à une baby-sitter. Tout son temps, il l'a passé soit avec moi, soit avec ma petite amie, et on s'est très bien occupés de lui.

– Ta « petite amie » ? crache Alexa. Tu présentes mon fils à ta pute du mois, maintenant ?

– *Notre* fils, grogne Drew. Et ce n'est pas la fille d'un mois. Contrairement à toi, je n'ai jamais présenté à Beck des personnes que je ne voyais qu'en passant. Toutes les fois où il m'a parlé d'hommes qui allaient et venaient chez toi, je n'ai pas ouvert la bouche et t'ai fait confiance pour te montrer prudente et respectueuse en sa présence. J'attends la même attitude en retour à l'égard d'Emerie.

– Emerie ? La fille que j'ai croisée dans le hall ? Tu baises avec la remplaçante ?

– Nous partageons ces bureaux. Elle est psychologue, pas assistante ou vacataire. Et de toute façon, qu'est-ce que ça pourrait bien te foutre, à toi, si elle faisait le ménage ici ? Au moins, elle a un job, elle.

Tu devrais essayer, ça t'aiderait peut-être à apprécier la valeur des bottes à mille dollars que tu portes.

– J'élève notre fils. C'est un boulot à plein temps.

– C'est drôle comme il redevient « notre » fils, quand je paie la facture de ce fameux boulot à plein temps, mais reste « ton » fils quand tu prévois de l'emmener sur le circuit NASCAR de ton péquenaud.

– Il vient avec moi, siffle-t-elle.

– Il reste ici.

– Je ne pense pas que tu aies envie de te battre sur ce point. Beck a le droit de connaître son père et de passer du temps avec lui.

Je me prépare à la tempête qui ne va pas manquer d'arriver.

– Justement, il passe du temps avec son père maintenant !!

– Je parlais de son père biologique.

– Je n'ai pas eu le choix, en l'occurrence, tout ça, c'est à cause de toi. Dieu sait que je ne t'aurais jamais épousée si j'avais su que tu étais une garce qui portait l'enfant d'un autre !

– Va te faire foutre !

– Fiche le camp d'ici, Alexa. Je te jure, va-t'en.

Même si je m'attendais au bruit, je sursaute quand elle ouvre en grand la porte du bureau de Drew en la cognant contre le mur. Alexa sort dans un vacarme de martèlements et de claquements de talons.

J'attends quelques minutes dans mon bureau, ne sachant pas trop s'il vaut mieux laisser à Drew le temps de se calmer ou tenter de le réconforter. Au bout d'un moment, n'entendant plus que le silence, je décide d'aller voir comment il va.

Son fauteuil est écarté du bureau et il est assis, les coudes plantés sur les genoux et la tête dans ses mains.

– Tu vas bien ? je lui demande d'une petite voix.

Il me répond sans lever les yeux. Sa voix est rauque.

– Oui.

J'avance de quelques pas hésitants.

– Qu'est-ce que je peux faire ?

Il secoue la tête à plusieurs reprises avant de la redresser.

– Tu peux faire que je sois le vrai père de ce petit garçon ?

Mon cœur se serre dans ma poitrine en voyant son expression défaite. Il a les yeux rougis et remplis de larmes, et moi, je ressens la douleur que je lis sur son visage.

Je m'agenouille devant lui.

– Tu es son vrai père, Drew.

Il m'écoute, mais je sens que mon message ne lui parvient pas. Alors je fais le choix de partager avec lui une histoire que je n'ai jamais racontée à personne.

– Quand j'avais dix-neuf ans, j'ai décidé que je voulais découvrir qui était ma mère biologique. J'ignore pourquoi. Rien ne clochait, je crois que j'étais juste curieuse. Bref, mon adoption était ouverte, donc les informations étaient consultables si je voulais. Ne souhaitant pas blesser mes parents, j'ai choisi de leur taire la démarche et me suis procuré les infos par moi-même.

Drew est attentif, maintenant.

– Un samedi, j'ai annoncé à mes parents que j'allais chez une amie. Au lieu de ça, j'ai traversé l'État en voiture, quatre heures de route, pour me rendre à l'adresse que j'avais de ma mère. Je suis restée dans la voiture, devant sa maison, et j'ai attendu qu'elle sorte. Ensuite, je l'ai suivie jusqu'à son travail, dans un restaurant. Au bout de quelques heures supplémentaires, j'ai enfin trouvé le courage d'entrer. Je l'avais observée par la vitre, je savais dans quelle section du restaurant elle servait et j'ai demandé une table près de la fenêtre afin qu'elle soit ma serveuse.

Même si c'est lui qui souffre, Drew tend le bras et exerce une pression sur mon épaule pour m'encourager à poursuivre.

– Qu'est-ce qui s'est passé ?

– Elle est venue prendre ma commande et, en bredouillant tout du long, j'ai réussi à commander un thé et des toasts sans jamais la lâcher des yeux. (Je marque une pause au souvenir de ce jour.) Elle était rousse.

Drew me caresse la joue.

– Bref, pendant qu'elle prenait une commande à une table voisine, mon téléphone a sonné et j'ai vu que c'était ma mère. J'ai laissé l'appel basculer sur la boîte vocale parce que je croyais qu'elle avait peut-être compris ce que je faisais et qu'elle était en colère. Pourtant, quand j'ai écouté son message, j'ai découvert qu'elle voulait juste s'assurer que j'allais bien. Elle disait qu'elle m'avait trouvée un peu tristounette la veille. Inutile de te décrire à quel point je culpabilisais. À mort. Quand la serveuse, ma mère biologique, est venue m'apporter mes toasts quelques minutes plus tard, je pleurais. Elle m'a dévisagée, mais elle ne m'a même pas demandé si tout allait bien. Elle n'avait qu'une hâte : larguer ses toasts sur la table et disparaître.

Je lâche un soupir.

– J'ai jeté un dernier regard vers la femme qui m'avait donné la vie et j'ai compris que ma mère, c'était la femme qui m'avait laissé le message vocal. La biologie me liait à cette serveuse, pourtant je ne ressentais rien de plus pour elle que pour une parfaite inconnue. Parce que c'était ce qu'elle était : une parfaite inconnue. J'ai jeté un billet de vingt sur la table et je suis partie sans me retourner.

Je croise le regard de Drew.

– Être parent, c'est un choix, pas un droit. Jusqu'à ce jour, je n'avais pas pigé pourquoi mes parents fêtaient le jour de mon arrivée chez eux chaque année. Tu es le papa de Beck, de la même façon que Martin Rose est le mien. N'importe qui peut devenir père, mais il faut être un vrai papa pour aimer et élever un enfant comme le sien.

– Viens par ici.

Drew me soulève du sol et m'installe sur ses genoux. Il glisse une mèche de cheveux derrière mon oreille. Ses yeux tout à l'heure en colère et tristes se sont réchauffés.

– D'où viens-tu ?

– Je me suis introduite ici par mégarde et je t'ai montré mes fesses, tu te rappelles ?

Il éclate de rire et je sens un peu de tension se dissiper quand il m'enlace et me dépose un baiser au sommet du crâne.

– Merci. J'avais besoin de ça.

Je suis ravie de l'avoir réconforté. Vu que Drew a eu Beck toute la semaine, c'est notre premier après-midi seul depuis tout ce temps.

– Je n'ai pas de rendez-vous avant deux bonnes heures, au cas où tu aurais besoin d'autre chose.

Il s'est mis debout, moi dans ses bras, presque avant que j'aie terminé ma phrase. Je lâche un hoquet, surprise par ce brusque mouvement. Et encore plus quand il se dirige vers la porte, moi qui m'attendais à ce qu'il m'écarte les cuisses ici même sur son bureau.

– Pas de sexe au bureau ? je lui demande.

– Le bureau, c'est pour le sexe, justement. Là, je veux te faire l'amour.

CHAPITRE 36

DREW

Je pourrais m'y habituer.

Je viens de sortir de la douche et entre dans la cuisine. Emerie est devant la cuisinière, dans une de mes chemises qui lui arrive aux genoux, en train de préparer quelque chose qui sent presque aussi bon qu'elle. Elle a mis de la musique et je reste dans l'encadrement de la porte pour la regarder onduler de droite à gauche tout en fredonnant une chanson que je ne reconnais pas.

Comme si elle avait senti ma présence, elle finit par se retourner.

– Le petit déjeuner est presque prêt, m'annonce-t-elle avec un sourire.

Je hoche la tête, mais je reste là quelques secondes encore pour le plaisir de la contempler. Il y a cinq jours, quand Alexa a débarqué telle une furie en affirmant qu'elle voulait emmener Beck sur les routes, j'ai pensé que ma semaine allait être pourrie ;

comme toujours après l'une de nos disputes. Mais Emerie a le don de me calmer, de m'inciter à voir les aspects positifs. Bon, ça a dû jouer aussi qu'elle ait passé toutes les nuits dans mon lit pour m'aider à apaiser mon stress, et que je me sois réveillé ce matin au contact de sa langue sur mon sexe, qui me léchait sous les couvertures comme si j'étais une sucette.

Tout sourire, elle m'adresse un clin d'œil en rougissant.

– Va t'asseoir. À mon tour de te nourrir.

Ouais, il est très possible que je m'habitue à ça.

***

– Ton premier rendez-vous est à quelle heure ? je lui demande.

On a terminé le petit déjeuner, puis je l'ai prise sur le plan de travail de la cuisine avant de ramasser et de laver la vaisselle pendant qu'elle se préparait. Maintenant, elle applique un truc sur ses cils, penchée vers le miroir.

– À dix heures. Mais je dois d'abord passer par mon appartement. Et toi ?

– Pas de rendez-vous avant cet après-midi, mais il faut que je rédige le premier jet d'une motion et la transmette au juge des affaires familiales d'ici là. Qu'est-ce que tu as besoin de récupérer chez toi ?

– Des vêtements. À moins que tu ne penses que je puisse m'en sortir avec ça, une ceinture et une paire d'escarpins ?

Elle montre ma chemise, ouverte, sous laquelle elle ne porte rien. Séduit par cet accès facile, je prends un sein dans ma paume avant de me pencher pour embrasser son téton érigé.

– Pourquoi est-ce que tu ne laisses pas des vêtements ici, pour les nuits où tu restes dormir, histoire de t'éviter la course jusqu'à chez toi, dans tes habits de la veille et sans sous-vêtements ?

J'ai parlé plus ou moins sans réfléchir, pourtant l'idée ne m'effraie pas, une fois émise. Bizarre.

Emerie lève les yeux vers moi.

– Tu m'offres un tiroir ?

Je hausse les épaules.

– Prends la moitié du dressing, si tu veux. Je n'aime pas te savoir en train de parcourir la ville en jupe et sans culotte le matin… même si je ne vois pas très bien pourquoi tu ne peux pas simplement la tourner à l'envers et la remettre comme ça.

Elle plisse le nez.

– C'est un truc de mec.

Une fois qu'elle a fini d'appliquer le maquillage qu'elle a dans son sac à main, elle s'habille et retourne à son appartement. J'appelle Alexa et lui laisse un message indiquant que je passerai prendre Beck pour le week-end vers dix-sept heures.

Soulagé d'être tombé sur sa boîte vocale plutôt que sur elle, je descends travailler, toujours de bonne humeur… pour être accueilli par un huissier qui attend devant la porte. Je suis avocat spécialisé dans les divorces, il n'est pas rare d'avoir la visite d'un huissier dès le matin. En revanche, il est plus rare que l'huissier en question vienne du tribunal d'Atlanta.

***

Je viens de relire pour la cinquième fois le même paragraphe de la motion.

Des changements ont eu lieu depuis le dernier arrêté de garde, qui nécessitent une modification des visites à l'enfant. Ces changements étaient inconnus au moment du décret final et justifient donc une révision des accords concernant la garde.

En lisant la partie suivante, je me suis assis sur ma chaise, plutôt que de me rendre directement à l'appartement d'Alexa, parce que je ne sais pas de quoi j'aurais été capable alors.

Comme indiqué en annexe, la paternité a été établie pour Levi Archer Bodine et non le défendeur, à qui le droit de visite a été attribué dans le décret de garde final.

La requérante demande une augmentation de sa période de garde d'une part égale à un droit de visite un week-end sur deux durant une période de huit heures comme attribué au défendeur. Le temps gagné par la requérante sera mis à profit pour permettre à l'enfant mineur d'être présenté à son père biologique.

De plus, le droit de garde du défendeur doit être réduit à la suite d'incidents récents dus à des négligences. À savoir une conduite du défendeur qui a mis l'enfant en danger par sa fréquentation d'une personne connue des services de justice.

En conséquence, la requérante a des raisons de s'inquiéter pour la sécurité de l'enfant mineur et requiert une modification immédiate du décret de garde.

Les documents annexés à la requête comprennent une copie de la condamnation la plus récente de la soi-disant criminelle et une du rapport des urgences. La criminelle, c'est Emerie et, bien entendu, il s'agit seulement d'un extrait partial des charges concernant l'accusation d'outrage à la pudeur. Rien ne mentionne en revanche qu'elle était adolescente au moment des faits et que la condamnation a été réduite le mois dernier. En plus de ce tas de merde, la copie du rapport des urgences comporte le diagnostic de brûlure accidentelle, ainsi qu'une déclaration sous serment d'une infirmière attestant que Beck a été amené par son père et la femme qui le gardait au moment de l'accident : Emerie Rose.

***

À la troisième tentative, voyant que je tombe encore sur sa boîte vocale, je n'en peux plus et décide de me rendre en personne chez Alexa. Ce n'est pas la meilleure idée du monde, considérant l'humeur dans laquelle je suis, mais j'ai besoin de crever l'abcès avec elle. Je n'ai qu'un moyen de pression sur cette femme, mais il se trouve que je l'ai en énormes quantités : l'argent. Je suis capable d'aller jusqu'à la payer pour régler cette affaire. *Encore.* Ce petit jeu, c'est sa manière de se venger de moi pour l'avoir empêchée d'emmener Beck en tournée pendant deux semaines sur le circuit NASCAR. Elle veut me montrer qui tient les rênes. Je connais mon ex-femme, elle est roublarde et prête à tout pour s'assurer de garder la main. Notre dispute et sans doute aussi sa rencontre avec Emerie lui ont donné l'impression qu'elle devait me remettre à ma place.

Les premiers coups que je frappe à sa porte restent sans réponse, ce qui ne fait que m'irriter encore plus et me pousse à cogner plus fort. Au bout de deux minutes impatientes, je sors ma clé. Quand j'ai fichu Alexa dehors et que je lui ai loué cet appartement, j'ai gardé un double des clés pour moi. Je n'ai jamais eu l'occasion de m'en servir, seulement là, j'en ai plus qu'assez qu'elle m'évite.

La serrure est coincée, mais à force d'agiter la clé à l'intérieur, j'ai le soulagement d'entendre le cliquettement bruyant de l'ouverture. Ne tenant pas à me faire assommer avec une poêle à frire, j'entrouvre la porte et crie.

– Alexa ?

Pas de réponse. Je répète :

– Alexa ?

Le vestibule est silencieux et aucun son ne me parvient non plus de l'intérieur de l'appartement. Décidant que la voie est libre et sûre, je pousse la porte en grand.

Et mon cœur s'arrête quand je découvre la scène.

CHAPITRE 37

EMERIE

Quelque chose ne va pas.

Les portes n'ont cessé de claquer pendant toute la dernière demi-heure de ma séance de thérapie téléphonique. Depuis dix minutes, s'y sont rajoutés les hurlements. L'une des voix est celle d'un Drew extrêmement furieux, l'autre celle de Roman, arrivé au bureau il y a peu. Il effectue souvent des enquêtes pour le compte de Drew, mais en l'occurrence, ce qui est en train de se produire semble bien plus personnel qu'une simple affaire.

Ayant présenté une énième fois mes excuses à mes patients (je leur mens en leur racontant que je vais devoir échanger quelques mots avec les ouvriers du bâtiment au sujet de leur langage), je raccroche et me dirige vers la porte fermée de mon bureau. Mais je m'immobilise en entendant mon nom.

– Emerie ? Qu'est-ce qu'elle vient faire là-dedans, bon Dieu ?

– En gros, Alexa a balancé au juge que je couche avec une repris de justice.

– Repris de justice ? Qu'est-ce qu'elle aurait fait ? Écopé d'un PV pour interdiction de stationnement ?

– C'est une longue histoire, mais elle a été arrêtée pour attentat à la pudeur le mois dernier.

– Quoi ?!

– Ça remonte à son adolescence. C'était une amende pour un bain de minuit qui a tourné à la convocation au tribunal parce qu'elle ne s'en était pas acquittée. C'est juste un écart de conduite… rien de plus sérieux qu'un PV, en effet. Mais évidemment, Alexa en fait des tonnes. La motion la qualifie ni plus ni moins que de repris de justice avec un penchant pour l'exhibitionnisme. Et elle a fait ajouter que c'est la repris de justice en question qui a récemment causé la brûlure de Beck.

– Merde.

– Ouais. Merde. Mais ce n'est pas le pire. Je pourrais plaider ça facile dans un tribunal new-yorkais, avec toutes les saletés que les juges entendent tous les jours. Mais elle a ouvert le nouveau dossier de garde du petit à Atlanta.

– Comment elle peut faire ça, puisque vous vivez tous les deux ici ?

– Je rentre tout juste de son appartement. Elle est partie. Le portier m'a expliqué qu'elle avait filé hier et laissé une adresse pour faire suivre son courrier. Son appart est vide. Elle a déménagé, putain !!

***

Drew n'est pas un gros buveur. Il aime prendre un verre de whisky à l'occasion, une bière ou deux, mais les avaler cul sec et à la file, ce n'est pas son truc.

Sauf ce soir.

Il a eu beau m'assurer que rien de tout ça n'est ma faute, je continue à me sentir terriblement coupable, en tant que catalyseur qui le fait passer pour un parent inapte.

Nous sommes dans son appartement, ayant tous les deux annulé nos obligations pour l'après-midi. J'ai promis à Roman que Drew serait à l'aéroport pour leur vol de demain matin. Ils vont à Atlanta, essayer de discuter avec Alexa, et je suis vraiment contente que Drew ne s'y rende pas seul. Il ne parvient même pas à prononcer le nom de son ex-femme sans grogner.

Je referme la porte après le départ de Roman, verrouille la serrure du haut, prends le verre de Drew sur le plan de travail de la cuisine et le vide dans l'évier. Il a les jambes plus longues que le canapé, et ses pieds dépassent de l'accoudoir. Je délace ses chaussures, puis entreprends de les lui ôter.

– Tu comptes me déshabiller ? bafouille-t-il. Laisse tomber les chaussures, passe direct au pantalon.

Je souris. Même saoul, il reste égal à lui-même.

– Il est presque vingt-trois heures. Ton vol est dans dix heures, je pense que tu as besoin de dormir un peu. Le petit matin risque de n'être pas très aimable avec ta tête.

Ses grandes chaussures tombent au sol avec un bruit sourd quand je les lui retire, suivies de ses chaussettes.

– Je ne peux pas perdre mon fils.

Mon cœur se brise au son angoissé de sa voix rauque.

– Tu ne le perdras pas. Si tu n'arrives pas à acheter Alexa, tu convaincras un juge que ton fils a besoin de toi et que sa place est à tes côtés.

– Il n'y a pas beaucoup de justice dans notre système. Les gens la tordent et la détournent tous les jours.

J'ignore quoi répondre à ça. J'ai juste envie de faire mon possible pour qu'il se sente mieux. Alors j'enlève moi aussi mes chaussures, je me glisse sur le canapé et je passe les bras autour de lui pour me pelotonner contre son torse.

– Je suis désolée de ce qui t'arrive. C'est tellement clair que tu l'aimes, ce petit bonhomme. Un juge ne manquera pas de le voir.

Il me serre contre lui en guise de réponse et, quelques minutes plus tard, alors que je crois qu'il s'est endormi, il reprend la parole. Ses mots sont à peine plus forts qu'un souffle.

– Tu veux des enfants, Oklahoma ?

– Oui. J'adorerais en avoir quelques-uns et peut-être en adopter aussi.

– Tu seras une super maman, un jour.

***

– On ne l'a pas trouvée. L'adresse qu'elle a laissée au portier, c'était celle de son frère. Un vrai loser, ce type, on est arrivés chez lui à quatorze heures, il était encore au lit. (Le ricanement de Drew résonne dans le téléphone.) Enfin, jusqu'à ce qu'il se retrouve suspendu dans les airs au bout des bras de Roman.

– Vous avez forcé l'entrée ?

– On n'a pas eu besoin. La porte n'était même pas fermée à clé. Crois-moi, y en a pas besoin : même les cafards refuseraient d'entrer dans ce taudis.

– Il vous a dit où est Alexa ?

– Il n'en savait rien.

– Il ment pour le compte de sa sœur ?

– Je ne pense pas. Il l'aurait balancée. Il avait tellement les jetons de Roman, ce petit merdeux de junkie, qu'il s'est pissé dessus. Et puis, je le connais. Il aurait essayé de me filer l'info contre l'argent de son prochain fixe, s'il en avait eu la moindre idée. C'est le genre qui vendrait sa mère pour vingt balles.

– Vous savez quoi, du coup ?

– Je suis arrivé au tribunal avant la fermeture et j'ai rempli une ordonnance restrictive en urgence pour demander au juge de la forcer à rentrer à New York. Notre accord relatif à la garde ne nous autorise ni l'un ni l'autre à sortir Beck de l'État sans la permission de l'autre parent. Ils vont ajouter cette motion à l'ordre du jour, avec sa demande de modification de la garde, pour après-demain. Si on ne la retrouve pas d'ici à jeudi, elle n'aura pas d'autre choix que de se pointer au moins au tribunal.

– Il y a quelque chose que je puisse faire ?

– Non. Merci, ma chérie. Entendre ta voix, ça suffit à me faire du bien.

Je souris.

– Je te rappellerai peut-être plus tard ce soir, et cette voix aura des choses cochonnes à te dire.

– Ah ouais ?

Je me mordille la lèvre.

– Je suis une joueuse d'équipe. Je veux aider de toutes les manières possibles.

– Je me débarrasserai de Roman, pour tout à l'heure. Il aime bien rester au bar et s'envoyer quelques whiskies à la fin de la journée. Je ne pense pas qu'il s'attarde trop aujourd'hui, après la soirée d'hier. Je préfère largement t'écouter jouir pendant que tu me racontes à quel point mon sexe te manque.

– Rendez-vous est pris. Je rentre bientôt à la maison.

– OK, ma chérie. Rappelle-moi une fois que tu es installée, alors.

– Drew ?

– Ouais ?

– Pour information : vous me manquez, ton sexe et toi.

Il gronde mon nom.

– Dépêche-toi de rentrer chez toi.

***

Je n'ai jamais donné dans le sexe au téléphone et j'ai vraiment très hâte d'appeler Drew. À tel point que j'ai enfilé un joli petit ensemble shorty et caraco en soie et mis du parfum pour l'occasion. Il est un peu plus de vingt-deux heures, donc j'imagine qu'il doit se préparer à se coucher aussi. Je prends mon portable et compose son numéro, souriant quand il me répond de sa voix bourrue.

– Tu es nue ?

– Non, mais je peux l'être.

J'ai la main sur l'interrupteur de la cuisine, prête à éteindre la lumière et à emporter le téléphone au lit avec moi, quand on frappe à la porte. Drew aussi l'a entendu.

– Il y a quelqu'un ?

– Je crois. Ne quitte pas.

Je me dirige vers la porte et regarde par l'œilleton, même si je sais d'avance de qui il s'agit. Ce n'est pas comme si j'avais des tonnes d'amis en ville, encore moins de ceux qui peuvent passer comme ça sans prévenir.

– Je peux te rappeler dans quelques minutes ?

– Je vais avoir envie de savoir qui c'est ?

– Sans doute pas. Accorde-moi quelques minutes pour me débarrasser de lui.

Une fois la communication coupée, j'attrape un pull dans le placard et l'enfile avant d'ouvrir.

– Baldwin ? Tout va bien ?

– Oui, ça va. Je voulais juste prendre de tes nouvelles. J'ai frappé, hier soir, mais tu n'étais pas là. Alors j'ai réessayé ce matin, mais tu n'étais toujours pas là. Et puis, tu n'as pas répondu à mes SMS aujourd'hui. Je commençais à m'inquiéter.

Mes sentiments pour Baldwin sont tellement confus que j'avais oublié à quel point il avait été un bon ami pour moi, pendant quelques années.

– Pardon, je ne voulais pas t'inquiéter. Ça va. Tout va bien. La journée a juste été un peu folle, hier, et celle d'aujourd'hui surchargée.

Le voyant peu convaincu, je décide d'opter pour l'honnêteté.

– Je vois quelqu'un, je suis restée chez lui la nuit dernière.

– Ah… (Il m'offre un sourire triste qui paraît forcé.) Alors, je suis content que tu ailles bien.

Comme je ne lui propose pas d'entrer, il fouille mon visage du regard, manifestement en quête de quelque chose. J'attends dans un silence gêné, plantée là à serrer mon gilet autour de moi.

Au bout du compte, Baldwin m'adresse un bref hochement de tête et ses yeux tombent sur mes jambes nues.

– C'est l'avocat ?

Pour une raison que je ne m'explique pas, ça m'agace qu'il l'appelle « l'avocat » et pas par son nom.

– Drew. Oui.

Il plonge dans mes yeux.

– Tu es heureuse ?

Je n'ai même pas besoin de réfléchir à la réponse.

– Oui.

Baldwin baisse brièvement les paupières et hoche de nouveau la tête en silence, puis :

– On pourra peut-être prendre un café cette semaine et discuter ?

Je lui souris.

– Bien sûr.

Un café chez *Starbucks*, c'est sans doute le meilleur moyen de relancer notre amitié. Cette relance sera d'ailleurs uniquement à effectuer de mon côté, car Baldwin n'a jamais vraiment été intéressé par moi d'une autre manière, à la différence de moi. Mais à présent que je fréquente quelqu'un d'autre, ça me mettrait mal à l'aise de sortir dîner avec lui. Peut-être un jour, plus tard, quand le temps aura passé entre les sentiments que j'éprouvais pour Baldwin et le début de ma nouvelle relation, mais pour l'instant je ne sais pas, je ne trouverais pas ça correct.

Après lui avoir souhaité une bonne nuit, je prends un moment pour rassembler mes pensées avant d'aller dans ma chambre et de rappeler Drew. Mes sentiments pour Baldwin, ils existent depuis si longtemps que je ne peux pas les éteindre complètement, cependant quelque chose a changé, sans l'ombre d'un doute. Même si une partie de moi sait que le confort sans retenue dont je me délectais avec Baldwin va me manquer, je me rends compte qu'il est plus important pour moi de respecter les limites que Drew souhaiterait me voir mettre en place, je le sais, comme ne pas inviter un homme dans mon appartement si tard, surtout quand je porte mon petit pyjama sexy.

Satisfaite, j'éteins les lumières et me glisse dans mon lit tout en composant le numéro de Drew sur mon portable.

– Coucou.

– Ton visiteur est parti ?

Une certaine inquiétude se mêle au ton habituellement assuré de Drew.

– C'était Baldwin. Il voulait prendre de mes nouvelles. Apparemment, il est venu frapper hier soir et ce matin, et il se tracassait parce que je n'avais pas répondu à ses SMS aujourd'hui non plus.

– Et tu lui as répondu quoi ?

– Que j'avais couché chez mon petit ami et que j'avais été très occupée, mais que tout allait bien.

– Ton petit ami ? C'est donc ce que je suis ?

J'entends du soulagement dans sa voix.

– Tu préfères que je t'appelle autrement ?

– Je ne sais pas. Qu'est-ce que tu as d'autre en magasin ?

– Hum… voyons voir… que penses-tu de « l'homme qui me donne plein d'orgasmes » ?

– On dirait mon nom indien.

J'éclate de rire.

– Ou bien « Propriétaire avec avantages » ou « Capitaine Prolactinator » ?

– Appelle-moi comme tu veux devant le professeur Crétin, du moment qu'il sait que tu es à moi.

À moi. J'aime bien comme ça sonne. Je ne sais pas trop comment c'est arrivé. Nous connaissant, ça a dû commencer à éclore pendant une dispute et fleurir alors qu'il me prenait sur son bureau, mais quoi qu'il en soit, nous en sommes arrivés là. Et je me rends compte que je n'ai nulle envie d'être ailleurs.

– Tu es seul ?

– Roman est en bas, au bar. Tenu par une barmaid. Je ne pense pas que ma compagnie va tellement lui manquer.

– OK, très bien. (Je tends la main vers ma table de chevet et ouvre le tiroir.) Tu as entendu ça ?

– Ne me dis pas que c'est encore l'autre qui frappe.

Sortant mon vibromasseur, je décide que Drew a besoin d'être un peu distrait de ces deux derniers jours si horribles. Je l'actionne et l'approche de mon téléphone, quelques secondes avant de le baisser vers mon corps.

– Est-ce que c'est… ?

– Mon vibro. Il s’ennuie un peu, depuis quelques semaines.

Drew lâche un grognement.

– Merde. J’aimerais être là-bas pour te regarder.

– Je pense que j’aimerais bien, moi aussi. Peut-être quand tu rentreras.

– Pas peut-être. Je viens direct à ton appartement à ma descente de l’avion.

Sa réaction m’excite. Je pose le vibromasseur sur mon clitoris et reprends d’une voix devenue rauque.

– Et si tu « venais » dans l’autre sens du terme, en attendant ?

CHAPITRE 38

DREW

– Elle est culottée, me chuchote Roman, pas si discrètement que ça.

Alexa vient d'entrer dans le tribunal de son pas assuré, accompagnée de son avocat, Atticus Carlyle. Elle nous adresse un sourire.

Mes poings se serrent instinctivement. Après être revenu bredouille d'une journée et demie de recherches, je me demande pourquoi je suis surpris qu'elle ait choisi ce connard. Je le hais presque autant qu'il me hait, l'enflure. C'est la quintessence du bon vieux gars du Sud : accent à couper au couteau, nœud papillon et allusion à Dieu dans toutes les introductions et les conclusions de ses plaidoiries. C'est aussi le seul avocat qui m'ait jamais poussé à perdre mes nerfs dans une salle d'audience. Or il se trouve que le juge qui nous a été assigné est justement celui qui m'a sanctionné, après mon pétage de câble. Je commence à avoir la sensation que rien de tout ça n'est une coïncidence.

Dans un effort pour conserver le semblant de calme qui me reste encore, je m'abstiens de regarder de l'autre côté de la salle. Le juge Walliford prend place et l'huissier en uniforme appelle nos numéros de dossier. Il passe quelques minutes à lire, ses lunettes perchées à la pointe de son nez, avant de relever les yeux.

– Tiens, tiens, tiens, voyez donc qui nous avons là. Comme on se retrouve, n'est-ce pas (*n'esseupâ*) ?

– Effectivement Votre Honneur, je réponds.

– Ben vrai, vôôôtrôônneureu. Content de vous revoir, ajoute l'avocat de la partie adverse de sa voix traînante.

Walliford déplace des papiers et ôte ses lunettes, avant de se caler contre le dossier de son fauteuil.

– Monsieur Jagger, pourquoi pensez-vous que cette affaire devrait être entendue dans un tribunal de New York, plutôt qu'ici à Atlanta ? Vous croyez que les rouages de la justice ne tournent pas à la même vitesse ici qu'à celle à laquelle vous êtes habitués, vous, les gens du Nord ?

Bordel, comment je suis censé répondre à ça ? J'ai déposé une demande qui se fonde sur le lieu de résidence pour un déplacement de l'affaire. Je m'éclaircis la gorge.

– Ce n'est pas ça, Votre Honneur, je suis sûr que cette cour est très efficace pour juger tout dossier présenté devant elle, mais étant donné que la plaignante et moi sommes résidents de New York, j'estime que la juridiction naturelle serait celle du comté de New York. Selon notre accord…

Là, Carlyle intervient, la tête la première.

– Vôôôtrôônneureu, ma cliente est résidente de notre bon État de Géorgie. Elle est née et a grandi ici. Au cours de son bref mariage avec M. Jagger, elle a été résidente temporaire de New York, mais elle a récemment acheté une maison dans le comté de Fulton et c'est donc ici, son État de résidence. (Il exhibe un papier et poursuit.) J'ai avec moi une copie du titre de propriété de sa nouvelle maison, son permis de conduire délivré à Atlanta et une copie du bail de l'appartement où elle résidait DE MANIÈRE TEMPORAIRE à New York. Vous constaterez d'ailleurs que le bail n'était même pas au nom de madame Jagger.

– C'est des conneries. Le bail était à mon nom parce que c'est moi qui payais le loyer. Elle y a vécu deux ans.

Je sais avant d'avoir terminé ma phrase que je viens de commettre une grosse erreur avec mon éclat. Le juge Walliford agite le doigt.

– Je ne tolérerai pas ce langage dans ma salle d'audience. Vous, les Nordistes, vous trouvez peut-être cela acceptable de vous exprimer ainsi, mais nous ne sommes pas dans un bar enfumé ou dans une ruelle malfamée. Je vous prie de respecter ce banc, ce sera ma dernière mise en garde, monsieur

Jagger. Après votre comportement de la dernière fois, dans ce même tribunal, je vous tiens à l'œil.

Et ça, c'était encore la meilleure partie de ma journée. Le juge Walliford a refusé ma demande de modifier les visites à New York et ordonné un procès complet pour décider du changement des droits de garde déposé par Alexa. Qui commencera dans deux semaines à compter de lundi. La seule chose qu'il a actée en ma faveur, ça a été notre planning de garde actuel, selon lequel j'ai Beck du vendredi au dimanche soir, ainsi que les mercredis soir pour le dîner. Bien qu'il soit clairement précisé que mes visites doivent se tenir, vous l'aurez deviné, dans « le bel État de Géorgie ».

J'attends que nous soyons sortis du bâtiment avant de tenter ne serait-ce que d'approcher Alexa. La dernière chose dont j'aie besoin, c'est qu'elle se mettre à brailler que je la harcèle et que Walliford me mette derrière les barreaux.

Je serre les dents.

– Alexa, je peux te parler, s'il te plaît ?

Carlyle la prend par le coude.

– Je ne pense pas que ce soit une bonne idée, Alexa.

Je l'ignore et regarde mon ex-femme droit dans les yeux.

– Tu me dois au moins ça. Ça fait plus de deux ans que j'ai découvert le pot aux roses, et j'ai encore sacrément mal. Pourtant, jamais je n'ai rien laissé paraître devant Beck, il reste pour moi ce qu'il était. Je me fous de ce qu'affirme un putain de test sanguin, c'est mon fils. (Elle détourne les yeux.) Regarde-moi, Alexa. Regarde-moi.

Quand elle croise enfin mon regard, je reprends :

– Tu me connais. Est-ce que je vais lâcher l'affaire même si je perds dans deux semaines ?

Son avocat s'interpose.

– Vous menacez ma cliente ?

Je continue à soutenir le regard d'Alexa.

– Non, je lui demande de faire passer notre fils en priorité et de ne pas s'entêter dans cette procédure.

Elle prend une profonde inspiration.

– Ce n'est pas *notre* fils. Allons-y, maître Carlyle.

Heureusement que Roman se tient près de moi. Il me passe les bras autour du torse pour m'empêcher de me lancer derrière elle tandis qu'elle s'éloigne.

***

Avant le vol de retour, je tente en vain de synchroniser mon calendrier avec mon téléphone portable, afin de passer quelques heures à feuilleter mon planning pour voir si je pourrais rester lundi, mardi et la moitié du mercredi à New York, puis revenir à Atlanta afin de dîner avec Beck le mercredi soir. Je resterais ensuite à Atlanta et télétravaillerais jeudi et vendredi, avant de repasser prendre Beck pour le week-end. Ça ne va pas être facile de caser une semaine de rendez-vous clients, de dépositions et de présence à la cour sur deux journées et demie. Mais je n'ai pas d'autre choix. Mon fils doit passer en priorité. Il est déjà assez perturbé par ce soudain changement et de ne plus pouvoir passer ses week-ends chez papa. En plus, j'ai dans l'idée que si je rate ne serait-ce qu'une seule visite, le juge Walliford en entendra parler. Je n'ai pas besoin de lui fournir des munitions supplémentaires contre moi.

Même si mon fils est ma priorité, j'ai un autre objectif à présent que je suis de retour sur le sol new-yorkais. N'étant pas certain de pouvoir attraper le dernier vol de retour depuis Atlanta, je n'ai pas annoncé à Emerie que j'avais une chance d'être rentré ce soir. Il est tard, presque minuit, pourtant j'indique quand même son adresse au chauffeur de taxi au lieu de la mienne.

Durant les six jours où j'ai été absent, on s'est parlé tous les soirs ; et presque chaque fois, ça s'est terminé par mon orgasme au son de son vibromasseur. Ça m'a aidé à calmer mes nerfs, mais en même temps, ça m'a aussi donné encore plus faim d'elle en chair et en os.

L'intérieur de son immeuble est plongé dans le silence. Je prends l'ascenseur sans que personne m'ait questionné, vu que son bâtiment n'a pas de portier. Je déteste ça, en fait. Il faut vraiment qu'elle se trouve un endroit plus sécurisé où vivre, n'importe quel connard peut se pointer à sa porte. D'ailleurs, c'est ce qui est sur le point de se produire. Ayant posé mes bagages pour frapper, je jette un coup d'œil en direction de l'appartement voisin.

Oui, il lui faut vraiment un appartement plus sécurisé.

Au bout de deux tentatives (la seconde fois je cogne si fort que je crains de réveiller des voisins), une Emerie à l'air tout endormi vient m'ouvrir.

Comme elle était couchée, elle a quitté ses lentilles et porte ses lunettes. *Bon Dieu ce qu'elle me plaît avec ces trucs sur le nez.*

– Salut. Qu'est-ce que tu... ?

Je ne lui laisse pas le temps de terminer, je ne lui dis même pas « bonjour ». Du moins pas avec des mots. Au lieu de quoi, je m'introduis chez elle et la repousse en arrière en lui prenant le visage entre mes mains d'un geste pas très délicat. Je l'embrasse longuement, avec fougue, en refermant la porte d'un coup de pied avant de la soulever afin que ses jambes viennent se nouer autour de ma taille. C'est génial, comme impression, ça me débarrasse de cette sensation merdique qui me colle aux basques depuis toute la semaine.

Quand je glisse sous son petit short de nuit sexy et que je me saisis de ses fesses à pleines mains, elle gémit dans ma bouche. L'envie me vient de la reposer et d'empoigner mon sexe, mais cela impliquerait de m'éloigner de la chaleur de ses cuisses, or ça, pas question ! Alors je parviens je ne sais comment à atteindre le canapé sans trébucher et je la jette dessus sans plus de cérémonie, avant de la recouvrir de mon corps.

– Putain ce que tu m'as manqué, je lui dis d'une voix rauque.

Le regard d'Emerie est flou et rempli de bonheur.

– Je l'avais deviné à ton « bonjour ».

Tout en m'affairant à lui retirer son short et ses sous-vêtements, je me mets à sucer son cou.

– Je t'ai manqué ?

Elle enfonce les ongles dans mon cou quand je délaisse le sien pour m'attaquer à son oreille.

– Oui, souffle-t-elle. Oui, beaucoup.

Je lui mordille le lobe et insinue deux doigts dans son sexe.

– Comment ? Tu mouilles pour moi ?

La réponse, je la connais déjà, évidemment, mais j'ai envie de l'entendre de sa bouche.

– Oui.

Je frotte mon pouce contre son clitoris.

– Oui quoi ?

– Oui, je mouille pour toi.

– Dis-moi que ta petite chatte est toute trempée pour moi. Je veux t'entendre me le dire.

Déjà je déboucle ma ceinture. Qui aurait cru que je sois aussi habile ? Je ne sais par quel prodige, j'ai réussi à nous déshabiller tous les deux d'une seule main tout en suçant son cou, son oreille, ses lèvres et en caressant sa petite chatte humide de mon autre main.

– Ma... petite chatte est trempée pour toi.

Bon Dieu, il n'y a rien de plus sexy qu'entendre Emerie me dire qu'elle est excitée par moi. La semaine écoulée n'est plus qu'un lointain souvenir, je n'ai qu'une idée en tête : plonger en elle.

– Tu m'as tellement manqué.

Je me répète, mais bon, j'ai beau le lui avoir déjà dit, ça reste très, très vrai. Il faut que je la pénètre, je n'en peux plus. Elle va devoir faire une croix sur les préliminaires, cette fois. Même si, au son de ses halètements, je devine que ça ne devrait pas trop la déranger. Je m'insinue lentement dans sa fente, et j'ai tant de peine à me contrôler que mon corps tout entier en tremble. Quand enfin je suis entièrement fiché en elle, je pourrais jurer que certaines de mes terminaisons nerveuses se sont réveillées pour la première fois depuis des années. Son sexe étroit enveloppe mon membre et ses jambes nouées autour de ma taille m'agrippent encore plus fort.

Punaise, je ne me rappelle pas la dernière fois où c'était aussi bon.

Je commence à bouger, trop pressé de me sentir aller et venir dans cet étau puissant, et très vite je me rends compte que je ne vais pas tenir longtemps. C'est trop bon. Emerie ouvre les yeux alors que je me retire et nos regards se nouent. Je saisis ses deux mains, entremêle nos doigts et les plaque au-dessus de sa tête. Je veux l'embrasser, mais je n'arrive pas à la quitter du regard. La façon dont elle halète à chaque assaut, ses petits gémissements lorsque je me retire, est un spectacle fascinant.

Ses mouvements copient les miens. En haut, en bas, dedans, dehors.

– Oh oui, Drew. Là, oui. Ne t'arrête pas.

Par miracle, je réussis à me retenir juste le temps qu'il faut pour qu'elle jouisse en premier. Je regarde l'orgasme transformer son visage : sa tête tomber sur le côté, ses yeux se fermer, ses lèvres sensuelles s'entrouvrir. C'est ce que j'ai vu de plus beau de ma vie.

Une fois qu'elle commence à redescendre de son nuage, je reprends ma cadence, pompant plus fort et plus vite, chassant son orgasme tandis que le mien monte, monte, monte. Pile au moment où je suis sur le point d'exploser, je comprends enfin pourquoi la sensation est aussi différente, pourquoi chaque nerf est sollicité comme pour la première fois.

Je n'ai pas mis de préservatif. *Merde.* Je vais devoir me retirer…

– Em, je n'ai pas…

J'essaie de lui expliquer pourquoi je vais lui gâcher la fin de ce moment, mais je manque de mots, ils m'échappent aussi vite que mon endurance.

– … de préservatif.

Elle me regarde droit dans les yeux.

– C'est bon, je prends la pilule. Jouis en moi. S'il te plaît.

Il n'est rien dont je n'aie plus envie que de me déverser en elle. Mon corps en brûle avec une ardeur animale, mais alors que je me laisse aller, j'ai aussi l'impression de lui donner quelque chose que je retenais à un niveau bien plus profond.

Pour la première fois depuis le soir où j'ai rencontré Alexa et qu'elle m'a affirmé prendre la pilule, je viens m'exposer au risque de faire confiance à quelqu'un. Sauf que, pour une raison qui m'échappe, ça ne m'apparaît pas comme un risque, avec Emerie. Ça me paraît juste normal.

CHAPITRE 39

EMERIE

Je sens le matelas s'enfoncer quand Drew se lève.

– Où tu vas ?

– Je ne voulais pas te réveiller. (Il contourne le lit et vient me déposer un baiser sur le front.) Il est tôt. Rendors-toi.

– Quelle heure il est ?

– Cinq heures trente.

Je me hausse sur un coude dans le noir.

– Pourquoi tu te lèves aussi tôt ?

– Il faut que je descende au bureau essayer de voir comment je peux caser, pour quelque temps, six journées de travail que j'ai déjà réduites à cinq dans seulement deux jours par semaine.

– J'en déduis que tu n'as pas consulté ton planning depuis un jour ou deux ?

– J'ai essayé, mais cette saleté de truc était verrouillée et n'a pas voulu se synchroniser.

Je me rallonge dans le lit et remonte la couverture.

– Ton premier rendez-vous n'est pas avant dix heures. Je ne pensais pas que tu rentrerais avant ce matin, sinon j'aurais fait débuter ta journée plus tôt. Je t'ai réorganisé les deux semaines à venir. Ça fait de longues journées, mais j'ai pu faire coïncider tous tes rendez-vous physiques sur deux jours par semaine. J'ai transformé un rendez-vous physique en conf'call et tu la feras depuis Atlanta jeudi de la semaine prochaine. Pour tout le reste, c'est réglé. J'ai aussi changé mon planning à l'inverse, afin que mes journées où tu es là soient légères et les autres bien remplies. Comme ça, je peux t'aider dans le travail de secrétariat, ce qui te permet d'avancer dans ta journée.

Drew reste silencieux une minute et je commence à craindre d'avoir outrepassé ma fonction. Je n'aurais peut-être pas dû toucher à son planning. Mais c'était pour l'aider de mon mieux. La chambre est plongée dans la pénombre et j'entends le froissement de ses vêtements, sans trop savoir s'il les enlève ou s'il les enfile, jusqu'à ce qu'il se réinstalle dans le lit. Son corps chaud se colle contre le mien. Il n'a toujours pas parlé, alors je me tourne face à lui.

– J'ai dépassé les bornes ?

Il me caresse la joue.

– Non, chérie. Tu n'as pas dépassé les bornes.

– Tu ne dis rien. J'ai cru que je t'avais agacé.

– Je réfléchissais, c'est tout.

– À quoi ?

– Au fait que je me sente chez moi, là, alors que je n'ai pas mis un pied dans mon appartement depuis une semaine.

C'est très probablement la chose la plus adorable qu'on m'ait jamais dite. En plus, il a raison. J'ai été toute tendue cette semaine, et je viens juste de me rendre compte que cette nervosité s'est apaisée à la seconde où j'ai regardé par l'œilleton cette nuit.

– Oui, je comprends ce que tu veux dire. Tu me calmes. Tu m'apaises, je pense que c'est plus ça.

– Ah oui ?

Il pose une main sur ma joue et caresse du pouce le creux de mon cou.

– Oui.

Il me dépose un baiser sur la pointe du nez.

– Tant mieux. Tu sais à quoi je pense, là ?

– À quoi ?

– À la manière dont je pourrais te remercier d'avoir organisé mon emploi du temps. J'hésite entre utiliser ma bouche et te dévorer en guise de petit déjeuner ou te prendre par-derrière tout en caressant ton anus.

Je glousse.

– Tu es vraiment un goujat. Tu es passé de tendre à cochon en dix secondes montre en main.

Celle qu'il avait dans mon cou tombe sur mon sein, dont il effleure le téton avant de le pincer… fort.

– Tu l'aimes bien, ma bouche de goujat.

Il a raison, après tout, je ne vais pas me battre pour le détromper.

– C'était quoi, mes options, au fait ?

– Ma bouche ou à quatre pattes, répond-il d'une voix où je perçois le sourire.

Je déglutis.

– Pourquoi se cantonner à une des deux ? Tu n'es pas attendu au bureau avant dix heures.

***

– Tu veux encore du café ?

Il est dix-huit heures passées et Drew a encore un client à recevoir et une dizaine d'autres à rappeler.

– J'adorerais, merci.

Je lui prépare son café juste comme il l'aime et le lui apporte dans son bureau. Il est en train de lire un dossier bleu dont j'ai signé la réception il y a une heure.

– Merci, répète-t-il sans lever les yeux.

– Tu me remercies beaucoup, aujourd'hui.

– Attends de voir ce que j'ai dans ma manche pour ce soir, répond-il.

Je sais qu'il est occupé, je ne veux pas lui prendre trop de son temps à batifoler. Il m'arrête au moment où j'arrive à sa porte.

– Chez moi ce soir ? Tu pourras rester dormir même si je m'en vais de bonne heure ou prendre un bain si tu veux. Ma nouvelle esclavagiste de secrétaire m'a prévu un début de journée à sept heures.

– Tu es sûr que tu ne dormirais pas mieux si je rentrais passer la nuit chez moi ? Tu as besoin de repos, avec tous les voyages et le stress que tu subis.

Drew lâche la liasse de feuilles qu'il lisait.

– Viens ici.

Je retourne me poster devant son bureau.

– Plus près.

Quand j'approche de son siège, il me surprend en m'attirant d'un coup sur ses genoux.

– Quatre heures de sommeil à côté de toi, c'est mieux que huit dans un lit vide.

– Méfie-toi, Jagger. Tu es en train de perdre ton acidité et de devenir tout sucre avec moi.

– Je suis tout sucre avec toi depuis le premier soir où tu as essayé de me flanquer hors de chez moi à coups de pied dans le derrière. Allez file. Va chercher tes affaires. Tu n'as pas besoin de traîner ici si tu as terminé, d'autant qu'ils annoncent de la neige pour ce soir.

Je m'empresse de suivre le conseil de Drew, à savoir aller remplir un petit sac de voyage et revenir.

Je passe tout le trajet de retour chez moi à penser à lui. Drew est le genre d'homme qui ne se laisse pas facilement apprivoiser en apparence, mais une fois que c'est fait, ça vaut largement les efforts consentis pour franchir ses barrières. Au cours de la semaine écoulée, j'ai la sensation que notre relation a vraiment pris une nouvelle voie.

Au point que je décide d'appeler mes parents tout en préparant mon sac, pressée de leur parler du nouvel homme dans ma vie, chose que je fais rarement. Ces derniers temps, disons, je ne sais pas, ces trois dernières années, c'était parce que je n'avais pas de nouveau petit ami. Mais aussi parce que je savais que ma mère allait s'inquiéter pour moi. Elle redoute que je sois blessée ou que j'aie par mégarde porté mon choix sur un tueur en série… parce que, bien entendu, tous les gens qui vivent dans une grande ville sont des tueurs en série potentiels. Alors je distille mes informations au compte-gouttes.

– C'est merveilleux, ma chérie. Comment vous vous êtes rencontrés ?

Euh… il s'est introduit dans mon bureau, puis il m'a sortie de prison le lendemain. Meilleur rencard de ma vie.

– En fait, c'est le propriétaire de mon nouveau bureau.

– Et c'est un gentil jeune homme ?

On ne s'est pas disputés… aujourd'hui.

– Oui, maman. Il est très gentil.

– Qu'est-ce qu'il fait dans la vie ?

Eh bien, il surfe sur les tendances misogynes qu'il a développées à cause des mensonges et des tromperies de son ex-femme et tâche d'extraire des hommes de leur mariage raté en laissant leur femme sans le sou.

– Il est avocat. Droit de la famille.

– Un avocat. Très bien. Et dans le droit de la famille. C'est une profession noble. Quand aurons-nous le plaisir de le rencontrer ?

– Je ne sais pas, maman. Il est très occupé avec son travail, en ce moment.

Et il se bat pour la garde de son fils… qui n'est pas son fils parce que sa garce d'ex-femme l'a utilisé comme vache à lait quand elle s'est retrouvée enceinte d'un autre homme.

Ma mère pousse un soupir.

– Bon, en tout cas assure-toi qu'il ait des valeurs. L'argent et un physique avenant, ça provoque souvent une cécité passagère.

– Oui, maman.

Nous discutons encore un peu, puis, ne me demandez pas d'où ça sort, une question m'échappe.

– Comment tu as su que papa était l'homme de ta vie ?

– J'ai arrêté de dire « je » quand j'envisageais l'avenir.

– Comment ça ?

– Avant de rencontrer ton père, tous mes projets n'étaient que ça : *mes* projets. Après notre rencontre, même au bout de quelques semaines seulement, j'ai cessé de voir l'avenir comme « mon » avenir mais comme le nôtre. Je ne m'en suis pas rendu compte tout de suite, mais quand je parlais des événements à venir, les samedis soir, les vacances, n'importe quoi, j'ai fini par réaliser que je m'étais mise à dire « nous » et plus « je ».

***

Je passe à l'épicerie sur le chemin du retour au bureau et prends de quoi nous faire à dîner. Drew va résider dans un hôtel d'Atlanta et travailler très dur le temps qu'il passera là-bas, du coup je me suis dit qu'il apprécierait un repas maison. Il rentre au moment où je sors les lasagnes du four.

– Hum, ça sent bon ici.

– J'espère que tu aimes les lasagnes.

– C'est mon deuxième plat préféré.

– Quel est le premier ?

Il vient se poster derrière moi, repousse mes cheveux sur une épaule et m'embrasse dans le cou. Sa réponse vibre contre ma peau.

– Toi.

– Calme-toi. Tu as besoin de profiter d'un bon repas tant que tu le peux. Tes semaines à venir vont être chargées.

J'ouvre le tiroir à droite de la cuisinière pour chercher une spatule et tombe sur deux petites voitures et un vieux téléphone à clapet au milieu des ustensiles de cuisine.

– Je me demandais justement où tu rangeais les petites voitures.

Drew s'esclaffe.

– Quand je demande à Beck de mettre de l'ordre dans ses affaires, il se contente de tout fourrer n'importe comment dans les tiroirs. L'an dernier, j'ai trouvé des crayons dans le bac à rangement des couverts. Il avait pris les cuillères et les avait toutes jetées à la poubelle. Face à mes questions, il a haussé les épaules et m'a expliqué qu'on n'en avait pas besoin parce que c'était plus facile de manger avec les mains, mais qu'en revanche, il n'y avait rien d'autre pour colorier.

Je souris.

– Pas faux.

Drew sort le téléphone à clapet du tiroir.

– Tu te rappelles, au début de notre rencontre, le jour où j'ai regardé les photos dans ton portable ?

– Oui. Tu m'avais dit que la meilleure façon de découvrir une personne, c'était de regarder les photos qu'elle a dans son téléphone au moment où elle s'y attend le moins. Ensuite, après avoir regardé les miennes, tu m'as passé ton appareil, mais il était vide. (Je lâche un soupir exagérément lourd.) Tu es vraiment un imbécile.

Il ouvre le vieux téléphone, appuie sur quelques touches et me le tend.

– Je monte me laver et me changer pour le dîner. C'est le portable de Beck. Il n'est pas en service, mais il aime bien l'utiliser comme appareil photo. Chaque fois que je suis assailli par les doutes quant à ma décision de vouloir rester dans sa vie, que je me demande si je ne fais pas n'importe quoi, si je ne devrais pas me mettre en retrait et laisser son père biologique prendre le relais, je contemple ces photos. Jette un œil.

Puis il va dans la chambre et je me verse un verre de vin, avant de m'asseoir à la table de la salle à manger pour découvrir les photos.

Le premier cliché montre Drew en train de se raser. Il est dans la salle de bains, seulement vêtu d'une serviette nouée autour de sa taille. Il a de la mousse à raser sur le côté gauche du visage et tient le rasoir près de son menton, où il a déjà tracé une ligne au milieu du savon. L'autre joue est déjà faite. Sur le côté, dans le reflet du miroir, je vois Beck, l'appareil photo dans une main et une spatule couverte de mousse blanche dans l'autre, dont il se sert comme d'un rasoir. Lui aussi a déjà nettoyé la moitié de son visage.

L'image suivante représente Beck dans un ruisseau. Elle a pu être prise dans le nord-ouest de l'État et sans doute il y a un an à peu près, vu l'évolution du visage de Beck depuis. Il porte des cuissardes, et un large sourire aux lèvres pour la photo ; il arbore fièrement un petit poisson qu'il a dû pêcher dans le cours d'eau.

Je continue à faire défiler les images : Beck et son père à la patinoire, assis côte à côte dans le métro, Drew qui lit *Harold et le crayon violet* dans le lit de Beck, Drew, Beck et Roman à vélo dans Central Park, une photo qui m'oblige à retourner l'appareil à l'envers avant de comprendre qu'en fait elle était bien à l'endroit : c'est Beck qui les a pris tous les deux alors que Drew le porte sur ses épaules, il s'est penché pour prendre leurs deux visages.

Cliché après cliché, leur vie ensemble m'est révélée, montrant à quel point Drew est effectivement le père de Beck, quoi qu'en dise le test d'un laboratoire.

La toute dernière me surprend. Je ne savais même pas que Beck avait ce téléphone, à l'époque où elle a été prise, et encore moins qu'il avait fait une photo. C'est l'après-midi où on est allés faire du patin à glace, avant que je ne tombe et me blesse à la cheville. Beck devait se tenir sur un côté de la patinoire, pendant que Drew et moi patinions ensemble, enfin, que j'essayais de patiner. J'ai les jambes largement écartées, c'était ma position, ce jour-là, et je ris en tombant dans une fente tout sauf gracieuse. Drew a un bras passé autour de ma taille, pour essayer de me relever, les yeux baissés vers moi, rieur lui aussi. On a l'air heureux, presque… comme si on était en train de tomber amoureux.

Mon cœur gonfle dans ma poitrine. Drew a raison. La meilleure façon de connaître quelqu'un, c'est de regarder ses photos en douce. En les observant, lui, il y voit l'amour d'un père pour son fils, un rappel de la raison pour laquelle il doit se battre. Moi, j'y vois un homme bien, un passionné forcené dès qu'il aime quelque chose, et prêt à tout pour le protéger. Je passe le doigt sur l'écran, sur la photo de nous, de moi en train de tomber, et je me rends compte que je suis tombée à plus d'un titre, ce jour-là.

Je dois cligner des paupières pour empêcher mes émotions de prendre le dessus. Je vais me lever et aller m'occuper du repas, tiens.

L'esprit occupé ailleurs, je ne fais pas attention et attrape le plat de lasagnes pour le retourner afin de les couper.

– Merde !

Je secoue la main et ouvre le robinet d'eau froide, que je fais couler sur la brûlure superficielle. *Décidément, elle ne me réussit pas, cette cuisinière.*

Bien sûr, Drew débarque à cet instant.

– Qu'est-ce qui s'est passé ?

– J'ai touché le plat chaud. Ce n'est pas grand-chose, ça pique juste un peu.

Drew retire ma main de sous le jet d'eau froide, l'inspecte et la remet sous l'eau.

– Je vais faire le service. Va t'asseoir. Je ne tiens pas à finir aux urgences pour la troisième fois cette année.

Nous passons la soirée à nous raconter les derniers événements, vu qu'on ne s'est pas vraiment parlé la veille ou ce matin, même si nos corps ont très bien communiqué. Drew me parle de la stratégie qu'il va mettre en place au tribunal pour la garde, et moi j'évoque de nouveaux patients que j'ai reçus. Le tout dans une ambiance étonnamment naturelle et routinière. Une fois le repas terminé, Drew remplit le lave-vaisselle pendant que je nettoie le plan de travail et la table.

– La photo de Beck en train de pêcher, elle a été prise où ? Il est adorable, avec ses petites cuissardes.

– Dans le nord-ouest de l'État de New York. Roman a une cabane dans les montagnes, à New Paltz. C'est rustique, mais il y a une vieille baignoire sur pattes qui te plairait. On devrait y aller au printemps.

– J'adorerais.

Quelques heures plus tard, nous sommes en train de nous brosser les dents avant de nous coucher quand Drew m'annonce :

– J'ai appelé Tess, aujourd'hui.

– Qui ça ?

– Ma secrétaire. Elle a dit que, d'après son médecin, elle pourrait reprendre à temps partiel d'ici deux semaines. Elle se remet mieux que prévu de son opération à la hanche et il faut qu'elle bouge, ça fait partie de sa rééducation.

– C'est super.

Dans le tourbillon qu'a été le mois écoulé, je n'ai pas vraiment cherché de nouvel espace de bureau. La première semaine, j'ai bien appelé un agent immobilier, qui m'a fait visiter des placards pour deux fois mon budget, dans des quartiers où je n'ai pas envie d'aller. Après ça, j'ai fait une pause. Mais là, l'idée démoralisante de ce que je peux payer comme local est moitié moins déprimante que celle de ne plus voir Drew au quotidien.

– Désolée. Il faut que je reprenne mes recherches d'un nouvel espace.

Drew fronce les sourcils.

– De quoi tu parles ?

Je me rince la bouche et réponds à son reflet dans le miroir.

– C'était notre accord : tu me laissais rester le temps que ta secrétaire revienne, en échange de mon aide pour répondre au téléphone en attendant que je me trouve un nouveau bureau.

Les mains posées sur mes épaules, il me fait pivoter face à lui.

– Tu ne t'en vas nulle part.

– Je n'ai pas les moyens de payer la moitié de ce que doit coûter le loyer de ton bureau.

– On va trouver une solution.

– Mais…

Il me cloue le bec d'un baiser, puis reste tout près de mon visage.

– On va se débrouiller. D'abord, on règle ce merdier à Atlanta, et ensuite on prendra le temps de discuter de tout ça, si tu veux bien. D'accord ?

Pour ne pas ajouter du stress à celui qu'il doit déjà ressentir, je hoche la tête.

– OK.

Mais une fois qu'on est couchés et que je me repasse la journée dans ma tête, je relie un peu les points des dernières heures écoulées.

« Roman a une cabane dans les montagnes, à New Paltz. On devrait y aller au printemps. »

« On va se débrouiller. D'abord, on règle ce merdier à Atlanta... »

« Comment tu as su que papa était l'homme de ta vie ?

J'ai arrêté de dire "je" quand j'envisageais l'avenir. »

Comme moi, Drew a opté pour le « on », qu'il en soit conscient ou pas.

Quand il se glisse dans le lit à mes côtés, je l'enlace étroitement. Peut-être, je dis bien peut-être, que ni lui ni moi n'avions trouvé la bonne personne avant… parce qu'on ne s'était pas encore rencontrés.

CHAPITRE 40

DREW

Ça a été les trois semaines les plus longues de ma vie.

L'huissier appelle la cour pour que la session commence. Le juge Walliford prend tout son temps, l'enfoiré (il dirait qu'il avance « au rythme du Sud », j'en suis certain), pour arriver jusqu'à son banc. Puis il s'assied et feuillette une liasse de dossiers. Roman est assis au premier rang du public, juste derrière moi. Il se penche et exerce une pression sur mon épaule pour m'exprimer son soutien tandis que j'attends d'apprendre la coupe que va subir mon droit de visite. Je le sens venir, j'ignore juste à quel point ça va être mauvais.

La dernière fois que j'ai été aussi nerveux, aussi à cran au sujet de la manière dont allait tourner ma vie, c'était le jour de mon mariage avec Alexa. Or on sait comment ça a fini, cette merde. Je tourne la tête vers mon ex-femme, habillée de manière très sobre, une fois n'est pas coutume. Elle, bien sûr, ne me rend pas mon regard, préférant garder les yeux braqués droit devant elle. Cette bonne femme, c'est quelque chose.

Enfin, Walliford cesse de farfouiller dans sa paperasse et s'éclaircit la gorge avant de se lancer dans une série de formalités rappelées pour mémoire.

– Numéro de dossiéééé 179920-16, Jagger contre Jagger. Demande en réduction de garde. Requête incidente en vue de réclamer une relocalisation et l'application de l'accord de garde précédemment signé.

Il lève les yeux pour la première fois.

– Avaaaant de commencer à annoncer mes décisions, je souhaite prendre un moment pour signaler qu'il ne s'agit pas d'une affaire facile. J'ai dû prendre en compte les droits des deux parties ici présentes, les droits d'un père biologique qui s'est vu privé de plusieurs années de liens avec son fils, ainsi que l'intérêt de l'enfant.

Il dirige son regard vers Alexa.

– Madame Jagger, je vous tiens pour largement responsable du bazar dans lequel nous nous trouvons aujourd'hui. Si vous aviez ne serait-ce qu'un doute infime concernant la paternité de cet enfant, il était de votre devoir de faire émerger la vérité à la naissance de ce petit innocent.

Pour la première fois, une lueur d'espoir m'apparaît. Walliford n'avait jamais montré vers qui penchait son cœur, jusqu'à présent, et j'avais cru qu'il était tombé sous le charme sudiste d'Alexa, dont elle n'a pas hésité à faire usage en couches bien épaisses depuis le début. Ce qui sort de sa bouche ensuite me sidère encore plus.

– Monsieur Jagger, je voudrais vous féliciter pour votre dévouement au jeune Beckett. Il est clair que vous aimez cet enfant et que vous vous souciez de lui aussi bien que si les résultats du test de paternité avaient été différents, il y a plusieurs années.

Intérieurement, je saute en l'air poing levé. Pourtant, je parviens à feindre l'humilité.

– Merci, Votre Honneur. Venant de vous, cela signifie beaucoup.

– Bien. Cela étant dit, passons à l'affaire qui nous occupe aujourd'hui. Concernant la demande de modification des modalités de garde déposée par madame Jagger, je ne vois rien qui justifie cette modification. L'ordre définissant le droit de visite d'Andrew M. Jagger est donc confirmé sans changement. (Il tourne les yeux vers Alexa.) Madame Jagger, le fait que votre requête d'augmenter votre droit de garde ait été déposée afin de permettre à monsieur Bodine d'entrer en contact avec votre fils est un pas dans la bonne direction. Cependant, il n'apparaît pas que monsieur Bodine se soit montré ne serait-ce qu'une fois au tribunal au cours de cette procédure. Pour être très honnête, son manque d'intérêt et de participation m'amène à m'interroger sur ses priorités et sur son intérêt pour son fils. Quoi qu'il en soit, il est le père de l'enfant et je vais accorder un droit de visite à monsieur Bodine. En revanche, ce temps devra entrer dans celui qui vous est imparti à vous avec votre fils et n'empiétera pas sur le temps de monsieur Jagger. En conséquence, cette cour accorde huit heures de garde par semaine à Levi Bodine. Une fois qu'une relation sera établie et que monsieur Bodine aura montré à cette cour son désir de s'impliquer dans la vie de son fils, j'envisagerai une augmentation de ses visites. Qui toutefois seront toujours prises sur votre temps, madame Jagger.

Je me tiens devant la cour, complètement hébété. Dans ma tête, je franchis le ruban jaune de la ligne d'arrivée, les bras levés. Je viens de terminer un marathon de presque quatre semaines. Et je n'en reviens pas d'avoir gagné.

Derrière moi, Roman lâche un « oui ! » triomphal et moi, je reste planté là, sidéré, avec l'impression que tout cela n'est qu'un rêve et que je vais me réveiller d'une seconde à l'autre pour être rattrapé par le cauchemar de la réalité.

Le juge Walliford en termine.

– Dernier point, concernant la contre-requête de monsieur Jagger visant à obliger le retour d'Alexa et Beckett Jagger dans leur demeure de New York, cette demande est refusée.

Minute. *Quoi ?*

– Votre Honneur, si je conserve mon droit de garde, comment pouvez-vous refuser ma demande que mon fils rentre à la maison ?

– N'est-ce pas évident, monsieur Jagger ? Votre fils va vivre ici, dans le grand État de Géorgie. Vous devriez envisager un déménagement.

Sur quoi il abat son marteau et se lève pour quitter la salle.

– Mais c'est des conneries ! J'ai un cabinet à New York. Alexa n'a même pas de travail ici.

Walliford s'immobilise.

– Cela vous fera mille dollars pour avoir usé de ce langage et de ce ton dans mon tribunal. Si ma décision ne vous convient pas, portez-la devant la cour d'appel.

***

Je m'appuie d'une main au mur des W.-C., le temps de pisser, puis je regagne mon tabouret de bar d'un pas mal assuré. Je n'ai aucune idée de l'endroit où sont passées ma cravate et ma veste, braguette toujours ouverte, chemise à moitié rentrée dans le pantalon et à moitié pendouillante. Bref, j'ai l'air aussi en vrac que je le suis.

– Je vais prendre un autre whisky *on the rocks*, j'annonce au barman, en poussant mon verre dans sa direction.

Il regarde Roman, puis moi à nouveau.

– Quoi ? Y vous faut la permission de mon père ? Filez-moi à boire, merde.

Est-ce que j'avais déjà mentionné que je suis encore plus con qu'à l'habitude quand je suis bourré ?

Mon portable vibre sur le comptoir. Emerie. C'est la troisième fois qu'elle appelle. Et la troisième fois que je ne décroche pas.

– Tu réponds toujours pas ? me demande Roman.

– Çasssèràquoi ? je bredouille.

– Ben par exemple à permettre à la dame de bien dormir cette nuit ? Parce que toi, tu vas pioncer à poings fermés, une fois que tu vas tomber vers dix-sept heures, espèce de sale égoïste. (Roman boit une gorgée de sa bière et la repose sur le bar.) Elle t'aime. Tu vas trouver la solution.

– Quelle solution ? C'est fini.

– Qu'est-ce que tu racontes ? Fais pas le con. C'est la première nana dont je te vois tomber vraiment amoureux. Depuis combien de temps on est amis ?

– Trop longtemps, apparemment, si tu te mets à me faire la leçon.

– Qu'est-ce que je t'ai dit derrière l'église, juste avant que tu épouses Alexa ?

Vu l'état dans lequel je suis, ma vie n'est guère qu'un vaste brouillard, pourtant ce fameux matin reste toujours très clair. J'y ai repensé plus d'une fois depuis, à la proposition de Roman qui parlait de me passer ses clés pour que je m'en aille. « Ma voiture est garée derrière, si tu veux t'enfuir. » Quand je lui avais rappelé qu'Alexa portait mon bébé et que j'agissais en adulte responsable, il avait répliqué : « On s'en fout, du devoir. »

Le barman m'apporte mon verre, et vu que je suis encore en mesure de me rappeler une partie de ma vie dont je n'ai nulle envie de me souvenir, je me dépêche de m'envoyer la moitié de son contenu.

Ensuite je me tourne vers Roman... enfin, vers deux Roman.

– Tu n'as jamais dit : « Je t'avais prévenu », par contre.

Il secoue la tête.

– Non. Et je le dirai pas non plus si tu rechignes à suivre mon conseil et que tu merdes avec Emerie, d'ailleurs. Je suis pas trop du genre à mettre le nez des gens dans leurs mauvaises décisions.

– Parfois, les décisions, c'est les circonstances qui les prennent pour toi.

Roman ricane.

– Ça, c'est des conneries et tu le sais. (Il marque une pause.) Tu te souviens de Nancy Irvine ?

Il me faut une minute pour fouiller dans les méandres abyssaux de mon cerveau mariné à l'alcool.

– Mademoiselle Varicelle ?

Il incline sa bière dans ma direction.

– Elle-même.

– Et alors ?

– Tu te rappelles le pacte qu'on avait passé de ne jamais draguer la même fille ?

– Ouais.

– Ben quand tu auras emménagé à Atlanta, en laissant Emerie le cœur brisé parce que tu es trop bête pour essayer de trouver un moyen de faire en sorte que ça fonctionne, je serai là pour la consoler… entre autres choses. Ouais, la vengeance est un plat qui se mange froid.

– Va te faire foutre.

– Qu'est-ce que ça peut te faire, de toute façon ? C'est juste une fille que tu as levée pour t'occuper en attendant mieux, non ? Elle ne vaut pas la peine que tu te soucies d'elle.

Comme par hasard, mon téléphone s'allume sur le prénom d'Emerie, m'indiquant l'arrivée d'un SMS. Je m'en saisis, ainsi que de mon verre, et me mets debout.

Vacillant, je me penche vers mon ami.

– Va te faire foutre.

Sur quoi je fonce vers l'ascenseur de l'hôtel.

CHAPITRE 41

DREW

Si je pouvais me fendre le crâne en deux pour en expulser quelques-uns des petits batteurs emprisonnés à l'intérieur, j'aurais peut-être une chance de me lever de mon canapé.

C'est un miracle que j'aie réussi à attraper l'avion, d'ailleurs. Jamais ça n'aurait été possible sans Roman, qui m'a traîné de ma chambre d'hôtel à six heures ce matin, encore plongé dans les vapeurs d'alcool. Putain de gueule de bois.

Maintenant, il est midi, ça fait plus d'une heure que je suis rentré à la maison. Et je viens enfin de m'acheter une paire de couilles pour répondre à Emerie.

Enfin, pour lui répondre par SMS.

Ouais, ça, c'est un mec qui a des couilles.

En plus, je lui mens. Ce n'est pas la première fois et ça ne sera certainement pas la dernière.

Drew : Désolé pour hier soir.
J'étais malade comme un chien.
Intoxication alimentaire.
Sushis avariés, je pense.

Les points de suspension se mettent aussitôt à danser.

Emerie : Contente que tu ailles bien.
J'étais inquiète. Qu'est-ce
qui s'est passé au tribunal ?

Admettre la vérité signifierait l'affronter, or je n'y suis pas encore prêt.

Drew : Le juge a ajourné sa décision
à la semaine prochaine.

Emerie : Zut. Enfin, c'est peut-être bon
signe. Au moins il réfléchit vraiment.

Je ne peux pas jouer les chochottes quand elle déploie de tels efforts pour rester positive.

Drew : Peut-être.

Emerie : Tu reviens quand ?

C'est là que je commence à me faire l'effet d'un vrai connard. Car c'est une chose de m'abstenir de lui révéler la décision du juge. Dans ma tête, j'ai la justification toute prête, j'évite de la perturber, mais être là, quelques étages au-dessus d'elle qui se trouve probablement au rez-de-chaussée en train de répondre à mes appels… Non, ça c'est de la pure couardise.

Un constat qui ne m'empêche pas de poursuivre sur ma voie de gros con.

Drew : Vais probablement prendre
le dernier vol ce soir. J'arriverai tard.

Emerie : Trop hâte de te voir.

Drew : Oui. Moi aussi.

Enfin une réponse qui n'est pas un mensonge.

***

Il y a un miroir dans le hall qui reflète le couloir menant aux bureaux privés. Je m'arrête en apercevant Emerie. Tellement, tellement belle. Tellement douce et honnête et pleine de toutes ces choses positives. Mes paumes deviennent moites tandis que je suis planté là à la contempler. Sa porte est fermée et elle inscrit quelque chose sur son ardoise, sans doute une maxime optimiste sur la manière de faire en sorte que les choses fonctionnent. Voilà qui va me donner la sensation d'être un plus gros sac à merde encore quand je le lirai.

J'ai passé les dernières vingt-quatre heures à réfléchir à la manière de procéder, à celle qui la blessera le moins. Il n'y a pas de raison de lui raconter ce qui s'est passé au tribunal. Elle croit que les relations peuvent survivre à tout, si les membres du couple y travaillent main dans la main. Pour moi, il n'y a aucun doute : elle va vouloir qu'on continue ensemble même si on est séparés par presque mille cinq cents kilomètres. Au début, ça pourrait fonctionner, d'ailleurs. Mais au bout du compte, ça finirait par s'effondrer. Comme toujours. Si ça se trouve, on ne se rendrait pas compte à quel point ça s'est dégradé avant que ça ne nous explose en pleine face. Emerie vient de s'installer dans sa nouvelle vie à New York, la laisser la vivre n'est que justice.

Du coup, tout ce qui me vient à l'esprit, c'est d'en finir vite. De ne pas faire traîner en longueur en tentant la relation à distance, parce que ça ne ferait que gaspiller son temps un peu plus. Elle a déjà gâché trois années de sa vie à s'accrocher à ce trouduc de Baldwin, je ne vais pas la faire mariner comme ça. Rupture rapide et complète. Comme quand on arrache un pansement. Ça brûle à mort sur le coup, mais une fois qu'on laisse passer l'air, qu'on cesse de couvrir la blessure, elle commence à guérir.

Elle rebouche son marqueur et recule d'un pas pour relire ce qu'elle vient d'écrire. Lentement, un sourire étire ses lèvres et le mal de tête dont je venais enfin de me débarrasser resurgit d'un coup, avec une vigueur démultipliée.

Je prends une profonde inspiration et me dirige vers mon bureau.

Emerie sort du sien pile au moment où je suis sur le point de passer.

– Salut, la marmotte, dit-elle en nouant les bras autour de mon cou. Dommage que tu n'aies pas traîné un peu plus longtemps, je m'apprêtais à monter te réveiller.

Elle m'embrasse sur les lèvres, avant de préciser :

– Nue.

– Emerie… (Je me racle la gorge, parce que ma voix est pitoyablement rauque.) Il faut qu'on…

Je n'ai pas le temps d'aller au bout de ma phrase, car avant de pouvoir prononcer le mot « parle », je suis interrompu par la sonnerie simultanée de nos deux téléphones et par le livreur d'UPS qui crie dans le hall. Je pourrais l'ignorer, mais non, je saute sur l'occasion de reporter l'inévitable, tel le connard sans couilles que je suis.

Ensuite, après le départ du livreur, le syndic de l'immeuble vient me parler de travaux qu'ils vont entreprendre, durant lesquels ils vont devoir couper l'eau à peu près deux heures demain. Quand je parviens enfin à m'extirper de cette conversation, mon client est arrivé, avec vingt minutes d'avance sur son rendez-vous. Comme je ne me vois pas le faire attendre dans le couloir pendant que je largue ma petite amie, ma conversation avec Emerie va devoir être reportée d'au moins une heure.

Sauf qu'un rendez-vous s'enchaîne sur un autre, une heure se transforme en deux, et soudain, il est presque dix-neuf heures. Pourtant, durant toute la journée, Emerie n'a rien fait d'autre que de se montrer souriante et heureuse de m'avoir retrouvé. Elle m'a même commandé mon déjeuner, puis elle est restée dans le hall à baratiner l'un de mes clients plus de dix minutes, le temps que je l'engloutisse. Voilà, tous mes prétextes se sont envolés et le bureau est enfin calme.

Je regarde par la fenêtre tout en buvant le café qui est apparu sur mon bureau comme par magie, il y a une demi-heure, quand Emerie est entrée. Je le sais au « clic-clic » de ses talons, pas parce que je me suis retourné.

Elle arrive derrière moi et m'enlace par la taille.

– Quelle journée de fou.

– Ouais. Merci pour tout. Le déjeuner, le café, d'avoir répondu au téléphone et à la porte toute la journée. Merci infiniment, quoi.

Elle pose la tête contre mon dos.

– C'est normal. On forme une bonne équipe, tu ne trouves pas ?

Je ferme les yeux. Merde. *Arrache le pansement, Drew, espèce de trouillard. Arrache-le, putain.* Je déglutis et pivote face à elle.

– Emerie, je ne suis pas taillé pour faire partie d'une équipe.

Elle rit, sans doute qu'elle n'a pas compris l'implication de mon aveu. Puis elle lève les yeux et voit ma mine sombre. Alors son sourire s'efface.

– De quoi tu parles ? Tu es un super coéquipier. Je prends les rênes quand tu as besoin de moi et tu fais pareil pour moi.

Arrache ce putain de pansement. Vite.

– Non, Emerie. Ça, c'est ce qu'un employé fait pour son employeur. Nous ne formons pas une équipe.

Elle a l'air de quelqu'un qui vient de se prendre un coup de poing. Sa lèvre inférieure si sensuelle tremble une fraction de seconde, avant qu'elle ne se ressaisisse. Et son attitude tout entière change. Les bras qu'elle avait nonchalamment le long du corps se replient dans une posture protectrice et elle redresse le dos. Le pire dans l'histoire, c'est qu'un bref instant, je suis excité de la voir passer ainsi en mode bagarre. Après tout, c'est en nous disputant que nous avons commencé tout ce bazar. Sauf que ni le moment ni le lieu ne sont bien choisis pour penser avec ma queue.

– Toute relation passe par des phases où un des deux a besoin de s'appuyer plus sur l'autre. Un jour viendra où j'aurai besoin de m'appuyer sur toi.

C'est la conseillère matrimoniale qui a pris la parole, et je me rends compte que je vais devoir me montrer plus abrupt. Alors au lieu d'arracher le pansement, je tranche carrément dans le vif.

– Je ne veux pas que tu t'appuies sur moi, Emerie. Je veux mettre un terme à ce qu'il y avait entre nous.

Elle recule d'un pas, alors j'enfonce le clou par une conclusion sans appel.

– Mon fils est ma priorité et il n'y a pas de place pour autre chose dans ma vie.

Sa voix, quand elle me répond, n'est qu'un souffle.

– Je comprends.

– Je suis désolé.

Par la force de l'habitude, je tends la main vers son épaule, histoire de la réconforter, mais elle s'écarte comme si j'avais la paume en feu.

– J'ai posé tes messages sur le bureau, reprend-elle, les yeux baissés. Et ton premier rendez-vous a été avancé à sept heures trente.

Il y a tant de choses que j'aurais dû dire, et pourtant je me contente de hocher la tête. Un geste qu'elle ne voit même pas.

Quand Emerie franchit la porte de mon bureau, je n'ai qu'une envie : effacer les cinq dernières minutes, remonter le temps et lui dire que je ne veux pas seulement être son coéquipier, que je veux être toute sa putain d'équipe. Au lieu de quoi, je reste planté à la regarder partir. Parce que ce serait encore plus difficile dans un mois ou un an. Parce que LES RELATIONS À DISTANCE NE FONCTIONNENT PAS. Il y aurait forcément un perdant parmi nous deux, si on continuait jusqu'à ce que l'un ait trompé l'autre.

Emerie disparaît dans son bureau et en ressort quelques minutes plus tard, vêtue de son manteau et chargée de son ordinateur portable, son sac à main sur l'épaule. Délicatement, elle referme la porte, si délicatement que j'ai failli ne pas l'entendre partir. C'est peut-être justement le but. Sauf que je l'entends et, quand je lève les yeux pour l'apercevoir une dernière fois, je constate qu'elle pleure. Je dois m'agripper à la chaise devant moi pour m'empêcher de lui courir après.

Et puis elle est partie.

Alors que je reste immobile pendant l'heure qui suit, avec tout un tas de bazar qui me tournicote dans la tête, la seule pensée qui émerge, c'est : qui est-ce que j'essaie de protéger, là ?

Elle ou… moi ?

CHAPITRE 42

DREW

Je ne pensais pas possible d'être encore plus mal que je ne l'ai été la semaine passée. Avec Alexa, on s'est disputés plus d'une heure quand je suis passé récupérer Beck, et puis elle a repris pile au même endroit quand je l'ai ramené deux jours plus tard. Mon fils ne s'est pas senti bien du week-end et n'a cessé de demander pourquoi on ne pouvait plus aller à la maison. Je n'ai pas su quoi lui répondre, et plus je laisse traîner, plus c'est compliqué.

Pour empirer encore la situation, mon vol de retour à New York a eu six heures de retard et ma dernière nuit de sommeil correcte remonte à celle qui a précédé la décision du juge. Même l'hôtesse de l'air m'a demandé si je me sentais bien. La vérité, c'est que non, je ne vais pas bien. Je suis malheureux et je n'arrive pas à envisager mon déménagement à Atlanta. Mais bon, ce n'est pas la véritable raison de la haine que je voue à la vie depuis peu.

Quand enfin mon avion atterrit à JFK, il est minuit. Je suis tellement épuisé que, au moins, je risque de tomber raide, cette nuit, de pouvoir enfin fermer les yeux. J'en ai tellement besoin. Hélas je commets l'erreur fatale de m'arrêter au bureau, juste pour jeter un coup d'œil.

Tout est calme. Je ne m'attendais pas à trouver Emerie encore là si tard, et puis de toute façon, elle m'évitait à tout prix avant que je parte pour Atlanta, se contentant de venir au bureau pour ses rendez-vous face à face et repartant aussitôt après. Je présume qu'elle effectue le reste de son travail de chez elle. En plus, ayant accès à mon planning, elle devait savoir que j'étais censé rentrer dans la soirée, du coup, je suppose qu'elle est restée loin d'ici.

Je lâche mes bagages à la réception et traverse l'espace tellement silencieux qu'il en est sinistre. La porte d'Emerie est fermée et je déploie des efforts surhumains pour passer devant sans m'arrêter, mais en vain. Bien qu'à peu près sûr qu'il n'y ait personne, je frappe d'abord, avant d'entrouvrir lentement la porte. La lumière du couloir éclaire assez la pièce pour que je voie à l'intérieur, en dépit de l'obscurité. Enfin, la pénombre doit me jouer des tours. Alors j'actionne l'interrupteur. Et mon cœur bondit tandis que je me fige.

Vide.

Le bureau est complètement vide !

Je cligne des paupières à plusieurs reprises dans l'espoir que mes yeux s'ajustent, mais non. Elle est partie. Et pour de bon, cette fois.

***

– J'ai besoin que tu prennes quelqu'un en filature.

– Bien le bonjour à toi aussi, cher ami.

Roman se laisse tomber sur le siège de l'autre côté de mon bureau.

Quand je lui ai envoyé un SMS à six heures du matin, il était déjà en chemin pour chez moi. N'ayant pas dormi de la nuit, j'ai décidé d'utiliser mon insomnie de manière productive et lui ai donc donné rendez-vous directement ici.

– Il se trouve qu'il n'a rien de « bon », ce jour.

Je jette le dossier que j'avais à la main et me frotte les yeux.

– Tu as une sale gueule, mec.

Roman se cale contre son dossier et pose ses pieds bottés sur mon bureau, les croisant au niveau des chevilles. En temps normal, je les lui aurais fait retirer sans ménagement, mais ce matin je n'en ai rien à fiche.

– Tous ces allers et retours, ça me crève.

– Ben ouais, c'est ça, la raison.

– C'est censé vouloir dire quoi, ça ?

– Rien. Qu'est-ce que tu attends de moi ?

– Je veux que tu suives Emerie.

– Quoi ? Mais pourquoi, putain ? Elle n'est pas de l'autre côté du couloir la moitié de la journée ?

– Elle a déménagé.

– C'est arrivé quand ?

– Au cours des derniers jours, je suppose, je ne sais pas exactement quand. Je suis rentré à minuit et son bureau avait été vidé.

– Ce qui explique sans doute pourquoi tu as la tronche d'un mec qui n'a pas dormi depuis deux jours.

– J'ai juste besoin de savoir si elle a trouvé un endroit sympa à louer. Je me suis dégoté une jolie petite maison en location de longue durée à Atlanta. Dave Monroe va me rejoindre à temps partiel ici, il s'occupera des clients qui acceptent d'être pris en charge par quelqu'un d'autre. Entre ça et le télétravail, j'envisage de pouvoir rentrer quelques jours deux fois par mois, au lieu de faire des allers et retours toutes les semaines. Il n'y a donc aucune raison pour qu'elle ne reste pas ici. Elle pourrait aisément m'éviter quand même.

– Donc tu vas vraiment le faire ? Abandonner ton cabinet et t'installer à Atlanta ?

– Qu'est-ce que j'ai d'autre, comme choix ? Je vais faire appel, mais il n'y a aucune garantie que ça change quoi que ce soit. Beck sent bien que je suis en pleine incertitude. Je ne peux pas vivre dans une chambre d'hôtel, il ne prendra jamais ses marques s'il ne peut pas avoir sa propre chambre et ses affaires. Il a besoin de se sentir chez lui, que je sois là si besoin : pour les événements scolaires, les rendez-vous chez le docteur… Il vient d'intégrer une équipe de hockey pour bouts de chou, qu'est-ce que je fais, si tous ses matchs tombent les jours où je suis à New York ? En plus, je ne peux pas faire cinquante-deux allers et retours par an, à caser quarante heures de travail sur deux journées. Ça va être trop dur, au bout d'un moment.

– Le bail de la maison que tu as trouvée, il court sur combien de temps ?

– Un an. (Je baisse les épaules, dépité.) Je pense que ça va prendre neuf mois avant que j'obtienne ne serait-ce qu'un rendez-vous pour commencer à exposer oralement mon appel en garde.

– Tu as déjà signé ?

– Pas encore. Je vois le proprio quand j'y retourne, à la fin de la semaine.

– Bien. Accorde-moi quelques jours supplémentaires.

– Pour quoi faire ?

– J'ai un gars à Atlanta qui bosse sur un truc pour moi.

– Tu veux m'en dire plus ou il ne vaut mieux pas ?

Roman sourit.

– Oh que non. Comme ça, tu ne peux pas être impliqué.

Je parviens à rire pour la première fois depuis… je ne sais plus trop. C'est tout Roman, ça : l'homme qui a toujours un plan pour couvrir mes arrières.

– Bon, quoi que ce soit, merci.

– Alors, tu veux que je fasse quoi, au sujet d'Emerie ? Que je la file, point barre ? Tu ne me donnerais pas un petit indice sur ce que je dois chercher ?

– Je veux juste m'assurer qu'elle va bien. Vois si elle a trouvé un espace de bureau et s'il est situé dans un quartier sûr.

Roman hausse un sourcil.

– Donc tu ne veux pas que je cherche à savoir si elle baise avec quelqu'un ?

Je serre la mâchoire si fort que je manque de me casser une dent.

– Non. Mais en supposant que tu l'apprennes quand même, tu ne me dis rien. Surtout si c'est avec ce trouduc de Baldwin, parce qu'il va s'amuser avec elle et puis la larguer ensuite.

– Comme toi ?

– Comment ça, putain ? Je ne me suis pas amusé avec elle, c'est moi qui me suis fait avoir. J'agis au mieux pour elle.

Roman se met debout.

– Je ne vais pas me disputer avec toi, mon pote. Je la surveille, si c'est ce que tu veux. Mais tu devrais peut-être te demander si ce qu'il y a de mieux pour Emerie, ça ne serait pas plutôt de la laisser prendre ses propres décisions sur la manière de gérer votre relation.

CHAPITRE 43

EMERIE

– Tu as été formidable.

Je lève les yeux de mes affaires de cours que je suis en train de ranger. Baldwin est posté dans l'encadrement de la porte.

– J'ai entendu les cinq dernières minutes, ajoute-t-il.

– Tu es trop gentil. J'étais dans un de ces états de nerfs…

Il sourit.

– Tu vas t'habituer. Mais sincèrement, ça ne se voyait pas.

Il y a deux jours, Baldwin m'a appelée pour m'annoncer que l'un des vacataires du département de psycho devait partir sans préavis, et il m'a demandé si ça m'intéressait de le remplacer. Ce qui m'assurerait avec une quasi-certitude le poste d'assistante pour lequel je passe un entretien demain. Alors j'ai accepté, même si je n'ai aucune envie de faire quoi que ce soit, ces jours-ci. Sortir de mon lit me demande déjà un effort surhumain.

Une fois mes affaires rangées, je me dirige vers la porte.

– Tu as cours ?

– Non, je viens de finir de corriger des copies et je voulais passer voir comment ça allait pour toi. Ça te dit qu'on déjeune ? Il y a un super petit bistrot à quelques pâtés d'immeubles qui sert les meilleures salades au thon ahi de la ville.

Le mois dernier, j'ai évité Baldwin par égard pour Drew, mais je n'ai plus aucune raison de le faire désormais. Bien que n'étant pas vraiment d'humeur à avoir de la compagnie, je sais que m'enfermer chez moi à m'apitoyer sur mon sort n'est pas vraiment sain.

– D'accord, avec plaisir.

Nous nous installons dehors sous les chaufferettes, car l'après-midi est radieux. À un moment donné, en allant aux toilettes, je repère un homme dans une voiture garée à quelques mètres de là. Je tournais le dos à la rue, pendant le repas, j'ignore donc depuis combien de temps elle est là, mais j'aurais juré que l'homme à l'intérieur est Roman. Une fois notre déjeuner terminé, je cherche la voiture des yeux, sauf qu'elle a disparu.

Plus tard dans la journée, après avoir vaqué à mes diverses occupations, je rentre à la maison pour une séance en ligne. Je n'arrive même pas à ouvrir la porte en entier tant mon mobilier de bureau encombre l'appartement. Ce n'était sans doute pas l'idée du siècle, de déménager avant d'avoir trouvé un autre endroit, mais je ne pouvais pas rester là-bas un jour de plus. Même quand Drew était absent, je n'arrivais pas à penser à autre chose qu'à lui. J'ai cru qu'en m'évitant de voir le bureau sur lequel on a fait l'amour, la salle de photocopies où on s'est rencontrés, ça m'aiderait à penser moins à lui. Hélas, mes pensées voyagent avec moi au lieu de rester là-bas.

Pendant que j'installe mon ordinateur portable de telle sorte que mes patients ne voient pas le bazar de la pièce remplie de meubles jusqu'à la gueule, on frappe à ma porte. Ça m'énerve que chaque fois mon cœur s'emballe à l'idée que ça puisse être Drew. Alors imaginez ma surprise en découvrant Roman par l'œilleton.

J'ouvre la porte.

– Roman ?

Il appuie les mains en haut de l'encadrement.

– J'ai pour instruction de te suivre.

– Il m'a bien semblé t'apercevoir au restaurant, aujourd'hui.

– Je peux entrer ? Je n'en ai pas pour longtemps.

– Euh… D'accord. Oui, entre. Mais je t'avertis, c'est le grand bazar, ici. J'ai installé mon bureau dans mon minuscule appartement et je n'ai la place de rien mettre, du coup il occupe à peu près tout mon salon.

J'ouvre la porte aussi grand que possible pour laisser passer Roman.

– Je peux t'offrir quelque chose à boire ?

Il lève une main.

– Merci, ça va.

Il y a des piles de dossiers partout sur le canapé. J'entreprends de les ramasser pour lui faire de la place.

– Tu veux t'asseoir ? Mets-toi à l'aise, comme ça tu pourras me raconter pourquoi tu me suis.

Il rigole.

– D'accord.

Je m'installe pour ma part sur mon fauteuil de bureau, face à lui, et attends qu'il commence.

– Drew m'a demandé de te filer. Il prétend vouloir s'assurer que ton nouveau bureau est situé dans un quartier sûr.

– Et si ça n'était pas le cas ? Qu'est-ce qu'il va faire de l'information ?

Roman hausse les épaules.

– On n'est pas toujours très logique quand on est un homme amoureux.

– Amoureux ? Tu as raté l'épisode où il m'a larguée ?

– Je ne pensais jamais dire ça de mon meilleur ami, je le connais depuis l'école élémentaire et il a toujours eu des nerfs en acier, mais il a peur.

– De quoi ?

– De tomber amoureux. Sa mère trompait son père et les a abandonnés quand il était môme.

Sa femme lui a menti sur le gamin dont elle était enceinte en lui laissant croire qu'il était de lui, tout en continuant de baiser avec le vrai père du petit pendant leur mariage. Il est tombé amoureux de ce petit bonhomme, et là, elle lui retire sa paternité. Sans compter que tous les jours, au boulot, les histoires de ses clients lui rappellent combien il est rare qu'une relation fonctionne, surtout dans les cas où les deux membres du couple ne passent pas beaucoup de temps ensemble. Il avait enfin trouvé du bon dans sa vie en te rencontrant. Je déteste le voir envoyer balader tout ça parce qu'il a trop peur de tenter sa chance. Est-ce qu'au moins il t'a dit que le juge autorisait Alexa à rester à Atlanta et qu'il allait y emménager ?

– Non.

Une douleur me vrille la poitrine. La manière dont il a mis un terme à notre relation s'explique un peu mieux, maintenant. Une partie de moi peut même comprendre pourquoi Drew est sceptique quant au fait que ça puisse fonctionner entre nous. Son passé lui a appris que si on tombe amoureux, la vie se charge de vous reprendre l'objet de votre amour. N'empêche, ça n'excuse pas ce qu'il a fait. Que sa décision soit justifiée ou non ne change rien au fait qu'il n'a même pas essayé de se battre pour nous. Qu'il ne m'a même pas expliqué ce qui se passait.

– Je suis navrée de ce qu'il traverse, Roman. Ça n'est pas juste, c'est vrai. Toutefois, même en admettant qu'en effet il tient toujours à moi, qu'est-ce que tu veux que j'y fasse ? Je ne peux pas effacer sa peur. Il n'a même pas voulu tenter l'aventure. Ça en dit long : à ses yeux, je ne valais pas de prendre le risque. Alors excuse-moi, mais j'ai la faiblesse de penser que je mérite mieux que ça.

Roman hoche la tête.

– Je comprends. C'est juste… Je t'ai vue avec ce prof, au déjeuner, ce midi.

– Baldwin et moi, on est amis. Oui, on a un passif… ou plutôt, j'ai un passif et j'ai éprouvé des sentiments pour lui. Mais ensuite je suis tombée amoureuse de Drew et ça m'a montré que les sentiments que je croyais nourrir pour Baldwin n'étaient pas vraiment de l'amour. Parce que jamais ça n'a été comme ça avec lui… Ce que je ressens pour Drew, c'est d'un tout autre ordre.

Roman sourit.

– Tu as dit « ressens », pas ressentais.

– Bien sûr. Je ne peux pas éteindre mes sentiments pour la simple raison que j'ai été blessée. Ça va me prendre du temps et des efforts de passer à autre chose.

– Tu veux bien m'accorder une faveur ? Ne déploie pas trop d'efforts tout de suite. J'ai encore l'espoir de réussir à lui remettre les idées en place.

CHAPITRE 44

DREW

Je ne suis pas du genre à transpirer.

J'ai vécu des affaires au tribunal où j'ai dû réagir dans le feu de l'action quand un témoin changeait sa version des faits et qu'un juge me dévisageait par-dessus ses lunettes ; je suis resté de marbre. Pourtant, bizarrement, aujourd'hui, j'ai dû m'éponger le front et mon mouchoir en papier est resté collé à mes paumes moites.

Pourquoi m'inflige-t-on ça aujourd'hui ? Je ne suis pas prêt. Beck n'est pas prêt. Mais ça n'a pas arrêté mon ex-femme. Elle a menacé de tout lui raconter quand je le ramènerais ce soir si ce n'était pas moi qui m'en chargeais. Et pour le coup, même si ce n'est pas une femme de parole, je suis certain qu'elle tiendrait cette promesse-là.

C'est la deuxième fois que je convoque la mémoire de mon père. « Arrache le pansement », c'était son image préférée. J'espère juste que le visage de mon fils ne ressemblera pas à celui d'Emerie quand j'ai rompu avec elle.

Je me tourne vers Beck, qui se marre devant un dessin animé, et regarde ma montre. *Merde.* Je n'ai plus le temps de repousser l'échéance.

– Beck ? Mon grand, il faut que je te parle de quelque chose avant que tu retournes chez maman ce soir. Tu veux bien éteindre la télé ?

Il se tourne vers moi, mon petit bonhomme si gentil, si facile à vivre.

– D'accord, papa.

Sur quoi il se lève, va chercher la télécommande sur le bureau et revient s'asseoir face à moi, m'accordant toute son attention. J'ai soudain la bouche sèche, ce qui ne facilite pas la prise de parole. J'aurai beau tourner autour du pot, je ne vois pas de manière facile d'annoncer ça à un enfant.

– Tout va bien ? Tu ressembles à moi quand j'ai mal au cœur. (Beck se relève.) Tu veux que j'aille chercher une bassine, comme tu fais quand je vais vomir ?

Je lâche un rire nerveux.

– Non, bonhomme. Je n'ai pas besoin de bassine. (*Du moins, je ne pense pas.*) Assieds-toi. C'est au sujet de moi et du fait que je suis ton papa.

Son expression s'assombrit.

– Tu ne vas plus être mon papa ? C'est pour ça que tu ne veux plus me prendre à ta maison ?

Je vais peut-être prendre la bassine, finalement.

– Oh, là, oh là. Non, pas du tout. Jamais je ne cesserai d'être ton papa. Mais… (*Et merde, c'est parti.*) Mais il y a des enfants qui ont de la chance et qui ont plus de deux parents.

Ses yeux s'allument.

– Tu vas te marier avec Emerie ?

Oh, bon Dieu. Ça fait mal, ça, et pas qu'un peu.

– Je ne pense pas que ça va arriver, Beck, non.

Son enthousiasme lui fait perdre les pédales.

– Parce que Mikayla, à l'école, elle a une belle-mère. Ses parents sont divorcés, comme maman et toi, et maintenant elle a deux mamans.

– Non. Enfin, oui. Non. Plus ou moins. Le truc, c'est que… en fait, je suis ton beau-papa.

– Donc j'ai deux papas ?

Il plisse le nez.

– C'est ça. Quand tu es né, ta maman et moi étions mariés. Je ne savais pas que tu n'étais pas mon…

Je sens les mots s'étrangler au fond de ma gorge et dois l'éclaircir à plusieurs reprises pour ne pas lui montrer à quel point je suis malheureux. Je tiens absolument à ce que Beck comprenne que ce que je suis en train de lui expliquer n'aura aucun effet sur notre relation, or me mettre à pleurer n'enverrait pas le message adéquat.

Alors je reprends :

– Je ne savais pas que tu n'étais pas… mon fils, biologiquement. Je ne l'ai su que des années après ta naissance.

– Si tu n'es pas mon papa biologique, alors, c'est qui ?

– Un homme qui s'appelle Levi. Maman dit que tu l'as déjà vu quelques fois.

De nouveau, ses prunelles brillent.

– Le pilote de voitures de course ?

Je me débats avec des émotions contradictoires. D'un côté, je suis dépité qu'il soit ravi d'être lié à ce connard, de l'autre, si ça rend la nouvelle plus facile à accepter pour lui, alors ça me va.

– Oui. Le pilote de voitures de course.

– Il a une voiture super cool ! Elle est décapotable et elle fait beaucoup de bruit.

Je m'oblige à sourire.

– Ta maman va commencer à te faire rencontrer Levi plus souvent. Mais ça ne changera rien entre toi et moi.

Il réfléchit à tout ce que je viens de lui dire un moment, avant de me demander :

– Tu m'aimes quand même ?

Beck a beau approcher les sept ans et commencer à trouver pas cool de me donner la main quand il arrive à l'école, là, ça ne tient plus. Je le hisse sur mes genoux et lui réponds, en le regardant droit dans les yeux :

– Je t'aime plus que tout au monde.

– Donc tu ne m'abandonnes pas parce que j'ai un nouveau papa ?

– Non, Beck. Je ne t'abandonnerai jamais. Les gens ne quittent pas quelqu'un quand ils l'aiment.

Ils restent ensemble pour toujours. C'est pour ça que j'emménage à Atlanta. Ta maman t'a emmené ici, et moi, je vais où tu vas.

– Mon papa biologique, il ne m'aimait pas, c'est pour ça qu'on habitait à New York avant ?

Waouh. Il en a, des questions compliquées.

– Je sais que c'est difficile à comprendre, mais Levi ne savait pas que tu étais son fils quand tu es né. Donc il n'a pas eu la possibilité de te connaître. Maintenant que c'est le cas, il va t'aimer aussi, j'en suis sûr.

Je me rends compte que le moment est venu pour moi d'avoir une longue conversation avec Levi, histoire de m'assurer que mon fils va devenir sa priorité, à lui aussi. S'il doit faire partie de sa vie, il a intérêt à ne pas le décevoir.

– Il va vivre ici aussi ?

– Je ne sais pas trop, mon bonhomme.

– Mais tu as dit que les gens ne partent pas quand ils aiment quelqu'un. Donc, s'il part, c'est qu'il ne m'aime pas ?

Punaise, je suis en train de merder en beauté.

– Parfois on n'a pas d'autre choix que de partir physiquement, même si on aime quelqu'un. Pour le travail, par exemple. Mais on trouve d'autres moyens pour continuer à être ensemble chaque jour. Quand j'ai dit que les gens n'abandonnent pas les gens qu'ils aiment, je ne voulais pas dire qu'ils devaient être présents à leurs côtés tous les jours. Il faut juste se montrer un peu plus inventif et trouver des moyens de passer du temps ensemble quand on ne peut pas être là en personne. Comme toi et moi le mois dernier, quand j'ai dû retourner à New York pour le travail.

– Comme se parler sur FaceTime avec l'iPhone de maman ?

– Exactement.

– Ou par Snapchat ?

– Je ne le connais pas, celui-là, mais si tu le dis…

Beck hoche la tête et reste silencieux un moment.

Ça fait beaucoup à assimiler, surtout pour un gamin de son âge. À ce jour, j'ai moi-même du mal à le digérer, alors…

– Tu as des questions, bonhomme ?

– Je peux continuer à t'appeler « papa » ?

Mon cœur se serre.

– Oui, carrément, même. Je serai toujours ton papa.

– Et Levi, je vais l'appeler comment ?

L'idée de mon fils appelant un autre homme « papa » m'est physiquement douloureuse. Mais ma souffrance à moi ne compte pas.

– Je suis sûr que toi, maman et Levi, vous allez réfléchir à ça.

Quelques minutes plus tard, Beck me demande s'il peut rallumer ses dessins animés. Il n'a pas l'air plus mal que ça. Moi, en revanche, j'ai l'impression que je viens de subir dix rounds d'un combat contre un poids lourd, les mains liées derrière le dos. Je suis mentalement et physiquement éreinté.

Cette nuit-là, après avoir redéposé Beck chez Alexa, je suis allongé sur mon lit d'hôtel, à me rejouer notre conversation en boucle. Pour moi, c'est important de me tenir aux choses que j'ai dites à mon fils aujourd'hui. Les gamins apprennent plus de l'exemple de leurs parents que de leurs leçons de morale. Je dois d'autant plus lui montrer que je suis là sur la distance que je ne contrôle pas les actes d'Alexa et de Levi.

Alors que je tente de m'endormir, une chose continue de me titiller et refuse de me laisser en paix. Une chose que j'ai dite. Je crois vraiment que mes paroles étaient vraies, mais si je suis honnête, je ne peux pas prétendre vivre selon mes préceptes. Et ça n'a rien à voir avec mon fils.

Les gens ne quittent pas quelqu'un quand ils l'aiment. Ils restent ensemble pour toujours.

***

Le lendemain matin, cette sensation irritante a germé. La racine était déjà là depuis plusieurs semaines, mais depuis ma conversation avec Beck, elle a poussé telle une vigne et élu domicile au creux de mon ventre, dans ma tête. Elle s'est entortillée autour de mon cœur, si étroitement que j'en ai du mal à respirer.

Je dois me traîner hors du lit afin d'arriver à l'aéroport à temps pour mon vol. Sur la banquette du taxi, je vérifie mon horaire de départ et m'agite. Je me connais, je sais que je peux fonctionner en boucle sur certains trucs, que j'ai besoin de savoir. Alors je finis par céder et j'envoie un SMS à Roman à cinq heures du matin.

Drew : Elle voit quelqu'un ?

Comme toujours, il me répond dans les minutes qui suivent. C'est la seule personne que je connaisse à avoir encore moins besoin de sommeil que moi.

Roman : Je croyais
que je n'étais pas censé te dire ça.

Drew : Dis-moi et c'est tout.

Roman : T'es sûr que tu vas
supporter ?

Oh putain. Non, je n'en suis pas sûr du tout. S'il pose la question, c'est mauvais signe.

Drew : Dis-moi.

Roman : Le voisin la drague.
Envoi de fleurs : énorme bouquet
de roses jaunes. Il l'a aussi emmenée
déjeuner l'autre jour
dans un resto branché avec grosse
addition et pas grand-chose à bouffer.

Merde.

Drew : Autre chose ?

Roman : J'ai commencé à lui filer
un peu le train, au gars. A dîné

avec une femme hier soir. Grande,
super jambes. À la moitié du repas,
ils ont eu l'air de se disputer.
Elle a joué la grande scène
du deux, genre je me lève et je jette
ma serviette sur la table,
avant de sortir en trombe. Je crois
qu'il l'a peut-être larguée.

Cette sensation désagréable au creux de mon ventre n'était donc pas là par hasard. Je vais la perdre pour toujours, si je ne fais rien. On arrive à l'aéroport, j'envoie un dernier message à mon pote avant de sortir du taxi.

Drew : Merci, Roman.

À quoi il répond aussitôt :

Roman : Va la récupérer.
Bouge-toi le cul.

***

Je suis presque aussi nerveux qu'hier quand j'ai dû apprendre la nouvelle à Beck. Mais il y a aussi quelque chose d'autre. Je suis déterminé. Je ferai ce qu'il faudra, tout ce qu'il faudra, mais j'obtiendrai le pardon d'Emerie et une seconde chance. J'ai merdé. Je pourrais faire porter le chapeau à un million d'épisodes de ma vie, mais la vérité vraie, c'est que j'ai merdé grave. Et je vais entreprendre de réparer.

Il y a un panneau « en panne » devant deux des ascenseurs de son immeuble. Je suis planté devant celui qui fonctionne, à taper du pied en regardant s'égrener les chiffres sur le cadran. Ça reste bloqué sur le neuf pendant trente secondes, et puis pareil au huitième. *Je n'ai pas le temps.* J'en ai déjà perdu assez. Balayant le hall du regard, je repère les escaliers et pars au trot. Le cœur battant, je les escalade deux à deux jusqu'au troisième étage.

Enfin je me retrouve devant la porte d'Emerie et, pour la première fois, je réalise que je n'ai aucune idée de ce que je vais lui dire. Deux heures d'avion et je n'ai pas été foutu de trouver une bonne phrase d'accroche. Heureusement que je suis du genre à agir dans le feu de l'action, en matière d'argumentations verbales.

Je prends une profonde inspiration, me campe sur mes pieds et frappe.

Lorsque la porte s'ouvre, je me rends compte à quel point je ne suis pas prêt.

Parce que c'est Baldwin qui me dévisage (de l'autre côté).

CHAPITRE 45

DREW

– Où est Emerie ?

– Elle s'habille. On a un petit déjeuner de travail à la fac, ce matin. Enfin, ça ne vous regarde pas, de toute façon.

Le professeur Crétin est toujours à l'intérieur de l'appartement, et moi je suis dans le couloir. Le symbolisme de cet état de fait me rend fou. Je le frôle pour pénétrer chez Emerie.

– Je vous en prie, entrez, marmonne-t-il d'un ton sarcastique.

Je me tourne face à lui et croise les bras.

– Laissez-nous, maintenant.

– Je vous demande pardon ?

– J'ai besoin de parler à Emerie seul à seule, donc j'apprécierais que vous disparaissiez.

Il secoue la tête.

– Non.

Je hausse les sourcils. Je ne pensais pas que cette tête de nœud aurait osé. À un autre moment, j'aurais même pu être impressionné par sa ténacité. Sauf qu'en l'occurrence, ça me fait juste chier.

J'avance d'un pas.

– Soit tu fiches le camp de toi-même, soit je te file un coup de main. Dans les deux cas, tu te tires. Alors, tu choisis quoi ?

Comprenant que je ne plaisante pas, il opte pour la solution de bon sens et rouvre la porte.

– Dites à Emerie qu'on se voit à l'université tout à l'heure.

– Ouais, ouais, je lui ferai passer le message sans faute.

Sur quoi, d'un coup de coude, je lui claque la porte au nez.

Je me retourne et découvre le salon d'Emerie encombré de meubles de bureau. Sachant que la pièce était à peine assez grande pour contenir un canapé et une table avant. À présent, elle est remplie comme un œuf d'un bureau, de fauteuils de bureau, d'étagères de rangement, d'un ordinateur et de ce qui va avec, plus tout le reste.

La porte de sa chambre grince et Emerie apparaît, les yeux baissés sur son téléphone tandis qu'elle fait défiler l'écran.

– Je viens d'ouvrir le trombinoscope des membres du département de biologie de la fac. Tu peux me redire qui on va rencontrer ? Je suis nulle pour retenir les noms.

Ma réponse la fige.

– Il n'y a que toi et moi.

Elle lève brusquement la tête et cligne des paupières à plusieurs reprises, comme si elle n'en croyait pas ses yeux de voir l'homme qui se tient dans son salon.

– Drew. Qu'est-ce que tu fais ici ? (Elle regarde derrière moi.) Et où est Baldwin ?

– Parti.

– Parti où ?

Je fixe mes pieds quelques secondes, puis je plante mon regard dans le sien. Je ressens une pression dans la poitrine en découvrant dans ses yeux la même tristesse qui règne derrière les miens.

– Tu l'aimes ? je lui demande d'une voix basse et gutturale.

Elle me dévisage pendant de longues secondes, les rouages tournent dans son cerveau. Et moi, je retiens mon souffle. Enfin, elle secoue la tête.

Ouf.

C'était tout ce que j'avais besoin de savoir. Le reste, on le gérera. J'obtiendrai son pardon, elle apprendra à me refaire confiance, mais je n'aurais pas pu l'empêcher d'être amoureuse d'un autre homme. Elle demeure plantée dans l'encadrement de la porte de sa chambre, et soudain il y a beaucoup trop d'espace entre nous. Je vais vers elle à grandes enjambées, sans me soucier que mon attitude soit celle d'un homme des cavernes. Le besoin irrépressible de la toucher dépasse toute idée de protocole.

Elle ne bouge pas. À mesure que j'avance, mon cœur bat plus fort. Elle ne bouge toujours pas quand je tends les bras, quand je prends son visage entre mes mains, ni quand je lui effleure doucement les lèvres des miennes, goûtant ses larmes. Prenant son immobilité comme un feu vert, ou du moins pas un orange clignotant, j'y retourne. Je plaque ma bouche sur la sienne et, oubliée la douceur, je l'embrasse avec férocité. Elle s'ouvre, gémit tandis que je l'attire contre moi. Le son de sa voix descend tout droit dans mon bas-ventre et le baiser affamé part rapidement en vrille. Elle sent incroyablement bon, son goût est aussi sucré que dans mes souvenirs et le contact de son corps pressé contre le mien… je n'ai jamais rien ressenti d'aussi bon.

Putain, mais quel idiot je suis. Comment j'ai pu abandonner tout ça ?

Notre baiser dure longtemps. Quand il s'interrompt, les doutes et la peur ne tardent pas à revenir la titiller. Sans compter la colère.

– Tu ne peux pas te pointer…

Je lui coupe la parole en écrasant mes lèvres sur les siennes. Cette fois, elle essaie de se débattre. Sans vigueur, elle me repousse, ce qui m'incite à l'enlacer encore plus étroitement. Au bout du compte, elle finit par se fatiguer et s'abandonner à nouveau. Quand nous mettons un terme à notre baiser, je garde mes lèvres à quelques centimètres des siennes, comme un rappel : je serai sur elle en un battement de cil si elle recommence.

– Accorde-moi juste une minute avant de m'arracher les yeux, d'accord ?

– Soixante secondes.

Je ne peux m'empêcher d'esquisser un sourire. *Dieu qu'elle m'a manqué, cette bouche.* Et pas seulement le contact de ses lèvres douces. Sa langue bien pendue aussi. Passant deux doigts sur sa joue, je me lance sans détour. D'une voix rauque, je dépose les armes à ses pieds.

– Je t'aime.

Un sourire plein d'espoir naît sur son beau visage. Et puis elle se rappelle ce que je lui ai fait subir ces dernières semaines et son sourire s'évanouit.

– Tu as une drôle de façon de le montrer. Tu m'aimes, alors tu me largues ?

– Le juge n'a pas changé mon planning de garde de Beck, mais il a autorisé Alexa à rester à Atlanta. Je dois déménager.

– Je sais tout ça. Roman m'a raconté.

– Roman ?

– Roman, oui.

– Putain, mais qu'est-ce que… ?

– Ça suffit avec tes « Putain mais qu'est-ce que… ». Au moins, Roman a eu la courtoisie de me renseigner sur le pourquoi de ton comportement de trou du cul.

– J'avais peur.

– Moi aussi. Pourtant je ne suis pas partie.

Je baisse les yeux.

– Je sais. Je pourrais te donner un million d'excuses sur mes raisons d'agir comme je l'ai fait, essayer de me justifier. Mais toutes ces raisons se ramènent à une seule et unique cause. (Je marque une pause et poursuis, mes yeux dans les siens.) J'avais peur.

– Et maintenant ? Tu n'as plus peur, maintenant ?

Je secoue la tête.

– J'ai fini par comprendre que j'avais plus peur de te perdre que de prendre le risque de souffrir. Je crois qu'on peut dire que je me suis acheté une paire de couilles.

Elle se radoucit. On dirait qu'elle a envie de me croire, mais qu'elle reste sceptique. Bon, je ne peux pas vraiment la blâmer.

– Qu'est-ce qui me dit qu'elles ne vont pas se recroqueviller et disparaître à nouveau ? (Sa voix se brise.) Tu m'as fait vraiment mal, Drew.

– Je suis tellement désolé. Je sais que là, ma parole n'a pas beaucoup de valeur pour toi, mais je te jure devant Dieu, Em, si tu m'accordes une seconde chance, je ne gâcherai pas tout, cette fois.

Ses yeux s'emplissent de larmes.

– Tu vas vivre à Atlanta et moi ici… Certains jours je travaillerai à la fac avec Baldwin. Comment veux-tu que ça fonctionne ?

– On fera en sorte que ça fonctionne. En prenant notre tour. Une semaine, tu viendras à Atlanta ; l'autre, je viendrai à New York. Ou bien une semaine sur deux, si c'est trop pour toi. Et entre-temps, on comblera avec des tas de sextos et de FaceTime. Je n'ai pas encore tout planifié, mais on trouvera. Ça ne sera pas facile, peut-être, mais ça en vaudra la peine. Je t'aime, Emerie. Je resterais sans boire pendant trois cents soixante-quatre jours, si je savais que c'est toi qui me rafraîchiras la dernière journée.

Une larme coule le long de la joue d'Emerie et je l'essuie de mon pouce.

– Je t'en supplie, Em, dis-moi que ce sont des larmes de joie.

– Je ne pense pas qu'une relation à distance fonctionne.

– On la fera fonctionner. S'il te plaît. S'il te plaît, accorde-moi une autre chance.

Elle secoue rapidement la tête.

– Non.

– Mais…

Je voudrais tenter encore de la persuader, mais elle me fait taire. En posant les lèvres sur les miennes.

C'est un baiser empli de tant de folles émotions que je les sens qui pulsent à travers mes veines et entre nous. Quand nous cessons de nous embrasser, elle est pantelante et moi paniqué. *Elle me dit « au revoir »*.

– À distance, ça ne marchera pas.

– Em, on fera en sorte que ça marche.

– Non. Je pars à Atlanta avec toi.

– On trouvera le… Attends… Quoi ? (Je la dévisage, incrédule.) Tu peux répéter ça ?

– J'ai dit que je partais avec toi à Atlanta.

– Et le boulot pour lequel tu as postulé à la fac ? Tes patients ?

– Je donne des TD jusqu'à la fin du semestre. Je viens de passer un entretien pour le poste de vacataire. Il se peut qu'ils ne m'embauchent même pas. Le semestre se termine dans trois mois. On fera les allers et retours d'ici là. Avec un peu d'expérience sur mon CV, j'aurai peut-être plus de chance de trouver un poste de vacataire là-bas. Quant à mes clients, la plupart sont délocalisables, leurs séances se faisaient par vidéo avant. J'en garderai peut-être quelques-unes face à face, et je reviendrai ici de temps en temps, si tu as encore des clients ici. Tu dois rester auprès de ton fils et je veux apprendre à le connaître aussi. Il fait partie de toi.

– Tu es sérieuse ? Tu as failli me filer une attaque, en affirmant que la relation à distance ne marcherait pas.

Elle sourit.

– Bien fait pour toi, après ce que tu m'as infligé ces dernières semaines.

Sans crier gare, je la soulève dans les airs. Elle pousse un petit cri, mais son sourire me rassure : elle est heureuse. Elle a les jambes nouées autour de ma taille, les bras passés autour de mon cou, et moi, je la serre tellement fort que j'ai peur de lui faire mal.

– Bon Dieu ce que je t'aime.

– T'as intérêt.

– C'est le cas.

Je reprends sa bouche dans un baiser passionné, tout en avançant jusqu'à trouver une surface dégagée où la poser. La surface en question se trouve être le comptoir de la cuisine, qui s'avère aussi à la hauteur parfaite. Mon sexe est déjà érigé rien qu'à sentir sa chaleur à travers mon pantalon.

Je ne sais comment, on parvient à s'arracher mutuellement nos vêtements sans jamais se déconnecter une seconde. Je suce la peau sous son lobe, mes doigts explorent la fente de ses fesses pendant qu'elle déboutonne mon pantalon. Quand il tombe au sol, je descends mon boxer et mon érection émerge, dressée contre mon ventre.

– Tu nous as manqué, je commente avec un regard vers mon entrejambe.

Elle rit.

– Vous m'avez manqué aussi, tous les deux.

J'ai tellement besoin d'être en elle. Tellement.

– Les préliminaires vont être courts, mais je me rattraperai après. Ce seront des post-liminaires.

Sur quoi je saisis mon membre, que j'abaisse afin de frotter mon gland contre sa moiteur, et je l'étale consciencieusement partout. Elle est trempée, prête déjà, moi follement impatient, alors j'entre en elle. Les yeux baissés vers nos ventres, Emerie regarde mon sexe disparaître dans le sien tandis que je m'insinue peu à peu.

Une fois entièrement installé, je relève son menton.

– Te regarder qui me regarde pendant que je te pénètre, c'est le truc le plus sexy que j'aie jamais vu de ma vie.

Elle sourit.

– Tant mieux, parce que j'ai beaucoup aimé regarder.

Je lui caresse la joue de la pulpe du pouce.

– Tout bien réfléchi, ce sourire, là, c'est peut-être ça, le truc le plus sexy que j'aie jamais vu de ma vie.

Je me mets à bouger, d'abord lentement, je glisse, dedans, dehors. Il y a quelque chose de différent, cette fois, comme si toutes les barrières entre nous avaient été retirées et que j'étais enfin libre de l'aimer.

Je l'embrasse sur les lèvres avec délicatesse.

– Je t'aime.

Elle fouille mon regard.

– Je t'aime aussi, Drew. Je ne le savais pas avant de le ressentir pour de vrai, mais à présent j'ignore si j'ai jamais été vraiment amoureuse avant toi.

J'ai l'impression qu'elle vient de me décerner une couronne. En cet instant, je suis un roi. Je ne sais pas vraiment ce que j'ai fait pour la mériter, mais je suis assez affamé pour m'en moquer. Elle est à moi, je la garde. Et cette fois, j'ai bien l'intention de la garder pour toujours.

Bien qu'il se soit écoulé seulement quelques semaines depuis la dernière fois que je lui ai fait l'amour, c'est trop long. J'essaie d'y aller lentement, mais soudain elle serre les jambes autour de moi et son sexe se crispe, empoigne le mien. Je sais que je ne vais plus tenir longtemps. Elle aime bien que je parle pendant l'amour, alors je lui susurre au creux de l'oreille tout ce que je veux lui faire : comme j'ai hâte d'enfouir mon visage entre ses jambes, de jouir sur ses seins, comment, plus tard, je vais la retourner sur le comptoir où elle est assise en ce moment et la prendre par-derrière pour éjaculer partout sur ses fesses, qui seront brûlantes et rouges de mes fessées.

Elle lâche un gémissement puissant, hurle mon nom en me suppliant d'y aller plus fort. J'accélère le rythme et, juste après que son corps s'agite de spasmes autour de moi, je jouis longtemps et intensément en elle. Les voisins ont dû tout entendre de notre finish spectaculaire ; j'espère en tout cas que l'un d'eux en particulier n'a rien manqué.

Une fois que notre respiration s'est un peu calmée, j'écarte une mèche folle sur sa joue et plonge dans ses yeux bleus repus.

– Alors comme ça, tu vas vraiment emménager à Atlanta avec moi ?

– Oui.

– J'ai trouvé une petite maison avec un jardin qui est disponible à la location. Tu pourrais peut-être venir la visiter et on déciderait si c'est bon ou si on veut quelque chose de plus grand.

– Ça fait six mois que je vis dans cette boîte à chaussures… n'importe quoi me paraîtra plus grand.

– Elle a trois chambres, une immense baignoire et le propriétaire m'a dit que je pouvais repeindre si je voulais.

– Tu es en train de m'autoriser à ajouter un peu de couleur dans ta vie ?

– Tu l'as déjà fait. Tu es le rouge de mon univers en noir et blanc.

ÉPILOGUE

EMERIE

Un an plus tard

– Tu l'as ?

Roman plante la main dans la poche de sa veste et en tire une enveloppe.

– Juste là. Je n'en reviens toujours pas que tu aies déterré ce merdier, ajoute-t-il en secouant la tête.

Je repère Drew qui arrive dans le couloir.

– Range. Il arrive.

Roman glisse l'enveloppe dans sa poche, dont il tire une flasque à la place. Il dévisse le bouchon et me la tend.

– Une gorgée ?

– Non, merci.

Drew entre au moment où Roman porte la vieille flasque en métal usé à ses lèvres.

– Tu continues à trimballer ce truc sur toi partout ?

– On ne sait jamais quand on peut avoir besoin d'un shot de Hennessy, mon ami.

Je suis même surprise que Drew ne se soit pas mis à boire, vu les journées qu'il a passées dernièrement. Je l'ai presque rendu fou, avec les préparatifs pour ce soir. Mes parents vont arriver d'ici quelques minutes, ainsi qu'une demi-douzaine de petits copains de Beck. Même si ça fait presque un an qu'on vit à Atlanta, c'est la première fois qu'on reçoit vraiment de la visite. Enfin, à l'exception de Roman, qui ne compte pas comme un invité. Il fait partie de la famille pour Drew et, au cours de l'année écoulée, il est devenu un membre de ma famille aussi. Il est le frère agaçant dont j'avais toujours rêvé.

Parfois, quand il vient nous voir, je les retrouve sur le canapé à deux heures du matin, en train de jouer à des jeux vidéo, Drew et lui. D'autres fois, il fait rater son avion à Drew quand celui-ci doit partir à New York pour ses affaires, parce qu'il l'a entraîné dans l'une de ses missions de surveillance. En revanche, il a toujours été là pour nous. La plupart des gens gardent des cicatrices de la varicelle. Drew en a gardé un ami pour la vie. Entre ces deux-là, ça coule de source.

Beck déboule du dehors comme une bombe. Ses vêtements sont trempés et de l'eau marronnasse coule de sa petite tête.

– J'ai arrosé les fleurs !

– Euh… tu as arrosé les fleurs ou c'est les fleurs qui t'ont arrosé ? Va prendre un bain avant que tout le monde n'arrive, j'ajoute en désignant la salle de bains.

– Je ne peux pas plutôt plonger tout nu dans la piscine ?

Il accompagne sa requête de petits bonds, les mains jointes en un geste de prière.

– Non, tu ne peux pas plonger tout nu dans la piscine. Les voisins vont te voir.

Les épaules basses, le petit fait la moue et se dirige vers la salle de bains d'un pas exagérément traînant.

– On va chercher de la bière, Roman et moi, m'annonce Drew. Tu as besoin de quelque chose pendant que j'y suis ? Que je passe prendre le gâteau que tu as commandé ?

– Mes parents font un détour par la boulangerie en venant. La tradition veut qu'ils paient le gâteau. Ne me demande pas pourquoi.

Menteuse.

Drew m'embrasse sur la joue.

– Comme tu veux. Au fait, ajoute-t-il tout bas, ça ne semblait pas te déranger que les voisins te voient, toi, quand tu étais nue dans la piscine, l'autre soir.

Oui, bon, d'accord, il marque un point. Même si, pour ma défense, ça ne fait que trois semaines qu'on a Beck pendant que sa mère est en lune de miel à Bali ; j'avais bu un verre de vin et Drew venait de rentrer du sport, ce qui avait gonflé ses muscles encore plus que d'habitude. Sans compter qu'il faisait sombre dehors, et puis… j'ai dit que ses muscles étaient particulièrement saillants ?

Dix minutes plus tard, je viens de terminer de préparer ma salade aux billes de melon quand la sonnette retentit.

J'ouvre la porte sur mes parents, les bras levés au ciel.

– Joyeux « Bienvenue chez nous » !

***

Je suis rentrée pour aller aux toilettes et en ressortant, je reste quelques minutes à observer la fête par la fenêtre de la cuisine. Tout se passe super bien dans le jardin. Mes parents discutent avec le nouvel associé de Drew et sa femme, Roman flirte avec la mère célibataire d'un des meilleurs amis de Beck (il se peut que j'aie signalé en amont à chacun d'eux que l'autre était célibataire), et Beck grimpe jusqu'à la cabane que son père et lui ont mis quatre mois à construire dans l'arbre, après notre emménagement ici.

Et aujourd'hui, c'est le jour de « Bienvenue chez nous ». Mes parents sont là, et cette année, ça va être encore plus spécial que d'habitude.

De la terrasse, Drew me voit les observer et s'excuse pour quitter la conversation qu'il avait avec l'un de ses nouveaux amis. Il se glisse dans la maison et vient se poster derrière moi, m'enlace par la taille et se joint à ma contemplation.

– Qu'est-ce qu'on regarde ?

– Ma vie.

– Ah oui ? (Il me fait pivoter vers lui et me donne un rapide baiser.) Maintenant, je regarde la mienne aussi.

Mon cœur soupire.

– J'adore quand tu me parles tendrement, comme ça.

– La nuit dernière, tu adorais quand je te parlais mal.

Je noue les bras autour de son cou.

– Peut-être tout simplement que je t'adore, toi.

– C'est vrai que je suis plutôt génial.

Je lève les yeux au ciel en riant.

– Égocentrique.

Il me dépose un baiser sur le front.

– Tes parents attendent le gâteau avec impatience. Je pense que ta mère a le bec sucré.

Mes parents me harcèlent avec ce gâteau depuis la minute où ils sont arrivés. Pas pour la raison qu'imagine Drew, cependant. Le soleil commence à tomber et on a déjà dépassé d'à peu près une heure le moment où j'aurais dû servir le dessert… mais je repousse. Ça fait plus de six mois que j'attends cet instant impatiemment, et soudain me voilà en proie à la panique.

– J'ai promis à Beck qu'il pourrait aider à porter le gâteau. Pourquoi est-ce que tu ne nous préparerais pas du café, pendant que je vais le chercher ?

Je trouve Beck et, quand je lui annonce que c'est l'heure, il revient à la maison en courant. Son sourire jusqu'aux oreilles me rappelle mon excitation lors de mon premier « Bienvenue chez nous ».

– Ben dis donc, ça doit être un sacré gâteau, commente Drew, en voyant l'expression enthousiaste de son fils.

– Il est dans ma chambre. Oncle Roman a dit qu'il l'avait mis sous mon oreiller, parce qu'il est plus fort qu'une fée, hurle Beck par-dessus son épaule, déjà à mi-chemin dans le couloir.

Drew fronce les sourcils et je lui tends la main sans explication supplémentaire.

– Viens.

La chambre de Beck est jaune vif. On l'a autorisé à choisir la couleur quand je me suis installée à Atlanta de manière permanente à la fin du semestre. Fidèle à sa parole, Drew ne s'est pas plaint de la couleur que j'ai ajoutée à la maison. Chaque pièce est plus vive que la précédente, à l'exception de notre chambre que j'ai peinte dans un gris très doux. Je l'ai choisi parce qu'en interrogeant Drew sur la couleur qui lui ferait plaisir pour notre chambre, il a répondu que j'étais toute la couleur dont il avait besoin. Alors j'ai exaucé son vœu dans la chambre, puisque c'est le lieu où il exauce tous les miens.

Beck se tient près de son lit, l'enveloppe derrière son dos. Il a l'air sur le point d'exploser tant il est surexcité et souriant.

Je lui adresse un hochement de tête.

– Vas-y.

Il sort l'enveloppe de derrière son dos et la tend à son père.

– Joyeux « Bienvenue chez nous ».

Hésitant, Drew saisit l'épaisse enveloppe blanche, puis se tourne vers moi.

– C'est pour moi ? Mais c'est ta journée à toi, chérie.

Je secoue la tête.

– Ouvre.

Il tire les documents de l'enveloppe et les déplie. Étant avocat, il n'aurait pas mis longtemps à deviner de quoi il retourne, même sans l'en-tête de la lettre qui annonce déjà tout. Il se fige pendant qu'il lit le début, puis relève vers moi des yeux sidérés.

Je lui fais « oui » de la tête.

Recevant par ce geste la confirmation de ce qui est écrit noir sur blanc en haut de sa feuille, Drew feuillette rapidement la dizaine de pages agrafées pour parvenir à la dernière. Je sais ce qu'il cherche : toutes les signatures qui lui certifieront que tout ça est bien officiel. Et les voilà, bien claires, nettes et précises, comme il aime. Les signatures du juge Raymond Clapman et de Levi Archer Bodine.

Quand il reporte son regard sur moi, je vois les yeux de Drew emplis de larmes.

– Comment… ?

– Joyeux « Bienvenue chez nous », papa. C'est moi, ton cadeau ! Maintenant, Emerie et toi, vous pourrez fêter ça le même jour !

Bien sûr, ce n'est là qu'une formalité. Drew a toujours été le père de Beck dans leur cœur à tous les deux, tout comme je suis la fille de mes parents. Néanmoins, parfois, officialiser les choses ajoute la cerise sur ce qui est déjà le plus beau des gâteaux. Plus tard, j'annoncerai à Drew qu'on va payer une pension alimentaire supplémentaire pendant au moins dix années encore, mais je sais qu'il n'en aura absolument rien à faire.

Quand j'ai accepté de reprendre à mon compte la pension alimentaire due par Levi en échange de sa signature sur la demande d'adoption, j'avais prévu de m'en acquitter sur mes propres deniers. Ce sera ma participation à l'éducation de l'enfant qui, au cours de l'année écoulée, est devenu le mien aussi.

Il s'est révélé que Levi n'était pas très partant pour devenir le père de Beck. Il n'était pas non plus intéressé par la présence, qu'il juge trop onéreuse, d'Alexa à ses courses. Apparemment, les autres filles avec lesquelles il couche n'y étaient pas très favorables non plus. Moins de deux semaines après qu'Alexa avait obligé Drew à annoncer à Beck qu'il n'était pas son père biologique, Levi l'a plaquée. Il n'en avait que faire, lui, d'apprendre à connaître Beck. Son seul lien avec le petit, c'était l'énorme chèque de pension alimentaire qu'il devait payer depuis leur séparation et qu'Alexa exigeait toujours scrupuleusement.

Alors, quelques mois plus tôt, tandis que Drew était à New York pour ses affaires et que le circuit NASCAR passait par la Géorgie, Roman et moi avons effectué un petit voyage d'une journée pour aller discuter avec Levi. Mon plan d'acheter sa décision était meilleur que celui concocté par Roman, qui impliquait l'intervention d'un ami d'ami de la police d'Atlanta pour mettre en scène l'arrestation de Levi sous prétexte de conduite en état d'ivresse et la menace de ruiner sa carrière de pilote s'il ne signait pas l'abandon de ses droits parentaux.

Pour ma part, je ne croyais pas beaucoup en mes chances de le convaincre de signer les papiers d'adoption en échange de la reprise du soutien financier auquel il était soumis, mais je n'avais rien à perdre et tout à gagner pour Drew. Or, parfois, il faut tenter sa chance. À présent qu'Alexa avait trouvé une nouvelle poule aux œufs d'or à laquelle s'accrocher, elle n'avait plus d'objection contre l'adoption. Au fond, elle savait que c'était juste et, au bout du compte, peu lui importait du moment qu'elle touchait son chèque mensuel et avait un homme à ses côtés.

Incrédule, Drew garde les yeux rivés aux papiers. Juste au moment où je le crois occupé à retenir ses larmes, j'en vois une qui s'écrase sur la page. En fait il pleure, il ne se retient pas, puis il ouvre grand les bras, en passe un autour de moi et l'autre autour de son fils pour nous attirer tous les deux contre lui. Et là, il ouvre les vannes. Ses épaules se mettent à tressauter et son corps à vibrer sous l'effet de ses sanglots silencieux.

Je ne parviens pas à m'en empêcher : je me mets à pleurer avec lui. Le moment est merveilleux, il me rappelle beaucoup le jour de mon arrivée chez mes parents et leurs larmes à eux. Je ne comprenais pas pourquoi ils en faisaient tout un plat, à l'époque, mais aujourd'hui, tout devient lumineux.

Une fois que nous avons séché nos larmes, Beck demande si on peut manger le gâteau, maintenant.

– Vas-y, mon bonhomme. Va chercher le gâteau et apporte-le dehors. Emerie et moi, on vous rejoint dans quelques minutes.

– OK, papa.

Sur quoi il sort en trombe, nous laissant tous les deux seuls.

Drew me dévisage, l'air stupéfait.

– Je n'en reviens pas que tu aies fait ça. Personne n'a jamais rien fait d'aussi important pour moi de toute ma vie.

Je recommence à avoir la gorge serrée.

– Roman m'a aidée.

Drew repousse une mèche de cheveux derrière mon oreille.

– Je n'en doute pas. Mais c'est toi qui m'as donné tout ce dont je rêvais.

Je serre ses doigts.

– Ce qui est normal, puisque tu m'as donné la même chose.

Il relâche ma main et recule d'un pas.

– Je ne t'ai pas encore tout donné. Mais j'en ai l'intention, si tu le veux bien.

La suite se déroule comme au ralenti. Drew plonge la main dans sa poche de devant et en sort un petit boîtier noir, avant de tomber sur un genou.

– J'ai ce truc dans ma poche depuis une semaine, à essayer de trouver comment te le donner. Je voulais que le moment soit spécial, alors je me suis dit qu'aujourd'hui ferait l'affaire, mais j'attendais aussi le bon moment. Or je n'en imagine pas de plus parfait, qu'est-ce que tu en dis ?

Je porte une main à ma bouche, les yeux baissés vers lui.

– Tu as raison, c'est parfait.

Drew serre ma main dans la sienne.

– Emerie Rose, depuis le jour où tu t'es introduite par effraction dans mon bureau, que tu l'as vandalisé et que tu m'as montré tes fesses, j'ai l'impression qu'il me manque une partie de moi lorsque je ne suis pas avec toi. Tu es la couleur dans mon univers en noir et blanc. Avant de te rencontrer, je ne comprenais pas pourquoi ça ne fonctionnait jamais avec personne. Mais je l'ai enfin compris : c'est parce qu'elles n'étaient pas toi. Alors s'il te plaît, dis-moi que tu veux bien m'épouser, parce que tu m'as déjà donné tout le reste. La seule chose qui manque à ma vie, c'est que tu portes mon nom.

J'ai l'impression de vivre un rêve. Les larmes coulent sur mes joues.

– C'est pour de vrai ? C'est vraiment en train d'arriver ?

– Vrai de vrai, chérie. Toi, moi, Beck… peut-être quelqu'un dans ton ventre et un autre qu'on adoptera un jour. On est déjà une famille. Tu m'as donné Beck de manière officielle aujourd'hui. Maintenant, donne-toi à moi de manière officielle. Dis « oui ».

– Oui ! Oui ! Oui !

Je suis tellement survoltée que je renverse Drew, qui a toujours un genou par terre, et nous tombons tous les deux au sol.

Où nous restons enlacés un moment, le temps que mon futur époux sèche mes larmes à coup de baisers.

– Ta demande était très mignonne. Oserais-je dire « romantique » ? Je ne te savais pas comme ça, Jagger.

Il roule de façon à se retrouver sur moi.

– Je suis comme ça. Mais je suis aussi autrement, et je vais te le confirmer dès que j'aurai viré tous ces gens de chez nous.

Je souris.

– Ah, revoici le pervers que je connais et que j'aime.

– Je veux juste que tu sois heureuse, chérie. (Il marque une pause.) Et nue.

Je le serai. Parce qu'entre les disputes, l'arrachage des vêtements et la « baise de compensation », je suis tombée follement amoureuse d'un homme inattendu au moment le plus incongru. Et il s'est avéré que c'était exactement ce dont nous avions tous les deux besoin.

REMERCIEMENTS

Avant tout, merci à mes lecteurs : jamais, dans mes rêves les plus fous, je n'aurais imaginé où ce voyage m'emmènerait quand j'ai commencé à écrire. Votre soutien et votre enthousiasme pour mes livres est un cadeau que je chéris. Merci de me permettre de vous raconter mes histoires et de faire partie de vos moments d'évasion !

À Pénélope : je pourrais remplir ce livre des « merci » que tu mérites, mais je vais résumer ça de mon mieux. Ma vie est une aventure avec toi et je ne me la figure pas sans toi. Merci de ton aide et de ton soutien constants, mais surtout de ton amitié indéfectible.

À Julie : tu es la définition de la force. Merci d'être toujours là pour moi.

À Luna : tu donnes vie à mes romans ! Merci beaucoup pour ton amitié, ton soutien incroyable et ta capacité à rendre les « Vi's Violets » intéressantes grâce à tes *teasers* magnifiques et à ta passion pour la lecture. J'ai hâte de te voir cette année !

À Sommer : merci de m'avoir laissée te rendre dingue… encore.

À mon agente, Kimberly Brower, qui est tellement plus que mon agente. J'ai déjà hâte de voir où nous emmèneront les nouvelles aventures de l'an prochain.

À Elaine et Jessica : merci d'améliorer mon histoire pour qu'elle coule aussi bien !

À Lisa, de TRSOR, et Dani, d'InkSlinger : merci d'organiser tout ce qui permet à ce livre d'être publié.

À tous les blogueurs géniaux : merci beaucoup, beaucoup pour tout ce que vous faites. Je vous suis sincèrement reconnaissante du temps que vous donnez avec tant de générosité pour lire mon travail, rédiger des critiques, créer des *teasers* et participer au partage de votre amour des livres ! Je suis honorée de vous compter parmi mes soutiens et amis. Merci ! Merci ! Merci !

Avec tout mon amour,

Vi

Composition et mise en pages
Nord Compo à Villeneuve-d'Ascq